Global Maritime Safety & Security Issues and East Asia

Maritime Cooperation in East Asia

Series Editors

VOLUME 8

The titles published in this series are listed at *brill.com/mcea*

Global Maritime Safety & Security Issues and East Asia

By

Suk Kyoon Kim

BRILL
NIJHOFF

LEIDEN | BOSTON

The author acknowledges that kind permission was granted by the publishers, including Taylor & Francis, to reproduce the following articles:
1. Portions of Chapter 8 were adapted from Suk Kyoon Kim, “The Expansion of and Changes to the National Coast Guards in East Asia,” *Ocean Development and International Law*, 49(4), 2018.
2. Portions of Suk Kyoon Kim and Seokwoo Lee, “The Legal Framework of Maritime Security in East Asia: A Comparative View,” in Harry N. Scheiber and Jin-Hyun Paik (eds.), *Regions, Institutions, and Law of the Sea: Studies in Ocean Governance*; (2013.05), pp.271–292, Brill/Martinus Nijhoff Publishers are updated and incorporated into relevant chapters.

The Library of Congress Cataloging-in-Publication Data is available online at http://catalog.loc.gov
LC record available at http://lccn.loc.gov/2019940284

Typeface for the Latin, Greek, and Cyrillic scripts: “Brill”. See and download: brill.com/brill-typeface.

ISSN 2405-934X
ISBN 978-90-04-38901-4 (hardback)
ISBN 978-90-04-38990-8 (e-book)

This book is printed on acid-free paper and produced in a sustainable manner.

Contents

Preface IX
List of Illustrations XII

1 **Defining Maritime Safety and Security** 1
I Safe Uses of the Sea 1
II Understanding of Maritime Safety and Security 3
III Maritime Safety and Security Domains 10

2 **Legal Framework for Maritime Safety and Security and IMO Law-Making** 13
I Introduction 13
II Legal Framework for Maritime Safety and Security in the UNCLOS 15
III Institutional Structure of the IMO and Its Roles 21
IV The IMO International Law-Making Process 28
V Enforcement by Flag, Coastal, and Port State 35
VI Status of IMO Conventions and Related Legal Instruments 39
VII Conclusion 54

3 **Safety of Navigation and Port State Control** 56
I Introduction 56
II Principal Regulations Governing the Safety of Navigation 57
III Ships and Navigational Safety Measures 64
IV Safety Measures to Prevent Marine Pollution 74
V Overview of Port State Control 82
VI Regional PSC Regimes 87
VII Conclusion 102

4 **Maritime Terrorism and the SUA Convention Regime** 104
I Introduction 104
II The Nature of Maritime Terrorism 105
III Objectives and Methods of Maritime Terrorism 113
IV Maritime Terrorist Organizations 120
V The SUA Convention Regime 125
VI Conclusion 145

5 **Contemporary Piracy: Nature and Reality** 148
I Emergence of Contemporary Piracy 148
II Definitions of Piracy and their Distinction from other Unlawful Acts at Sea 149
III Typology of Contemporary Piracy 156
IV Aspects of Contemporary Piracy Attacks: Trends, Features and Violence 162
V Costs of Piracy 170
VI Global Counter-Piracy Efforts and Policy Reponses 173
VII Efforts of East Asian Countries to Combat Piracy 183
VIII Conclusion 194

6 **ISPS Code and Port & Cargo Container Security** 196
I Introduction 196
II Adoption of the ISPS Code 197
III Regulations of the ISPS Code 200
IV Implementation of the ISPS Code of East Asian Countries 214
V U.S. Maritime Security Legislations 217
VI U.S. Port and Cargo Container Security Programs 220
VII Conclusion 226

7 **Enforcement of Proliferation Security Initiative (PSI) and Challenges** 228
I Evolution of the Proliferation Security Initiative 228
II Nature of the PSI 234
III Interdiction Principles and Participation in the PSI 235
IV The PSI and International Law 243
V Enforcement of Interdictions 259
VI Challenges to the PSI 263
VII Conclusion 266

8 **Growing Roles of Coast Guards in East Asia** 267
I Introduction 267
II Overview of Coast Guards in East Asia 268
III Roles and Duties of Coast Guards 277
IV Status of Coast Guard Ships in International Law: Rights and Responsibilities 281
V Build-Ups of Coast Guards in East Asia 286

VI Reinforcement of Major Coast Guards in East Asia 288
VII Conclusion 302

9 **Conclusion** 304

Index 315

Preface

Following the previous book published worldwide in 2017, titled *Maritime Disputes in Northeast Asia: Regional Challenges and Cooperation*, this publication *Global Maritime Safety & Security Issues and East Asia* is the second attempt to share my research results and the experiences gained throughout my career in the Korea Coast Guard (KCG). Encouraged by the successful publication of the first volume, I was primarily motivated by some factors to engage in writing another book about maritime safety and security.

First, a lingering question in my mind throughout my research journey in various issues of maritime affairs was how the commonly used terms, 'maritime safety' and 'maritime security' can be defined and distinguished conceptually from each other. They are in common usage in the maritime domain, but they are not legal terms, and thus there is no definition in international law. The two fields are understood to be distinctive in terms of their nature and focus. In common usage, however, maritime safety is often used to encompass facets of maritime security, and their usage is often muddled. This occasionally brings about confusion in understanding and addressing threats in the two fields.

Second, I have noticed that most publications dealing with maritime threats concentrate largely on maritime security issues. In substance, the two subjects of maritime safety and security are very closely linked to each other, and thus I have felt that these two subjects need to be covered together in a book. In addition, I have had a desire to approach these two subjects from a practical perspective, rather than a legal one — likely as a result of my career in the Korea Coast Guard.

Third, I intended to explore how global maritime safety and security measures and regimes are being implemented and enforced in the regional context of East Asia. East Asian countries such as China, Japan and Korea are principal stakeholders in a wide array of global safety and security measures and regimes, and thus it would be significant to explore their implementation of the global regimes.

This book is composed of two parts. Chapters 1, 2 and 3 are primarily concerned with matters concerning maritime safety. Chapter 1 is an introduction, which examines previous researches on the usage of the two terms and attempts to define them, distinguishing the realms of the two subjects.

Chapter 2 highlights the legal framework of maritime safety and security and the process of law-making thereof in the International Maritime Organization (IMO). It outlines a wide array of legal instruments that provide the international standards and rules for maritime safety and security and the law-making process in the international maritime body under the United Nations.

Chapter 3 covers safety measures applied to the safety of ships and navigation and the protection of the marine environment and Port State Control (PSC). This chapter describes the principal safety rules and standards that must be met in ship design and construction in accordance with the type of ships and the safety equipment that must be installed on ships. It also gives an account of the safety measures of navigation and preventive measures for marine pollution. It describes PSC programs, which are a principal instrument of port states to ensure compliance with safety rules and standards, and implementation by the regional PSC regimes to prevent substandard ships and marine pollution.

Chapters 4 through 8 are concerned with maritime security regimes and their implementation by states. Specifically, Chapter 4 deals with aspects of maritime terrorism and the Convention for the Suppression of Unlawful Act Against the Safety of Navigation (SUA Convention), which is a principal international legal framework to address maritime terrorism. This chapter discusses the definitional problem of maritime terrorism in line with terrorism on land, for which there is no universally agreed-upon definition. The aspects of maritime terrorism are examined in comparison with piracy and other unlawful acts at sea. In terms of international cooperation to address the threats of maritime terrorism, the aspects of the SUA Convention are examined.

Chapter 5 deals with the contemporary piracy issue, which is the largest threat to the safety of navigation today. Along with the legal nature of piracy in international law, various aspects of contemporary piracy, such as the status and trends of piracy occurrences worldwide and international counter-piracy measures, are explored.

Chapter 6 describes the details of the International Ship and Port Security Code (ISPS Code) and U.S. port and cargo container security measures. This chapter outlines the adoption of the ISPS Code as an amendment to the 1974 Safety of Life at Sea (SOLAS) Convention to enhance the security of ports and ships engaged on international voyages in the aftermath of the 9/11 terrorist attacks. It examines the requirements for ships, companies and port facility management under the code. In addition, it outlines the legal basis for U.S. port and cargo container security measures and their implementation.

Chapter 7 deals with aspects of the Proliferation Security Initiative (PSI) and the challenges with respect to its enforcement. It focuses on the legal challenges concerned with the implementation of the PSI.

Chapter 8 explores the growing roles and significance of coast guards as the enforcers of maritime safety and security measures as well as the defenders of maritime interests of states. Prior to the examination of the growing roles and expansion of coast guards in East Asia in relation to maritime disputes, it provides the details of coast guards, including duties, typology of existence, and legal status of coast guard ships. This chapter takes a closer look at a regional trend in East Asia, in which countries are expanding their coast guards in the wake of growing regional maritime disputes.

Lastly, Chapter 9 outlines the key points of discussion in the previous chapters.

I am proud and humbled to be publishing this book as well. This book would not be possible without those who inspired and helped me in my work. I would render special gratitude to Professor Zou Keyuan at Central Lancaster University, who encouraged me to write this book. I also extend my special thanks to Professor Seok-woo Lee at Inha University, Korea. Along with my first book, he has arranged an opportunity for me to publish this book as one of the series of '*Maritime Cooperation in East Asia*.' I also extend my thanks to Brill to allow me to publish it following the previous book. I also would like to thank Professor Ted McDorman, editor of *Ocean Development and International Law* for allowing me to publish the article about coast guard — Chapter 8 in this book. I am also grateful to Laura Schreier, Johanna Lee and Malathy Chandrasekaran who were involved in editing and publication.

I also express my gratitude to Dong Kyu, Kim, who is my friend as well as mentor in life. He has always encouraged me, recognizing my dream and hope. Lastly, I express love to my wife Hansil, son Chanhyo, and daughter Hyunji, who always support me.

Illustrations

Figures

1 Trend of shipping losses, Lloyd's List Intelligence Casualty Statistics 2
2 Institutional structure of the IMO, IMO Convention Part VI, Arts. 16 – 26 27
3 LRIT system architecture, European Maritime Safety Agency 75
4 Trend of inspection rate (%) (2007–2017), Tokyo MOU Annual Report 2017 97
5 Trend of detention rate (%) (2007–2017), Tokyo MOU Annual Report 2017 97
6 Deficiencies by main categories (%) (2017), Tokyo MOU Annual Report 2017 98
7 Trend of detention ratio (%) (2004–2017), USCG Annual PSC Report 2017 99
8 Types of safety deficiencies leading to detentions (2017), USCG Annual PSC Report 2017 100
9 Trend of global piracy occurrences (2008–2017), adapted from IMB Annual Piracy Reports 163
10 Status of piracy attacks off the Somali coast (2007–2017), adapted from IMB Annual Piracy Reports 166
11 Types of violence to crew (2008–2017), adapted from IMB Annual Piracy Reports 169
12 Types of vessels attacked (2012–2017), adapted from IMB Annual Piracy Reports 169
13 Trend of China's increase of large coast guard vessels (1000 tons or greater), Ministry of Foreign Affairs Japan 294

Tables

1 Status of the IMO council members (2016–2017), IMO Convention Part VI, Arts. 16–26 25
2 Top 10 flags of registration 2016, UNCTAD, *Review of Maritime Transport 2016* 36
3 Status of IMO conventions and other legal instruments, adapted from the IMO 41
4 Status of navigational safety conventions of East Asian countries, adapted from Status of IMO Treaties 63
5 Status of regional PSC MOU s, Kim Yoon Chul, *International Maritime Treaties* (Dasom, 2013) (translated by author) 88
6 Selection scheme, Paris MOU, Annex 8 93
7 CSI operational ports, Adapted from the U.S. CBP, *CSI Fact Sheet* 223

8 Status of PSI participants (as of 2018), adapted from U.S. Department of State, *'Proliferation Security Initiative Participants'* 240
9 UNSCRs on North Korea, adapted from *UNSCR Resolutions* 246
10 Typology of coast guards 278
11 Status of the merged maritime enforcement agencies, Park Moon Jin, 'Restructuring of Chinese Maritime Organizations and Implications' (translated by author), *Dokdo Journal*, vol. 21 290

CHAPTER 1

Defining Maritime Safety and Security

I Safe Uses of the Sea

Human beings enjoy innumerable benefits from the sea — especially in terms of food, resources, transport and recreation. In particular, maritime transport is a key factor that has contributed to the modernization and economic development of the world. Maritime transport has led to the cost-efficient, swift transfer of goods and resources, as well as the transportation of people, across the world. In the age of globalization, the world economy is tightly interconnected and overwhelmingly dependent on seaborne trade. Maritime transport is the backbone of globalization and lies at the heart of cross-border transport networks that support supply chains and enable international trade.[1]

Over the past decades, total seaborne trade has more than quadrupled, and approximately 90 percent of world trade and two-thirds of its petroleum are transported by sea.[2] In 2015, estimated world seaborne trade surpassed 10 billion tons in volume for the first time.[3] International shipping transports approximately 80 percent of global trade by volume and over 70 percent of global trade by value.[4] Given the significance of seaborne trade and the uses of the sea, the sea lanes and supporting shore infrastructure are often referred to as the 'life lines' of the modern global economy. Thus, the safety and security of navigation and shipping are critical to global trade and, by extension, the global economy itself.[5]

International shipping is, however, involved many different dangers. As maritime transport has increased in tandem with rapid growth in the global trade, maritime casualties and incidents have grown correspondingly. Ships and seafarers are exposed to a variety of dangers and harms stemming from

1 UNTACD, 'Review of Maritime Transport 2016,' available at http://unctad.org/en/PublicationsLibrary/rmt2016_en.pdf.
2 The International Chamber of Shipping, 'World Seaborne Trade' available at http://www.ics-shipping.org/shipping-facts/shipping-facts.
3 UNTACD (n 1).
4 *Ibid.*
5 U.S. Navy, 'A Cooperative Strategy 21st Century Sea Power,' available at http://www.navy.mil/local/maritime/150227-CS21R-Final.pdf.

 | DOI:10.1163/9789004389908_002

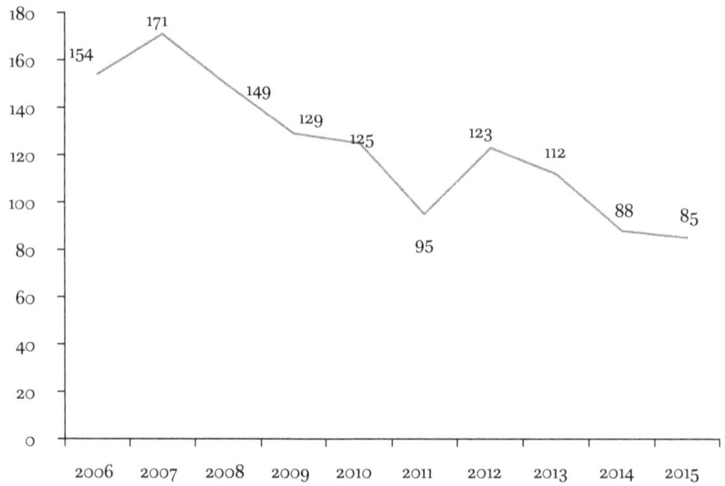

FIGURE 1 Trend of shipping losses
SOURCE: LLOYD'S LIST INTELLIGENCE CASUALTY STATISTICS

natural, accidental or human causes. They are also exposed to a wide array of unlawful acts and threats at sea and onshore such as piracy, armed robbery and terrorist acts. With the uses of the sea proliferating, the marine environment has been polluted by a variety of pollutants from ships, onshore and inland.

Regarding maritime casualties, there were a total 2,687 reported international shipping casualties (incidents) and 85 losses in 2015. This was a significant improvement over the 10-year average losses of 123. Large shipping losses have declined by 45 percent over the past decade. This has been driven by an increasingly robust safety environment and self-regulation.[6] However, despite these improvements (shown on Fig. 1), the harsh nature of the sea means that the risk of maritime casualties and losses remains high.

Also, as coastal and marine tourism and recreation activities grow, the safety of passenger ships is also becoming a critical concern. As seen in the *Sewol* ferry disaster[7] in Korea in April 2014, the risk of maritime accidents by ferry boats,

6 'Safety and Shipping Review 2016,' Allianz Global Cooperate & Specialty, available at http://www.agcs.allianz.com/assets/PDFs/Reports/AGCS_Safety_Shipping_Review_2016.pdf.

7 On 16 April 2014, the *Sewol* ferry, a 6,825-ton, roll-on roll-off passenger ship, with 476 passengers and crew on board, was en route to Jeju Island when it sank off the coast of the Jindo Island, southwest of Korea. The passengers included 345 high school students on a field trip, 14 teachers, 104 general passengers and 33 crew members. This deadliest ferry accident left 295 dead and 9 missing, and 172 rescued. Passing through the Maengol Strait at 18 knots, the ferry, loaded with 2142.7 tons of cargo, began to list sharply to the left when it made a left turn around 08:49 and capsized around 10:25 am.

which carry many passengers, remains high. Recent casualties have raised significant concerns over passenger ship safety.

Because ships and seafarers remain vulnerable to maritime incidents, the most critical concern in maritime transport is how to enhance safety and security at sea. This may involve questions of both how to protect life and property at sea, as well as how to protect the marine environment from pollution. Ultimately, it relates to questions of how to ensure safe navigation and protect shipping from maritime threats.

II Understanding of Maritime Safety and Security

Various Definitions

The two terms 'maritime safety' and 'maritime security' might be the most commonly used terms in the maritime world. Although affairs concerning maritime safety and security are dealt with separately in practice, there is no generally agreed-upon distinction between the two terms in international law and theory. They are often used interchangeably, and their meanings are interpreted differently depending on who is using them and in what context. However, their distinction is crucial as it affects the structure, organization and responsibilities of the agencies involved.[8] Furthermore, these definitions may directly relate the establishment of states' maritime safety and security policies.

In the absence of universally agreed-upon definitions of maritime safety and security, researchers have made attempts to define their meanings. As a result, the definitions vary with these researchers' perspectives, and their applications to the maritime domain are varied. This sometimes results in confusion in classifying the realm of maritime safety and security, and addressing who is responsible for the two maritime domains. Against this backdrop, the definitions of maritime safety and security by researchers and agencies are introduced below. According to Del Pozo and his colleagues, maritime safety and security are defined as follows[9]:

Maritime safety: "The combination of preventive and responsive measures intended to protect the maritime domain against, and limit the effect

8 Del Pozo, Dymock, Feldt, Hebrard & Monteforte, 'Maritime Surveillance in Support of CSDP' (April 2010), The Wise Pen Team Final Report to EDA Steering Board, available at http://www.realinstitutoelcano.org/wps/wcm/connect/44d0718042982ce1bb66bb24ab1546e8/The_wise_pen_team_final_report_april_2010.pdf?MOD=AJPERES&CACHEID=44d0718042982ce1bb66bb24ab1546e8.

9 *Ibid.*

of accidental or natural danger, harm, and damage to the environment, risk or loss."

Maritime security: "The combination of preventive and responsive measures to protect the maritime domain against threats and intentional unlawful acts."

Recognizing the three maritime functions of maritime countries as maritime safety, maritime security and maritime defense, Urbanski and his colleagues from the Polish Naval Academy define maritime safety and security as[10]:

Maritime safety: "The safety of life and property at sea from environmental and operational threats, as well as the safety of maritime environment from pollution by the ships."

Maritime security: "The security from terrorism, piracy and similar threats, as well as effective interdiction of all the illicit activities on sea such as pollution of the marine environment; illegal exploitation of sea resources; illegal immigration; smuggling drugs, persons, weapons and other things that can be used for terrorist activities."[11]

Urbanski and his colleagues argue that "maritime safety is achieved as the result of the existing maritime safety legal framework; operating the global and regional navigational infrastructure, but mainly as the result of operation of the highly specialized maritime operational services."[12] They include: "ships classification, survey, certification and inspection services; aids to navigation service; hydrographic and navigational information service; search and rescue (SAR) service; marine environment protection service; combating the environmental pollutions service; Vessel Traffic Services (VTS); ensuring the security of the ships and port facilities service, etc." On the other hand, they argue that "maritime security is achieved as the result of the operation of the proper national maritime services such as coast guard, maritime police, customs services, immigration service, etc."[13]

Fransas and her colleagues describe maritime safety with the four following components,[14] instead of defining the term explicitly: (i) external safety, such as safe fairways, ports, safety equipment, environmental conditions;

---

10 J. Urbanski, W. Morgas & M. Miesikowski, 'The Present and Expected Changes in Maritime Safety, Security and Defense Functions' (2009) 3(2), *International Journal on Marine Navigation and Safety of Sea Transportation*, 11–17, p. 11.

11 *Ibid.*

12 *Ibid.*

13 *Ibid.*

14 Fransas, Nieminen & Rytkkonen, 'Maritime Safety and Security Literature Review' (2012), *Series B Research and Reports*. No 77, University of Applied Science, p. 12.

(ii) internal safety, such as the ship's structure, the ship's damage stability, assessment of commercial premises, etc.; (iii) human factors; (iv) environmental impacts resulting from complex interactions between the above-mentioned factors.

Examining various maritime security definitions by different agencies such as the U.S. Navy, the International Maritime Organization (IMO) and the United Nations, Klein concludes that maritime security means "the protection of a state's land and maritime territory, infrastructure, economy, environment and society from certain harmful acts occurring at sea."[15] She argues that "in the absence of a universal definition the international community should take a comprehensive approach to the issue."[16]

Bueger takes an alternative approach to the maritime security discourse.[17] Rather than contemplating the definition of 'maritime security,' he concentrates on identifying the relations of maritime security to other concepts that deal with the governance of maritime space. Describing maritime security as "one of the latest buzzwords of international relations," he argues that "maritime security can be understood in a matrix of its relation to other concepts, such as marine safety, seapower, blue economy and human security." "The concept of 'seapower' concerns the role of military force and the maritime dimension of inter-state war and threats to national survival." "Marine safety addresses the safety of ships and maritime installations with the primary purpose of protecting maritime professionals and the marine environment." "The concept of 'blue economy' is linked to maritime security since sustainable management strategies not only require the enforcement and monitoring of laws and regulations, but a secure maritime environment provides the precondition for managing marine resources." "Human security considers the living conditions of coastal communities dependent on the sea, in particular, their food security and the risk of their marginalization in land focused governments."

Bueger's relations approach to the concept of maritime security appears to be very comprehensive and far-reaching in addressing the scope of maritime security. Notably, marine safety is subsumed under maritime security. Despite identifying various aspects of maritime security in relations to other relevant concepts, it appears that it remains vague and the challenge of defining maritime security in an explicit phrase has not been addressed.

15 Natalie Klein, *Maritime Security and the Law of the Sea* (Oxford University Press, New York, 2011), p. 11.

16 *Ibid.*

17 Christian Bueger, 'What is Maritime Security?' (2015) 53, *Marine Policy*, pp. 159–164.

An alternative approach to defining the concept of maritime security is also taken by Rahman.[18] Rather than defining maritime security, he identifies five prisms through which 'maritime security' in a non-traditional sense is often viewed. The five perspectives include: (i) security of the sea itself; (ii) ocean governance; (iii) maritime border governance; (iv) military activities at sea; and (v) security relation of the maritime transportation system.

Germond understands the concept of maritime security from a geopolitical perspective.[19] Likewise, he does not address the definition of maritime security in generic terms. Instead, he argues that "maritime security has to do with (illegal and disruptive) human activities in the maritime *milieu* that is a certain geographically delimited space. Thus, states are differently impacted by maritime security threats depending on their actual geographical location." Indeed, geographical location is a vital factor which affects the maritime security of a state, but it might be one among a wide range of maritime security factors.

The U.S. Navy takes a task-oriented approach, claiming that "maritime security is a non-doctrinal term." The tasks and operations defined as maritime security include: "to protect sovereignty and maritime resources; to support free and open seaborne commerce; to counter maritime related terrorism, weapons proliferation, transnational crime, piracy, environmental destruction, and illegal seaborne immigration."[20] The U.S. Navy divides maritime security into 'individual' and 'collective' categories. "Individual maritime security operations involve actions taken by a single nation-state to provide for its safety and security, consistent with its rights." "Collective maritime security operations are required to unite actions of like-minded nation-states to promote mutual safety and security at sea."

The IMO has drawn a distinction between maritime safety and security since the 1980s. Under the auspices of its Maritime Safety Committee (MSC),

18 Chris Rahman, 'Concepts of Maritime Security,' (2009) 07(09), *Discussion Papers, Center for Strategic Studies New Zealand.* See also Luts Feldt, Peter Rolle and Ralph D. Thiele, 'Maritime Security – Perspective for a Comprehensive Approach,' (April 2013), no. 22, Institute for Strategic, Political, Security and Economic Consultancy (ISPSW): They also provide the elements that are part of maritime security, which include: international and national peace and security; sovereignty, territorial integrity and political independence; security of sea lines of communications; security protection from crimes at sea; resource security, access to resources at sea and to the seabed; environmental protection; and security of all seafarers and fishermen.

19 Basil Germond, 'The Geographical Dimension of Maritime Security,' (2015)54, *Marine Policy*, p. 138.

20 U.S Coast Guard, 'Naval Operations Concept 2010: Implement Maritime Strategy,' available at https://www.uscg.mil/history/docs/2010NOC.pdf.

the IMO refers to maritime safety as "preventing or minimizing the occurrence of accidents at sea that may be caused by substandard ships, unqualified crew or operator error," whereas "maritime security is related to protection against unlawful and deliberate acts."[21]

The United Nations (UN) describes the nature of maritime safety and security. The UN refers to maritime safety as follows: "It is principally concerned with ensuring the safety of life at sea, safety of navigation, and the protection and preservation of the marine environment."[22] The UN places an emphasis on the role of the shipping industry in this regard and on its fulfillments for ensuring safety. The fulfillments include the following: "vessels must be safely constructed, regularly surveyed, appropriately equipped (e.g., with nautical charts and publications) and adequately manned; crew must be well trained; cargo must be properly stowed; and an efficient communication system must be on board."[23] Concerning the meaning of maritime security, the UN says that "it, at its narrowest conception, involves protection from direct threats to the territorial integrity of a state, such as armed attack from a military vessel."[24]

The UN's definition of maritime security, in a broad sense, includes "security from crimes at sea, such as piracy, armed robbery against ships, and terrorist acts." The definition of maritime security by the UN covers "intentional and unlawful damage to the marine environment, including from illegal dumping and the discharge of pollutants from vessels and the depletion of natural resources, such as from illegal, unreported and unregulated (IUU) fishing."[25] The UN states that "various approaches have been taken to maritime security, depending on the state's perspective of the interests that may be threatened, either directly or indirectly, by activities in the oceans and seas."[26]

Components of the Definitions of Maritime Safety and Security

As discussed in various definitions of maritime safety and security above, it is difficult to draw a clear distinction between the two terms. The definitions vary depending on users and the context. However, we can figure out some common and distinctive components of the definitions. The meanings, differences and

21 Klein (n 15), p. 8, Citing Kenneth G. Hawkes, *Maritime Security* (Cornell Maritime Press, Centreville, 1989).

22 UN General Assembly, 'Oceans and the Law of the Sea: Report of the Secretary General' (10 March 2008) UN Doc A/63/63, para. 35.

23 *Ibid.* para 39.

24 *Ibid.*

25 *Ibid.*

26 *Ibid.*

connectivity of the two terms can be understood better and more explicitly by highlighting key components.

First, a commonly accepted distinction between maritime safety and security is whether the risks, dangers or harms occurring at sea are 'accidental' or 'intentional.' Maritime safety is concerned primarily with 'accidental' or 'natural' dangers and harms. On the other hand, maritime security is related to 'intentional' and 'unlawful' acts in the maritime domain.

Second, both maritime safety and security involve 'tasks' and 'activities' to keep the sea safe and secure. A source of confusion in drawing a distinction between the two terms is that they are often differently understood either as an 'activity' or a 'condition.'[27] The definitions discussed above expressly or implicitly indicate that the concepts of maritime safety and security are involved in 'activities,' which are either proactive or responsive, to protect life and property against dangers and threats at sea. Del Pozo and his colleagues expressly define that they are "a combination of preventive or responsive measures." The UN is in line with their definitions, with respect to maritime safety in particular, by emphasizing the fulfillments that the shipping industry is required to carry out.

Third, maritime safety focuses on proactive measures for the safety of ships and crew on board, whereas maritime security is more concerned with responsive activities to threats and attacks against ships and crew, the marine environment, marine resources, or installations onshore and offshore, and the rights of a state.

Fourth, tasks to enhance maritime safety are concerned primarily with the protection of the safety of ships, property and the crew onboard. Consequently, the shipping industry and ship operators are primarily tasked with the responsibility of ensuring maritime safety. While maritime safety is within the state or global legal framework, the rules and regulations are implemented at the industry or operational level.

In this context, maritime safety is ensured primarily by the shipping industry, shipping associations, ship owners, crew and seafarers, classification society, hydrographic services, VTS, port authority, etc. For maritime security, it is used at the narrowest concept as military operations against infringement on the maritime right of a state, as the UN described. The underlying objective of maritime security is to protect the maritime rights of a state and to safeguard the territorial integrity of a state at sea. Thus, the tasks of ensuring maritime security are carried out primarily by state-level agencies, which are responsible

27 Del Pozo, Dymock, Feldt, Hebrard & Monteforte (n 8), p. 44.

for law enforcement against unlawful acts or to uphold the protection of sovereignty. The agencies may include the military, coast guard, customs services, immigration services, fishery protection agencies, etc.

Conclusion

In terms of definition, as discussed above, it is difficult to draw an explicit distinction between maritime safety and maritime security. Maritime safety often encompasses the concept of maritime security. Otherwise, it is understood that maritime safety is subsumed under maritime security. The two terms are often used imprecisely, inconsistently, or in ways that overlap each other. Further problems occur in translation to and from other languages, where the terms can have the same, mixed, or overlapping meanings.[28] However, distinctive or common components that constitute the concepts of maritime safety and security can be drawn from the various definitions.

Based on the definitions discussed above, my conclusion is that both maritime safety and security are principally a set of 'measures' and 'activities' to ensure safe navigation and to protect the marine environment and the rights of a state at sea. While both are 'activities' and 'tasks,' either preventive or responsive, maritime safety is concerned primarily with preventive activities to protect life and property at sea and is the responsibility of the shipping industry and actors at the operational level. On the other hand, maritime security is more focused on responsive activities to protect life and property at sea and is primarily to the responsibility of relevant state agencies. The domain of maritime security is concerned with protecting the maritime interests and rights of a state, primarily against external threats.

In conclusion, 'maritime safety' can be defined as "an array of preventive and responsive efforts and activities to protect life and property at sea, and to preserve the marine environment, by regulating and managing ships and seafarers, as well as using technological advances against natural and accidental dangers and harms." Meanwhile, 'maritime security' can be defined as "comprehensive preventive and responsive efforts and activities to safeguard the territorial integrity of a state and to protect the security of ships, individuals, and states by implementing a variety of security regimes against intentional and unlawful acts and threats at sea."

A prominent distinction between the two domains might be whether the cause of dangers or threats is 'natural,' 'accidental,' or 'intentional.' Maritime safety is concerned with efforts or activities at sea to protect life and property

28 Del Pozo, Dymock, Feldt, Hebrard & Monteforte (n 8), p. 44.

and the marine environment from dangers and harms inflicted by 'natural' or 'accidental' causes. On the other hand, maritime security is principally concerned with measures and activities at sea to address threats and unlawful acts which derive from 'intentional' causes.

Even though they are conceptually distinctive in some respects, the two frameworks have common and mutually reinforcing objectives, as the UN describes: "a secure maritime space is certainly a safer one, and a maritime regime that prioritizes safety is less vulnerable to criminal activity and other threats."[29] Consequently, "efforts to enhance either maritime security or safety lead to improvements in both, and result in cascading effects on the conduct and regulation of other activities in the sea."[30]

III Maritime Safety and Security Domains

It is not an easy task to draw a boundary between maritime safety and security in the maritime domain. However, it is necessary to attempt to divide the domains of maritime safety and security based on conceptual distinctions, given that the two maritime domains carry different meanings and applications, and differ in terms of their implications for enforcement agencies.

Amongst various maritime regimes, which are inherently interconnected and overlapping, the maritime safety domain can be categorized largely by the following subjects:

- *Safety of ships*: The safety of ships involves safety standards, regulations, procedures and measures to enhance safety on ship design, construction, equipment, seaworthiness, survey and classification, etc.
- *Safety of crew*: The safety of crew is concerned with regulations and measures to enhance the safety of ships and crews and with measures to reduce casualties caused by human error and the management of the shipping company. This may include standards of training, certification, working and living conditions of the crew, and the safety management of the shipping company.
- *Safety of navigation*: The safety of navigation is a crucial part in improving the maritime safety of ships and crew, given the number of casualties and loss of life and property occurring during navigation. This may involve the publication of navigational information and charts, navigation equipment,

29 UN General Assembly (n 22), para. 36.
30 *Ibid.*

routing systems, reporting systems, safety of cargo, hydrographic surveys, radio communications, vessel traffic services (VTS), port state control, etc.

- *Search and rescue* (SAR): Casualties that occur due to the perilous nature of the sea underscores the importance of search and rescue regimes. The duty to render assistance to people in distress at sea is a well-established maritime tradition, which is reflected in various international laws. The duty is implemented by maritime tradition, international instruments, radio communication, ship reporting, aviation and SAR cooperation regimes, etc.
- *Safety of the marine environment*: The marine environment is affected by a variety of pollutants, such as the dumping of wastes, oil spills from ships, spillage from on- and offshore installations, and the discharge of pollutants from inland. The regimes to preserve the marine environment include a variety of prevention, preparedness, and response instruments, and safety standards employed to prevent pollution from marine accidents.

In the absence of a generally agreed-upon definition of maritime security, the UN has identified specific threats to maritime security, and implied that maritime security is concerned with addressing these specific threats.[31] The maritime security threats identified by the UN include: (i) piracy and armed robbery against ships; (ii) terrorist acts involving offshore shipping installations and other maritime interests; (iii) illicit trafficking in arms and weapons of mass destruction; (iv) illicit traffic in narcotic drugs and psychotropic substances; (v) smuggling and trafficking of persons by sea; (vi) illegal, unreported fishing; and (vii) intentional and unlawful damage to the marine environment.

Building on the U.N.'s description and the nature of maritime security — which is also concerned with protecting the territorial integrity of states and the freedom of navigation — the domain of maritime security can be classified into the following main categories:

- *Security of territorial integrity*: This concerns international maritime regimes to protect the right of free navigation and the territorial integrity of a state. These regimes are concerned with innocent passage, freedom of the high seas, and transit passage, etc. Security of territorial integrity is concerned with security regimes against terrorism, illicit trafficking of arms and weapons of mass destruction, and drug smuggling. These regimes may include anti-terrorism measures, the Proliferation Security Initiative (PSI), and interdiction of vessels carrying illicit items, pursuant to international law.
- *Security of navigation*: In the maritime world, the biggest threat to free and secure navigation is acts of piracy and armed robbery against ships. Thus,

31 *Ibid.*, para. 53–113.

the security of navigation is focused primarily on counter-measures to protect ships, seafarers and cargo from piracy attacks and armed robbery. The measures to combat piracy and armed robbery are implemented at a state, regional and global level, either on a bilateral or multilateral cooperation basis.

- *Security of cargo*: This is concerned with cargo security regimes and instruments to ensure the security of cargo transport against the smuggling of illicit items, drugs, arms and weapons of mass destruction, and against attempts to use cargo as a means of terrorism. The cargo security regimes mostly created by the U.S. in the aftermath of the 9/11 terrorist attacks include the Container Security Initiative (CSI), the Secure Freight Initiative (FSI), Customs-Trade Partnership Against Terrorism (C-TPAT), 24-hour advance rule, etc.
- *Security of ports and on-offshore installations*: A port is a place where cargo is loaded and discharged from ships, and a place where various dangerous, noxious and flammable chemical cargo and energy resources such as oil, liquefied natural gas (LNG) and liquefied profane gas (LPG) are stored. On-offshore installations and facilities on and off shores are mostly located near ports. Any disruption in major ports by terrorist attack or explosion could inflict enormous damages to ports and on-offshore installation and facilities, crippling the functions of ports. Security of ports is concerned with protecting ports from a variety of external threats and keeping them operational.
- *Security of fishery resources*: Seafood is critical to global food security. Security of fishery resources is threatened by overfishing, caused by Illegal, Unreported and Unregulated (IUU) fishing.

CHAPTER 2

Legal Framework for Maritime Safety and Security and IMO Law-Making

I Introduction

The development of international regimes for maritime safety and security has a long history. They have gradually been formulated ever since humans were actively engaged in sea-faring and navigation across the oceans. In the early stage, maritime safety and security regimes were established in the form of regional traditions, practices or customs. Most maritime safety and security regimes codified in international shipping treaties were created in the 20th century, when international commerce and seaborne trade surged.

Out of various international transport methods, shipping has become the most prevalent form of international transport in the modern world due to its cost-efficiency and effectiveness. That is, ships can transport an enormous amount of cargo around the world at extremely low cost. With explosive industrial growth and globalization, and technology advances in the last century, international commerce surged. This resulted in a booming shipping business worldwide.

However, the safety of shipping was of particular concern since numerous serious maritime accidents occurred, inflicting enormous loss of life and damage to property, and ultimately discouraging shipping and sea-going. Marine pollution, caused either by oil spills, the dumping of wastes or the discharge of pollutants from ships, also became a serious problem. In particular, an upsurge in tankers carrying oil, chemicals and other noxious and dangerous goods posed a grave threat to the marine environment. Challenged by these unprecedented problems, the international community engaged in efforts to enhance the safety of navigation and to prevent and control marine pollution. To this end, as a core effort, a large number of international treaties on shipping were adopted from the middle of the 19th century onwards. The treaties were aimed at setting global safety standards that would be applicable to all shipping around the world, and at preventing and controlling marine pollution across the oceans.

The International Maritime Organization (IMO), which came into existence in 1958 and is a permanent international maritime body of the United Nations

 | DOI:10.1163/9789004389908_003

(UN), has served as a core international body in formulating a regulatory maritime framework. In tandem with explosive growth in shipping, the role of the IMO has become highly important as a regulatory framework setter. The IMO has developed a number of new conventions, which have set maritime safety standards to improve the safety of ships and crew, and instruments to prevent and control maritime pollution. The IMO has also ensured that existing legal instruments keep pace with changes in shipping technology and demands in the maritime world. As a result, since its creation, the IMO has adopted more than 50 international conventions and agreements and also adopted numerous protocols and amendments.[1] The safety regulations adopted by the IMO are mostly multilateral conventions, requiring state parties to ratify and enact domestic legislation.

Under the auspices of the UN, the international community created the 1982 United Nations Convention on the Law of the Sea (UNCLOS), which entered into force in 1994. The UNCLOS, referred to as 'the constitution of the sea,' is a global legal framework that provides for all the uses of the sea. The UNCLOS sets forth the principles of the uses of the sea as well as a legal framework to ensure the safety and security of ships and crew and the rights of states at sea.

Pursuant to the UNCLOS, the IMO, other UN agencies, and international organizations including the Food and Agriculture Organization (FAO), the International Labor Organization (ILO), the International Hydrographic Organization (IHO), and the International Atomic Energy Agency (IAEA), have developed a wide array of rules and standards for safety and security in the maritime domain. They are mostly in the form of multilateral conventions and agreements, which have binding force as international law once they become effective.

This chapter will explore the international legal framework that governs safety and security regimes with respect to shipping and marine pollution. It will examine the rights and responsibilities of states to enforce the maritime safety and security regimes. It will also examine the institutional structure and the law-making process of the IMO and discuss relationships between the UNCLOS and IMO legal instruments. This chapter will involve reviewing the provisions prescribing the principles of safety and security under the UNCLOS, but the focus will be on the law-making of IMO and its legal instruments.

1 IMO, 'Introduction of IMO,' available at the IMO website: http://www.imo.org/en/About/Pages/Default.aspx.

II Legal Framework for Maritime Safety and Security in the UNCLOS

Charter of the United Nations

The Charter of the United Nations (UN) provides for underlying principles governing international relations, and for the maintenance of international peace and security, including on the seas. All member states are obliged to settle their disputes by peaceful means and to refrain from threats or use of force against the territorial integrity or political independence of any state, or in any other manner inconsistent with the purposes of the UN.[2] In conformity with the principle of dispute settlement prescribed in the Charter, member states are required to settle their maritime disputes in a peaceful manner.

The Charter provides for the principal organs of the UN, which include a General Assembly, a Security Council, an Economic and Social Council, a Trusteeship Council, an International Court of Justice, and a Secretariat. Amongst them, the Security Council plays an essential role in ensuring maritime security.

The Security Council is responsible for the maintenance of international peace and security, including on the seas, and all member states are obliged to accept and carry out the decisions of the Security Council.[3] The International Court of Justice (ICJ) is a principal judicial organ of the UN. The ICJ plays a critical role in solving international disputes, including maritime disputes over boundary delimitation and territorial integrity at sea. All members of the UN are *ipso facto* the members of the ICJ.[4] Each member of the UN is obliged to undertake to comply with the ICJ in any case to which it is a party.[5]

The United Nations Convention on the Law of the Sea

On 10 December 1982, the UN Conference on the Law of the Sea adopted the United Nations Convention on the Law of the Sea (UNCLOS).[6] The UNCLOS created a variety of new ocean regimes governing all uses of the sea and its resources. Principal legal regimes for the uses of the sea, the rights of a coastal state, and the freedom on the high seas include: the breadth of the territorial sea up to 12 nautical miles; a foreign vessel's innocent passage through territorial waters; transit passage in the straits used for international navigation; a

2 Charter of the United Nations, Art. 2.
3 *Ibid.*, Art. 25.
4 *Ibid.*, Arts., 92 & 93.
5 *Ibid.*, Art. 94.
6 United Nations Convention on the Law of the Sea (Montego Bay, 10 December 1982, in force 16 November 1994) 1833 *UNTS* 396.

coastal state's sovereign rights in a 200-nautical mile exclusive economic zone; a coastal state's rights over the continental shelf for exploration and exploitation; all states' rights to exercise the freedom of the high seas.

Together, the UNCLOS provides for various legal regimes with respect to safety and security in the maritime domain. It prescribes a wide range of responsibilities and rights varying with the status of a state, which is a 'flag,' 'coastal,' or 'port' state. The UNCLOS is a framework convention, also termed an 'umbrella convention,' many of provisions of which are general principles and doctrines concerning the duties or rights of states. These provisions are implemented through specific operative regulations in other international treaties or national legislation adopting the rules and standards contained in the international agreements.

These relationships are reflected in several provisions of the UNCLOS which require states to "take account of," "conform to," "give effect to," and "implement" the relevant international rules and standards developed by or through the "competent international organization" (i.e., IMO).[7] Under the UNCLOS, the relevant international rules and standards are referred to as "applicable international rules and standards," "internationally agreed rules and standards," "generally accepted international regulations," "applicable international instruments," or "generally accepted international regulations, procedures and practices."[8] These provisions explicitly establish an obligation on parties to the UNCLOS to apply IMO rules and standards. The specific form of such application relies to a great extent on parties' interpretation of the phrases to "take account of," "conform to," "give effect to," or "implement" in relation to IMO provisions.[9]

The duties or responsibilities of states set forth in the UNCLOS with respect to safety and security at sea, in terms of the enforcement of international rules and standards, may be outlined as follows:

A. Safety and security regimes concerned with exercising the right of innocent passage.
   1. Coastal state's right to adopt laws and regulations relating to innocent passage.
      The coastal state may adopt laws and regulations relating to innocent passage through the territorial sea concerning[10]: (i) the

7 IMO, 'Implications of the United Nations Convention on the Law of the Sea for the International Maritime Organization,' LEG/MISC.8 (2014), p. 8.
8 *Ibid.*
9 *Ibid.* p. 10.
10 UNCLOS, Art. 21(1).

safety of navigation and the regulation of maritime traffic; (ii) the protection of navigational aids and facilities and other facilities or installations; (iii) the protection of cables and pipelines; (iv) the conservation of the living resources of the sea; (v) the prevention of infringement of the fisheries laws and regulations of the coastal state; (vi) the preservation of the environment of the coastal state and the prevention, reduction and control of pollution; (vii) marine scientific research and hydrographic surveys; (viii) the prevention of infringement of the customs, fiscal, immigration or sanitary laws and regulations of the coastal state. The right of the coastal state to adopt the laws and regulations concerning innocent passage does not apply to the design, construction, manning or equipment of foreign ships except the implementation of generally accepted international rules or standards.[11]

2. Obligation of foreign ships to use sea lanes and traffic separation schemes.
   (i) Foreign ships when exercising innocent passage through the territorial sea of the coastal state are obliged to comply with the laws and regulations adopted by the coastal state and those concerned with the prevention of collision at sea.[12].
   (ii) Foreign ships exercising the right of innocent passage are obliged to use sea lanes and traffic separation schemes designated or prescribed by the coastal state.[13] The coastal state is required to take into account in designation or prescription of sea lanes or traffic separation schemes, of: (i) recommendations of the competent international organization; (ii) any channels customarlly used for international navigation; (iii) special characteristics of particular ships and channels; (iv) density of traffic.
3. Obligation of foreign nuclear-powered ships and ships carrying nuclear or other inherently dangerous or noxious substances. Such ships are required to carry documents and observe special precautionary measures when exercising innocent passage, established for such ships by international agreements.[14].

11 *Ibid.*, Art. 21(2).
12 *Ibid.*, Art. 21(4).
13 *Ibid.*, Art. 22(1).
14 *Ibid.*, Art. 23.

B. Safety measures for artificial islands, installations and structures in the EEZ. The coastal state, which is entitled to exercise sovereign rights over the construction, operation and use of artificial islands, installations, and structures in its EEZ, is obliged to take safety measures for them.[15]

1. Due notice of the construction of artificial islands, installations or structures and giving warning of their presence.
2. Removal of any installations or structures abandoned or disused to ensure safety of navigation. Appropriate publicity must be given to the depth, position and dimension of any installations or structures not entirely removed.
3. Establishment of safety zones, which shall not exceed a distance of 500 meters aground them.
4. Respect of the safety zones and compliance with international standards regarding navigation in the vicinity of artificial islands, installations, structures and safety zones.

C. Duties of ships during transit passage.
Ships exercising transit passage in the strait used for international navigation are obliged to comply with the following rules.[16]

1. Refrain from any threat or use of force against the sovereignty, territorial integrity or political independence of states bordering the strait and compliance with principles of international law embodied in the Charter of the United Nations.
2. Compliance with international regulations, procedures, and practices for safety at sea and for the prevention, reduction and control of pollution from ships.

D. Duties of the flag state.

1. The flag state is obliged to take measures for ships flying their flag to ensure safety at sea with regard, *inter alia*, to:[17]
   (i) the construction, equipment and seaworthiness of ships.
   (ii) the manning of ships, labor conditions and training of crews, taking into account of the applicable international instruments.
   (iii) the use of signals, the maintenance of communications, and the prevention of collisions.
2. The safety measures that the flag state is required to take include:[18]

15 *Ibid.*, Art. 60(3)(5)-(7).
16 *Ibid.*, Art. 39 (1) & (2).
17 *Ibid.*, Art. 94(3).
18 *Ibid.*, Art. 94(4).

(i) survey of ships by a qualified surveyor to ensure that ships have on board such charts, nautical publications and navigational equipment and instruments as are appropriate for the safe navigation of the ship.

(ii) to ensure that each ship is in the charge of a master and officers who possess appropriate qualifications in particular in seamanship, navigation, communications and marine engineering, and that the crew is appropriate in qualification and numbers for the type, size, machinery, and equipment of the ship.

(iii) to ensure that the master, officers and the crew are fully conversant with and required to observe the applicable international procedures and practices and to take necessary steps for their observance.

E. States' obligations in respect of pollution by dumping.

1. to adopt laws and regulations to prevent, reduce and control pollution of the marine environment by dumping.
2. to take other measures to prevent, reduce and control such pollution.
3. to endeavor to establish global and regional rules, standards and recommended practices and procedures to prevent, reduce and control such pollution.

F. States' obligations in respect of pollution from vessels.

1. to establish international rules and standards to prevent, reduce and control pollution of the marine environment from vessels and promote the adoption of routing systems designed to minimize the threat of accidents which might cause pollution of the marine environment.
2. to adopt laws and regulations for the prevention, reduction and control of pollution of the marine environment from vessels flying their flag or registry.
3. to give due publicity to the requirements and to communicate them to the competent international organization when establishing particular requirements for the entry of foreign vessels into their ports or internal waters or for a call at their off-shore terminals.
4. to adopt laws and regulations for the prevention, reduction and control of marine pollution from vessels exercising the right of innocent passage within their territorial sea and from vessels navigating the EEZ.
5. to include those means, standards and rules relating to prompt notification to coastal states, whose coastline or related interests may be affected by incidents.

G. Enforcement by flag states.

1. to ensure compliance by vessels flying their flag or their registry with applicable international rules, standards, laws and regulations for the prevention, reduction and control of pollution of the marine environment from vessels.
2. to provide for the effective enforcement for such rules, standards, laws and regulations.
3. to take appropriate measures to ensure that the vessels flying their flag or their registry are prohibited from sailing, until they can proceed to sea in compliance with the requirements of international rules and standards.
4. to ensure that vessels flying their flag or their registry carry on board certificates by or issued pursuant to international rules and standards.

H. Measures relating to seaworthiness of vessels to avoid pollution.
States are obliged to take administrative measures to prevent the vessels from sailing when it has been ascertained that a vessel within one of their ports or at one of their off-shore terminals is in violation of applicable international rules and standards relating to seaworthiness of vessels and thereby threatens damage to the marine environment.[19]

Along with such responsibilities and duties, the UNCLOS stipulates other provisions with respect to the enforcement of maritime safety and security measures.

A. Duty to render assistance persons in distress[20].

1. Every state is obliged to require the master of a ship flying their flag, the crew or the passengers, without serious danger to the ship:
   (i) to render assistance to any person found at sea in danger of being lost.
   (ii) to proceed with all possible speed to the rescue of persons in distress, if informed of their need of assistance.
   (iii) after a collision, to render assistance to the other ship, its crew and its passengers and where possible, to inform the other ship of the name of its own ship, its port of registry and the nearest port at which it will call.
2. States are obliged to promote the establishment, operation and maintenance of an adequate and effective rescuc service regarding safety on and over the sea

19 *Ibid.*, Art. 219.
20 *Ibid.*, Art. 98.

B. Duty to cooperate in the repression of piracy and in the suppression of illicit trafficking in narcotic drugs and psychotropic substances[21].
   1. States are obliged to cooperate to the fullest possible extent in the repression of piracy on the high seas or in any other place outside the jurisdiction of any state.
   2. States are also obliged to cooperate in the suppression of illicit trafficking in narcotic drugs and psychotropic substances.

C. Duty to avoid adverse consequences in the exercise of the powers of enforcement.
   1. States are obliged not to endanger the safety of a foreign vessel during enforcement:
      (i) not to endanger the safety of navigation.
      (ii) not to create any hazard to a vessel.
      (iii) not to bring it to an unsafe port or anchorage.
      (iv) not to expose the marine environment to an unreasonable risk.

III Institutional Structure of the IMO and Its Roles

Introduction

The shipping industry is inherently international, and thus it is vital that shipping is subject to generally agreed-upon uniform international regulations and rules at the global level on matters such as ship construction standards, navigational rules, standards of crew competence and regulations of pollution from ships.

The UNCLOS functions as a framework convention dealing with the comprehensive uses of the sea and matters of safety and security at sea. The UNCLOS is a law-making treaty in that it provides for only the principles regulating the uses of the sea, and for general requirements and criteria to ensure maritime safety and security, without creating specific rules and standards, which are applicable to ships and navigation at the operational level.

The creation of the operative rules and standards concerning matters of maritime safety and security, in particular, is delegated to "competent international organization(s)," which may include the International Maritime Organization (IMO), the International Labor Organization (ILO), the Food and Agriculture Organization (FAO), the International Hydrographic Organization

21 *Ibid*, Arts. 100 & 108.

(IHO), the International Atomic and Energy Agency (IAEA), and other related international organizations.

States are required to refer to the proposals or recommendations of the competent international organization(s). When the term is used in the singular in the UNCLOS, it applies exclusively to the IMO, given the global mandate of the organization as a specialized agency within the United Nations system.[22] Amongst those agencies, the principal international agency in terms of international rule-making with respect to the safety and security of shipping and other matters at sea is the IMO.

In conformity with the provisions of the UNCLOS, rules and standards concerning maritime safety and security are adopted by the IMO as various legal instruments and oblige member states to enforce them. Against this backdrop, the below explores the institutional structure of the IMO and the law-making process. It also examines the IMO's roles in the law-making process and assesses its accomplishments as a rule-setter in the maritime domain.

Functions of the IMO

The IMO is a specialized agency of the United Nations, in the field of shipping and on the effect of shipping on the marine environment, in accordance with Article 57 of the Charter of the UN.[23] The IMO is responsible for the safety and security of shipping and the prevention and control of marine pollution from ships. The IMO is the global standard-setting authority for the safety, security and environmental performance of international shipping.[24] Since its creation, the IMO has played a key role in international law-making in maritime safety and security.

The IMO was first created by the Convention on the Inter-Governmental Maritime Consultative Organization (IMO Convention), which was adopted by the United Nations in 1948 and entered into force in 1958. The Inter-Governmental Maritime Consultative Organization was changed to the International Maritime Organization (IMO) in 1982 in accordance with an amendment to the convention.

Under the IMO Convention, the principal purposes of IMO are:[25] (i) to provide the machinery for international cooperation in governmental regulations and practices relating to shipping for international trade; (ii) to set the highest practicable standards for matters concerning maritime safety, efficiency of

22 IMO (n 7).

23 IMO Convention, Art. 64.

24 IMO (n 1).

25 IMO Convention (n 23), Art. 1.

navigation, and prevention and control of marine pollution from ships; (iii) to promote the availability of shipping for international commerce by removing discriminatory action and unnecessary restrictions; (iv) to consider any matters concerning shipping and the effect of shipping on the marine environment referred to it.

Pursuant to these purposes, the IMO is designed to perform the functions of:[26] (i) to consider and make recommendations to governments on matters related to the above-mentioned purposes; (ii) to provide for the drafting of conventions, agreements or other instruments and to recommend them to governments and to intergovernmental organizations; (iii) to provide machinery for consultation among members and the exchange of information among governments; (iv) to perform functions associated with the aforementioned matters; (v) to facilitate technical co-operation within the scope of the organization.

Institutional Structure of the IMO

In terms of the IMO's institutional structure, it consists of an assembly, a council, and five main committees, which include: (i) the Maritime Safety Committee; (ii) the Marine Environment Protection Committee; (iii) the Legal Committee; (iv) the Technical Cooperation Committee and (v) the Facilitation Committee; and a number of sub-committees to support the work of the main technical committees (See Fig. 2).

A. Membership[27]

Membership in the IMO is open to all states, subject to certain provisions. As of 2018, 173 states are parties to the IMO Convention and accordingly they become members of the IMO. All members are entitled to participate in meetings of the IMO bodies responsible for drafting and adopting recommendations containing safety and anti-pollution rules and standards. All states, whether or not they are members of the IMO or the UN, are invited to participate in the various IMO conferences responsible for adopting new IMO conventions and amending existing conventions.

B. The Assembly[28]

The Assembly is the highest governing body of the IMO, and it is composed of all member states. It meets once every two years in regular sessions, but extraordinary sessions may be convened upon request by one-third of member states. The functions of the assembly are: (i) to establish any temporary or, upon recommendation of the council, permanent

26 *Ibid.*, Art. 2.

27 *Ibid.*, Part III, Arts. 4–10.

28 *Ibid.*, Part V, Arts. 12–16.

subsidiary bodies; (ii) to elect the members to be represented on the council; (iii) to receive and consider the reports of the council and to decide upon any question referred to it by the council; (iv) to approve the work programme; (v) to vote on the budget and determine financial arrangements; (vi) to perform the functions of the organization; (vii) to recommend to members for the adoption of recommendations and guidelines concerning maritime safety, the prevention and control of marine pollution from ships and other related matters; (viii) to promote technical co-operation, taking into account the special needs of developing countries; (ix) to refer to the council for consideration or decision any matters within the scope of the organization.

C. The Council[29]

The Council is the executive body of the IMO, composed of 40 members elected by the Assembly. The Council performs all the functions of the IMO, except the function of making recommendations, which is reserved for the Assembly by Article 15(j). Primary functions of the council include: (i) to coordinate the activities of the organs; (ii) to consider the draft work programme and budget estimates and submit them to the Assembly; (iii) to receive reports, proposals and recommendations of the committees and other organs and submit them to the assembly and member states with comments and recommendations; (iv) to appoint the Secretary-General, subject to the approval of the Assembly; (v) to make a report to the assembly at each regular session on the work performed by the organization; (vi) to submit to the assembly financial statements of the organization, together with the council's comments and recommendations; (vii) to enter into agreements or arrangements concerning the relationships of the IMO with other organizations, subject to approval by the Assembly. The Council members elected by voting are classified into three categories (See Table 1).

- Category A: 10 states with the largest interest in providing international shipping services.
- Category B: 10 other states with the largest interest in international seaborne trade.
- Category C: 20 other states not elected under Category A or B above which have special interests in maritime transport or navigation, and whose election to the Council will ensure the representation of all major geographic areas of the world.

29 *Ibid.*, Part VI, Arts. 16–26.

TABLE 1 Status of the IMO council members (2016–2017)

Category	Member
Category A	China, Greece, Italy, Japan, Norway, Panama, Korea, Russia, U.K, U.S.
Category B	Argentina, Bangladesh, Brazil, Canada, France, Germany, India, Netherlands, Spain, Sweden
Category C	Australia, Bahamas, Belgium, Chile, Cyprus, Denmark, Egypt, Indonesia, Kenya, Liberia, Malaysia, Malta, Mexico, Morocco, Peru, Philippines, Singapore, South Africa, Thailand, Turkey

SOURCE: IMO CONVENTION PART IV, ARTS. 16–26

D. Maritime Safety Committee[30]

The Maritime Safety Committee (MSC) is the highest technical body of the IMO, and consists of all member states. The MSC will meet at least once a year. The functions of the MSC prescribed in the Convention include: (i) to consider any matter within the scope of the IMO concerned with aids to navigation, construction and equipment of vessels, manning from a safety standpoint, rules for the prevention of collisions, handling of dangerous cargoes, maritime safety procedures and requirements, hydrographic information, log-books and navigational records, marine casualty investigation, salvage and rescue, and any other matters directly affecting maritime safety; (ii) to provide machinery for performing any duties assigned to it by the IMO Convention or any duty within its international instrument and accepted by the IMO; (iii) to submit to the Council proposals for safety regulations or for amendments to safety regulations; and recommendations and guidelines which MSC has developed; and a report on the work of the Committee.

E. Marine Environment Protection Committee[31]

The Marine Environment Protection Committee (MEPC), which consists of all member states, is responsible for: (i) performing functions to prevent and control marine pollution from ships; (ii) facilitating the enforcement of the conventions concerned with the prevention and control of

30 *Ibid.*, Part VII, Arts. 27–31.

31 *Ibid.*, Part IX, Arts. 37–41.

marine pollution from ships; (iii) providing for the acquisition of scientific, technical and any other related information on the prevention and control of marine pollution from ships; (iv) promoting cooperation with regional organizations concerned with the prevention and control of marine pollution from ships; (v) considering and taking appropriate action with respect to any other matters falling within the scope of the organization; (vi) submitting to the Council proposals for regulations and their amendments, recommendations and guidelines which the committed has developed; (vii) a report on the work of the Committee.

F. Sub-Committees: the MSC and the MEPC, the two main Technical Committees of the IMO, are supported in their work by a number of subcommittees. They are open to all member states and include:
   1. Sub-Committee on Human Element, Training and Watchkeeping (HTW).
   2. Sub-Committee on Implementation of IMO Instruments (III).
   3. Sub-Committee on Navigation, Communications and Search and Rescue (NCSR).
   4. Sub-Committee on Pollution Prevention and Response (PPR).
   5. Sub-Committee on Ship Design and Construction (SDC).
   6. Sub-Committee on Ship Systems and Equipment (SSE).
   7. Sub-Committee on Carriage of Cargoes and Containers (CCC).

G. Legal Committee[32]

The Legal Committee (LE), which consists of all member states, is empowered to deal with any legal matters within the scope of the IMO. The LE was established as a subsidiary body to deal with legal questions which arose in the aftermath of the *Torrey Canyon* disaster.[33] The LE is responsible for: (i) considering any legal matters within the scope of the organization; (ii) taking all necessary steps to perform any duties assigned to it by the convention or by the assembly or the council, or any duties with the scope of the IMO; (iii) submitting to the council drafts of international conventions and of amendments to international conventions that the committee has developed; (iv) a report on the work of the Committee.

H. Technical Co-operation Committee[34]

The Technical Co-operation Committee (TC), which consists of all member states, is empowered to deal with any matter within the scope of the IMO concerned with the implementation of technical cooperation in the

32 *Ibid.*, Part VIII Arts. 32–36.

33 IMO (n 1).

34 IMO Convention (n 23), Part X, Arts. 42–46.

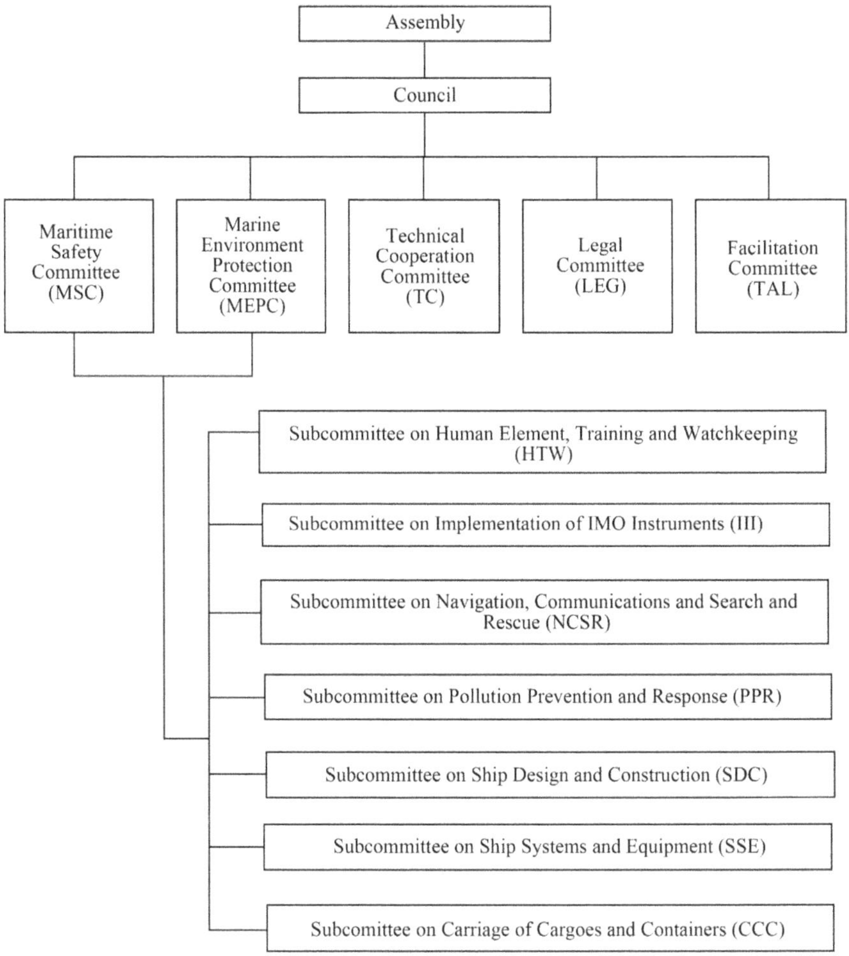

FIGURE 2 Institutional structure of the IMO
SOURCE: IMO CONVENTION PART IV, ARTS. 16–26

technical cooperation field. The TC was established in 1969 as a subsidiary body of the council and was institutionalized by means of an amendment of the IMO Convention which entered into force in 1984.[35]

I. Facilitation Committee[36]

The Facilitation Committee (FC), which consists of all member states, was established as a subsidiary body of the council in 1972 and became fully institutionalized in 2008 as a result of an amendment of the IMO

35 IMO (n1).
36 IMO Convention (n 23), Part XI, Arts. 47–51.

Convention. The FC is empowered to deal with IMO's work in eliminating unnecessary formalities and 'red tape' in international shipping by implementing all aspects of the Convention on Facilitation of International Maritime Traffic 1965.[37] The FC is also responsible for dealing with any matter within the scope of the IMO concerned with the facilitation of international maritime traffic. In recent years, the FC's work, in accordance with the wishes of the assembly, has been to ensure that the right balance is struck between maritime security and the facilitation of international maritime trade.[38]

J. Secretariat[39]

The secretariat, which is composed of the secretary-general and other personnel that the IMO may require, is responsible for the administrative work to support the functions of the IMO. The secretary-general and staff are obliged not to be influenced by any government or any external authority.

IV The IMO International Law-Making Process

Law-Making Process

To carry out the purposes of the IMO —the promotion of safe, secure, and environmentally sound shipping — a top priority is to adopt the highest practicable rules and standards with respect to maritime safety and security, efficiency of navigation, and prevention and control of pollution from ships. The law-making process of the IMO is very complicated. As a special agency of the UN in the field of shipping and marine pollution, the IMO has adopted numerous international conventions and agreements containing specific rules and standards concerning the safety and security of shipping and the prevention and control of marine pollution from ships. The IMO has also adopted numerous protocols and amendments. As stated earlier, the IMO is responsible for more than 50 international conventions and agreements. The below outlines the law-making process in the IMO.

A. Adoption of a Convention

Maritime disasters, which inflicted enormous damage to life, property and the marine environment, prompted the international community to take action

37 *Ibid.*

38 IMO (n 1).

39 IMO Convention (n 23), Part XII, Arts. 52–57.

to prevent such events from recurring. These efforts resulted in the adoption of new international conventions concerning maritime safety and security and the protection of the marine environment. This can be illustrated in the cases of the *Titanic* disaster in 1912, which led to the creation of the International Convention for the Safety of Life at Sea (SOLAS) in 1914, and the *Torrey Canyon* incident in 1967, which prompted the adoption of the International Convention for the Prevention of Pollution from Ships (MARPOL) in 1973. The aftermath of the 1978 *Amoco Cadiz* oil spill incident and the 1987 *Herald of Free Enterprise* disaster led to the adoption of the International Safety Management (ISM) Code in 1993, which was incorporated into the SOLAS Convention in 1994. In addition, the findings of research studies contributed to the adoption of a new convention, as it was a case in the 2004 International Convention for the Control and Management of Ships' Ballast Water and Sediment.

To adopt or amend a convention, all the member states of the IMO are authorized to suggest the need for a new convention or an amendment to an existing convention. Typically, the suggestion is made by one of the IMO committees or sub-committees. The IMO has six main bodies that relate to the adoption and implementation of conventions. The Assembly and the Council are the main organs, and the Committees involved are the Maritime Safety Committee, the Marine Environment Protection Committee, the Legal Committee, and the Facilitation Committee. Technology advances in shipping and other related industries are discussed by member states in these bodies, and any of them can suggest the need for a new convention and amendments to existing conventions.[40] The respective Committee is assisted by various subcommittees in drafting a new convention.

When a Committee suggests the need for a new convention, it is referred to the Council, and as necessary, to the Assembly. If the suggestion is authorized to proceed, the Committee in question considers the matter in greater detail and ultimately draws up a draft instrument. In some cases, the subject may be referred to a specialized Sub-Committee for detailed consideration. The representatives of all the member states are invited to participate in the process of drawing up a draft convention.

The views and advice of intergovernmental and international nongovernmental organizations whose interests and activities are related to the purposes of the IMO[41] are also invited to partake in the process. Their practical and diverse views, based on experience in the subject matter, contribute to the work of the IMO.

40 IMO (n 7).

41 IMO Convention, Art. 66.

The draft convention, which is agreed upon in the committee concerned, is reported to the Council and the Assembly. The Committee recommends to the two bodies that a diplomatic conference be convened to discuss the draft for formal adoption. All the member states of the IMO and all the member states of the UN and any of its specialized agencies are invited to attend the conference. The organizations of the UN and other international organizations in official working relationships with the IMO are also invited to send observers, who can provide their expert views and advice to the representatives of member states. Prior to the conference, the draft convention is circulated to invited member states and other international organizations for their review and comments.

In the conference, the draft convention, together with the comments from governments, is examined. Necessary changes are made by consensus of the participating representatives. Through this process, a draft convention, which is acceptable to all or the majority of the governments present, is agreed upon and adopted by the conference. All participating countries have an equal footing in adopting a convention. The convention is deposited with the Secretary-General. The Secretary-General sends the copies of the convention to the member states for signature, which is usually open for 12 months. Signatories may ratify or accept the convention while non-signatories may accede.

B. Signature, Ratification, Acceptance, Approval and Accession

Since its creation in 1969, the Vienna Convention on the Law of Treaties (Vienna Convention) has served as a framework convention for treaties by providing for the authoritative guide regarding the formation and effects of treaties. In this context, IMO law-making complies with much of the principles in the Vienna Convention, including the means of consent to the treaty.

Concerning signature as a means of expressing consent, the Vienna Convention stipulates the cases where the signature of the representative of a state is recognized as "the consent of a state to be bound by a treaty"[42]: (i) the treaty provides that the signature shall have that effect; (ii) the negotiating states were in agreement that the signature should have that effect; (iii) the state intended to give the full powers to its representative or was expressed during the negotiations.

A state may sign a treaty 'subject to ratification, acceptance or approval.' In such a condition, a state is obliged to refrain from acts which would defeat the object and purpose of the treaty until: (i) it has made its intention clear not to

---

42 The Vienna Convention on the Law of Treaties, 1969, Art. 12(1).

become a party to the treaty; or (ii) it has expressed its consent to be bound by the treaty, pending the entry into force of the treaty.[43]

Typically, most multilateral conventions contain a clause of state's consent subject to ratification. It signifies that the signature as a means of consent alone does not suffice to bind the state to the treaty, and the instrument of ratification should be deposited with the depositary of the treaty. The origin of ratification was to ensure that a state representative did not exceed his powers or instructions with regard to the making of a particular treaty. However, many states make use of this option for multilateral conventions to ensure that any necessary legislation is enacted and other constitutional requirements fulfilled before entering into treaty commitments.[44]

The terms 'acceptance' and 'approval' are also used as the means of the consent of a state. They are the same in their effect with ratification, but the two words are less formal and non-technical and preferred by some states, which might have constitutional difficulties with the term 'ratification.'[45] Most multilateral conventions are open for signature for a specified period of time. Accession is the method used by a state to become a party to a treaty to which it did not sign whilst the treaty was open for signature. Consent by accession is possible where: (i) the treaty provides; (ii) the negotiating states were in agreement; (iii) subsequently agreed that consent may be expressed by means of accession.[46]

C. Entry into Force

Each convention contains appropriate provisions stipulating the conditions which have to be met before it enters into force. By the time the convention comes into force, it becomes binding upon the contracting governments that have ratified it. The conditions vary, but typically the more important and more complex the convention, the more stringent are the conditions for its entry into force.[47]

The SOLAS Convention 1974 provided that entry into force requires acceptance by 25 states whose merchant fleets comprise not less than 50 percent of the world's gross tonnage. For the International Convention on Tonnage Measurement of Ships 1969, the requirement was acceptance by 25 states whose combined merchant fleets represent not less than 65 percent of world

43 *Ibid.*, Art. 18(a).

44 IMO (n 1).

45 *Ibid.*

46 The Vienna Convention on the Law of Treaties, 1969, Art. 15.

47 IMO (n 1).

tonnage. When the appropriate conditions have been fulfilled, the convention enters into force for the states that have accepted generally, after a grace period to provide states the time to take the steps necessary for implementation.[48]

In the case of some conventions that affect a few states or deal with less complex matters, the entry into force requirements may not be so stringent. For example, the Convention Relating to Civil Liability in the Field of Maritime Carriage of Nuclear Material 1971 came into force 90 days after being accepted by five states. The Special Trade Passenger Ships Agreement 1971 came into force after three states (including two with ships or nationals involved in special trade) had accepted it.[49] For the important technical conventions, it is necessary that they be accepted and applied by a large section of the shipping community. Thus, it is essential that they should, upon entry into force, be applicable to as many of the maritime states as possible.

A government's acceptance of a convention signifies that the contracting government is obliged to enforce the measures required by the convention. For the enforcement of the measures required in the convention, national law has to be enacted or amended. Along with legislative measures, other possible necessary arrangements by states may include the creation of new bodies at the governmental or industry level, funding, recruitment, training and appointment of inspectors etc. Accordingly, adequate notice should be provided to shipowners, shipbuilders and other related industry so that they can take account of the requirement measures in their future acts and plans. Given such national legislation and arrangements, typically IMO conventions enter into force an average of five years after adoption.

D. Enforcement

Contracting states enforce the provisions of IMO conventions as far as their own ships are concerned and impose penalties for infringements. A state's jurisdiction to enforce measures in the conventions varies with the status of a state jurisdiction. As stated earlier, the UNCLOS distinguishes state jurisdiction into three different categories: flag, coastal, and port state jurisdiction. The IMO legal instruments, conforming to the UNCLOS, specify how state jurisdiction should be exercised so as to ensure compliance with safety of shipping and anti-pollution regulations, which will be discussed in detail later.

The enforcement of the provisions of conventions entirely rests with contracting governments, except a particular case in the International Convention on Standards of Training, Certification and Watchkeeping for Seafarers

48 *Ibid.*
49 *Ibid.*

(STCW) 1978, under which the IMO has been given the authority to inspect the training, examination and certification procedures of the contracting parties. The contracting governments are required to provide relevant information to IMO's Maritime Safety Committee, which will judge whether or not the state concerned meets the requirements.[50]

E. Amendment

Technologies and techniques in the shipping industry are changing very rapidly. As a result, not only are new conventions required, but existing ones need to be updated. However, it was very difficult to amend the early conventions because in most cases, amendments to the conventions required the consent of two-thirds of the contracting parities. Despite an urgent need for the implementation of amendments, this requirement in practice led to long delays in bringing the amendments into force.[51]

As a consequence, many of the initial amendments to IMO treaties never came into effect. To address this problem, the IMO introduced a new prompt amendment procedure in the early 1970s, which is referred to as 'tacit acceptance.' Under the tacit acceptance system, amendments to technical regulations enter into force at a particular time after a certain period unless a certain number of state parties oppose the adoption of the amendment within that period. At a particular time after a certain period, it is deemed that the amendment has been accepted by the member states which do not oppose the amendment. The tacit acceptance system enables prompt entry into force of the amendments to the technical regulations of IMO conventions, which need to keep up with rapidly changing technologies and techniques.

The tacit acceptance system was first applied to the amendment to the International Regulations for Preventing Collisions at Sea opened in October 1972. The purpose of the amendment was to update the Collisions Regulations and to separate them from the SOLAS Convention. The effectiveness of the tacit acceptance system has been illustrated in the case of the 1974 SOLAS Convention, which has been amended on many occasions. Under the convention, an amendment to most of the annexes is deemed to have been accepted at the end of two years from the date on which it is communicated to contracting governments unless the amendment is objected to by more than one-third of contracting governments, or contracting governments owing not less than 50 percent of the world's gross merchant tonnage. The period may be varied by

50 STCW Convention, Annex Chapter 1, Reg. 1/7.

51 IMO (n 1).

the Maritime Safety Committee with a minimum limit of one year.[52] Generally, amendments enter into force within 18 to 24 months.

Despite having the merit of expediency, the tacit acceptance system was challenged by least-developed countries or developing countries, which were not capable of keeping pace with rapid developments in international regulations due to a lack of resources and technical expertise.[53] This has resulted in a disparity of compliance between developed and developing countries, making the uniform implementation of conventions across the world difficult. However, it has been proved that tacit acceptance procedures are very useful in expeditiously updating technical regulations contained in the IMO conventions, particularly those concerned with the marine environment.[54] The tacit acceptance system has been incorporated into the majority of the IMO's technical conventions and has been extended to some other instruments.

Forms of IMO Legal Instruments

The international laws that the IMO produces can be classified largely into two types: a resolution and an international convention.

A. Resolutions

A vast majority of IMO Resolutions are adopted by the bodies of the assembly, the MSC and the MEPC. All IMO member states are entitled to participate in adopting the Resolution by those bodies. The IMO Resolutions incorporate recommendations on the implementation of rules and standards not contained in IMO treaties. These Resolutions are normally adopted by consensus and accordingly reflect global agreements by all IMO member states.[55]

Technical Codes or Guidelines included in the Resolutions become mandatory by incorporation into national legislation. This is, for instance, the case of the International Maritime Dangerous Goods Code (IMDG Code), which came into mandatory effect on 1 January 2004, following the entry into amendments to SOLAS Chapter 7.[56] In several cases, Codes and Guidelines initially contained in non-mandatory IMO Resolutions are incorporated at a later stage into IMO Treaties. For instance, the International Code for the Construction and Equipment of Ships Carrying Dangerous Chemicals in Bulk (IBC Code)

52 IMO (n 1).
53 Md. S. Karim, *Prevention of Pollution of the Marine Environment from Vessels* (Springer, Switzerland, 2015), p. 33.
54 *Ibid.*
55 IMO (n 7), p. 10.
56 *Ibid.*

has been incorporated into both the International Convention for the Safety of Life at Sea 1974 (SOLAS) and the International Convention for the Prevention of Pollution from Ships (MARPOL).[57]

B. Treaties

A primary purpose of the IMO is to set the highest practicable standards for matters concerning maritime safety, efficiency of navigation, and prevention and control of marine pollution from ships. In accordance with this purpose, the IMO has produced a large number of treaties that contain operative rules and standards concerning maritime safety, navigation, maritime pollution and maritime security. IMO treaties exist in the form of multilateral conventions, protocols and agreements, which are required of state parties to ratify and enact domestic legislation to be implemented. A majority of IMO treaties are in the form of multilateral conventions, which have a binding force as international law once a certain number of state parties ratify. The IMO has adopted more than 50 international conventions and agreements and also adopted numerous protocols and amendments (See Table 3).

V Enforcement by Flag, Coastal, and Port State

Flag State

For many centuries, the system of open registries, under which the owner of a ship and the flag of the ship are from different countries, has been customary. A unique maritime system has developed under the open registries — that is, the Flags of Convenience (FOCs). The FOC is defined as a “flag of any country allowing the registration of foreign-owned and foreign-controlled vessels under conditions which, for whatever reason, are convenient and opportune for the persons who are registering the vessels.”[58]

‘Flagging out,’ which means that shipowners register their ships with foreign countries, has become a long-held tradition in the international shipping community for various reasons. The economic benefits that shipowners enjoy from ‘flagging out’ might be the biggest attraction. Under the open registries, a shipowner may choose a more economically advantageous foreign country and register his or her ships with the country and fly its flag. By flagging out to a developing or least-developed country, the shipowner from a developed

57 *Ibid.*

58 Boleslaw Adam Boczek, *Flags of Convenience: An International Legal Study* (Harvard University Press, Cambridge, 1962), p. 2.

TABLE 2 Top 10 flags of registration 2016

Country	Number of Vessels	Vessel Share of World Total (%)	Share of World Total Dead-Weight (%)
Panama	8,513	8.97	18.51
Liberia	3,153	3.50	11.42
Marshall Islands	2,942	3.24	11.07
Hong Kong	2,515	2.77	8.96
Singapore	3,605	3.97	7.04
Malta	2,101	2.31	5.26
Bahamas	1,450	1.59	4.40
China	4,052	4.46	4.20
Greece	1,386	1.52	4.07
Cyprus	1,053	1.16	1.84

SOURCE: UNCTAD, *REVIEW OF MARITIME TRANSPORT 2016*

country may enjoy the benefits of lower registration fees and taxes, less stringent regulations, lower wages for crews and lower costs for compliance with regulations.

As a result, the majority of shipowners, mostly from developed countries, remain competitive against fleets owned by the shipping companies that are based in developing countries. Additionally, the system of open registries has been an opportunity for FOC countries to make a large amount of income from registration fees and taxation. As of 2016, the tonnage registered under a foreign flag is 70.2 percent of the world total.[59] (See Table 2)

In terms of share of the world's total dead weight, Panama, Liberia and the Marshall Islands continue to be the largest vessel registries, accounting for 18.5 percent, 11.4 percent and 11.1 percent, respectively. The FOC countries include some landlocked countries, like Mongolia.

Despite various benefits of the FOCs, many problems arise, and they are inherently linked to a wide range of maritime issues — particularly, issues concerned with the enforcement of safety obligations. The regime of the flags of convenience is often used to avoid stringent regulations for the safety of ships and onerous regulations for manning on board ships. Once registered with flag states, most of the flag of conveniences ships remain out of those flag states'

59 United Nations Conference for Trade and Development (UNCTAD), '*Review of Maritime Transport 2016*,' p. 44.

control. They do not implement rules and standards in international conventions, and the conditions and safety requirements for mariners on board ships are compromised. Moreover, it is argued that the increasing pollution of oceans and beaches is the result of poorly maintained and operated vessels flagged by FOC s.[60]

Reflecting the tradition of the flags of convenience, and pursuant to the 1958 Geneva Convention on High Seas, the UNCLOS provides the provisions of the open registry. Article 91(1) stipulates that "every state shall fix the conditions for the grant of its nationality to ships, for the registration of ships in its territory, and for the right to fly its flag. Ships have the nationality of the state whose flag they are entitled to fly. There must exist *a genuine link* between the state and the ship."

The interpretation of "a genuine link" has been up for debate. The International Tribunal for the Law of the Sea (ITLOS) ruled in the *M/V SAIGA* (No. 2) Case that the provision of 'a genuine link' is to ensure the implementation of the flag state's duties, not to provide criteria to judge the validity of the open registration of ships.[61] The enforcement of the provisions of IMO conventions is primarily the responsibility of the flag state.

The UNCLOS provides that states are obliged to exercise their jurisdiction in administrative, technical and social matters over ships flying its flag.[62] They are required to undertake specific safety measures, prescribed in the UNCLOS, for ships flying its flag at sea.[63] In relation to the maritime zones, state parties to IMO treaties, pursuant to such provisions of the UNCLOS, are obliged to exercise jurisdiction over ships flying their flag, irrespective of the maritime zone where the ships are located. The differences in the rights and obligations of states in the various maritime zones do not change the obligations on flag states to implement safety measures and measures to prevent, reduce and control pollution on board their vessels.[64]

---

60 Devinder Grewal, 'International Ship Safety Regulations' in Wayne K. Talley, *Maritime Safety, Security and Piracy* (informa, London, 2008), p. 16.

61 The *M/V SAIGA* (No. 2) Case (Saint Vincent and the Grenadines v. Guinea), para. 82–83: "*...there is nothing in article 94 to permit a state which discovers evidence indicating the absence of proper jurisdiction and control by a flag state over a ship to refuse to recognize the right of the ship to fly the flag of the flag state.... The conclusion of the Tribunal is that the purpose of the provisions of the Convention on the need for a genuine link between a ship and its flag state is to secure more effective implementation of the duties of the flag state, and not to establish criteria by reference to which the validity of the registration of ships in a flag state may be challenged by other states.*"

62 UNCLOS, Art. 94(1).

63 *Ibid.*, Art. 94(2).

64 IMO (n 1).

Coastal State

In relation to the flag state jurisdiction, the coastal state jurisdiction under the UNCLOS to prescribe and enforce laws and regulations is very restrictive. The coastal state jurisdiction with regard to maritime safety and security and the protection of the marine environment is primarily concerned with innocent passage through territorial waters and navigation in the exclusive economic zone (EEZ), as discussed earlier.

Principally, IMO treaties do not regulate the nature and extent of coastal state jurisdiction. Only the UNCLSO provides the extent to which the coastal state may enforce laws and regulations against foreign ships exercising the right of innocent passage in the territorial water and navigating the EEZ.[65] Pursuant to the UNCLOS, the coastal state may adopt laws and regulations concerned with the degree of innocent passage through the territorial sea and with the principle for the prevention, reduction and control of marine pollution from foreign vessels exercising innocent passage in the territorial sea.[66]

The same principle applies to transit passage in straits used for international navigation or to archipelagic sea lane passage in archipelagic waters. In the EEZ, the coastal state's prescriptive jurisdiction is limited to the adoption of laws and regulations, in conformity with and for the implementation of international rules and standards established by the IMO for the prevention, reduction and control of marine pollution from vessels.[67]

Prior to the UNCLOS, coastal state jurisdiction with regard to navigation was solely regulated by two specific IMO conventions: (i) the Convention Relating to Intervention on the High Seas in Cases of Oil Pollution 1969; and (ii) the Protocol Relating to Intervention on the High Seas in Cases of Pollution by Substances Other than Oil 1973. These instruments specifically regulate the right of the coastal state to intervene on the high seas in the case of pollution casualties. The basic principles in these instruments are codified in article 221(1) of the UNCLOS.[68]

Port State

As illustrated above, a vast majority of ships operate under the flags of convenience (FOCs) system. Many of the flag states have no meaningful link with the FOCs. The flag states find no incentive to prescribe stringent laws and

65 UNCLOS, Arts. 21, 22 & 58.
66 *Ibid.*, Arts. 21(1) & 211(4).
67 *Ibid.*, Art. 211(5).
68 IMO (n 7), p. 13.

regulations against the FOC s.[69] Moreover, a vast majority of the FOC countries, either developing countries or the least-developed countries, rarely have the instruments and capability to inspect the ships flying their flag and enforce the rules and standards imposed by national laws or international conventions.

As substandard ships not complying with the rules and standards are increasingly a threat to the safety of the sea and the marine environment, the international community has strengthened the port state jurisdiction against foreign ships voluntarily in port, which is called the port state control (PSC). Voluntary access to port implies acceptance by the foreign ship of the port state jurisdiction in order to ensure compliance with IMO regulations.[70]

The UNCLOS grants the port state a right to undertake investigation or institute proceedings against a vessel voluntarily in port. The investigations and proceedings are in respect to any discharge from the vessel outside the maritime zones under the jurisdiction of the port state that are in violation of the IMO's international rules and standards.[71] The port state is given authority to take administrative measures to prevent the sailing of ships that are in violation of international rules and standards concerned with the seaworthiness of ships, which threaten the marine environment.[72] The PSC in this regard will be discussed in greater detail later.

The safety regime of the enforcement by port states was applied even before the creation of the UNCLOS. The 1969 International Convention on Civil Liability for Oil Pollution Damage (CLC) included a provision that a port state to this convention must ensure that foreign vessels visiting its port must have insurance or other security required by this convention. This approach was further expanded by the MARPOL Convention in 1973.[73]

VI Status of IMO Conventions and Related Legal Instruments

The IMO has produced a large number of treaties concerned with the safety and security of shipping and the prevention and control of pollution from ships. Except for some conventions that had already existed by the time the IMO came into existence in 1958 (e.g., the International Convention for the Safety of Life at Sea 1948 and the International Convention for the Prevention

69 Karim (n 53), p. 33.
70 IMO (n 7), p. 13.
71 UNCLOS, Art. 218(1).
72 *Ibid.*, Art. 219.
73 Karim (n 53), p. 36.

of Pollution of the Sea by Oil 1954), most conventions and instruments in shipping were formulated by the IMO law-making process. The treaties are mostly in a form of multilateral conventions or other legal instruments.

IMO treaties can be classified largely into four main categories of convention: (i) maritime safety; (ii) marine pollution; (iii) liability and compensation in relation to pollution damage; (iv) maritime security. Other than these, a number of conventions are concerned with facilitation, tonnage measurement, and salvage. As illustrated in Table 3, the vast majority of IMO conventions fall within the scope of maritime safety and marine pollution. This might indicate that the activities of the IMO have focused primarily on efforts to ensure maritime safety and the protection of the marine environment.

Table 3 shows that the SOLAS Convention is a core IMO convention in the field of maritime safety, under which many mandatory codes and other legal instruments — including guidelines, either mandatory or non-mandatory — have been formulated to prescribe safety obligations in detail. With growing concern over marine pollution, the IMO has made enormous efforts to prevent, reduce and control marine pollution.

This has led to the formulation of a variety of marine pollution conventions. The International Convention for the Prevention of Pollution from Ships 1973, as modified by the Protocol of 1978 relating thereto (MARPOL 73/78), is a key convention in the field of marine pollution. Likewise, in the SOLAS Convention, the MARPOL 73/78 contains many different technical and practicable codes and other legal instruments to implement the provisions of the Convention. Along with growing marine pollution, liability and compensation related to pollution damage have risen to an important area of concern by the IMO.

In terms of maritime security, the Convention for the Suppression of Unlawful Acts Against the Safety of Maritime Navigation (SUA 1988) is a principal treaty designed to prevent and combat illegal use of force against ships, crews and passengers on board ships. The Protocol of the SUA Convention extends its coverage to the fixed platforms on the continental shelf.

Outside this, maritime security measures are stipulated in other IMO conventions, particularly in the SOLAS Convention. The amendments to the 1974 SOLAS Convention set out a number of measures to strengthen maritime security and prevent and suppress acts of terrorism against shipping. Of particular note is that these amendments created a new SOLAS chapter dealing specifically with maritime security, which in turn contains the mandatory requirement for ships to comply with the new International Ship and Port Facility Security Code (ISPS Code). Table 3 lists IMO treaties and the related mandatory Codes and Guidelines that the IMO has produced.

TABLE 3 Status of IMO conventions and other legal instruments

Category	Convention (effective)	Codes and other instruments made under the Convention (effective)
Maritime safety	– International Convention for the Safety of Life at Sea (SOLAS), 1974 (May 1980)	– International Code for the Construction and Equipment of Ships Carrying Dangerous Chemicals in Bulk (IBC Code) (July 1986) – International Code for the Construction and Equipment of Ships Carrying Liquefied Gases in Bulk (IGC) (July 1986) – International Code for the Safe Carriage of Grain in Bulk (Grain Code) (Jan. 1994) – International Code of Safety for High-Speed Craft (1994 HSC Code) (Jan. 1996) – Sub-chapter 1.9 of the Code of Safe Practice for Cargo Stowage and Securing (CCS Code) (Jan. 2002) – Guidelines for the Authorization of Organizations Acting on Behalf of the Administration (July 1996) – Specifications on the Survey and Certification Functions of Recognized Organizations Acting on Behalf of the Administration (July 1996) – Guidelines on the Enhanced Program of Inspections During Surveys of Bulk Carriers and Oil Tankers (Jan. 1996)

TABLE 3 *(cont.)*

Category	Convention (effective)	Codes and other instruments made under the Convention (effective)
		– International Management Code for the Safe Operation of Ships and for Pollution Prevention (International Safety Management (ISM) Code) (July 1998) – International Life-Saving Appliances (LSA) (July 1998) – International Code for Application of Fire Test Procedures (FTP Code) (July 1998) – International Code for the Safe Carriage of Packaged Irradiated Nuclear Fuel, Plutonium and High-Level Radioactive Wastes on Board Ships (INF Code) (Jan. 2001) – International Code for Fire Safety Systems (FSS Code) (July 2002) – International Maritime Dangerous Goods (MDG) Code (Jan. 2004) – International Code for the Security of Ships and Port Facilities (ISPS Code) (July 2004) – Technical Provisions for Means of Access for Inspections (Jan. 2005) – Standards and Criteria for Side Structures of Bulk Carriers of Single-Skin Construction (July 2006)

- Standards for Owners' Inspection and Maintenance of Bulk Carrier Hatch Covers (July 2006)
- Performance Standard for Protective Coatings for Dedicated Seawater Ballast Tanks in all Types of Ships and Double-Sided Skin Spaces of Bulk Carrier (July 2008)
- International Code of International Standards and Recommended Practices for a Safety Investigation into a Marine Casualty or Marine Incident (Casualty Investigation Code) (Jan. 2010)
- International Code on Intact Stability, 2008 (2008 Ships and Double-side Skin Spaces of Bulk Carriers Performance Standard for Protective Coatings) (July 2008)
- International Code of International Standards and Recommended Practices for a Safety Investigation into a Marine Policy or Marine Incident (Casualty Investigation Code) (Jan. 2010)
- International Code on Intact Stability 2008 (2008 IS Code) (July 2010)
- International Maritime Solid Bulk Cargoes (IMSBC 2008) (Jan. 2011)
- International Goal-Based Ship Construction Standards for Bulk Carriers and Oil Tankers (Jan. 2012)

TABLE 3 (*cont.*)

Category	Convention (effective)	Codes and other instruments made under the Convention (effective)
		– Performance Standard for Protective Coatings for Cargo Oil Tanks of Crude Oil Tankers (Jan. 2012) – Performance Standard for Protective Coatings for Alternative Means of Corrosion Protection for Cargo Oil Tanks of Crude Oil Tankers (Jan. 2012) – International Code on the Enhanced Program of Inspections during Surveys of Bulk Carriers and Oil Tankers (2011 ESP Code) (Jan. 2014) – Code on Noise Levels on Board Ships (NOISE Code) (July 2014) – Code for Recognized Organization (RO Code) (Jan. 2015) – Code for Ships Operating in Polar Waters (Polar Code) (Jan. 2017)
	– Protocol of 1978 relating to the International Convention on the Safety of Life at Sea, 1974 (SOLAS PROT 1978) (May 1981)	

- Protocol of 1988 Relating to the International Convention for the Safety of Life at Sea, 1974 (SOLAS PROT 1988) (Feb. 2000)
- Convention on the International Regulations for Preventing Collisions at Sea, 1972 (COLREG 1972) (July 1977)
- Special Trade Passenger Ships Agreement (STP), 1971 (Jan. 1974)
- Protocol on Space Requirements for Special Trade Passenger Ships, 1973 (SPACE STP 1973) (June 1977)
- International Convention on Load Lines (LL), 1966 (July 1968)
- Protocol of 1988 Relating to the International Convention on Load Lines (LL), 1966 (LL PROT 1988) (Feb. 2000)
- International Convention for Safe Containers (CSC 1972) (Sept. 1977)
- Convention on the International Mobile Satellite Organization (IMSO C 1976) (July 1976)

TABLE 3 (*cont.*)

Category	Convention (effective)	Codes and other instruments made under the Convention (effective)
	– Operating Agreement on the International Maritime Satellite Organization (INMARSAT) (INMARSAT OA) (July 1979)	
	– Torremolinos Protocol of 1993 Relating to the International Convention for the Safety of Fishing Vessels, 1977 (SFV PROT 1993) (Not yet in force)	
	– Cape Town Agreement of 2012 on the Implementation of the Provisions of the 1993 Protocol relating to the Torremolinos International Conference for the Safety of Fishing Vessels, 1977 (Cape Town Agreement 2012) (Not yet in force)	
	– International Convention on Standards of Training, Certification and Watchkeeping for Seafarers, 1978 (STCW 1978) (Apr. 1984)	– Seafarers' Training, Certification and Watchkeeping (STCW) Code
	– International Convention on Standards of Training, Certification and Watchkeeping for Fishing Vessel Personnel, 1995 (STCW-F) (Sept. 2012)	

	– International Convention on Maritime Search and Rescue, 1979 (SAR 1979) (June 1995)	
Marine pollution	– International Convention for the Prevention of Pollution from Ships, 1973, as Modified by the Protocol of 1978 Relating Thereto (MARPOL 73/78) (Oct. 1983)	– International Code for the Construction and Equipment of Ships Carrying Dangerous Chemicals in Bulk (IBG Code) (April 1987) – Code for the Construction and Equipment of Ships Carrying Dangerous Chemicals in Bulk (BCH Code) (April 1987) – Code for Recognized Organization (RO Code) (Jan. 2015) – Code for Ships Operating in Polar Waters (Polar Code) (Jan. 2017)
	– Protocol of 1997 to Amend the International Convention for the Prevention of Pollution from Ships, 1973, as Modified by the Protocol of 1978 Relating Thereto (MARPOL PROT 1997) (May 2005) – International Convention on Oil Pollution Preparedness, Response and Co-operation, 1990 (OPRC 1990) (May 1995) – 2000 Protocol on Preparedness, Response and Co-operation to Pollution Incidents by Hazardous and Noxious Substances (OPRC/HNS PROT 2000) (June 2007)	

TABLE 3 (*cont.*)

Category	Convention (effective)	Codes and other instruments made under the Convention (effective)
	– Convention on the Prevention of Marine Pollution by Dumping of Wastes and Other Matter, 1972 (LC 1972) (Aug. 1975) – 1996 Protocol to the Convention on the Prevention of Marine Pollution by Dumping of Wastes and Other Matter, 1972 (LC PROT 1996) (Mar. 2006) – International Convention on the Control of Harmful Anti-Fouling Substances on Ships, 2001 (AFS 2001) (Sept. 2008) – International Convention for the Control and Management of Ships' Ballast Water and Sediments, 2004 (BWM 2004) (Sept. 2017)	
Liability and compensation	– International Convention Relating to Intervention on the High Seas in Cases of Oil Pollution Casualties, 1969 (INTERVENTION1969) (May 1975)	

- Protocol Relating to Intervention on the High Seas in Cases of Oil Pollution by Substances other than Oil, 1973(INTERVENTION PROT 1973) (Mar. 1983)
- International Convention on Civil Liability for Oil Pollution Damage, 1969 (CLC 1969), (June 1975)
- Protocol to the International Convention on Civil Liability for Oil Pollution Damage, 1969 (CLC PROT 1992) (April 1981)
- Convention relating to Civil Liability in the Field of Maritime Carriage of Nuclear Material, 1971 (NUCLEAR 1971) (July 1975)
- International Convention on the Establishment of an International Fund for Compensation for Oil Pollution Damage 1971 (FUND 1971) (Oct. 1978)
- Protocol to the International Convention on the Establishment of an International Fund for Compensation for Oil Pollution Damage, 1971 (FUND PROT 1976) (Nov. 1994)

TABLE 3 (*cont.*)

Category	Convention (effective)	Codes and other instruments made under the Convention (effective)
	– Protocol of 1992 to Amend the International Convention on the Establishment of an International Fund for Compensation for Oil Pollution Damage 1971 (FUND PROT 1992) (May 1996) – Protocol of 2000 to the International Convention on the Establishment of an International Fund for Compensation for Oil Pollution Damage, 1971 (FUND PROT 2000) (June 2001) – Protocol of 2003 to the International Convention on the Establishment of an International Fund for Compensation for Oil Pollution Damage, 1992 (FUND PROT 2003) (Mar. 2005) – Athens Convention Relating to the Carriage of Passengers and their Luggage by Sea, 1974 (PAL 1974) (Apr. 1987)	

- Protocol to the Athens Convention Relating to the Carriage of Passengers and their Luggage by Sea 1974 (PAL PROT 1976) (Apr. 1989)
- Protocol of 1990 to Amend the Athens Convention relating to the Carriage of Passengers and their Luggage by Sea 1974 (PAL PROT 1990) (Not yet in force)
- Protocol of 2002 to the Athens Convention Relating to the Carriage of Passengers and their Luggage by Sea 1974 (PAL PROT 2002) (Apr. 2014)
- Convention on Limitation of Liability for Maritime Claims, 1976 (LLMC 1976) (Dec. 1986)
- Protocol of 1996 to Amend the Convention on Limitation of Liability for Maritime Claims, 1976 (LLMC PROT 1996) (May 2004)
- International Convention on Liability and Compensation for Damage in Connection with the Carriage of Hazardous and Noxious Substances by Sea, 1996 (HNS 1996) (Not yet in force)

TABLE 3 (*cont.*)

Category	Convention (effective)	Codes and other instruments made under the Convention (effective)
	– Protocol of 2010 to the International Convention on Liability and Compensation for Damage in Connection with the Carriage of – Hazardous and Noxious Substances by Sea, 1996 (HNS PROT 1996) (Not yet in force) – International Convention on Civil Liability for Bunker Oil Pollution Damage, 2001 (BUNKERS 2001) (Nov. 2008)	
Maritime Security	– Convention for the Suppression of Unlawful Acts Against the Safety of Maritime Navigation (SUA 1988) (Mar. 1992) – Protocol of 2005 to the Convention for the Suppression of Unlawful Acts Against the Safety of Maritime Navigation (SUA 2005) (July 2010) – Protocol for the Suppression of Unlawful Acts Against the Safety of Fixed Platforms Located on the Continental Shelf (SUA PROT) (Mar. 1992)	

	– Protocol of 2005 to the Protocol for the Suppression of Unlawful Acts Against the Safety of Fixed Platforms Located on the Continental Shelf (SUA PROT 2005) (July 2010)
Others	– Convention on Facilitation of International Maritime Traffic (FAL), 1965 (Mar. 1967) – International Convention on Tonnage Measurement of Ships, 1969 (Tonnage 1969) (July 1982) – International Convention on Salvage,1989 (SALVAGE 1989) (July 1996) – Nairobi International Convention on the Removal of Wrecks, 2007 (Nairobi WRC 2007) (Apr. 2015) – Hong Kong International Convention for the Safe and Environmentally Sound Recycling of Ships, 2009 (HONG KONG CONVENTION) (Not yet in force)

SOURCE: ADAPTED FROM THE IMO

VII Conclusion

Since its creation, the IMO has played a key role in establishing practicable standards for maritime safety, navigation and marine pollution. The IMO has greatly contributed to make the sea safer and more environmentally sound through the adoption of a variety of new conventions and protocols and related codes and guidelines, and by making amendments to existing conventions. The IMO conventions have been formulated by the consensus of member states. Thus, the rules and standards imposed by the conventions become global norms that member states are bound to.

Most IMO conventions have employed the tacit acceptance system in amendments to conventions so that it facilitates the amendment process, and enables the IMO to promptly reflect rapidly changing technologies and techniques in shipping. However, the IMO law-making process has some inherent weaknesses and challenges that need to be addressed.

First, most of rule-making of IMO has been developed in the aftermath of major maritime accidents. Given that the best safety policy would be to take necessary measures in advance to prevent maritime accidents from occurring and reduce the risk, the focus of IMO rule making should be more concerned with a proactive approach, rather than a reactive approach. Thus the IMO should be more concerned with the assessment of risk related to maritime safety.

Second, the IMO rule-making needs to enhance safety requirements for the ships engaged on domestic voyage, such as ferry, to reduce the risk of disastrous ferry boat accidents. The safety requirements of ferry boats below a certain size fully rests with a state, and as a consequence, in many countries, particularly underdeveloped countries, the safety of ferry boats used for major public transport remains vulnerable.

Third, the implementation of the rules and standards contained in IMO conventions entirely rests with state parties, making the enforcement of conventions non-uniform across the world.[74] Except in a few cases, as illustrated in the STCW Convention, the IMO itself has no means and jurisdiction to enforce the provisions of conventions.

Fourth, the tacit acceptance system has facilitated the amendment process and thus allowed IMO conventions to be more flexible when change is necessary. However, frequent amendments within short timeframes occasionally make it difficult for some developing countries to keep pace with developments

74 Grewal (n 60), p. 28.

in IMO conventions. This leads to non-compliance by some developing countries, which lack the expertise of officials and the resources needed to meet the requirements imposed by amendments.

Fifth, most the flag of convenience ships, which do not have a close link with flag states, operate at a substandard level while staying out of the control of flag states in terms of enforcement of international shipping rules and standards. Given that over 70 percent of registered ships around the world are flagged out to foreign countries, the port state control by IMO legal instruments needs to be further strengthened in order to ensure compliance with generally accepted IMO rules and standards.

CHAPTER 3

Safety of Navigation and Port State Control

I Introduction

Shipping involving navigation across the ocean in harsh conditions might be one of the most dangerous of all the world's industries. For this reason, shipping is one of the most heavily regulated industries to ensure the safety of ships and navigation. It was among the very first industry to adopt widely implemented international safety standards and regulations. Regulations concerning shipping are developed at the global level because shipping, which is inherently international, requires uniform regulations concerning construction standards, navigational rules and standards of crew competence. Otherwise, the application of divergent standards and rules by states and regions might cause enormous confusion in the safety of navigation.

The shipping industry is regulated by various international agencies. As discussed in Chapter 2, the main international body in formulating safety rules and standards is the International Maritime Organization (IMO). The IMO has adopted a comprehensive framework of detailed regulations, in the form of international conventions and resolutions, which include technical codes and guidelines for the safety of ships and the protection of the marine environment. The rules and standards set out in the conventions and resolutions are subject to the implementation and enforcement of flag states, coastal states and port states, depending of their jurisdiction.

Flag states, which assume principal responsibility for enforcing safety rules and standards, as prescribed in the UNCLOS,[1] are required to ensure that ships flying their flag comply with the international safety standards of navigation and the marine environment. Flag states enforce the rules and standards through inspections of ships conducted by a network of international surveyors, much of which is delegated to classification societies.[2] The inspection of ships by flag states is supplemented by port state control, under which authorities in any country that a ship may visit can inspect foreign flagged ships to ensure that they comply with international rules and standards. Port state

---

1 UNCLOS, Art. 94.

2 International Chamber of Shipping (ICS), 'The Regulation of International Shipping,' Shipping Facts.

 | DOI:10.1163/9789004389908_004

control officials are authorized to detain foreign ships if they do not conform to international rules and standards.

This chapter deals with the requirements and measures for the safety of navigation and the protection of the marine environment. It intends to give an overall picture of principal safety standards and rules, which are very complex and laid down in various international regulations, as well as safety measures of navigation. This chapter also examines port state control, which plays an essential role in ensuring compliance with international safety standards because 70.2 percent of the world total fleet is under the flag of convenience system.[3]

II Principal Regulations Governing the Safety of Navigation

Standards and rules for navigational safety and pollution prevention are provided in a number of different international conventions adopted by the IMO and the International Labor Organization (ILO). This part outlines principal conventions and regulations governing the safety of navigation and pollution prevention.

Principal Conventions

1 The International Convention for the Safety of Life at Sea, 1974 (SOLAS 1974)

Concerning the safety of ships and navigation, the SOLAS is generally regarded as the most important international legal framework. For the most part, international safety standards for merchant shipping are formulated in the rules, codes and procedures adopted within the framework of SOLAS. First adopted in 1914 in response to the *Titanic* disaster, the Convention lays down a comprehensive range of minimum standards for ship safety and essential safety equipment to be fitted onboard, including construction, design, fire protection, lifesaving appliances, radio communications, safety of navigation, carriage of cargoes and safety measures for high-speed craft. The SOLAS also requires regular ship surveys and the issuance of compliance certificates by flag states.

The current SOLAS Convention, amended in 2002, is composed of 16 chapters, which include: Chapter I General provisions; Chapter II-1

3 UNCTAD, 'Review of Maritime Transport 2016,' available at http://unctad.org/en/PublicationsLibrary/rmt2016_en.pdf.

Construction-subdivision and stability, machinery and electric installations; Chapter II-2 Fire protection, fire detection and fire extinction; Chapter III Life-saving appliances and arrangements; Chapter IV Radio communications; Chapter V Safety of navigation; Chapter VI Carriage of cargoes; Chapter VII Carriage of dangerous goods; Chapter VIII Nuclear ships; Chapter IX Management for the safe operation of ships; Chapter X Safety measures for high-speed craft; Chapter XI-1 Special measures to enhance maritime safety; Chapter XI-2 Special measures to enhance maritime security; Chapter XII Additional safety for bulk carriers; Chapter XIII Verification of compliance; Chapter XIV Safety measures for ships operating in polar waters.

Contracting governments to the SOLAS are required to fully implement the standards and requirements and undertake to promulgate relevant laws and regulations. They are also required to take all steps necessary to implement the standards and requirements.[4] As of 2017, the number of contracting states is 163, which constitute approximately 99.14 percent of the gross tonnage of the world's merchant fleet.[5]

2 The Convention on International Regulations for Preventing Collisions at Sea, 1972 (COLREG 1972)

The COLREG 1972 is generally referred to as 'rules of the road,' as it sets out navigation rules to be followed by ships and other vessels at sea to prevent collisions between two or more vessels. The COLREG 1972 was first adopted by the IMO in October 1972 and entered into force in July 1977. It was designed to update and replace the Collision Regulation of 1960. One of the most important elements in the COLREG 1972 was the recognition given to traffic separation schemes, which will be discussed below.

The COLREG 1972 is composed of 38 rules, divided into five sections: Part A General (Rules 1–3); Part B Steering and Sailing (Rules 4–19); Part C Lights and Shapes (Rules 20–31); Part D Sound and Light Signals (Rules 32–37); Part E Exemptions (Rule 38). There are four annexes which include: (i) Annex I Positioning and technical details of lights and shapes; (ii) Annex II Additional signals for fishing vessels fishing in close proximity; (iii) Annex III Technical details of sound signal appliances; (iv) Annex IV Distress goals, which lists the signals indicating distress and need of assistance.

4 SOLAS, Art. 1.

5 IMO, 'Status of multilateral Conventions and instruments in respect of which the International Maritime Organization or its Secretary-General performs depositary or other functions,' posted on 11 October 2017.

3 The International Convention on Load Lines, 1966 (CLL 1966)

The CLL 1966 sets the minimum permissible freeboard, according to the season of the year and the ship's trading pattern. It has long been recognized that limitations on the draught to which a ship may be loaded make a significant impact on the safety of ship. These limits are given in the form of freeboards, which constitute the main objective of the convention, besides external weathertight and watertight integrity.[6] The International Convention on Load Lines was first adopted in 1930 on the basis of the principle of reserve buoyancy, although it was recognized then that the freeboard should also ensure adequate stability and avoid excessive stress on the ship's hull as a result of overloading.[7] The CLL 1966 was adopted by the IMO in April 1966 and amended by the 1988 Protocol and further revised in 2003. The 1988 Protocol was adopted to harmonize the survey and certification requirement of the 1966 CLL with the relevant provisions in the SOLAS and the International Convention for the Prevention of Pollution from Ships 1973/1978 (MARPOL 73/78).

The CLL 66 sets out the provisions that determine the freeboard of ships by subdivision and damage stability calculations. In accordance with the CLL 66/88, all assigned load lines must be marked amid ships on each side of the ship engaged in international voyages, together with the deck line. The determinations of the freeboard of ships are calculated and/or verified by classification societies, which issue the International Load Line Certificate in accordance with the legislation of participating states. The convention includes three annexes, which contain various regulations for determining load lines, including details of marking and verification of marks, conditions of assignment of freeboard, and special provisions for ships intended for the carriage of timber.

4 The International Safety Management Code (ISM Code)

The ISM Code, or the International Management Code for the Safe Operation of Ships and for Pollution Prevention, is designed to improve the safety of international shipping and to reduce pollution from ships by establishing an international standard for the safe management and operation of ships and for pollution prevention.

The origin of the code goes back to the late 1980s, when there was mounting concern about poor management standards in shipping. Investigations

---

6 IMO, 'International Convention on Load Lines,' available at http://www.imo.org/en/About/conventions/listofconventions/pages/international-convention-on-load-lines.aspx.

7 *Ibid.*

into a number of serious accidents, such as the *Herald of Free Enterprise*, found that they were caused by human error. The IMO adopted in October 1989 the 'Guideline on Management for the Safe Operation of Ships and for Pollution Prevention,' whose purpose was to provide those responsible for the operation of ships with a framework for the proper development, implementation and assessment of safety and pollution prevention management in accordance with good practice. After some experience in the use of the guidelines, in 1993 the IMO adopted the ISM Code, which was made mandatory under SOLAS Chapter IX (management for the safe operations of ships) in 1994.

The ISM Code establishes safety-management objectives and requires a safety management system (SMS) to be established by the 'Company,' which is defined as the shipowner or any person, such as the manager or bareboat charterer, who has responsibility for operating the ship. The company is required to establish and implement a policy for achieving these objectives, including providing the necessary resources and shore-based support. Companies and their ships are subject to regular audits to ensure that a safety management system is in place, including adequate procedures and lines of communication between ships and their manager ashore.

5 The International Convention on Standards of Training, Certification and Watchkeeping for Seafarers, 1978 (STCW 1978)

The STCW sets minimum standards relating to training, certification and watchkeeping for seafarers internationally that states are required to meet or exceed. The STCW was the first to establish basic requirements on training, certification and watchkeeping for seafarers on an international level. Previously the standards of training, certification and watchkeeping of officers and ratings were set out by individual governments, usually without reference to practices in other countries.

As a result, standards and procedures varied widely, causing confusion and ineffectiveness. The regulations provided in the Convention, which contains basic requirements, are supported by sections in the STCW Code, which enlarge and explain the basis requirements in the convention. Part A of the code is mandatory and provides for the minimum standards of competence required of seagoing personnel in detail. Part B of the code contains recommended guidance, which is intended to help states implement the convention.

The STCW has undergone a major revision in 2010, called the 'Manila Amendments' to keep training standards in line with new technological and operational requirements that require new shipboard competencies. The principal amendments include: (i) improved measures to prevent fraudulent practices associated with certificates of competency; (ii) new work and rest hours for seafarers; (iii) new grades of certificate of competency for able seafarers in both deck and engine; (iv) new requirements relating to training in modern technology; (v) new requirements for security training; (vi) additional medical standards; (vii) specific alcohol limits.

For those working in the fishing industry, the IMO has developed a separate convention, which is the International Convention on Standards of Training, Certification and Watchkeeping for Fishing Vessel Personnel (STCW- F), 1995. The convention sets the standards for certification of fishing vessel personnel on vessels of greater than 24 meters in length and more than 750kW engine power.

6 The International Convention for the Prevention of Pollution from Ships, 1973/1978 (MARPOL 1973/1978)

The MARPOL Convention is a key international convention dealing with the prevention of pollution of the marine environment by ships from operational or accidental causes. The Convention, which aims at the complete elimination of intentional pollution of the marine environment by oil and other harmful substances and the minimization of accidental discharge of such substances, concerns the prevention of pollution from oil, bulk chemicals, dangerous goods, sewage, garbage and atmospheric pollution spilled by the operation of ships or through accidents. The Convention also includes ship safety provisions such as those that require tankers of 5,000 dwt and more to be fitted with double hulls.

The Convention was first adopted in 1973 by the IMO, and the Protocol of 1978 was adopted in response to a number of subsequent tanker accidents during the period of 1976–1977. As the 1973 MARPOL Convention had not yet entered into force when the 1978 Protocol was adopted, the protocol incorporated the Convention. As a result, the current MARPOL Convention 73/78, which entered into force in 1983, is a combination of the 1973 Convention and the 1978 Protocol. The MARPOL 73/78 includes six technical annexes: (i) Annex I Regulations for the Prevention of Pollution by Oil (effective in October 1983); (ii) Annex II Regulations for the Control of Pollution by Noxious Liquid Substances in Bulk (effective in October 1983); (iii) Annex III Prevention of Pollution by Harmful Substances Carried by Sea in Packaged Form (effective in July 1992); (iv) Annex IV Prevention of Pollution by Sewage from Ships (effective in September 2003); (v) Annex V Prevention of Pollution by Garbage from Ships (effective in December 1988); (vi) Annex VI Prevention of Air Pollution from Ships (effective in May 2005). As of 2017, 155 states are parties to the MARPOL 73/78, accounting for 99.14 percent of the world's shipping tonnage.[8]

Status of East Asian Countries

Table 4 outlines the status of East Asian countries with respect to the conventions concerned with navigational safety. For China, Japan and Korea, they have a keen interest in ensuring the safety of navigation since they are heavily dependent on sea-borne trade. They have actively participated in regime building for the safety of navigation and are committed to the implementation of safety regulations as the parties to key conventions.

For North Korea, it has acceded to a number of key conventions for maritime safety, such as the International Convention for the Safety of Life at Sea (SOLAS) and the Convention on the International Regulations for Preventing Collisions at Sea (COLREG). Concerning the International Convention on Maritime Search and Rescue (SAR), in particular, North Korea has yet to accede. The SAR Convention requires parties to establish search and rescue regions within each sea area with the agreement of the parties concerned and to accept responsibility for providing search and rescue services for a specified area. North Korea, as a party to the SOLAS, is responsible for the necessary arrangements for distress communication and coordination in its area of responsibility and for the rescue of persons in distress at sea around its coasts.[9] However, without the establishment of SAR regions and coordination between SAR organizations, procedures for the entry into the waters of North Korea of rescue units, especially the territorial seas and the 50-nautical-mile Military Boundary Zones, is complicated and time consuming.[10]

In terms of marine pollution control, North Korea is a party to the International Convention for the Prevention of Pollution from Ships (MARPOL). However, North Korea has not joined the 1999 International Convention on Oil Pollution Preparedness, Response and Co-operation (OPRC), and the 2000 Protocol on Preparedness, Response and Co-operation to Pollution Incidents by Hazardous and Noxious Substances. Given a higher risk of marine pollution incidents in the semi-enclosed seas in East Asia, North Korea's participation in the OPRC Convention and its Protocol is required for a closer cooperation with neighbor countries in dealing with possible major pollution incidents.

---

8 IMO, 'Status of Treaties,' available at http://www.imo.org/en/About/Conventions/StatusOfConventions/Documents/Status%20of%20Treaties.pdf.

9 Suk Kyoon Kim, 'Korean Peninsula Maritime Issues,' *Ocean Development and International Law*, 41(2), p. 167.

10 *Ibid.*

TABLE 4 Status of navigational safety conventions of East Asian countries

	China	Japan	ROK (South Korea)	DPRK (North Korea)
SOLAS Convention 74	X	X	X	X
SOLAS Protocol 78	X	X	X	X
SOLAS Protocol 88	X	X	X	X
CLL Convention 66	X	X	X	X
CLL Protocol 88	X	X	X	X
COLREG Convention 72	X	X	X	X
STCW Convention 78	X	X	X	X
STCW-F Convention 95				
SAR Convention 79	X	X	X	
Facilitation Convention 66	X	X	X	X
MARPOL 73/78	X	X	X	X
MARPOL Protocol 97	X	X	X	X
London Convention 72	X	X	X	
London Convention Protocol 96	X	X	X	
OPRC Convention 90	X	X	X	
OPRC/HNS 2002	X	X	X	
NAIROBI WRC 2007	X			X

SOURCE: ADAPTED FROM STATUS OF IMO TREATIES

*X: ratification

*SOLAS Convention: The International Convention for the Safety of Life at Sea; CLL Convention: The International Convention on Load Lines; COLREG Convention: The Convention on International Regulations for Preventing Collisions at Sea; SAR Convention: The International Convention on Maritime Search and Rescue; STCW Convention: The International Convention on Standards of Training, Certification and Watchkeeping for Seafarers; STCW-F: The International Convention on Standards of Training, Certification and Watchkeeping for Fishing Vessels Personnel; MARPOL: The International Convention for the Prevention of Pollution from Ships; London Convention: The Convention on the Prevention of Marine Pollution by Dumping of Wastes and Other Matter; OPRC Convention: The International Convention on Oil Pollution Preparedness, Response and Co-operation; OPRC-HNS: The Protocol on Preparedness, Response and Co-operation to pollution Incidents by Hazardous and Noxious Substances; NAIROBI WRC: The Nairobi International Convention on the Removal of Wrecks

III Ships and Navigational Safety Measures

Ship Construction and Equipment

The most vital part in ensuring navigational safety might be concerned with the construction of ships and installation of adequate equipment in compliance with safety standards. Construction of ships carrying specialized cargoes or passengers involves a wide array of technologies and requirements to ensure the safety of navigation. As illustrated in the adoption of the SOLAS Convention in response to the *Titanic* disaster, the IMO, in an effort to enhance the safety of ships and navigation, has developed a wide range of international conventions and other instruments that set out minimum standards and requirements of ship design, construction, structure, equipment, machinery installations and electric installations, and fire protection of all types of vessel and craft. The conventions and other mandatory instruments include[11]:

- 1974 SOLAS Convention (chapters I, II-1, II-2, III, X, XI-1, XII and other relevant chapters) and the 1988 Protocol relating thereto;
- MARPOL 73/78 (Annexes I and IV and other relevant annexes, as appropriate);
- International Life-Saving Appliances (LSA) Code;
- International Code on Intact Stability, 2008;
- International Code of Safety for High-Speed Craft (HSC Code), 1994 and 2000;
- Guidelines on the enhanced program of inspections during the surveys of bulk carriers and oil tankers (IMO Res. A. 744(18));
- Condition Assessment Scheme (CAS); and
- Fire Safety System (FSS) Code, 2001

Amongst those, the SOLAS Convention is the chief instrument that sets comprehensive minimum standards that ships are obliged to comply with to ensure the safety of ships and navigation. Chapter II-1 and II-2 of the SOLAS Convention cover structure, subdivision and stability, machinery, electrical installations, fire protection, fire detection and fire extinction. This part outlines safety measures relating to construction of ships provided in the aforementioned chapters of the Convention.

Design and Construction

The structure of ships is required to comply with the applicable requirements of Parts A and A-1 of Chapter II-1 of SOLAS. In addition, ships must be designed,

11 IMO, 'Maritime Safety,' IMO website, available at http://www.imo.org/en/OurWork/Safety/Cargoes/Pages/Default.aspx.

constructed and maintained in compliance with the structural, mechanical and electrical requirements of a classification society which is recognized by the flag state.

Subdivision and Stability

For stability standards, ships are required to comply with the relevant requirements of the International Code on Intact Stability, 2008 and the relevant requirements relating to intact stability of Part B-1 of Chapter II-1 of SOLAS. For subdivision standards, ships are required to comply with the applicable subdivision and damage stability requirements of Parts B, B-1, B-3 and B-4, and the applicable requirements of Part A of Chapter II-1 of SOLAS.

Machinery Installations

Ships are required to have machinery installations, including steering gear, that comply with the applicable requirements of Part A and Part C of Chapter II-1 of SOLAS. Ships must be provided with sufficient parts and materials for machinery installation, which take into account the intended service of the ship and the risk to the ship from the failure of any part of the machinery. Where alternative design and arrangements for machinery installations are sought, the application is required to comply with the applicable requirements of Part E of Chapter II-1 of SOLAS.

Electrical Installations

The electrical installations to be fitted on ships must comply with the applicable requirements of Part A and Part D of Chapter II-1 of SOLAS. Where approval for alternative design and arrangements for electrical installations are sought, the application is required to comply with the applicable requirements of Part F of Chapter II-1 of SOLAS.

Life-Saving Appliances and Arrangements

Ships whose keels were laid or were at a similar stage of construction on or after 1 July 1998 are required to have life-saving appliances and arrangements that comply with the applicable performance standards of the International Life-Saving Appliance (LSA) Code adopted by the resolution of MSC 48(66) in 1996. Such ships are required to have life-saving appliances and arrangements that comply with the applicable performance standards of Chapter III of SOLAS.

Fire Protection, Fire Detection and Fire Extinction

In 2002, a comprehensive new set of requirements for fire protection, fire detection and fire extinction on board ships entered into force as a new revised

Chapter II-2 of SOLAS, incorporating technological advances in fire detection and extinction as well as lessons learned from fire incidents over the years.[12]

The regulations are designed to ensure that: Fires are first of all prevented from occurring — for example, by making sure that materials such as carpets and wall coverings are strictly controlled to reduce the fire risk; secondly, that any fires are rapidly detected; and thirdly, that any fire is contained and extinguished.[13] Designing ships to ensure easy evacuation routes for crew and passengers is a key element of the Chapter.[14] Specifically, passenger ships are required to have fire protection that complies with all applicable requirements of Chapter II-2 of SOLAS. Non-passenger ships and tankers are required to have fire protection that complies with all applicable requirements of Chapter II-2 of SOLAS.

Ships' Routeing

The ships' routeing system refers to the establishment of an international and mandatory way for ships to follow predetermined routes that help them avoid hazards to navigation at sea. Navigational hazards include, but are not limited to, the risk of collision with traffic in areas of high-transit volume, shallow water areas, and areas where certain ships have the potential to damage the marine environment and ecology.[15]

The purpose of ships' routeing systems is to improve the safety of navigation in converging areas and in areas where the density of traffic is great and where freedom of movement of shipping is inhibited by restricted searoom, the existence of obstructions to navigation, limited depth, or unfavorable meteorological conditions.[16] The practice of predetermining routes for shipping originated in 1898 by shipping companies operating passenger ships across the North Atlantic. Related provisions were subsequently incorporated into the SOLAS Convention. Regulation 10(1) of SOLAS Chapter V lays down the requirements of ships' routeing, of which principal provisions include:

- Ships' routeing systems are recommended for use by, and may be made mandatory for, all ships, certain categories of ships or ships carrying certain cargoes
- The initiation of establishing a ship's routeing system is the responsibility of the government(s) concerned

12 *Ibid.*
13 *Ibid.*
14 *Ibid.*
15 IMO, *Ships' Routeing*, 2017 Edition.
16 *Ibid.*

- Ships' routeing systems should be submitted to the IMO. Where two or more governments have a common interest in a particular area, they should formulate joint proposals for the delineation and use of a routeing system on the basis of an agreement between them. States are required to comply with the measures adopted by the IMO
- A ship is obliged to follow the mandatory ships' routeing system adopted by the IMO that applies to its category or the cargo it carries, unless there are compelling reasons not to use a particular ships' routeing system
- Mandatory ships' routeing systems are subject to the review of the contracting government(s) concerned

Concerning the procedure of establishing ships' routeing system, governments intending to establish a new routeing system or to amend an existing one must submit proposed routeing measures to the IMO's Sub-Committee on Navigation, Communication and Search and Rescue. The Sub-Committee evaluates the proposal and makes a recommendation regarding its adoption. The recommendation is then passed to the MSC for its adoption.

1 Traffic Separation Schemes

Ships' routeing systems include traffic separation schemes and other measures to improve safety at sea, including two-way routes, recommended tracks, deep-water routes,[17] precautionary areas[18] and areas to be avoided.[19] Amongst ships' routeing, traffic separation schemes may be the most salient. Traffic separation schemes and other ships' routeing systems have been established in most of the major congested shipping areas of the world, such as the Malacca Strait. As a result, the number of collisions and groundings has been dramatically reduced.[20]

A traffic separation scheme is a routeing measure aimed at separating opposing streams of traffic by appropriate means and by the establishment of traffic lanes.[21] The first traffic separation scheme was established in the Dover Strait in 1967. It was first operated in a voluntary basis. The effectiveness of the system was proved in a study showing that collisions between 1956 and 1960

17 Deep-water routes are established primarily for the safety of ships whose ability to maneuver is constrained by their draught.

18 Precautionary areas are the areas where ships need to navigate with particular caution for safety reasons.

19 Areas to be avoided indicate areas that ships should avoid navigating through for reasons of exceptional danger or especially sensitive ecological and environmental factors.

20 IMO (n 11).

21 'Traffic lane' indicates areas within defined limits in which one-way traffic is established. Natural obstacles, including those forming separation zones, may constitute a boundary.

in the Strait were 60 in total, but 20 years later, following the introduction of traffic separation schemes, this total was cut to only 16. On this basis, the IMO adopted a resolution stating that observance of all traffic separation schemes be made mandatory.

The UNCLOS allows for coastal states to require foreign ships exercising innocent passage to use the designated traffic separation schemes in its territorial waters.[22] States bordering straits used for international navigation may designate sea lanes and prescribe traffic separation schemes for navigation in straits where necessary to promote the safe passage of ships.[23] Traffic separation schemes also apply to archipelagic states.[24] The designated traffic separation schemes should clearly indicate the sea lanes and traffic separation schemes on charts to which due publicity is given.[25]

Rule 10 of the COLREG provides specific rules that ships using traffic separation schemes are required to comply with. The principal rules include requirements that:

- A vessel must proceed in the appropriate traffic lane in the general direction of traffic flow for that lane;
- A vessel must avoid crossing traffic lanes, but if obliged to do so, the ship must cross on a heading as closely as possible to a right angle compared with the general direction of traffic flow;
- A fishing vessel shall not impede the passage of any vessel following a traffic lane;
- A vessel shall not use an inshore traffic zone when she can safely use the appropriate traffic lane within the adjacent separation scheme;
- A vessel of less than 20 meters in length or a sailing vessel shall not impede the safe passage of a power-driven vessel following a traffic lane.

2 Ship Reporting

As part of routeing systems, mandatory ship reporting systems are in place in areas where there are special environmental or navigational concerns. In areas where a mandatory reporting system applies, ships are required to report to shore-based authorities without delay when entering in and, if necessary, when leaving the areas covered by the system. A ship may be required to provide the ship's name, cargo and other information. This enables the ship to be identified on radar and its course plotted throughout the system.

22 UNCLOS Art. 22.
23 *Ibid.*, Art. 41.
24 *Ibid.*, Art. 53.
25 *Ibid.*, Arts. 22, 41 & 53.

Safe Carriage of Cargoes

Since the carriage of cargoes on board ships involves a great deal of hazards and risks to ships and persons on board, special precautions in dealing with cargoes are required. Improper stowage and securing of cargoes, for example, has resulted in numerous serious ship casualties and caused injury and loss of life, not only at sea but also during loading and discharge.[26] The shipment of solid bulk cargoes is associated with hazards relating to structural damage due to improper cargo distribution, loss or reduction of stability during a voyage, and chemical reactions of cargoes. The rapid increases since the 1950s in the use of freight containers for the consignment of goods at sea and the development of specialized container ships prompted the adoption of the 1972 Convention for Safer Containers.

The increase in the maritime transport of harmful substances and marine pollution prompted the IMO to adopt relevant mandatory provisions of the SOLAS and the International Maritime Dangerous Goods (IMDG) Code, which governs the carriage of dangerous goods in packaged form. Furthermore, the International Convention for the Prevention of Pollution from Ships (MARPOL) prohibits the carriage of harmful substances in ships except in certain circumstances to prevent pollution to the environment. Given the high importance of safe carriage of cargoes, SOLAS Chapter VI (Carriage of cargoes) and VII (Carriage of dangerous goods) set out in detail the rules and standards for safety matters concerning cargo operations according to the types of cargoes.

Other than the SOLAS, the IMO has developed a number of relevant conventions and relevant instruments, either mandatory or recommendatory, concerning the safety of cargo carriage. The conventions and instruments to deal with matters of the carriage of cargoes are outlined below. They include, but are not limited to[27]:

- 1974 SOLAS (Chapter VI and VII);
- MARPOL (Annexes III and V);
- International Convention for Safe Containers (CSC) 1972;
- International Maritime Dangerous Goods (IMDG) Code and related supplements;
- International Maritime Solid Bulk Cargoes (IMSBC) Code and related supplements;
- International Code for the Construction and Equipment of Ships Carrying Liquefied Gases in Bulk (IGC Code);

---

26 IMO (n 11).

27 *Ibid.*

- International Code for the Safe Carriage of Packaged Irradiated Nuclear Fuel, Plutonium and High-Level Radioactive Wastes on Board Ships (INF Code);
- International Code for the Safe Carriage of Grain in Bulk; and
- Code of Safe Practice for Cargo Stowage and Securing (CSS Code)

The non-mandatory instruments include, but are not limited to[28]:

- Code for Safe Practice for Solid Bulk Cargoes (BC Code);
- Code for the Construction and Equipment of Ships Carrying Liquefied Gases in Bulk (GC Code);
- Code for Safe Practice for Ships Carrying Timber Deck Cargoes;
- Code Safe Practice for the Safe Loading and Unloading of Bulk Carriers (BLU Code);
- Recommendations on the Safe Transport of Dangerous Cargoes and related Activities in Port Areas;
- Guidelines for the Preparation of the Cargo Securing Manual;
- Emergency Response Procedures for Ships Carrying Dangerous Goods;
- Medical First Aid Guide for Use in Accidents Involving Dangerous Goods (MFAG);
- Reporting procedures, including inspection programs for cargo transport units carrying dangerous goods; reporting of incidents involving harmful substances and/or marine pollutants; reporting of casualties involving dangerous cargoes;
- IMO/ILO/UNECE Code of Practice for Packing of Cargo Transport Units;
- Recommendations on the Safe Use of Pesticides in Ships; and
- Any recommendations and guidelines relevant to the carriage of bulk cargoes

Vessel Traffic Services (VTS)

Vessel traffic services include a variety of shore-side systems, which range from the provision of simple informational messages to ships (such as the position of other traffic or meteorological hazard warnings) to extensive management of traffic within a port or waterway.[29] When ships enter a VTS area, they report to the authorities, usually by radio, and are tracked by the VTS control center. Ships must keep watch on a specific frequency for navigational or other warnings, as they may be contacted directly by the VTS operator if there is a risk of an incident or, in areas where traffic flow is regulated, to be given advice on when to proceed.[30]

---

28 *Ibid.*

29 *Ibid.*

30 *Ibid.*

Recognizing the value of VTS, the IMO adopted in 1997 Resolution A. 857(20), which has replaced Guidelines for Vessel Traffic Services[31] adopted in 1985. The Guideline states that VTS is particularly appropriate in such as[32]: (i) high-traffic density; (ii) traffic carrying hazardous cargoes; (ii) conflicting and complex navigation patterns; (iv) difficult hydrographical and meteorological elements; (v) shifting shoals and other local hazards; (vi) environmental considerations; (vii) interference by vessel traffic with other marine-based activities; (viii) a record of maritime casualties; (ix) narrow channels, port configuration, bridges and similar areas where the progress of vessels may be restricted.

The Guideline makes a distinction between a port or harbor VTS and a costal VTS. A port VTS is mainly concerned with vessel traffic to and from a port or harbor, while a coastal VTS is mainly concerned with vessel traffic passing through the area.[33] A VTS could be a combination of both types. The type and level of services rendered could differ between both types of VTS: In a port or harbor VTS, a navigational assistance service and/or a traffic organization service is usually provided for, while in a coastal VTS usually only an information service is rendered.[34] Concerning the use of VTS, the Guideline states that participation of ships in a VTS may be either voluntary or mandatory, depending on governing rules and regulations. The Guideline makes clear that decisions concerning the actual navigation and the maneuvering of the vessel remain with the master.[35]

The benefits of implementing a VTS are that it allows identification and monitoring of vessels, strategic planning of vessel movements and provisions of navigational information and assistance. It can also assist in the prevention of pollution and coordination of pollution response.[36] A revised SOLAS Chapter V, adopted in 2000, set outs the provisions concerning VTS. Regulation 12-vessel traffic services states:

- Contracting governments undertake to arrange for the establishment of VTS where, in their opinion, the volume of traffic or the degree of risk justifies such services.
- Contracting governments planning and implementing VTS, wherever possible, shall follow the guidelines developed by the organization. The use of VTS may only be mandatory in sea areas within the territorial seas of a coastal state.

---

31 IMO, Resolution A. 578(14).

32 IMO, Res. A. 857(20) Guidelines for Vessel Traffic Services, 3.2.2.

33 *Ibid.*, 2.1.2.

34 *Ibid.*

35 *Ibid.*, 2.6.2.

36 *Ibid.*, 2.1.3.

- Contracting governments shall endeavor to secure the participation in, and compliance with, the provisions of vessel traffic services by ships entitled to fly their flag.

Automatic Identification Systems (AIS)

Regulation 19 of SOLAS Chapter V (Carriage of requirements for shipborne navigational systems and equipment) provides navigational systems and equipment to be carried on board ships, in accordance with the size and type of ships. The automatic identification system (AIS) is mandatory equipment out of a range of systems and equipment for navigational safety.

In 2000, the IMO adopted a new resolution requiring all ships to carry automatic identification systems capable of providing information about the ship to other ships and to coastal authorities automatically. The Regulation requires AIS to be fitted aboard all ships of[37]: (i) 300 gross tonnage and upwards engaged on international voyages; (ii) cargo ships of 500 gross tonnage and upwards not engaged on international voyages; (iii) passenger ships irrespective of size.

The Regulation requires that AIS shall[38]:

- Automatically provide information on the ship's identity, type, position, course, speed, navigational status and other safety-related information to appropriately equipped shore stations, other ships, and aircraft;
- automatically receive such from similarly fitted ships;
- monitor and track ships and
- exchange data with shore-based facilities.

AIS must be operated in accordance with the guideline adopted by the IMO.[39] Ships fitted with AIS are required to maintain AIS in operation at all times except where international agreements, rules or standards provide for the protection of navigational information.[40]

Long-Range Identification and Tracking (LRIT)

LRIT is a designated IMO system designed to collect and disseminate the global vessel position information received from contracting parties to the IMO. The LRIT system, which aims to provide a global system for the identification and tracking of ships, enables states to provide prompt and effective services

37 SOLAS, Reg. 19.2.4.
38 *Ibid.*, Reg. 19.2.5.
39 IMO Resolution A. 917(22) 'Guideline for the Onboard Operational Use of Shipborne Automatic Identification Systems (AIS).'
40 SOLAS, Reg. 19.2.7.

through providing accurate information on the location of ships in distress, as well as ships in the vicinity that could lend assistance. Also, it helps a government efficiently respond to the security risk by identifying the ship's location in sufficient time.

The LRIT system is mandatory in accordance with V/19-1 of the 1974 SOLAS Convention. The LRIT regulation applies to the following ships engaged on international voyages: (i) all passenger ships, including high-speed craft; (ii) cargo ships, including high-speed craft of 300 gross tonnage and above; (iii) mobile offshore drilling units. As shown in Fig. 3, the LRIT system consists of:

- LRIT shipborne equipment, which provides position information to the Communication Service Provider
- Communication Service Providers (CSP); which provide the communication infrastructure and services to ensure the secure transfer of LRIT messages between the ship and ASP
- Application Service Providers (ASP); which provide a communication interface and add information to the LRIT message between the CSP and the LRIT Data Center
- LRIT Data Center; which collects and provides LRIT information to its users according to its Data Distribution Plan
- LRIT Data Distribution Plan (DDP); which defines rules and access rights (i.e., which users can receive what LRIT information)
- International LRIT Data Exchange; which routes LRIT information between LRIT Dater Centers according to the DDP.

The system specifies that flag states should ensure that its flag ships transmit a minimum of four positions per day (once every six hours). LRIT information is stored and available for those users entitled to access it. LRIT users include the following[41]:

- Flag states may request information on the location of their vessels around the world
- Coastal states may request information on ships up to 1000 nautical miles from their coasts, irrespective of their flag
- Port states may request information on those ships that have declared one of their ports as a destination, irrespective of their location or flag
- Search and rescue authorities

41 European Maritime Safety Agency, 'Vessel Tracking Globally: Understanding LRIT,' available at file:///C:/Users/%EA%B9%80%EC%84%9D%EA%B7%A0/Downloads/eulritdatacentre_web%20(1).pdf.

Hydrographic Services

In accordance with Regulation 27 of Chapter V of SOLAS, contracting states are required to have adequate and up-to-date nautical charts and nautical publications, such as sailing directions, lists of lights, notices to mariners, tide tables and all other nautical publications necessary for the intended voyage. Regulation 9 of Chapter V sets out the obligations of hydrographic services, which include:

- to undertake to arrange for the collection and compilation of hydrographic data and the publication, dissemination and keeping up to date of all nautical information necessary for safe navigation
- to undertake to cooperate in carrying out the following nautical and hydrographic services:
    - (i) to ensure that hydrographic surveying is carried out, as far as possible, adequate to the requirements of safe navigation
    - (ii) to prepare and issue nautical charts, sailing directions, lists of lights, tide tables and other nautical publications, where applicable, satisfying the needs of safe navigation
    - (iii) to promulgate notices to mariners in order that nautical charts and publications are kept, as far as possible, up to date; and
    - (iv) to provide data management arrangements to support these services
- to undertake to ensure the greatest possible uniformity in charts and nautical publications and to take into account, whenever possible, relevant international resolutions and recommendations.
- to undertake to coordinate their activities to the greatest possible degree in order to ensure that hydrographic and nautical information is made available on a world-wide scale as timely, reliably and unambiguously as possible.

IV Safety Measures to Prevent Marine Pollution

Introduction

The safety of ships and navigation is directly related to marine pollution. With oil spills by tankers significantly increasing over the last few decades, marine pollution has become a major concern of the international community. Accidents of oil tankers resulted in a vast amount of oil being spilled into the sea, inflicting enormous damage to the marine environment. In addition, there is also a growing concern over the risk of spill of hazardous and noxious substances, in tandem with increasing traffic volume transporting those substances.

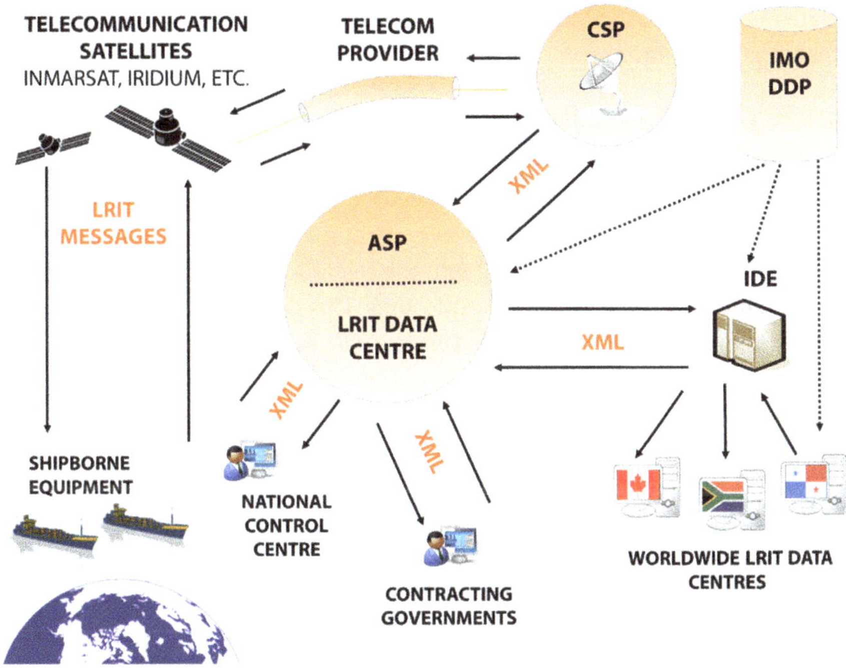

FIGURE 3 LRIT system architecture
SOURCE: EUROPEAN MARITIME SAFETY AGENCY

Despite mounting concern about marine pollution, little attention was paid to marine pollution until the 1958 UN Conference on the Law of the Sea provided the general obligations of states to prevent marine pollution by oil and radioactive wastes in articles 24 and 25 of the High Sea Convention.[42] Afterward, the international community has actively engaged in the formulation of marine pollution treaties to address marine pollution problems.

While the UN Convention on the Law of the Sea (UNCLOS) provides the global framework to address the problem of marine environment, a variety of conventions and legal instruments set forth the specified standards and requirements to prevent and control marine pollution from various sources. The sources of marine pollution are largely identified with five categories, which include: (i) marine pollution from ships; (ii) dumping of wastes; (iii) land-based pollution; (iv) sea-bed exploration and exploitation; (v) and airborne pollution. This part will examine safety aspects of marine pollution and

42 R.R Churchill and A.V. Lowe, *The Law of the Sea* (Manchester University Press, Manchester, 1999), 3rd ed. p. 333.

related treaties and legal instruments concerned with the prevention and control of marine pollution.

Marine Pollution from Ships

Marine pollution from ships is caused by either normal operations or accidents. Oil spills are a main source of marine pollution from ships. For accidental causes, some oil as well as other noxious cargoes like chemicals, liquid gas and radioactive materials spill into the sea as a result of serious accidents such as collisions, strandings and explosions. This happened in the cases of oil tankers the *Torrey Canyon* in 1967, *Amoco Cadiz* in 1978, *Exxon Valdes* in 1989, *Sea Empress* in 1989, *Prestige* in 2002 and *Hebei Spirit* in 2007.

As recently as on 6 January 2017, an Iranian oil tanker *Sanchi*, which was transporting 130, 6000 tons of condensate, an ultra-light crude oil, from Iran to South Korea collided with the *CF Crystal*, a Hong Kong register carrying grain from the U.S., 160 miles off the coast of Shanghai. As a consequence, the oil tanker caught on fire, leaving the tanker's 32 crew members missing. The Chinese government speculated that much of the oil — between 40 and 70 percent — would evaporate in hours.[43] However, if those fumes drift toward towns and cities, it could inflict health problems, leading to coughing and asthma.[44] In terms of the amount of oil, the resulting spill would be double the oil spillage by the sinking of the *Prestige* off the coast of Spain in November 2002, which leaked 63,000 tons of oil into the Atlantic, damaging beaches in France, Spain and Portugal and forcing the closure of Spain's richest fishing grounds.

For operational reasons, ships may discharge some oil with bilge water and ballast water into the sea. Also, the discharge of sewage or throwing garbage overboard into the sea creates marine pollution. But the greatest amount of pollution from ships comes from their cargoes, mainly oil. As illustrated earlier, the MARPOL Convention serves as the principal legal instrument to prevent marine pollution from ships. The MARPOL Convention addresses comprehensive sources of pollution from ships, which include: oil; noxious liquid substances carried in bulk; harmful substances carried by sea; sewage; garbage; and air pollution from ships.

1 Ballast Management

Pollution caused by ballast water discharged during the normal operation of ships is a serious cause of ecological problems within the marine environment.

43 Amanda Erickson, 'A Giant Oil Tanker Is on Fire and Could Explode in the East China Sea,' *The Washington Post*, 9 January 2017.

44 *Ibid.*

Ballast water is pumped in to maintain safe operating conditions throughout a voyage. It serves to reduce stress on the hull, provides transverse stability, improves propulsion and maneuverability and compensates for weight changes in various cargo load levels and due to fuel and water consumption.[45] While ballast water is essential for safe and efficient modern shipping operations, it may pose serious ecological, economic and health problems due to the multitude of marine species carried in ships' ballast water.

Recognizing the significance of ballast water management, the IMO adopted in 2004 the International Convention for the Control and Management of Ships' Ballast Water and Sediment (BMW Convention), which entered into force in September 2017. The Convention sets forth the obligations of states and ships: (i) undertake to implement the provisions of requirements in the convention and the annex[46]; (ii) each ship is required to carry a ballast book, which should be maintained on board the ship for a minimum period of two years[47]; (iii) ships are required to carry out ballast water management that meets given standards[48]; (iv) additional measures taken by states must meet a specified standard or requirement[49]; (v) ships performing ballast water exchange are required to do so with an efficiency of at least 95 percent volumetric exchange of ballast water[50]; (vi) ballast water management systems used to comply with this convention must be approved by the administration taking into account guidelines developed by the IMO.[51]

2 Tanker Safety Measures to Prevent Accidental Pollution

Tanker safety measures are of particular importance of the shipping industry. As demonstrated by serious accidents over the past decades, accidents of tankers carrying dangerous goods, such as oil, gas and chemicals, have disastrous effects to the marine environment, with thousands of tons of oil spilled into the sea. The safety measures for tankers are incorporated in various safety conventions and codes. The principal safety measures are outlined below.

- **More Stringent Safety Measures**

  The SOLAS Convention sets forth more stringent safety requirements for tankers, given their higher risk of accidents, including fire, compared to

---

45 IMO (n 11).
46 BMW Convention, Art. 2.
47 BMW Annex, Reg. B-2.
48 *Ibid.*, Reg. B-3.
49 *Ibid.*, Reg. C-1.1.
50 *Ibid.*, Reg. D-1.2.
51 *Ibid.*, Reg. D-3.

ordinary cargo ships. For a measure to prevent the explosion of empty tanks filled with flammable gas, the inert (non-explosive) gas system is applied. The normal method is to fill these tanks with inert gas. They are cleaned and pumped into the empty tanks, or into the spaces left above the oil in loaded tanks. The inert gas system is required on all new tankers and most existing tankers of 20,000 dwt and above.[52]

– **Requirement of Double Hull and Double Bottom**

In the aftermath of serious oil tanker accidents, in 1992 the MARPOL Convention 73/78 was amended to make it mandatory that tankers of 5,000 dwt and more ordered after 6 July 1993 would be fitted with double hulls and double bottoms or an alternative design approved by the IMO.[53] The requirement for double hulls that applies to new tankers has been also applied to existing ships under a program that began in 1995.[54]

In accordance with the requirement, all tankers are subject to conversion (or being taken out of service) when reached a certain age (up to 30 years old). This measure was adopted to be phased in over a number of years because shipyard capacity is limited and it would not be possible to convert all single-hulled tankers to double hulls without causing immense disruption to the world trade and industry.[55]

Following the *Erika* incident[56] off the coast of France in December 1999, the IMO decided to accelerate the phase-out of single hull tankers. As a result, the IMO adopted a revised phase-out schedule for single hull tankers, which entered into force in September 2003. Furthermore, the *Prestige* incident[57] in 2002 further accelerated the phase-out schedule for single hull tankers.

52 IMO (n 9).
53 MARPOL, Annex I, Reg. 19.
54 *Ibid.*, Reg. 20.
55 IMO (n 9).
56 The *Erika*, an oil tanker owned by a Malta shipping company, sank off the coast of France in 1999, causing a major environmental disaster. As the *Erika* entered the Bay of Biscay, with a heavy cargo of around 20,000 tons of fuel oil, it ran into a heavy storm. On 12 December 1999, the *Erika* broke in two and sank, releasing thousands of tons of oil into the sea, killing marine life and polluting shores around Brittany, France. The investigations into the *Erika* incident undertaken by France and Malta concluded that age, corrosion, insufficient maintenance and inadequate surveys were all contributing factors to the structural failure of the ship. This incident, on top of other accidents involving oil tankers, prompted states to undertake additional international measures to eradicate substandard vessels, particularly substandard oil tankers.
57 The *Prestige*, a 26-year-old, Greek-operated, single-hulled oil tanker, officially registered in the Bahamas, sank on 19 November 2002 in Galicia, Spain. The *Prestige* encountered a winter storm while sailing in the Atlantic Ocean and it burst a tank. As a consequence, the ship began to take on water from high waves and the engine shut down. Refused by the

- **Carriage of Heavy-grade Oil**
  In December 2003, more revisions were made to further accelerate the phase-out schedule, which entered into force in April 2005.[58] Revised Annex I, which entered into force in 2007, banned the carriage of heavy-grade oil by single-hull tankers of 5,000 tons dwt and above after the date of entry into force of the regulation (5 April 2005) and in single-hull oil tankers of 600 tons dwt and above but less than 5,000 tons dwt, not later than the anniversary of their delivery date in 2008.[59]
- **Enhanced Inspections**
  Since 1995, all tankers and bulk carriers aged 5 years and over have been subject to a specially enhanced inspection program which is intended to ensure that any deficiencies such as corrosion or wear and tear resulting from age or neglect are detected. Guidelines on enhanced surveys on tankers and bulk carriers are contained the IMO Assembly Resolution A. 744(18), adopted in November 1993.[60]
- **Special Requirements for Those Working on Tankers**
  The International Convention on Standards of Training Certification and Watchkeeping for Seafarers, 1978, as amended in 1995 (STCW), includes several requirements aimed specifically at those working on tankers.[61]

3 Safety of Carriage of Chemicals by Ship

The safety of carriage of chemicals by ships is covered by the SOLAS Convention and the MARPOL Convention. Carriage of chemicals in bulk is governed by regulations in SOLAS Chapter VII- Carriage of Dangerous Goods and MARPOL Annex II- Regulations for the Control of Pollution by Noxious Liquid Substances in Bulk.

The two Conventions require chemical tankers to comply with the International Bulk Chemical Code (IBC Code), which prescribes the international standards for the safe carriage of dangerous chemicals and noxious liquid substances in bulk by sea. The Code specifically prescribes the design and

French, Spanish and Portuguese governments to dock in their ports for fear of oil pollution, the *Prestige* ultimately split in half and sank after several days of sailing and towing. The *Prestige,* carrying 77,000 tons of heavy fuel oil, spilled 76,000 tons of oil into the sea, polluting the seabed and contaminating the coastline, especially along the territory of Galicia. The oil spill was the largest environmental disaster in the history of both Spain and Portugal.

58 MARPOL, Annex I, Reg. 21.

59 *Ibid.*

60 IMO (n 11).

61 *Ibid.*

construction standard for ships involved in the transport of bulk liquid chemicals. It also identifies the equipment that must be carried to minimize the risk to the ship, its crew and the environment, taking into account the nature of the products that the ship is transporting.[62] Chemical tankers built before 1 July 1986 are required to comply with the Code for the Construction and Equipment of Ships Carrying Dangerous Chemicals in Bulk (BCH Code), which is the predecessor of the IBC Code.[63]

MARPOL Annex II sets out a pollution categorization system for noxious and liquid substances, classified into four categories: (i) Category X[64]; (ii) Category Y[65]; (iii) Category Z[66]; and (iv) Other Substances.[67] The Annex includes a number of other requirements reflecting modern stripping techniques which specify discharge levels for products that have been incorporated into Annex II. For ships constructed on or after 1 January 2007, the maximum permitted residue is 75 liters for products in categories X, Y and Z.[68] Chemicals carried in packaged form, in solid form or in bulk are regulated by Part A of SOLAS Chapter VII- Carriage of Dangerous Goods.

Part A- Carriage of Dangerous Goods in Packaged Form, which requires ships to comply with the International Maritime Dangerous Goods (IMDG) Code, sets out the provisions for the classification, packing, marking, labeling and placarding, documentation and stowage of dangerous goods. MARPOL

62 *Ibid.*

63 *Ibid.*

64 Category X indicates noxious liquid substances which, if discharged into the sea from tank cleaning or deballasting operations, are deemed to present a major hazard to either marine resources or human health, and therefore are justifiably prohibited from being discharged into the marine environment.

65 Category Y indicates noxious liquid substances which, if discharged into the sea from tank cleaning or deballasting operations, are deemed to present a hazard to either marine resources or human health or are deemed to cause harm to amenities or other legitimate uses of the sea, and therefore are justifiably limited by quality or quantity from being discharged into the marine environment.

66 Category Z indicates noxious liquid substances which, if discharged into the sea from tank cleaning or deballasting operations, are deemed to present a minor hazard to either marine resources or human health, and therefore require less stringent restrictions on the quality and quantity of the discharge into the marine environment.

67 Other Substances indicate substances that have been evaluated and found to fall outside Category X, Y or Z because they are considered harmless to marine resources, human health, amenities or other legitimate uses of the sea when discharged into the sea from tank cleaning or deballasting operations. The discharge of bilge or ballast water or other residues or mixtures containing these substances are not subject to any requirements of MARPOL Annex II.

68 IMO (n 8).

Annex III also sets out regulations for the prevention of pollution by harmful substances in packaged form. The Annex includes general requirements for the issuing of detailed standards of packing, marking, labeling, documentation, stowage, quantity limitations and notifications for preventing pollution by harmful substances.

4 Prevention of Pollution by Sewage from Ships

The main source of marine pollution is the discharge of land-based sewage into the sea. Nevertheless, the sewage discharged from ships is also a major contributing factor to marine pollution. MARPOL Annex IV sets forth a set of regulations regarding the discharge of sewage into the sea. It also provides regulations concerning the ships' equipment and systems for the control of sewage discharge and the provision of port reception facilities for sewage, and requirements for survey and certification.

For the most part, the discharge of sewage into the sea is prohibited. Given that the oceans are capable of assimilating and dealing with raw sewage through natural bacterial action, however, Annex IV of MARPOL allows the discharge of sewage beyond a specified distance from the nearest land[69]: (i) to discharge comminute and disinfected sewage at a distance of more than 4 nautical miles; (ii) to discharge sewage that is not comminuted or disinfected at a distance of more than 12 nautical miles. States are required to provide for adequate reception facilities at ports and terminals for the reception of sewage without causing delay to ships.[70] In addition, when a ship has in operation an approved sewage treatment plant certified by the administration to meet operational requirements, the discharge of sewage into the sea, under certain conditions, is permitted.[71]

Prevention of Marine Pollution by Dumping

The Convention on the Prevention of Marine Pollution by Dumping of Wastes and Other Matter, 1972 (London Convention) is designed to promote the effective control of all sources of marine pollution and take all practicable steps to prevent pollution of the sea by the dumping of wastes and other matter. The regulation in the 1996 London Protocol, which replaced the Convention, prohibits the dumping of any wastes or other matter with exception of those listed in Annex I.[72]

---

69 MARPOL Annex IV, Reg. 8.

70 *Ibid.*, Reg. 10(a).

71 *Ibid.*, Reg. 10(b).

72 1996 Protocol to London Convention, Art. 4.1.1.

The permissible wastes and other matter set forth in Annex I include: (i) dredged material; (ii) sewage sludge; (iii) fish waste, or material resulting from industrial fish processing operations; (iv) vessels and platforms or other man-made structures at sea; (v) inert, inorganic geological material; (vi) organic material of natural origin; (vii) bulky items primarily comprising iron, steel and similarly unharmful materials; and (viii) carbon dioxide from carbon dioxide capture processes for sequestration. The materials listed in (vii) and (viii) are subject to certain conditions to be dumped into the sea. The materials listed in Annex I are required a permit from the authorities. Contracting states are required to legislate the procedures and requirements for the issuance of permit.[73]

V Overview of Port State Control

Introduction

Port Sate Control (PSC) generally means the inspection of foreign ships in national ports to verify that the condition of the ships and their equipment comply with the requirements of international regulations and that the ship is manned and operated in compliance with these rules.[74] From the perspective of the power of authorities, PSC is defined as "the power of actors from a state to board, inspect and when appropriate detain a merchant ship flying a foreign flag that enters its ports."[75]

PSC is distinguished from Port State Jurisdiction (PSJ). Whereas PSC is primarily limited to the administrative measures of a port state against substandard ships in its ports, such as detaining a ship in a port until corrective measure have been taken or ordering it to proceed the nearest shipyard for repairs, PSJ encompasses the authority of a port state to prosecute the foreign ship for the breach of international or domestic legislation concerning pollution or safety standards committed in its port or before entering the port.[76] PSJ, which is broader than PSC, derives from the territorial sovereignty that states enjoy in their internal waters under customary international law.[77]

---

73 *Ibid.*, Art. 4.1.2.

74 IMO (n 11).

75 John Hare, 'Port State Control: Strong Medicine to Cure a Sick Industry,' *Georgia Journal of International and Comparative Law* 26 (Summer 1997): 571, cited in Elizabeth DeSombre, *Flagging Standards* (The MIT Press, Cambridge, 2006), p. 87.

76 Churchill & Lowe (n 42), p. 276.

77 *Ibid.*

The need for PSC has been previously discussed in Chapter II, which can be outlined as: to prevent growing maritime casualties by substandard ships and thereby also prevent marine pollution. As was discussed in that chapter, the flag of convenience system has been a primary reason for the growing number of substandard ships. The primary responsibility of ensuring that ships comply with standards and safety requirements rests with flag sates.

However, given that 70.2 percent of the world's total tonnage is flagged out to open registries, which are mostly underdeveloped countries that use this system for financial gain, flag states are often not capable of fulfilling their responsibility. Instead, Port State Control, which was originally intended to back up the implementation of the flag state, proved to be very effective to prevent and control substandard ships. Thus, PSC has become an essential maritime safety regime, which has greatly contributed to the safety of navigation and the prevention of marine pollution. This chapter explores aspects of PSC in relation to the safety of navigation and the prevention of marine pollution.

Legal Basis for Port State Control

Regarding the legal basis of port state control, a number of international agreements developed over the past three decades, many of them under the auspices of the IMO.[78] Above all, the authority of a port state to prevent substandard ships from accessing its ports and inspect them can be found in territorial sovereignty in accordance with customary international law. The port is part of state's internal waters, which, in contrast to territorial waters, have the same legal status as a part of land. As such, a foreign ship in its ports is subject to the exclusive authority of the state and to national legislation as well as international agreements. The principal international agreements with respect to the legal basis of PSC are outlined below.

1 MARPOL 74/78

The MARPOL Convention provides authority to port states by allowing officers appointed or authorized by states to inspect ships "for the purpose of verifying whether the ship has discharged any harmful substances in violation of the provisions of the regulations."[79] States are also allowed to "inspect a ship when it enters the ports or offshore terminals under their jurisdiction, if a request for an investigation is received from any state with sufficient evidences that the ship has discharged harmful substances or effluents containing such

78 DeSomber (n 75).

79 MARPOL 73/78, Art. 6.2.

substances in any place."[80] Other than those, the regulations of PSC are provided in annexes, which include: Regulation 10 of Annex I;[81] Regulation 15 of Annex II;[82] Regulation 8 of Annex III;[83] Regulation 11 of Annex IV;[84] Regulation 8 of Annex V[85] and Regulation 10 of Annex VI.[86]

2 SOLAS 1974

The first provision of PSC in the international convention is found in the SOLAS Convention 1914, which could not afford to enter into force due to the First World War. The proposed provision of PSC is as below:

> Every ship holding a Safety Certificate. ... is subject in the ports of the other Contracting States to control by officers duly authorized by their governments in so far as this control is directed towards verifying that there is on board a valid Safety Certificate, and if necessary, that the conditions of the vessel's seaworthiness correspond substantially with the particulars of that certificate; that is to say, so that the ship can proceed to sea without danger to the passengers and the crew.[87]

The current SOLAS Convention sets forth the provisions of PSC in several chapters. Regulation 19 of Chapter I, which adopts much of the wording of

80 *Ibid.*, Art. 6.5.

81 "States are required to investigate if there has been a violation of the prohibition of any discharge of oil and oily mixture into the sea from ships and the special areas when visible traces of oil are observed on or below the surface of water in the immediate vicinity of a ship or its wake."

82 "A ship in a port of another state is subject to inspection by officers duly authorized by such state concerning operational requirements where there are clear grounds that the master or crew are not familiar with essential shipboard procedures relating to the prevention of pollution by liquid noxious substances."

83 "A ship in a port of another state is subject to inspection by officers duly authorized by such state concerning operational requirements where there are clear grounds that the master or crew are not familiar with essential shipboard procedures relating to the prevention of pollution by harmful substances."

84 "The discharge of sewage into the sea is prohibited except in certain circumstances."

85 "A ship in a port of another state is subject to inspection by officers duly authorized by such state concerning operational requirements where there are clear grounds that the master or crew are not familiar with essential shipboard procedures relating to the prevention of pollution by garbage."

86 "A ship in a port or an off-shore terminal under jurisdiction of another state is subject to inspection by officers duly authorized by such state concerning operational requirements where there are clear grounds that the master or crew are not familiar with essential shipboard procedures relating to the prevention of air pollution from ships."

87 SOLAS 1914, signed in London on 20 January 1914, Art. 6.1.

PSC in the 1914 SOLAS, provides: (i) "every ship when in a port of another contracting government is subject to control by officers duly authorized by such government in so far as this control is directed towards verifying that the certificates issued ... are valid."; (ii) "such certificates, if valid, shall be accepted unless there are clear grounds for believing that the condition of the ship or of its equipment does not correspond substantially with the particulars of the certificates or that the ship and its equipment are not in compliance with the provisions of ..." (iii) "in the circumstances given in paragraph (b) or where a certificate has expired or ceased to be valid, the officer carrying the control shall take steps to ensure that the ship shall not sail until it can proceed to sea or leave the port for the purpose of proceeding to the appropriate repair yard..."

The regulations of PSC are also provided in other chapters. "The administration, another contracting government at the request of the administration or an organization recognized by the administration are required to periodically verify the proper functioning of the ship's safety-management system."[88] "A ship when in a port of another contracting party is subject to control of officers of such government."[89] "When there are grounds for believing that the master or crew is not familiar with essential shipboard procedures relating to the safety of ships, the contracting government carrying out the control is required to take such steps that do not allow the ship to sail until the situation has been brought to order."[90] "When a ship in port is not in compliance with the requirements of the ISPS Code, states are required to impose any one or more control measures, which may include inspection of the ship, delaying the ship, restriction of operations including movement within the port, or expulsion of the ship from port."[91] "Such measures may additionally or alternatively include other lesser administrative or corrective measures."[92]

3 UNCLOS

The state's right of territorial sovereignty under customary international law, which is a primary legal source of port state control, is reflected in the UNCLOS. The UNCLOS provisions of PSC build on nascent aspects of international law that sees ports as part of the sovereign territory of a state, and thus an area to which states have the ability to restrict access.[93]

---

88 SOLAS 73/78, Chapter IX, Reg. 6.2.
89 *Ibid.*, Chapter XI-1, Reg. 4.
90 *Ibid.*
91 *Ibid.*, Chapter XI-2, Reg. 9.1.2 & 1.3.
92 *Ibid.*
93 DeSomber (n 75), p. 89.

The UNCLOS lays out the ability of states to, "establish particular requirements for the prevention, reduction, and control of pollution of the marine environment as a condition for the entry of foreign vessels into their ports or internal waters or for calls at their offshore terminals."[94] "When a vessel is voluntarily within a port or an off-shore terminal of a state, that state may institute proceedings in respect of any discharge from the vessel outside the internal waters, territorial sea or exclusive economic zone of that state in violation of international rules and standards."[95] "States which, upon request or on their own initiative, have ascertained that a vessel within one of their ports or at one of their off-shore terminals is in violation of international rules and standards relating to seaworthiness of vessels and thereby threatens to the marine environment, are required to take administrative measures to prevent the vessel from sailing."[96] Such state may "allow the vessel to proceed only to the nearest repair yard and, upon removal of the causes of the violation, and the vessel to continue immediately."[97]

4 Other International Agreements

The legal sources of PSC are found in other international conventions. There are some provisions for port state control within international law under the auspices of the International Labor Organization (ILO) and these actually sowed the seeds of the current port state control regime.[98]

In particular, the Convention concerning Minimum Standards in Merchant Ships (Merchant Shipping (Minimum Standards) Convention, 1976) stipulates the provision relating to port state control on safety or health[99]: "a state in whose port a ship calls and receives a complaint or obtains evidence that the ship does not conform to the standard of the Convention is required to submit a report to the flag state and the international labor office." "The state may take measures necessary to rectify any conditions on board which are clearly hazardous to safety or health." "The state is required to notify the measures taken of the nearest maritime or consular or diplomatic representative of the flag state." "The state should not unreasonably detain or delay the ship." Such complaints may be lodged by "a member of the crew, a professional body, an association, a trade union, or generally, any person with an interest

94 UNCLOS, Art. 211.
95 *Ibid.*, Art. 218(1).
96 *Ibid.*, Art. 219.
97 *Ibid.*
98 DeSomber (n 75), p. 90.
99 Merchant Shipping (Minimum Standards) Convention, 1976, Art. 4.

in the safety of the ship, including an interest in safety or health hazards to its crew."

In addition, the STCW Convention, TONNAGE Convention, COLREG Convention, Load Line Convention, BMW Convention, CLC Convention and AFS Convention also serve as the legal basis of PSC.

VI Regional PSC Regimes

Overview

As PSC proved to be an effective means of preventing substandard ships, states within various regions have grouped together under memorandums of understanding (MOUs) with respect to port state control.[100] Regional PSC regimes have developed: to eliminate so-called 'port shopping,' to enhance the efficiency of port states' inspections by means of harmonization between port states and by increasing information-sharing, and to reduce the burden of repetitive inspections of foreign states.[101]

The origins of PSC lie in the Hague MOU signed in 1978.[102] In response to the implicit control granted to port states under the Merchant Shipping (Minimum Standards) Convention 1976 (ILO 147), eight European states[103] signed a memorandum of understanding in the Hague in 1978 to create a method for implementing the provisions and others contained in IMO agreements.[104] Before this agreement could become fully operational, the *Amoco Cadiz* oil spill incident[105] refocused attention away from labor standards and onto environmental and safety issues on ships.[106]

100 Ho-Sam Bang & Duck-Jong Jang, 'Recent Developments in Regional Memorandums of Understanding on Port State Control, *Ocean Development & International Law* (2012) 43(2), p. 171.

101 *Ibid.*

102 Z. Oya Özçayir, 'The Use of Port State Control in Maritime Industry and Application of the Paris MOU' (2009) 14 *OCLJ* 208, cited in Anton Kulchytsky, 'Legal Aspects of Port State Control' (2012), Master thesis, Lund University, Sweden.

103 They include: Belgium, Denmark, France, West Germany, the Netherlands, Norway, Sweden and the United Kingdom.

104 DeSomber (n 75), p. 91.

105 The oil tanker *Amoco Cadiz* ran aground on Portsall Rocks, 5 km (3.1 miles) from the coast of Brittany, France, on 16 March 1978, following a steering gear failure. The ship ultimately split in three and sank, spilling the entire cargo of 223,000 tons of crude oil and 4,000 tons of bunker fuel into the sea over a period of two weeks. This incident was recorded as the largest oil spill of its kind in history to that date.

106 *Ibid.*

TABLE 5 Status of regional PSC MOUs

MOU	Foundation year	Number of participating states	Goal of inspection (%)	Region	Location of secretariat
Paris MOU	1982	27	Priority I: 100% Priority II: to be used for completing percentage of annual total of inspections	Europe	The Netherlands
Viña de Mar MOU	1992	13	20	South America	Argentina
Tokyo MOU	1993	20	80	Asia/Pacific	Japan
Caribbean MOU	1996	14	15	Central America	Barbados
Mediterranean MOU	1997	10	15	Mediterranean Sea	Egypt
Indian MOU	1998	19	10	Indian Ocean	India
Abuja MOU	1999	14	15	Africa	Nigeria
Black Sea MOU	2000	6	15	Black Sea	Turkey
Riyadh MOU	2004	6	10	The Gulf	Saudi Arabia

SOURCE: KIM YOON CHUL, *INTERNATIONAL MARITIME TREATIES* (DASOM, 2013) (TRANSLATED BY AUTHOR)

In the aftermath of the incident, which served as a catalyst in strengthening PSC in Europe, the Paris MOU, which evolved from the Hague MOU, was created in 1982. The successful operation of the Paris MOU promoted the creation of other regional MOUs. Furthermore, the IMO Assembly Resolution A. 682(17) adopted in 1991 acknowledged the performance of the Paris MOU in combating substandard ships and called on the parties to consider concluding more regional arrangements.[107]

As outlined in Table 5, there are currently nine regional PSC MOUs, which cover nearly all the regions of the world, and the U.S. Coast Guard has its own PSC Program. The regional MOUs include: (i) Paris MOU; (ii) Viña del Agreement; (iii) Tokyo MOU; (iv) Caribbean MOU; (v) Mediterranean MOU; (vi) Indian Ocean MOU; (vii) Abuja MOU; (viii) Black Sea MOU; (ix) Riyadh MOU.

In terms of the legal nature of an MOU, it is an administrative agreement which does not create internationally binding obligations for state parties.[108] MOU may be concluded when states attempt to record certain matters in writing, but wish to do so in a manner that it is not intended to create legal rights and obligations under international law.[109] An MOU simply expresses a convergence of will between the parties, indicating an intended common line of action, rather than creating a legal commitment.[110]

Regional PSC MOUs aim to build a framework of cooperation among the maritime authorities of a region or a group of states with similar position on PSC. They provide for uniformity and harmonization for the application, among participating states, of the right of a port state to ascertain that calling ships are in compliance with internationally agreed-upon rules and standards on maritime safety and protection of the marine environment within its jurisdiction.[111]

Paris MOU

1 Creation of the Paris MOU

The Paris MOU, created in January 1982, came into force on 1 July 1982. It aims: to prevent the operation of substandard ships; to avoid distorting competition between ports; to achieve an improved and harmonized system of port state control; and to strengthen cooperation and the exchange of information.[112] The Paris MOU has served as a prototype for subsequent regional PSC MOUs

107 Bang & Jang (n 100), p. 171.
108 Kulchytsky (n 102), p.23.
109 R. Jennings and A. Watts, eds. *Oppenheim's International Law*, 9th ed. (Longman, Essex, 1992), pp. 1202–1203, cited in Bang & Jang (n 100), p. 172.
110 *Ibid.*
111 Kulchytsky (n 102), p.23.
112 Paris MOU, Preamble.

and thus many of provisions of other regional MOUs are identical to those of the Paris MOU. The Paris MOU is composed of eight sections and has 12 annexes. As of 2018, 27 maritime authorities from European states and Canada are participating in the Paris MOU.

The MOU was reinforced by the European Community (EC) Directive on PSC adopted in 1995 and revised in 2009. In line with the EC Directive, the Paris MOU was amended in May 1996 and in May 2010. The 1995 EC Directive was adopted because the Paris MOU was more fluid than a treaty and had not been applied in a uniform way, with wide differences in the number of inspections and detentions carried out by different states.[113]

The directive acts as a legislative umbrella over the Paris MOU, making its enforcement and application more consistent throughout Europe. The directive creates an operational strength, which distinguishes the Paris MOU from the other regional MOUs.[114] However, not all participants in the Paris MOU are members of the EU, and thus PSC activities need to be well coordinated by the Secretary of the MOU.[115]

2 Inspection

The procedure for inspection on board a ship is provided in Annex 9. An inspection on board a ship may begin with a check of the certificates and documents, and the overall condition and hygiene of the ship. When clear grounds are found that the condition of the ship or its equipment or crew or the working and living conditions of seafarers does not meet the relevant requirements of a relevant instrument, a more detailed inspection will be carried out.

The examples of 'clear grounds' are listed in Article 6 of the annex. An expanded inspection, which includes a check of the overall condition, including the human element, is carried out in the risk areas, which include: documentation; structural condition; water/watertight condition; emergency systems; radio communication; cargo operations including equipment; fire safety; alarms; living and working conditions; navigational equipment; life-saving appliances; dangerous goods; propulsion and auxiliary machinery; and pollution prevention.

3 Ship Risk Profile

Pursuant to Annex 7, all ships in the information system are assigned either as high, standard or low risk based on generic and historic parameters.[116]

113 Bang & Jang (n 100), p. 173.
114 *Ibid.*
115 *Ibid.*
116 Paris MOU, Annex 7, Art. 1.

Generic parameters include: types of ship; age of ship; flag state; recognized organization performance; and company performance. Historic parameters include: number of deficiencies recorded in each inspection within the previous 36 months; and number of detentions within previous 36 months.[117] Of particular note is that the Black, Grey and White list for flag state performance is established annually, taking into account the inspection and detention history over the preceding three years.

Each parameter has criteria, and the parameter is measured with a weighting point which reflects the relative influence of each parameter on the overall risk of the ship.[118] The level of ships' risk is determined by adding up these points.

- High Risk Ships (HRS) are ships that meet the criteria to a total value of five or more weighting points.[119]
- Low Risk Ships (LRS) are ships that meet all the criteria of the Low Risk Parameters and have had at least one inspection in the previous 36 months.[120]
- Standard Risk Ships (SRS) are ships which are neither HRS nor LRS.[121]

4 Selection Scheme for Inspection

The Paris MOU is based on a ship's risk profile, according to which the inspection and selection scheme determines the scope, frequency and priority of inspections.[122] Inspections are divided into two categories: (i) periodic and (ii) additional. Periodic inspections are carried out at intervals determined by the ship risk profile, while additional inspections might be triggered by overriding or unexpected factors and conducted in between periodic inspections.[123] Ships become due for period inspection in the following time windows:[124]

- For HRS: between 5–6 months after the last inspection in the Paris MOU region.
- For SRS: between 9–12 months after the last inspection in the Paris MOU region.
- For LRS: between 24–36 months after the last inspection in the Paris MOU region.

117 *Ibid.*, Table 6.
118 *Ibid.*, Art. 3.
119 *Ibid.*, Art. 4.
120 *Ibid.*, Art. 5.
121 *Ibid.*, Art. 6.
122 *Ibid.*, Annex 8, Art. 1.
123 *Ibid.*, Arts. 2 & 3.
124 *Ibid*, Art. 4.

The selection scheme is divided into two priorities: (i) Priority I and (ii) Priority II. Ships that fall within Priority I must be inspected because either the time window has closed or there is an overriding factor. Ships that fall within Priority II may be inspected because they are within the time window or the port state considers that an unexpected factor has warranted an inspection. In the case of unexpected factors, the need to undertake an additional inspection is left to the discretion of the authority.[125] The priority and the level of selection will be shown for each ship in the information system.[126] The overriding factors listed below are considered sufficiently serious to trigger an additional inspection at Priority I.[127]

- Ships reported by another member state or the secretariat, excluding unexpected factors;
- Ships involved in a collision, grounding or stranding on their way to port;
- Ships accused of an alleged violation of the provisions on discharge of harmful substances or effluents;
- Ships that have been manoeuvred in an erratic or unsafe manner whereby routing measures as adopted by the IMO or safe navigational practices and procedures have not been followed;
- Ships that have been suspended or withdrawn from their class for safety reasons after last PSC inspection;
- Ships that cannot be identified in the database.

Unexpected factors indicate a possible serious threat to the safety of the ship and the crew, or to the environment, which requires an additional inspection for professional judgment. Annex 8 sets out the factors, which include[128]:

- Ships reported by pilots or relevant authorities that may include information from Vessel Traffic Services about ships' navigation;
- Ships that did not comply with the reporting obligations;
- Ships reported with outstanding ISM deficiencies (three months after the issuing of the deficiency);
- Previously detained ships (three months after the detention);
- Ships that have been the subject of a report or complaint by the master, a seafarer, or any person or organization with a legitimate interest in the safe operation of the ship, ship on-board living and working conditions, or the prevention of pollution, unless the member states concerned deems the report or complaint to be manifestly unfounded;

---

125 *Ibid.*, Art. 8.
126 *Ibid.*, Art. 9.
127 *Ibid.*, Art. 11.
128 *Ibid.*, Art. 12.

TABLE 6 Selection scheme

Priority	Level	Category of inspection
I	Overriding factor	Additional
Ship must be	HRS not inspected in last six months	Periodic
inspected	SRS not inspected in last 12 months	Periodic
	Ships not inspected in last 36 months	Periodic
II	HRS not inspected in last five months	Periodic
Ship may be	Ships with unexpected factors	Additional
inspected	SRS not inspected in last 10 months	Periodic
	LRS not inspected in last 24 months	Periodic

SOURCE: PARIS MOU, ANNEX 8

- Ships reported to have problems concerning their cargo, particularly noxious or dangerous cargo;
- Ships where information from a reliable source has reported that their risk parameters differ from the ones that have been recorded, thereby increasing the risk level;
- Ships carrying certificates issued by organizations that were once recognized by the Paris MOU, but whose recognition has been withdrawn since the last inspection in the Paris MOU region.

The selection scheme discussed above is outlined at Table 6.

5 Detention

Detention of ships may be undertaken in exceptional circumstances where certificates are missing, expired or invalid. Moreover, as a result of a more detailed inspection, a ship may be suspended when the overall condition of a ship and its equipment, also taking the seafarers and their living and working conditions into account, is found to be obviously sub-standard. The suspension may continue until the responsible parties have taken the steps necessary to ensure that the ship complies with the requirements of the relevant instruments.[129]

In the case of detention, authorities are to immediately notify the responsible parties and provide an inspection report.[130] Deficiencies are to be rectified

129 *Ibid.*, Sec. 3.6.

130 *Ibid.*, Sec. 3.7.

before the ship is allowed to sail if they constitute a hazard to safety, health or the environment. Where the deficiencies cannot be remedied in the port of inspection, the authority may allow the ship to proceed to the nearest repair yard for repairs.[131] The owner or the operator of a ship has a right of appeal against a detention decision or refusal of access. However, the appeal itself does not cause the detention or refusal of access to be suspended.[132]

6 Refusal of Access of Ships

The distinctive feature of the Paris MOU is to ban ships from accessing ports if they have been systematically found to be substandard. A ship is not allowed to access ports and anchorage of member states where a ship[133]:

- Flies the flag of a state appearing on the Grey List and has been detained or has been issued with a prevention of operation order under the system of mandatory surveys for the safe operation of regular ro-ro ferry and high-speed passenger craft services more than twice in the course of 24 months in a port or anchorage within the region of the MOU;
- Flies the flag of a state appearing in the Black List and has been detained or has been issued with a prevention of operation order under the system of mandatory surveys for the safe operation of regular ro-ro ferry and high-speed passenger craft services more than twice in the course of the preceding 36 months in a port or anchorage within the region of the memorandum.

The refusal of access order will be lifted after a period of three months has passed from the date of issue of the order. If the ship is subject to a second refusal of access, the period shall be 12 months. The subsequent detention in a port or anchorage shall result in the ship being refused access to any port or anchorage. A third refusal of access order may be lifted after a period of 24 months has passed and only if[134]:

- The ship flies the flag of a state whose detention rate falls neither into the Black List nor the Grey List;
- The statutory and classification certificates of the ship are issued by organization(s) which are recognized by one or more of the member states;
- The ship is managed by a company with a high performance rating and the conditions are met.

131 *Ibid.*, Sec. 3.8.

132 *Ibid.*, Sec. 3.12.

133 *Ibid.*, Sec. 4.

134 *Ibid.*

Any ship not meeting the above criteria after a period of 24 months will be permanently refused access to any port or anchorage.[135]

Tokyo MOU

1 Organizational Structure

The Memorandum of Understanding on Port State Control in the Asia-Pacific region, known as the Tokyo MOU, was formed in Tokyo on 1 December 1993 and came into effect on 1 April 1994. As of 2018, there are 20 full members and 13 observers.[136] The full members include: Australia, Canada, Chile, China, Fiji, Hong Kong (China), Indonesia, Japan, Korea, Malaysia, Marshall Islands, New Zealand, Papua New Guinea, Peru, the Philippines, Russia, Singapore, Thailand, Vanuatu and Vietnam.

The objectives of the Tokyo MOU, nearly identical to those of the Paris MOU, are: to establish an effective port state control regime in the Asia-Pacific region through the cooperation of its members and the harmonization of the members' activities; to eliminate substandard shipping; to promote maritime safety and security; and to safeguard seafarers working and living on board ships.

As a governing body of the MOU, the Port State Control Committee monitors and controls the implementation and ongoing operation of the MOU. The Committee consists of representatives from the member authorities, cooperating member authorities and observers. For the purposes of the MOU, a database system called the Asia-Pacific Computerized System (APCIS) is established to exchange information on port state control.

2 Implementation of Inspection

Modeled on the Paris MOU, procedures for inspection, rectification, detention and selection schemes under the Tokyo MOU are virtually identical to those in the Paris MOU. As in the Paris MOU, the Tokyo MOU also builds on the 'priority based selection scheme,' in targeting ships to be inspected. The system sets a higher priority for ships having a higher targeting factor value.[137] The members are required to first inspect ships exceeding an average detention percentage over a 3-year rolling period and those having several recent deficiencies.[138]

Despite an inherently identical structure of port state control as the Paris MOU, however, slight variations exist between the two MOU s. In terms of ship

135 *Ibid.*

136 The observers include: North Korea, Macao (China), Samoa, Solomon Islands, Tonga, U.S. Coast Guard, IMO, ILO, Paris MOU, Viña del Mar Agreement, Indian Ocean MOU, Black Sea MOU and Riyadh MOU.

137 Tokyo MOU, Sec. 3.3.1.

138 *Ibid.*, Sec. 3.3.

risk profile, for the Tokyo MOU, ships that meet the criteria to a total value of four or more weighting points fall within High Risk Ships, as opposed to a total of five or more weighting points in the Paris MOU.

For intervals of periodic inspection, the Tokyo MOU has shorter time windows, under which High Risk Ships are eligible for inspection two to four months since a previous inspection; for Standard Risk Ships, five to eight months; for Low Risk Ships, nine to 18 months. The Tokyo MOU qualifies the ships on the White List that have undergone an IMO audit as Low Risk Ships. For the Tokyo MOU, in accordance with the procedures of the New Inspection Regime (NIR), which has been effective from 1 January 2014, flags whose total number of inspections over a 3-year rolling period does not reach the minimum of 30 are not included in the Black-Grey-White list.

Consequently, some flags cannot afford to meet the criteria for their ships to qualify as Low Risk Ships, despite having undergone the IMO audit. The Tokyo MOU aims very high in terms of inspections for calling vessels — it aims to inspect 80 percent of calling vessels, compared to other regional MOUS' 10–15 percent inspection rate.

The Annual Report on Port State Control in the Asia-Pacific Region 2017 shows the status and trends of PSC in the region in the past decade. In the period between 2007 and 2017, a total of 308,448 ships were inspected. The average inspection rate over the same period was 67.5 percent, peaking at 71 percent in 2016. (see Fig. 4)

The average detention rate was 4.76 percent over the same period, a higher detention rate than the Paris MOU of 3.81 percent in the period between 2008 and 2017. Of particular note is that the detention rate has been trending constantly downward over the recent years off its 2008 peak of 6.90 percent. (see Fig. 5) This may indicate that PSC under the Tokyo MOU has greatly contributed to the prevention of substandard ships. On the other hand, it may also indicate that compliance of flag states to safety and marine pollution standards and rules has improved over the years.

Of the categories of deficiencies discovered in inspections over the same period, as illustrated in Fig. 6, fire safety measures are the biggest single factor at 18.01 percent (the biggest factor overall is "Others," which is not detailed, at 41.15 percent). Fire safety is followed by safety of navigation with 15.37 percent, lifesaving appliances with 12.86 percent, and load lines with 6.94 percent.

USCG PSC Program

The U.S., which does not belong to any regional MOU s, has its own unique port state control system. The responsible agency for PSC in the U.S. is the U.S Coast Guard (USCG). The details of the USCG are discussed in Chapter 8. It is

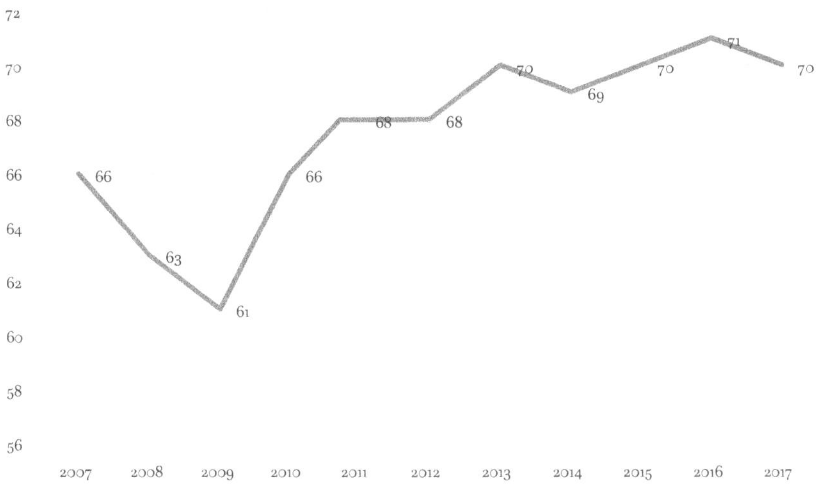

FIGURE 4 Trend of inspection rate (%) (2007–2017)
SOURCE: TOKYO MOU ANNUAL REPORT 2017

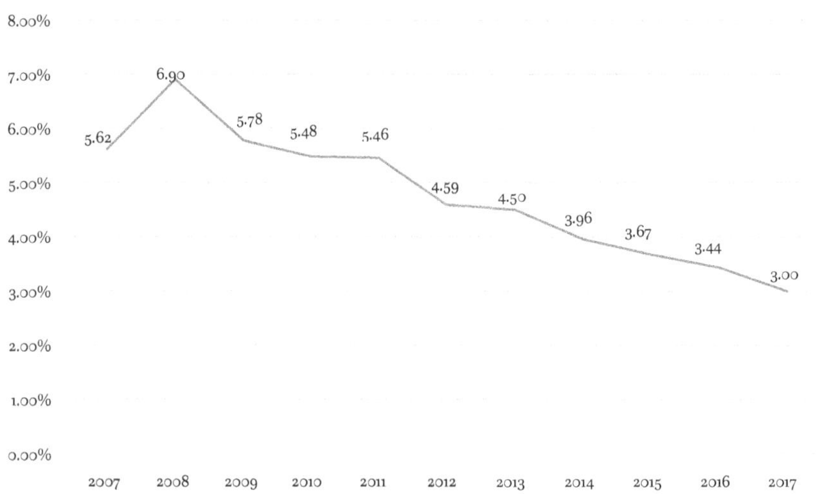

FIGURE 5 Trend of detention rate (%) (2007–2017)
SOURCE: TOKYO MOU ANNUAL REPORT 2017

worth noting in relation to PSC that the Commandant of the USCG is authorized to designate any officer as a Captain of Port (COTP) for such ports or adjacent high seas over which the U.S. has jurisdiction to facilitate the execution of Coast Guard duties prescribed by law.[139] The USCG has been tasked with full

139 14 U.S. Code §3, sec. 634.

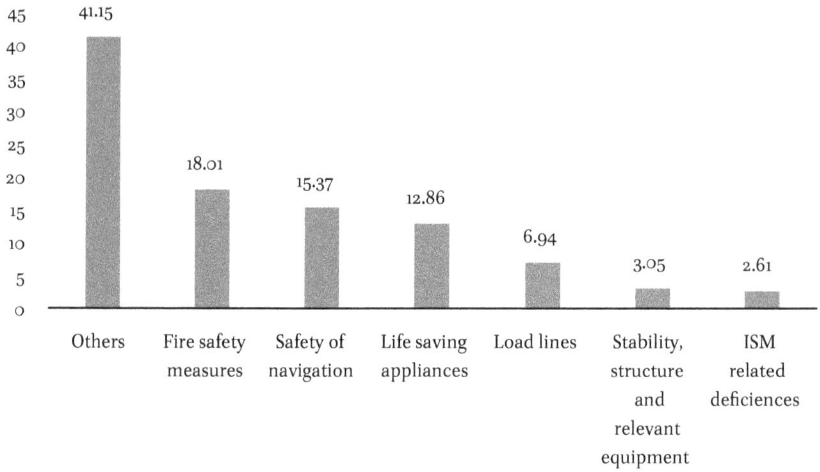

FIGURE 6 Deficiencies by main categories (%) (2017)
SOURCE: TOKYO MOU ANNUAL REPORT 2017

PSC duties since 1 May 1994.[140] Previously, the USCG had been responsible for limited aspects of navigational safety and pollution prevention, particularly tankers and passenger vessels.

The USCG PSC program is distinguished from the regional PSC MOUs in many respects. The selection of ships for inspection is decided in accordance with ratings evaluated by use of the Targeting Matrix. The Targeting Matrix is composed of columns of parameters, which include: (i) Column I Ship Management; (ii) Column II Flag State; (iii) Column III Recognized Organizations; (iv) Column IV Vessel History; and (v) Column V Ship Particulars. Total targeting scores, which are the sum of columns I–V, determine ships' priorities.

The priority of inspection is classified into Priority I, Priority II and Non-Priority Vessel (NPV).[141] Priority I vessels are: (i) ships with 17 or more points on the matrix; (ii) ships involved in a maritime casualty that may have affected seaworthiness; (iii) USCG COTP determines a vessel to be a potential hazard to the port or the environment; (iv) ships whose classification society has a detention ratio equal to or greater than 2 percent. For those ships, port entry may be restricted until the Coast Guard examines the vessel.[142]

Priority II vessels are: (i) ships with seven to 16 points on the matrix; (ii) ships with outstanding requirements from a previous examination in this or

140 46 U.S. Code §§3301–3318.
141 USCG, 'Port State Control in the United States,' *2016 Annual Report*, p. 6.
142 *Ibid.*

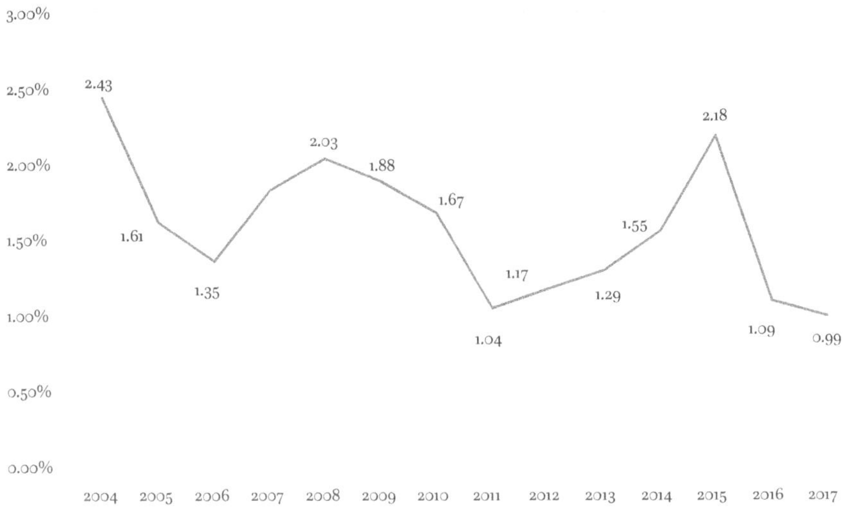

FIGURE 7 Trend of detention ratio (%) (2004–2017)
SOURCE: USCG ANNUAL PSC REPORT 2017

another U.S. port that requires clearing; (iii) ships that have not been examined within the past 12 months per Column IV. For those vessels, cargo operations or passenger embarkation/debarkation may only be restricted if the sector commander/COTP determines that the vessel poses a safety or environment risk to the port.[143]

Non-Priority Vessels are ships with six or fewer points on the matrix. Those vessels pose a low safety and environmental risk. The USCG may select and examine vessels using the Port State Control random selection process.[144]

If a vessel has scored either a Priority I or Priority II and has had a USCG PSC examination within the past six months with no serious deficiencies, the sector commander may downgrade the vessel to NPV. If the sector commander downgrades a vessel, it will be added to the pool of random examinations.[145] The USCG targets flag administrations for additional PSC examinations if their detention ratio scores are higher than the 3-year running ratio and if an administration is associated with more than one detention in the past three years.[146]

As shown in Fig. 7, the detention rate of USCG PSC in the period between 2004 and 2017 is generally lower than those of the Paris and Tokyo MOU s. Over

143 *Ibid.*
144 *Ibid.*
145 *Ibid.*
146 *Ibid. p. 7.*

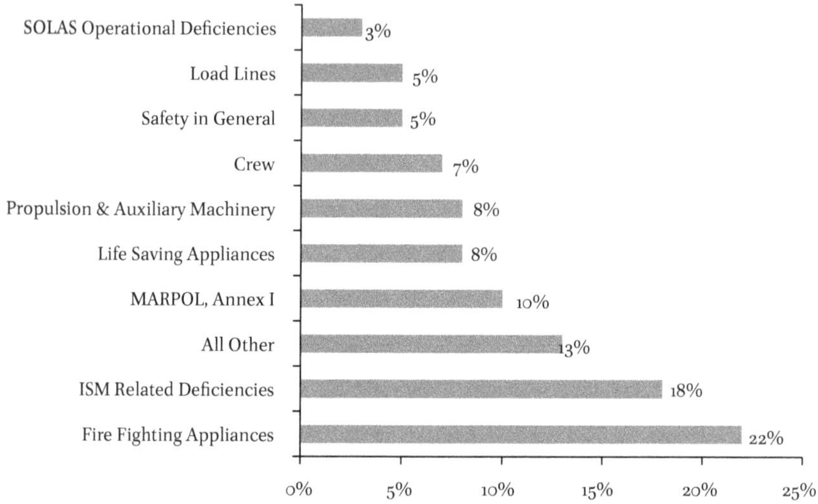

FIGURE 8 Types of safety deficiencies leading to detentions (2017)
SOURCE: USCG ANNUAL PSC REPORT 2017

a recent 5-year period, the average detention rate was 1.42 percent, of which the lowest was 0.99 percent in 2017.

As illustrated in Fig. 8, the leading type of safety deficiency in 2017 was fire-fighting and protection systems, similar to the Tokyo MOU. Fire safety issues are the most common area for detainable deficiencies. A significant number of remote-operable fuel shutoff valves on various fuel and lube oil tanks were found disabled in the open position, which could not be operated from outside the space in the event of a fire.[147]

Features of Regional MOUs and Challenges

As illustrated earlier, currently there are nine regional PSC MOUs and one USCG PSC Program across the world. Following the Paris MOU, other regional MOUs were created in the same mold. As such, the principal structures of MOUs are nearly identical, but there exist slight variations in the implementation of PSC, according to each MOU.

Regarding the annual inspection rate goal, a majority of regional MOUs inspect between 10 to 20 percent of ships calling to their ports. The Mediterranean MOU and the Riyadh MOU are the lowest, aiming for 10 percent. Notably, the Tokyo MOU states set a very high rate of inspection of calling vessels, at

147 *Ibid.*, p. 12.

80 percent. The Paris MOU gives priority to calling ships using the ship risk profile, and it aims to inspect all calling ships with Priority I.

Apart from individual features, a number of common principles are found in the regional MOUs. First, the no-preferential treatment principle and the discrimination principle co-exist in targeting ships to be inspected. According to the no-preferential treatment principle, ships of non-party states or those below conventional size should not be given preferential treatment in order to ensure that they undergo equivalent surveys and inspections, and that an equivalent level of safety and protection of the marine environment is ensured.[148]

On the other hand, the discrimination principle is applied to inspection regimes. That is, port states are encouraged to determine which ships to inspect based on the record of an individual ship, the type of ship it is, and most importantly, the characteristics of the flag state in which it is registered.[149] In addition to the inspection record of individual ships, certain types of ship are more likely to be inspected: oil and chemical tankers, gas carriers, and bulk carriers are given a higher priority for inspection than are other types of ships. Older ships are also of greater concern.[150]

Another principle is that each PSC authority is required to apply the relevant instruments that are in force and to which its state is a party. In the case of amendments to a relevant instrument, each authority will apply those amendments that are in force and that its state has accepted. An instrument so amended will then be deemed to be the relevant instrument for that authority.[151] As a result, there might be different practices of application of instruments even within the same MOU region, varying with member states' status with respect to the relevant instruments. This is quite undesirable for the matter of uniformity and harmonization in members' activities, especially in those regions where cooperation on PSC is weak.[152]

Despite the best efforts at coordinated inspections within the MOU regions, national variations continue. It has been suggested that some states fill out paperwork without conducting anything but cursory inspections, and that others scrupulously fulfill their inspection targets by inspecting those with good records.[153]

148 Kulchytsky (n 102), p.18.
149 DeSomber (n 75), p. 93.
150 *Ibid.*
151 Paris MOU, Sec. 2.3; Tokyo MOU, Sec. 2.4; Indian MOU, Sec. 2.3; Black Sea MOU, Sec. 2.3.
152 See Kulchytsky (n 102), p.18.
153 DeSomber (n 75), p. 97.

These problems are closely linked to the qualification of port state control officers (PSCOs). PSCOs carrying out inspections of operational requirements should be qualified as[154]: (i) a master or chief engineer and have appropriate seagoing experience; or (ii) have qualifications from a recognized institution and have specialized training; or (iii) a qualified officer of administration. Furthermore, for independence and impartiality of inspections, PSCOs and the persons assisting them should have no commercial interest, either in the port of inspection, or in the ships inspected, nor should PSCOs be employed by or undertake work on behalf of recognized organizations.[155]

Unqualified PSCOs who do not have adequate competence or skills in a maritime-related field and those who are not able to communicate in English with the key crew are problematic in some states. It is also charged that some inspectors in the European system can be brought off.[156] Notably, the Tokyo MOU and the Caribbean MOU, in contrast to the rest of MOUs, have not provided ethics provisions to address the problem of bribery existing in some PSC regions.[157]

VII Conclusion

Shipping is one of the most heavily regulated industries to ensure the safety of ships and navigation. Over the past decades, the international community, particularly on the initiative of the IMO, has adopted a large number of legal instruments to deal with issues concerning various aspects of the safety of navigation. Although it began with the safety of ships, the focus has expanded to regulate navigational safety, the marine environment and maritime security.

The safety rules and standards in legal instruments are subject to the implementation of flag states, coastal states and port states, depending on their jurisdiction. The vast portion of implementation of the rules and standards rests with flag states. As described earlier, more than 70 percent of ships engaged in international shipping are flagged out to foreign states, i.e., the flags of convenience. The flags of convenience, which operate open registries mostly for financial gains, are not capable of ensuring that their ships comply with the safety regulations. As such, the largest challenge to maritime safety might

154 IMO Assembly Resolution A. 1052(27), 1.9.5.

155 *Ibid*, 1.8.3.

156 William Langewiesche, *The Outlaw Sea: A World of Freedom, Chaos, and Crime* (North Point Press, New York, 2004), pp. 92–93, cited in Elizabeth R. DeSomber (n 75), p. 97.

157 Kulchytsky (n 102), p.20.

be how to effectively implement the safety standards and rules to prevent substandard ships and to protect the marine environment.

Port State Control (PSC) has played a vital role in ensuring navigational safety and the protection of marine environment, serving as a supplementary safety net to flag state control. The significance of PSC has significantly increased over recent years. In fact, PSC, under an umbrella of regional MOU regimes, takes the place of the flag state control. Given the vast majority of flags of convenience out of world total fleets, the status of PSC's is likely to become more significant and expanded.

Despite its increasing significance to ensuring ship safety and protection of marine environment, the PSC MOUs, not legally binding regimes, but merely a coalition of cooperation in the MOU region, have a fundamental challenge that needs to be addressed. For variations in member states' status with respect to the relevant instruments, the regional MOUs have no effective means, other than voluntary cooperation of member states, to enforce harmonized activities within the MOU regions. This is quite undesirable for the matter of uniformity and harmonization in members' activities, especially in those regions where cooperation on PSC is weak.

In order to address this problem, an adoption of PSC agreements that replaces the regional MOUs needs to be considered. That is, the regional PSC MOUs need to be transformed to multilateral regional treaties to ensure the enforcement of PSC among member states in a harmonized manner. In addition, there should be more efforts at the regional MOUs level to enhance the expertise and vocational ethics of inspectors and transparency of inspection.

Nonetheless, the responsibilities and obligations that flag states should bear are not exempted or lessened. Rather, flag states' commitment to the safety of ships under their flag should be encouraged and strengthened.

CHAPTER 4

Maritime Terrorism and the SUA Convention Regime

I Introduction

In the post-Cold War era, non-conventional security threats derived from racial, ethnic, regional, religious and cultural conflicts have superseded the conventional security threats that had been based on the ideological conflicts of the Cold War era. Non-conventional security threats, such as terrorism, piracy, cyberattacks or weapons of mass destruction (WMD) pose a grave threat to the peace and security of the contemporary world. Of those, the most salient and volatile threat in peacetime must be terrorism. In fact, terrorism is not a newly emerged security threat in the post-Cold War era — it has a long history, dating back to ancient times. However, it has been a subject of concern for the international community since the 1960s, following a series of aircraft hijackings.[1] In the aftermath of the 9/11 terrorist attacks on the United States in 2001, in particular, terrorism has become the most imminent global security threat in peacetime. As such, counter-terrorism has risen to a top global agenda item that the international community as a whole needs to fight together.

Under these circumstances, the maritime domain is perceived to be highly vulnerable to terrorist attacks, as evinced in the number of maritime terrorism incidents in recent years. Given that the aim of terrorist attacks is to increase loss of life, economic damage, and public fear to the greatest extent possible, these attacks look for maritime targets such as vessels, ports, offshore facilities and plants. Attacking these places can inflict crippling damage to the economy and shipping of a state, as well as draw considerable public attention. However, the risks and consequences of maritime terrorism appeared not to have been prioritized in the past, and as a consequence a lesser focus on counter-terrorism efforts was accorded. This might happen because the risk of terrorism in the maritime domain is not so tangible to the public, and furthermore

1 A. Conte, *Human Rights in the Prevention and Punishment of Terrorism* (Springer, Berlin, 2010), p. 7.

 | DOI:10.1163/9789004389908_005

maritime terrorism is not regarded an imminent threat due to a relatively small number of attacks over the years.

However, currently the maritime domain is not only a direct target of terrorism, but also is used as a channel for terrorist organizations to attempt terrorist attacks on land. The latter is executed in the form of transporting terrorists or illicit materials to be used for terrorism. In particular, the proliferation of WMDs transported by sea is a grave concern of the international community. Recognizing the vulnerability and enormous negative impact of maritime terrorism, the international community has exerted a variety of efforts to prevent and combat maritime terrorism. As an integral part of counter-terrorism measures, the international community has adopted a number of multilateral treaties. The Convention for the Suppression of Unlawful Acts Against the Safety of Maritime Navigation (SUA Convention) is a key instrument, serving as a legal base of international cooperation in counter-maritime terrorism efforts.

This chapter will explore various aspects of maritime terrorism in relation to land-based terrorism and international law. The subjects cover the definition and nature of maritime terrorism, types and scenarios of maritime terrorism, and efforts to prevent and fight maritime terrorism. As an essential part of counter-maritime terrorism regimes, the SUA Convention will be examined in depth. Given a wide range of counter-maritime terrorism efforts, this chapter will deal with only the SUA regime, and other regimes will be discussed in later chapters.

II The Nature of Maritime Terrorism

Definition of Terrorism

The Oxford Dictionary defines 'terrorism' as "the unlawful use of violence and intimidation, especially against civilians, in the pursuit of political aims." Despite the fact that terrorism is one of the most frequently referenced terms in international law and the contemporary world, there is no universally adopted legal definition of terrorism yet.

The origin of the term 'terrorism' has a long history that goes back to the 1789 French Revolution — the establishment described the conduct of revolutionaries as 'terrorism.' 'Terrorism' is derived from the 'Reign of Terror' or the 'Terror' (*Terreur* in French) in the period between June 1793 and July 1794, during which the official number of people executed in Paris by the repressive and violent government were up to 16,594. The term 'terror' or 'terrorism' has gained common usage after the numerous terrorist attacks of the past decades.

Most notably, the 9/11 terrorist attacks brought terrorism to the forefront of international politics and the global security agenda.

The definition of terrorism is very controversial. As of 2018, a total of 18 international conventions and protocols related to fight terrorism have been adopted since the 1970s. The conventions deal with specific forms of terrorist conduct and are thereby precise in nature and not of general application. Furthermore, they are not a solution in themselves, since treaties are only binding upon state parties.[2]

The United Nations (UN) has adopted a number of resolutions condemning acts of terrorism and urging member states' actions to fight terrorism. Among them, the UN General Assembly Resolution 49/60[3] contains a provision describing terrorism: "criminal acts intended or calculated to provoke a state of terror in the general public, a group of persons or particular persons for political purposes are in any circumstance unjustifiable, whatever the considerations of a political, philosophical, ideological, racial, ethnic, religious or any other nature that may be invoked to justify them."

The UN Security Council Resolution 1556 defined terrorism as[4]: "criminal acts, including against civilians, committed with the intent to cause death or serious bodily injury, or taking of hostages, with the purpose to provoke a state of terror in the general public or in a group of persons or particular persons, intimidate a population or compel a government or an international organization to do or to abstain from doing any act, which constitute offences within the scope of and as defined in the international conventions and protocols relating to terrorism."

Prior to the UN, 24 member states of the League of Nations in 1937 adopted the Convention for Prevention and Punishment of Terrorism, in which terrorism was defined as "all criminal acts directed against a State and intended or calculated to create a state of terror in the minds of particular persons or a group of persons or the general public." The convention did not come into force due to the lack of ratifications, which were attributed to mainly dissent over the definition of the term.[5]

The U.S. Department of Defense defines 'terrorism' as "the unlawful use of violence or threat of violence, often motivated by religious, political, or other

2 *Ibid.*, p. 19.

3 UN General Assembly Resolution, A/RES/49/60, 'Measure to Eliminate International Terrorism' adopted on 17 February 1995.

4 UN Security Council Resolution, S/RES/1566(2004), 'Threat to international peace and security caused by terrorist acts, adopted on 8 October 2004.

5 Conte (n 1). p. 20.

ideological beliefs, to instill fear and coerce governments or societies in pursuit of goals that are usually political."[6] The United States Federal Criminal Code[7] has defined 'international terrorism' as "... activities that involve violent ... or life-threatening acts ... that are a violation of the criminal law of the United States and ... appear to be intended: (i) to intimidate or coerce a civilian population; (ii) to influence the policy of a government by intimidation or coercion; or (iii) to affect the conduct of a government by mass destruction, assignation, or kidnapping ..."

Exploring the definitions of terrorism, a number of principal components are found: (i) criminal acts; (ii) the threat or the use of violence to cause death or injury against civilians; (iii) provocation of terror in the public; (iv) intimidation or coercion of a population or a government organization or international organization to do or abstain from doing any act; and (v) political or religious ends.

The Comprehensive Convention on Terrorism, proposed by India in 1996, intends to criminalize all forms of international terrorism and deny terrorists, their financiers and supporters, any access to funds, arms and safe havens. The Convention has been negotiated over the last two decades. Notwithstanding its urgency and the international community's efforts to define terrorism in international laws, it has failed to reach a consensus.

This happens mainly due to difficulty in agreeing on a basis for determining when the use of violence is legitimate. A heated controversy in this regard is concerned with whether the definition of terrorism can be applied to state terrorism — in which acts of terrorism are conducted by governments against their own people — or in support of international terrorism.

Another controversy is concerned with how to distinguish acts of terrorism from the acts of a liberation movement. Palestinian militants, for example, call Israel terrorist and Kurdish militants call Turkey terrorist. The ambivalent nature of terrorism is often described in a cynical saying that goes "one state's terrorist is another state's freedom fighter." As such, the absence of a universally agreed-upon definition of terrorism has become a major obstacle in rallying international counter-terrorism efforts.

Definition of Maritime Terrorism

As with terrorism generally, there exists no universally agreed-upon definition of maritime terrorism in international laws and scholarly literatures.

6 U.S. Department of Defense, *Dictionary of Military Associated Terms*, available at https://fas.org/irp/doddir/dod/jp1_02.pdf.

7 18 U.S. Code §2331(definition).

Principally, the concept of maritime terrorism is understood in the context of two global phenomena: terrorism and piracy.

First, the nature of maritime terrorism is understood to fall within the context of terrorism and thus is seen as an extension of land-based terrorism to the maritime domain. The concept of maritime terrorism primarily builds on that of terrorism, but the uniqueness of the maritime domain is highlighted in terms of access to the sea. Thus, just as with defining terrorism, the same controversies may arise when defining maritime terrorism.

Derek Johnson and his colleagues define maritime terrorism,[8] based on the components that constitute 'the offence' under the 1988 Convention for the Suppression of Unlawful Acts against the Safety of Maritime Navigation (SUA). The SUA prescribes the offence as: (i) any attempt or threat to seize control of a ship by force; (ii) to damage or destroy a ship or its cargo; (iii) to injure or kill a person on board a ship; or (iv) to endanger in any way the safe investigation of a ship that moves from the territorial waters of one State into those of another State or into international waters. In the context of the extension of land-based terrorism to the maritime domain, Rubert Herbert-Burns and Zuker Lauren define maritime terrorism as pertaining to terrorist acts committed "within or with the intent of compromising the features of the maritime domain."[9]

Second, maritime terrorism is distinguished from piracy. The concept of maritime terrorism needs to be understood within the framework of legal regimes under the UN Convention on the Law of the Sea (UNCLOS). The UNCLOS establishes a number of maritime zones, including internal waters, territorial seas, contiguous zones, exclusive economic zones, continental shelves and the high seas, according to which a coastal state's jurisdiction differs, and acts of violence are differently characterized.

The concept of maritime terrorism was initially understood within the context of piracy whereby any unauthorized act of violence on the high seas would be characterized as 'piracy.'[10] Whereas piracy is characterized as acts of violence on the high sea or outside the jurisdiction of a coastal state, committed for economic purposes,[11] maritime terrorism is acts of violence perpetrated,

8 Derek Johnson, Erika Pladdet & Mark J. Valencia, 'Introduction: Research on Southeast Asian Piracy,' in Dereck Johnson & Mark Valencia (eds), *Piracy in Southeast Asia: Status, Issues and Responses* (Institute of Southeast Asian Studies, Singapore, 2005).

9 Rupert Herbert-Burns & Zuker Lauren, 'Drawing the Line Between Piracy and Maritime Terrorism,' (2004) 16(4), *Jane's Intelligence Review*, pp. 30–35.

10 Natalie Klein, *Maritime Security and the Law of the Sea* (Oxford University Press, New York, 2011), p. 147.

11 UNCLOS, Art. 101.

irrespective of maritime zones, for political motivations. Nonetheless, the line between piracy and maritime piracy has been blurred. This may happen because terrorist groups are engaged in piracy to finance their activities, as demonstrated in some cases in which terrorists attack ships primarily for financial purposes. It appears that maritime threats have become increasingly intertwined and less discernable.[12]

Maritime terrorism is also distinguished from armed robbery against ships in terms of its purpose and where the crimes were committed. As with piracy, the purpose of armed robbery is for financial gains. By contrast, armed robbery against ships is acts of violence committed within the jurisdiction of a coastal state. The International Maritime Organization (IMO) defines armed robbery against ships as "any illegal act of violence or detention or any act of depredation, or threat thereof, other than an act of piracy, committed for private ends and directed against a ship or against persons or property on board such a ship, within a State's internal waters, archipelagic waters and territorial sea."[13]

The Council for Security Cooperation in the Asia Pacific (CSCAP) Working Group in 2009 has offered an extensive definition of maritime terrorism: "the undertaking of terrorist acts and activities within the maritime environment, using or against vessels or fixed platforms at sea or in port, or against any one of their passengers or personnel, against coastal facilities or settlements, including tourist resorts, port towns or cities ..."

The definition attempts to highlight the characteristics of maritime terrorism by encompassing a wide range of terrorist targets in the maritime domain, but it is not sufficient to describe the nature of terrorism. The definition has not described an integral part of terrorism, which is political ends. Furthermore, the definition has not addressed the inherent problems with the aforementioned definition of terrorism, i.e., what use of violence constitutes terrorism (more specifically, directed at whom, by whom and for what ends).

Joyner describes maritime terrorism as "the systematic use or threat to use acts of violence against international shipping and maritime services by an individual or group to induce fear and intimidation in a civilian population in

12 Patch, John C. 'The Overstated Threat' in *Modern Piracy and Maritime Terrorism: The Challenge of Piracy for the 21st Century* (eds. by M.R Haberfeld and Agostino von Hassell), cited in Eric Shea Nelson, 'Maritime Terrorism and Piracy: Existing and Potential Threats,' (2012) 3(1), *Global Security Studies*, p. 18.

13 IMO Res. A. 1025 (26) (Annex, para. 2.2), 'Code of Practice for the Investigation of the Crimes of Piracy and Armed Robbery Against Ships.'

order to achieve political ambitions and objectives."[14] It appears that Joyner's definition reflects the very nature of terrorism, with an explicit description of political objectives, but the characteristics of the maritime domain are not sufficiently described, with only a limited coverage of international shipping and maritime services.

Many of maritime terrorism definitions discussed above build on the definitions of land based terrorism. Notably, the coverage of the definitions is very broad and inclusive, thus encompassing the various kinds of unlawful acts at sea within the scope of maritime terrorism. This could blur the line with other unlawful acts at sea while ignoring or according a lesser focus on the very nature of maritime terrorism, which builds on a political, ideological or religious motivation.

By all accounts of the components of maritime terrorism, it may be described as "acts of violence or the threat of use of violence against vessels, passengers or infrastructure on and offshore to intimidate a population or compel a government or an international organization to do or to abstain from doing any act, in order to achieve political or religious objectives."

Relationship between Maritime Terrorism and Piracy

As illustrated above, the concepts of maritime terrorism and piracy are discernable in terms of primarily their purposes, i.e., political ends, as opposed to financial gains. In addition, regarding the targets and methods of assault, those used and chosen by pirates and terrorists may vary. Pirates tend to choose small vessels rather than large ones.

However, a trend of piracy attacks in recent years, particularly off the Somali Coast and the Gulf of Aden, shows that piratical incidents occur more often against larger vessels such as bulk carriers. Nonetheless, what is obvious is that pirates target ships that are most vulnerable.[15] And ships that are most susceptible to piracy attacks are those that lack surveillance technology, are easy to board, and have small crews.[16] Unlike piracy, maritime terrorists target vessels that will have some effect on the political objectives that they are trying to achieve. Thus, targets that are chosen by terrorists fall into four categories[17]: (i) ships as iconic

---

14 Christopher C. Joyner, 'Suppression of Terrorism on the High Sea: 1988 IMO Convention on the Safety of Maritime Navigation' (1989) 19 *Israel Yearbook on Human Rights*, cited in Natalie Klein (n 10).

15 Eric Shea Nelson, 'Maritime Terrorism and Piracy: Existing and Potential Threats,' (2012)3(1), *Global Security Studies*, p. 17.

16 *Ibid.*

17 Martin N. Murphy, *Small Boats, Weak States, Dirty Money: Piracy and Maritime Terrorism in the Modern World* (Columbia Up, New York 2008), cited in Eric Shea Nelson (n 15).

targets; (ii) ships as economic targets; (iii) ships as mass casualty targets; and (iv) ships as weapons.

Similar to pirates, terrorists often use small boats to carry out attacks against unsuspecting ships. Terrorists prefer small boats because of their speed and acceleration, maneuverability, and ability to evade radar detection.[18] Despite their differences, some contend that these two maritime threats have become increasingly intertwined and less discernable.[19]

Furthermore, some argue, particularly since the 9/11 attacks in the U.S., that maritime piracy should be considered an act of terrorism. This argument claims that that the root causes and factors that enable both piracy and terrorism are similar, and that the tactics of each overlap, particularly in hijacking and hostage-taking.[20]

The inflexible distinction of acts of piracy and maritime terrorism is likely to cause confusion for enforcement agencies in combating these unlawful acts, which are required to undertake multi-purpose tasks at sea. For example, in 2008, the German Navy frigate *Emden*, on patrol in the Gulf of Aden to intercept *Al Qaeda*'s vessels, encountered pirate vessels attacking a Japanese tanker. However, since the *Emden* was mandated to intervene only if the pirates were defined as terrorists, it had no choice but to let the pirates go.[21]

However, the conflation of the two distinct and separate maritime threats may also pose some problems in addressing those threats. Since piracy and maritime terrorism are distinct in their motivations, they require different solutions that will involve a complex mix of economic, political and military responses.[22] Conflating the two threats is likely to pose a challenge to law enforcement. It is entirely legal that the owner of a ship kidnapped by pirates pays a ransom to pirates for the release of crews. However, if piracy becomes a form of terrorism, this would change because in many countries, including the U.S., knowingly making payments to terrorist groups is not allowed.[23]

18 *Ibid.*

19 John Patch, 'The Overstated Threat,' *In Modern Piracy and Maritime Terrorism: The Challenge of Piracy for the 21st Century* (eds by M.R. Haberfeld and Agostino von Hassell), cited in Eric Shea Nelson (n 15), p. 18.

20 Yong, A, J and Valencia, M. J, 'Conflation of Piracy and Terrorism in Southeast Asia: Rectitude and Utility, *Contemporary Southeast Asia* (2003), 25(2).

21 Douglas R. Burgess Jr. 'Piracy is Terrorism,' *The New York Times*, 5 December 2008.

22 Donna J. Nincic, 'The Radicalization of Maritime Piracy: Implications for Maritime Security,' *Journal of Energy Security*, 14 December 2010, available at http://www.ensec.org/index.php?option=com_content&view=article&id=269:the-radicalization-of-maritime-piracy-implications-for-maritime-energy-security&catid=112:energysecurity-content&Itemid=367.

23 *Ibid.*

A worrisome trend regarding acts of piracy and terrorism is that some terrorist groups have chosen acts of piracy to finance their activities, as noted above. This phenomenon is particularly notable in Southeast Asia and West Africa. Some terrorist groups that have the ability to operate in the maritime realm have chosen acts of piracy to finance their land-based operations. The Philippine terrorist group *Abu Sayyaf*, for example, has committed acts of piracy against ships sailing off the Philippine coast.

As recently as October 2016, the 10 gunmen of the *Abu Sayyaf* boarded a 11,391-ton Korean cargo ship off the Philippine coast and kidnapped crews for a ransom payment. In West Africa, militant groups, such as *Boko Haram* and the *Movement for the Emancipation of the Niger Delta,* have engaged in committing piracy in the form of kidnapping oil tankers or attacking on and offshore oil infrastructure. Given this phenomenon, some argue that a type of nexus between pirates and terrorists may have been formed.

Terrorists and pirates have shared interests in ensuring that corrupt and weak states remain corrupt and weak, since as an extension of land-based operations, maritime terrorism and piracy thrive only when conditions on shore permit them to do so.[24] The two groups could build a cooperative relationship on a case-by-case basis for financial rewards. Then, pirates are able to assist terrorists who lack skills and experience at sea in exchange for the protection for pirates' land-based activities and sharing a ransom payment.[25]

However, a formal nexus between pirates and terrorists is unlikely, given the clandestine nature of these maritime perpetrators. Some terrorist groups are well trained and skilled seafarers to the extent that they are capable of conducting maritime operations by themselves, without assistance from pirates. Furthermore, on the part of terrorists, a partnership with pirates is likely to be a quite risky deal due to a higher possibility that they might leak the terrorists' plots. While terrorists seek to obtain leverage, influence and power through the publicity generated by their violence,[26] pirates do not seek publicity because it brings unwanted attention from law enforcement officials, and the more frequent their attacks become, the more likely they are to be apprehended.[27]

Despite their similarities and differences, what is indisputable is that both piracy and terrorism are acts of violence at sea that pose a great danger to

24 Nelson (n 15), p. 23.

25 *Ibid.*

26 Hoffman Bruce, *Inside Terrorism* (Columbia Up, New York, 2006), cited in Eric Shea Nelson, 'Maritime Terrorism and Piracy: Existing and Potential Threats,' *Global Security Studies* (2012) 3(1), p. 18.

27 Murphy (n 17).

peace and stability in the maritime domain, and they should be addressed for safe navigation and the secure use of the sea. For counter-terrorism measures, the international community needs to clarify what constitutes maritime terrorism and piracy, and what actions may be taken against the perpetrators of these acts.[28]

III Objectives and Methods of Maritime Terrorism

Objectives of Maritime Terrorism

Maritime terrorism may seek low-level objectives in order to achieve a higher level of political ends. Terrorists may seek to create human casualties, economic losses, environmental damage, or other negative impacts, alone or in combination, with either minor or major consequences.[29] The targets that terrorists choose may vary, depending on the objective that they are willing to pursue. If human casualties are the principal objective, for instance, passenger vessels such as cruise ships and ferries may be more attractive terrorist attacks than cargo and other vessels.[30]

The case in point might be the bombing of the Philippine *Superferry* 14 in 2004, which resulted in 116 casualties. A 3.6-kilogram (8-pound) TNT placed in a hollowed-out TV set exploded on the *Superferry*, a 10,000-ton ferry with 899 passengers and crew onboard, an hour after its departure from Manila. The investigation found that the bombing was conducted by the *Abu Sayyaf* Group combined with elements from the *Jemaah Islamiyah* and the *Rajah Solaiman Revolutionary Movement*. The incident has been listed as the most destructive act of terrorism in maritime history.

If economic loss is the primary objective, terrorists may seek to carry out different types of attacks, with potentially few human casualties but significant impacts to critical infrastructure or commerce.[31] Given that today roughly 80 percent of global freight moves by sea, much of it in the form of cargo that is transported on the basis of a 'just enough, just in time' inventory system,[32] any

---

28 Nelson (n 15), p. 25.

29 Paul Parfomak & John Frittelli, 'Maritime Security: Potential Terrorist Attacks and Protection Priorities,' *CRS Report for Congress*, 14 May 2007, Congressional Research Service.

30 *Ibid.*

31 *Ibid.*

32 Michael D. Greenberg, Peter Chalk, Henry H. Willis, Ivan Khilo & David S. Oritz, 'Maritime Terrorism: Risk and Liability,' *RAND Corporation*, 2006, pp. 15–16.

disruption of sea-borne trade by terrorism could cause massive economic destabilization. Attacks on oil tankers and on and offshore energy facilities may generate significant economic externalities.

The suicide attack against the *M/V Limburg*, a French oil tanker, in October 2002 might be a pertinent case in point. The incident resulted in only three deaths (two of which were bombers), but it directly contributed to the short-term collapse of the international shipping business in the Gulf of Aden and nearby waters and led to a $0.48/barrel hike in the price of Brent crude oil. As a consequence, the tripling of war-risk premium was levied on ships calling at the Gulf of Aden. In addition, the suicide bombing caused insurance rates among Yemeni shippers to rise 300 percent and reduced Yemeni port shipping volume by 50 percent in only one month after the attack.[33] This caused the Yemeni economy to lose an estimated $3.8 million a month in port revenues.[34]

The disruptive economic dimension of maritime terrorism has been singled out as having specific pertinence to *Al Qaeda*. Osama bin Laden, before being killed in 2011, had emphasized that attacking key pillars of the Western commercial and trading system was integral to his war on the U.S. and its major allies.[35] This was highlighted in a statement of *Al Qaeda* that was issued following of the bombing of the M/V *Limburg*: "*By hitting the oil tanker in Yemen, the mujahedeen hit the secret line, and the lifeline of the crusader's nation. They reminded the enemies of the heavy cost of blood and the enormity of losses that they will pay as a price for their continued aggression on our community and looting of our wealth.*"[36]

Terrorists may also seek to cause a crippling environmental damage with a decisive attack on oil tankers or ships carrying hazardous and noxious substances or on and offshore oil facilities. A major oil spill from the stricken oil tanker is liable to devastate the marine environment in the immediate vicinity of the release and, if left to drift, could conceivably degrade elongated stretches of fertile coastline.[37] For some developing states in Africa and Asia that rely heavily on fish for both indigenous consumption and overseas export earnings,

33 U.S. Department of State, 'Yemen's Economy Suffering due to October Terrorist Attack,' 8 November 2002.

34 Greenberg, Chalk, Willis, Khilo & Oritz (n 32).

35 *Ibid.*

36 'Statement Attributed to bin Laden Praises Recent Attacks," *CNN*, 14 October 2002, available at http://edition.cnn.com/2002/WORLD/meast/10/14/bin.laden.statement/index.html.

37 Greenberg, Chalk, Willis, Khilo & Oritz (n 32).

such effects have the potential to feed into wider socioeconomic unrest and could possibly act as a trigger for political instability.[38]

Typology of Terrorist Attacks

High-profile maritime terror attacks that have happened in the past few decades can be classified into a number of types, in accordance with both the *modus operandi* and targets of attacks. They may include hijacking of ships, bombing, ramming, use of the sea for land-based terrorism, and attacks on port facilities.

1 Hijacking of Ships

The hijacking of ships has been the most typical type of piracy attack off the Somali coast over the last decade. As will be demonstrated in the later chapter, the *modus operandi* of this type of piracy assault involves the hijacking of a vessel underway, and holding the crew hostage for a period of time for a ransom payment. When a negotiated ransom is paid, the crews held hostage are released for the most part without being harmed. Unlike hijacking by piracy attacks, which are motivated by solely financial gains, terrorists commit hijacking of ships, holding crews and passengers hostage, to claim political demands and to bring international attention to their cause. As a consequence, in many cases, casualties are involved.

– **Hijacking of *Santa Maria* (1961)**

The hijacking of *Santa Maria*, a 21,000-ton Portuguese cruise ship, occurred on 23 January 1961. The cruise ship was hijacked by a group of 70 Portuguese and Spanish political rebels led by Henrique Galvao, a Portuguese political exile, to bring international attention to the Estado Nova regime in Portugal and the Franco fascist regime in Spain. When the cruise ship was seized by the rebels, it was on a holiday cruise in the southern Caribbean, with 600 passengers and 300 crew members onboard. The rebels boarded the ship disguised as passengers, killed one officer and injured several others in the process of taking control of the ship. The ship was held for 14 days before the U.S. Navy stepped in and the terrorists finally surrendered to the Brazilian Navy in exchange for political asylum. The incident was recorded as the first modern-day hijacking at sea.

– **Hijacking of *Achille Lauro* (1985)**

On 7 October 1985, *Achille Lauro*, an Italian cruise ship with 748 passengers onboard, was kidnapped by four gunmen representing the Palestine Liberal

38 *Ibid.*

Front in Egypt's territorial waters. The hijackers asked for the release of Palestinian prisoners from Israeli jails. In response to Israel's refusal, the hijackers executed a Jewish-American in a wheelchair and threw him overboard. Egypt negotiated the release of hostages and took the hijackers into custody, but did not arrest them. Subsequently, the hijackers took an Egyptian flight to Tunisia. Under U.S. pressure, Tunisia did not allow the aircraft to land. U.S. Navy fighters forced the airplane down at a NATO airfield in Italy where a standoff occurred between U.S. and Italian authorities over which government had jurisdiction. The Italian government denied U.S. requests for extradition and tried the hijackers in Italy. The leader of the hijacking was eventually allowed to leave Italy through Yugoslavia.

– **Hijacking of a Turkish Passenger Ferry in the Black Sea (1996)**

The Black Sea hostage-taking incident occurred on 16 January 1996 on the Black Sea during the first Chechen War. The Turkish ferry *Avrasaya*, with 177 passengers and 55 crew on board, was kidnapped by a group of nine gunmen in a Turkish port. The hijackers threatened to blow up the ferry unless Russian forces ceased their attacks against the Chechen rebels. The hostages were released without any casualties when the hijackers surrendered to the Turkish authorities.

– **Hijacking of the *M/V Penrider* (2003)**

The Malaysian oil tanker *Penrider* was seized by armed raiders in August 2003 near the Malaysian coast. The raiders attacked the oil tanker and held three crew members hostage and demanded a ransom. They were released when the owner of the ship paid $100,000 for a ransom. The raiders, disguised as pirates, were believed to be the rebels of the *Free Ache Movement*, an Islamic terror group which fights to establish an Islamic state in the province of Ache in Indonesia.

2 Bombing of Ships

The bombing of ships involves either the detonation of explosives placed on the ship or the ramming of a small boat carrying explosives to a target vessel. Ramming a small boat into a target vessel is a typical method used by suicide bombers.

– **Suicide Bombing of the *USS Cole* (2002)**

The suicide bombing against the U.S. Navy guided-missile destroyer *USS Cole* took place on 12 October 2002 when the destroyer was refueling at the Yemeni port of Aden. A small fiberglass boat carrying explosives and two suicide bombers approached the port side of destroyer and rammed. The assault involved approximately 180–320 kg (400–700 pounds) of explosives, creating a big gash in the ship's port side. Seventeen sailors were killed and 39 were injured in the blast. It was found that the suicide attack was organized and directed by *Al Qaeda.*

– **Suicide bombing of the *M/V Limburg* (2002)**

The *M/V Limburg*, a French crude oil tanker of 157,000 tons, was attacked by suicide bombing on 6 October 2002. The attack involved a small boat, packed with 100–200 kilograms of TNT. The small boat rammed the *M/V Limburg* as it was preparing to take on a pilot-assisted approach to the Ash Shihr Terminal off the coast of Yemen. The oil tanker was lifting 297,000 barrels of crude oil at the time of attack. It was estimated that 90,000 barrels of oil spilled into the water. The attack killed one crewman and two terrorists. The attack was significant because it marked *Al Qaeda*'s first successful strike against an oil target.

– **Bombing of the *Superferry 14* (2004)**

As illustrated earlier, the bombing of the *Superferry 14* on 27 February 2004 resulted in 116 casualties. A 3.6-kilogram (8-pound) TNT placed in a hollowed-out TV set exploded on the *Superferry*, a 10,000-ton ferry with 899 passengers and crew onboard. The terrorist from *Abu Sayyaf* placed the explosive and it exploded an hour after its departure from Manila.

3 Transport of Weapons and Terrorists

Several incidents where terrorists attempted to transport weapons used for terrorism and terrorists by sea were interdicted. Although the transport of weapons and terrorists is not a commitment of direct terrorism assaults, it is very significant in that those attempts were directly linked to terrorist attacks by providing means of terrorism. The interception of ships carrying weapons used for terrorism may have significant implications for international efforts to prevent the proliferation of weapons of mass destruction (WMD s). The interdictions for the purpose of the Proliferation Security Initiative (PSI) will be demonstrated in Chapter 7.

– **Use of a Coaster to Transport Weapons (1973)**

A coaster *Claudia,* owned by a German arms trafficker, was intercepted by the Irish Navy while attempting to land a consignment of weapons intended for the *Provisional Irish Republican Army* (PIRA). On board were five tons of munitions that included 250 Soviet-made assault rifles, pistols, mines, grenades and other explosives. It was found that PIRA had asked the trafficker to acquire those weapons and explosives and that the order had been filed by Libya.

– **Use of a Freighter to Transport Weapons (2002)**

Karine A, a 4,000-ton Palestinian freighter, was seized by Israeli forces in the Red Sea on 3 January 2002. The freighter was carrying a wide range of arms, including rockets, anti-tank missiles, long-range mortar bombs, mines, sniper rifles, ammunition, and more than two tons of high explosives. Allegedly the consignment was bound for either the Palestinian Authority or Hezbollah, to be used for attacks against Jewish targets in Israel.

– **Use of a Fishing Vessel to Transport Weapons (2003)**

The Abu Hassan, an Egyptian fishing vessel, was intercepted and seized by the Israeli Navy on 21 May 2003, on the charge of smuggling weapons into the Gaza Strip. The Egyptian owner of the fishing boat was recruited by *Hezbollah* and trained specifically to carry out maritime support missions. The fishing vessel was carrying a *Hezbollah* explosives expert and a radio-activation system, detonators, and compact discs with instructions on how to prepare explosives.

– **Transport of Terrorists by Sea (2008)**

A series of Mumbai terrorist shootings and bombings were carried out by 10 members of the Pakistan-based terrorist group, the *Lashkar-e Tayyiba*, for four days between 26 November and 29 November 2008 across Mumbai, India. The terrorist attacks resulted in 164 people killed and 308 wounded. The Mumbai attacks were planned and directed by *Lashkar-e-Tayyiba* militants inside Pakistan. The gunmen were trained and sent by sea to Mumbai. Then the terrorists came ashore by inflatable speed boats.

4 Attack on Port Facilities

In the wake of the 9/11 attacks in the U.S., a likely — and much-feared — scenario, is that terrorists hijack a ship carrying oil, liquified natural gas or radiological materials, and ram the ship into a major port such as New York, detonating it. Because ships, storage facilities, energy plants and industry infrastructure are densely located in ports, the detonation of any ship loaded with explosives or flammable materials in a port by ramming or other means of attack would be likely to cause devastating subsequent explosions. The scale of damage inflicted by explosions and pollutant leaks into a densely populated city would be unimaginable. The following sections outline various non-terrorism-related explosions that nonetheless demonstrate the potential risks of a detonation in port.

– **Halifax Explosion (1917)**

The Halifax explosion is a maritime disaster that occurred in Halifax, Canada on 6 December 1917. The explosion took place when *SS Mont Blanc*, a French cargo ship laden with high explosives, collided with the Norwegian vessel *SS Imo*, a chartered unladen cargo ship, in a narrow strait off the Halifax Harbor. The fire on *Mont Blanc* made the ship uncontrollable and it continued to drift toward a pier in the harbor. Approximately 20 minutes after collision, the fire set off the high explosives. The blasts devastated a district of Halifax, killing approximately 2,000 people and injuring 9,000 others. The blast was the largest man-made explosion before nuclear weapons were developed, releasing the equivalent energy of roughly 2.9 kilotons of TNT.

– **Explosions in the Port of Tianjin (2015)**

On 12 August 2015, a series of explosions occurred at a container storage station at the Port of Tianjin, China. The explosions resulted in 173 deaths, injuring hundreds of others. According to an investigation, an overheated container of dry nitrocellulose was the case of the initial explosion. Fires caused by the initial explosions continued to burn, repeatedly causing secondary explosions, with eight additional explosions occurring on 15 August. Allegedly over 40 kinds of hazardous chemicals, including ammonium nitrate and potassium nitrate in amounts of up to 3000 tons, were stored in the storage station. Among those chemicals, 700 tons of sodium cyanide, which is highly toxic and deadly, were stored at the site.

Scenarios of Potential Maritime Terrorist Attacks in the Future

The U.S. Coast Guard, the U.S. Navy and other federal agencies have identified scenarios for potential maritime terrorist attacks in port for maritime security exercises. They include[39]:

- Various types of explosives attacks on a ship in port.
- Hostage-taking and executions aboard a vessel in port
- A marine mine attack on a navy frigate in port
- Underwater explosive devices planted on multiple vessels in port
- A nuclear device aboard an incoming vessel in a 55-galllon drum
- Attack on a port with a biological disease agent
- Detonation of a 'dirty' bomb in a shipping container at multiple U.S. ports

Potential maritime terrorist attacks would not be necessarily confined to port. Extending the realm to other maritime spaces, more extensive scenarios in addition to the above-mentioned scenarios can be envisaged. They include:[40]

- Use of a commercial container ship to smuggle chemical, biological or radiological (CBR) materials for unconventional attacks carried out on land or at major commercial ports

39 Suk Kyoon Kim, *Maritime Disputes in Northeast Asia: Regional Challenges and Cooperation*, (Brill, Boston, 2017), p. 156, cited from Paul Parfomak & John Frittelli, 'Maritime Security: Potential Terrorist Attacks and Protection Priorities,' *CRS Report for Congress*, 9 January 2007, Congressional Research Service, pp. 9–10.

40 See Greenberg, Chalk, Willis, Khilo & Oritz (n 32); See also Parfomak & Frittelli (n 39).

- Use of a 'Trojan Horse' such as a fishing trawler, resupply ship, tug or similar innocuous- looking vessel, to transport weapons and other battle-related materials
- Hijacking of a vessel as a fund-raising exercise to support a campaign of political violcncc directed toward ethnic, ideological, religious or separatist designs
- Attacking a cruise liner or passenger ferry to cause mass casualties by detonating an on-board or submersible improvised explosive device, or ramming the vessel with a fast-approach, small attack craft
- Use of a small, high-speed boat to attack an oil tanker or offshore energy platform to affect international petroleum prices or cause major pollution
- Bombing and sinking of a liquefied propane gas (LPG) or oil tanker in a major commercial and naval shipping channel to block or disrupt maritime traffic
- Hijacking of an LNG carrier that is then detonated as a 'floating bomb' or used as a collision weapon
- Ramming and dirty bombing a ferry with a hijacked cargo ship
- Coordinated bombing of docks and bridges, and mining of the harbor at a major commercial port

Identifying the scenarios of potential maritime terrorist attacks is significant in preventing and responding to maritime terrorism. Understanding the probability of these scenarios enables the responsible authorities to prioritize maritime security activities and allocate limited resources efficiently. The more vulnerable and high-value the maritime targets, the more resources and security they require.

IV Maritime Terrorist Organizations

Status of Maritime Terrorist Organizations

Attacks against maritime targets by terrorists are very rare. According to the data covered by the Global Terrorism Database (GTD), 199 of 98,000 attacks in the last 40 years, which is less than 0.2 percent of the total, were carried out against maritime targets.[41] As of 2016, the U.S. Department of State (DOS) has designated 61 foreign terrorist organizations across the world.[42] The DOS has

41 Justin V. Hastings & Victor Asal, 'When Terrorism Goes to Sea: Terrorist Organizations and the Move to Maritime Targets,' *Terrorism and Political Violence* (2015) 27(4), pp. 722–740.

42 U.S. Department of State, 'Country Reports on Terrorism 2016,' available at https://www.state.gov/documents/organization/272488.pdf.

identified 10 of the designated terrorist organizations as having maritime capabilities, or at least having demonstrated maritime capabilities in the past.[43] The organizations on the list include:
- Al Qaeda
- Abu Nidal Organization
- Abu Sayyaf Group (ASG)
- Basque Fatherland and Liberty
- Hamas
- Hezbollah
- Jemaah Islamiya (JI)
- Lashkar e-Tayyiba
- Liberation Tigers of Tamil Eelam(LTTE)
- Palestine Liberation Front — Abu Abbas Faction

Several terrorist groups that are believed to have maritime capabilities or that have engaged in maritime terrorism are not on the list. They include *Al Shabaab*, *Al Qaeda* in the Arabian Peninsula (AQAP), *Hizbul Islam* operating in the Gulf of Aden region, *Boko Haram* and the *Emancipation of the Niger Delta* operating in the Gulf of Guinea.[44] The disparities are also illustrated by the findings of Hastings & Asal, who have examined the data of the GTD and found that 14 terrorist groups have conducted at least once maritime attack between 1998 and 2005. The terrorist groups that have engaged in maritime attacks include[45]:
- People's Revolutionary Army (Columbia)
- Aden Abyan Islamic Army (AAIA)
- Tawhid and Jihad
- Palestinian Islamic Jihad (PIJ)
- Sudan People's Liberation Army
- Liberation Tigers of Tamil Eelam (LTTE)
- New People's Army (NPA)
- Jemaah Islamiya (JI)
- Abu Sayyaf Group (ASG)
- Moro Islamic Liberation Front (MILF)
- Free Ache Movement (GAM)
- Revolutionary Armed Forces of Columbia (FARC)
- Hamas
- Al Qaeda

43 See U.S. Department of State, 'Country Reports on Terrorism 2010,' available at https://www.state.gov/documents/organization/170479.pdf.

44 Nincic (n 22).

45 Hastings & Asal (n 41).

The terrorist organizations on the list of the DOS are principally land-based. Given that there are relatively quite a small number of maritime attacks by only a few terrorist organizations, none of those terrorist organizations appears to have fully engaged in maritime attacks. Thus, acts of maritime terrorism are likely to be supplementary to land-based operations by the terrorist organizations.

Several reasons for the quite limited scale of terrorist attacks on maritime targets, despite the potentially vast and cascading effects of maritime terrorism, can be identified from an operational perspective.

First, for operations at sea, terrorist organizations must have the ability to operate vessels and to do seafaring. It would not be easy for land-based terrorist organizations to acquire such capabilities. Second, they would have to recruit personnel who have experience and expertise in sea-faring and have knowledge in operating navigational equipment. Otherwise, the group would have to set up training facilities to train and educate recruits. Third, vessels used for maritime attacks need to be equipped with costly seaworthy communication and navigation equipment. Fourth, the probability of a successful attack maritime targets greatly depends on sea conditions, such as tide, wave and wind. Moreover, maritime targets are not stationary, so it is quite difficult to target them correctly.

A maritime attack that was attempted by *Al Qaeda* but failed may demonstrate the nature of maritime terrorism. *Al Qaeda* attempted to attack the *USS The Sullivans* in January 2000 by a suicide bombing using a small boat. But the boat sank before it reached the target because it was overloaded with the explosives, a tactical error that more experienced seamen would not have made.[46] Nonetheless, operational difficulties do not negate the possibility of maritime terrorism, but may illustrate the challenges that terrorists may face in when attempting to attack seaborne targets.

Major Contemporary Terrorist Organizations with Maritime Capability

Of the terrorist organizations that are believed to have maritime capabilities, some prominent examples are described below.

– ***Abu Sayyaf Group***

The *Abu Sayyaf Group* (ASG), which was responsible for the *Superferry 14* bombing in 2004, is the most violent terrorist group in the Philippines. The group claims to promote an independent Islamic state in western Mindanao

46 *Ibid.*

and the Sulu Archipelago. The ASG is estimated to have 400 members. The ASG has committed kidnappings-for-ransom, bombings, ambushes of security personnel, public beheadings, assassinations and extortion. The ASG is primarily funded through kidnapping-for-ransom operations and extortion. It is known that the ASG has links to *Jemaah Islamiya*, a regional terrorist group whose operatives have provided training to ASG members and have helped facilitate several ASG terrorist attacks.

– ***Boko Haram***

The Nigeria-based *Boko Haram* (BH) is responsible for numerous attacks in Nigeria, Cameroon, Chad and Niger that have killed thousands of people since its reemergence in 2009. In 2015, BH pledged its allegiance to the Islamic State of Iraq and Syria (ISIS). In 2014, BH killed approximately 5,000 Nigerian civilians in various attacks, of which the kidnapping of 276 female students from a secondary school brought a global attention to its atrocities. The membership of BH is estimated to be several thousands. It is known that BH has engaged in acts of piracy in the form of kidnapping and attacks on oil rigs and on and offshore oil infrastructure in the Gulf of Guinea.

– ***Free Ache Movement***

The *Free Ache Movement* was a separatist group seeking the independence of the Ache region from Indonesia. Prior to signing a peace agreement with the Indonesian government in 2005, it had been linked to a number of piracy acts intended to raise money through hijacking ships or robbing crews on their own in the Malacca Strait.[47]

– ***Jemaah Islamiya***

The *Jemaah Islamiya* (JI), which means an 'Islamic Congregation,' is a Southeast Asia-based terrorist organization dedicated to the establishment of an Islamic state in the region. The activities of JI span Brunei, Indonesia, Malaysia, Singapore, the southern Philippines and southern Thailand. In recent years, JI has been focusing on its operations and increasing its presence in Indonesia. JI has carried out many attacks in the region. Significant attacks include the 2002 Bali bombing and the 2003 Marriot Hotel bombing in Jakarta. In January 2015, the 44 Philippine policemen and three civilians were killed when a police squad was ambushed on an island in Mindanao.

– ***Liberation Tigers of Tamil Eelam***

The *Liberation Tigers of Tamil Eelam* (LTTE), founded in 1976, is a Tamil secessionist group in Sri Lanka. LTTE's campaign to create an independent

---

47 Parfomak & Frittelli (n 29).

state of Tamil Eelam led to the Sri Lankan civil war, which ran from 1983 to 2009 when LTTE was defeated by Sri Lanka government forces. Despite its defeat, LTTE's international network of sympathizers and financial supporters has persisted. LTTE founded a naval subgroup, known as the *Sea Tigers*, in 1984 to perform the vital task of smuggling supplies to LTTE. Over time, *the Sea Tigers* expanded its operations and began to target the Sri Lank Navy. *The Sea Tigers* had a number of suicide-bomber vessels. For over two decades, *the Sea Tigers* sank many Sri Lank naval ships with much loss of life: eight major vessels; 20 fast attack craft; and 28 inshore patrol craft.[48] Many merchant ships were attacked in an attempt to cause maximum disruption of trade routes during the 25 years of hostilities.[49] LTTE has engaged in acts of piracy. It has been suspected of hijacking several civilian ships in international waters. The main targets were ships flying Philippines, Greek, Indonesian, Panamanian, Belize, Chinese, Jordanian, Cambodian and Indian flags.[50]

– ***Al Qaeda***

Al Qaeda (AQ), established in 1988, seeks to eliminate Western influences and presence from the Muslim world, topple 'apostate' governments of Muslim countries and to establish a pan-Islamic caliphate government according to its own interpretation of Sharia law that would ultimately be at the center of a new international order.[51]

AQ conducted the 9/11 terrorist attacks on the United States, killing nearly 3,000 people. AQ was behind the *USS Cole* bombing in 2000 and the French oil tanker *M/V Limburg* in 2001. Prior to the arrest of the chief maritime planner Al Nashiri, called "*Prince of the Sea*," it was believed that the plot to attack Western shipping interest in the Strait of Gibraltar has been at the final stage. AQ was believed to have owned at least 23 ships, most of which operated through front companies located in Liberia, Tonga, Panama, Belize and the Isle of Man.[52] Allegedly Bin Laden had used fishing trawlers procured for family businesses

48 Sri Lanka Ministry of Defense, *Humanitarian Operation Factual Analysis: July 2006-M2009*, July 2011, available at http://slembassyusa.org/wp-content/uploads/2011/08/Sri-Lankan-Humanitarian-Operation-Factual-Analysis.pdf.

49 *Ibid.*

50 Sanjeewa Karunaratne, 'LTTE's Era of Sea Piracy Has Ended,' *Asian Tribune*, 21 May 2009.

51 U.S. Department of State, 'Country Reports on Terrorism 2016,' available at https://www.state.gov/documents/organization/272488.pdf.

52 Koknar, 'What Al Qaeda Could Do with 'Terror Navy'?,' 2005, cited in RAND Corporation, *Maritime Terrorism: Risk and Liability*, 2006.

located in Madagascar and parts of Asia to transport weapons, ammunition and explosives.[53]

Despite the removal of core leaders of AQ, including Bin Laden in May 2001, AQ remains a focal point of 'inspiration' for a worldwide network of affiliated groups, such as *Al Qaeda* in the Arabian Peninsula (AQAP), *Al Qaeda* in the Islamic Maghreb, *Al-Nusrah Front*, *Al Shabaab* and *Al Qaeda* in the Indian Subcontinent and other violent Sunni Islamic extremist groups.[54]

– ***Al Shabaab***

Al Shabaab (AS) was the militant wing of the former Somali Islamic Court Council that took over parts of southern Somalia during the second half of 2006. Since the end of 2006, AS and associated militias have undertaken a violent insurgency using guerrilla warfare and terrorist attacks against the transitional government of Somalia. AS is believed to have 7,000–9,000 fighters composed of a mixture of Somali recruits and foreign terrorist fighters. AS carried out a number of terrorist attacks, including a significant attack against the Westgate Mall in Nairobi, Kenya in 2013, resulting in the death of at least 65 civilians. Reportedly, there was a growing link and cooperation between AS, which was desperate for funding and resources, and other criminal gangs as well as pirates.[55] On the contrary, some argue that AS has been terrific at stamping out piracy from its ports due to its harsh interpretation of Shariah and the personal animus between profit-seeking pirates and Islamist militants.[56]

V The SUA Convention Regime

A New Legal Regime for Counter-Maritime Terrorism

While acts of piracy are an age-old phenomenon plaguing mankind, terrorism at sea has only manifested itself in recent times through the *Achille Lauro* hijacking in 1985, which served as a wake-up call.[57] In the hijacking incident, as illustrated earlier, four kidnappers held ship's crew and passengers — hailing from a number of different countries including Italy, the United States and

53 Joshua Sinai, 'Future Trends in Worldwide Maritime Terrorism, Connections' *The Quarterly Journal* (2004) 3(1), cited in RAND Corporation (n 52).

54 *Ibid.*

55 Jonathan Saul & Camlia Reed, 'Shabaah-Somali Pirates Links Growing: UN Adviser,' *Reuters*, 21 October 2011.

56 Currun Singh, 'Al Shabaab Fights the Pirates,' *The New York Times*, 22 October 2013.

57 Helmut Terk, 'Combating Terrorism at Sea: The Suppression of Unlawful Acts Against the Safety of Navigation,' *15 U. Miami Int'l & Comp. L. Rev.* 337 (2008).

Austria — hostage, demanding the release of 50 Palestinian prisoners held in Israel. The Italian government, which took the hijackers into custody, exercised criminal jurisdiction, denying the U.S. request for extradition.

In examining the hijacking incident, there was an argument that the incident could be considered as an act of piracy as defined in Article 15 of the 1958 Geneva Convention on the High Seas and Article 101 of the 1982 UN Convention on the Law of the Sea (UNCLOS).[58] However, some countries, such as Austria, Italy and Egypt, asserted that the hijacking incident did not fall within acts of piracy defined in the Conventions because the hijackers did not act for 'private ends,' and the seizure did not meet the two-ship requirement.[59]

As such there was an obvious legal gap, which would be filled by creating a specific convention relating to maritime terrorism.[60] These definitive requirements of piracy under the UNCLOS prevent numerous maritime terrorist acts from being classified as piracy, including a 'maritime 9/11 situation' where passengers or crew already aboard a vessel hijack the ship and use it as a weapon.[61] As was apparent in the *Achille Lauro* hijacking, the lack of establishment of criminal jurisdiction in combating maritime terrorism was problematic. Against this backdrop, the international community reached a consensus that legal measures were necessary to deal with acts of maritime terrorism which were not covered by the existing legal framework, and to ensure that the perpetrators were made duly accountable. More specifically, there was a need for rules relating to the arrest, prosecution and subsequent detention of those responsible for acts of maritime terrorism.[62]

The hijacking of the *Achille Lauro* constituted one of the first genuine acts of maritime terrorism recorded in modern history.[63] The international community, outraged by the terrorist acts, engaged in creating a new legal regime to counter terrorist acts at sea. Toward this end, the 14th Assembly of the International Maritime Organization (IMO), held in November 1985, considered the issue and supported a proposal by the United States that measures to prevent unlawful acts should be developed.

---

58 *Ibid.*

59 H.E Jose Luis Jesus, 'Protection of Foreign Ships against Piracy and Terrorism at Sea: Legal Aspects,' 18 *Int'l, J. Marine & Coastal L.* 363, 384 (2003), cited in Helmut Tuerk(n 57).

60 Tuerk(n 57), p. 343.

61 Tammy M. Sittnick, 'State Responsibility and Maritime Terrorism in the Strait of Malacca: Persuading Indonesia and Malaysia to Take Additional Steps to Secure the Strait' (2005) 14(3), *Pacific Rim Law and Policy Journal* 743–769, p. 749.

62 *Ibid.*

63 *Ibid.*, p. 339.

The Assembly adopted Resolution A. 584(14), 'Measures to Prevent Unlawful Acts Which Threaten the Safety of Ships and the Security of Their Passengers and Crew.' Subsequently in 1986, the Maritime Safety Committee (MSC) issued a circular (MSC/Circ. 443) on 'Measures to Prevent Unlawful Acts Against Passengers and Crews on Board Ships.'[64]

In November 1986, the governments of Austria, Egypt and Italy proposed a new international convention to deal specifically with the issue of maritime terrorism modeled on existing anti-terrorism conventions, particularly the Hague and Montreal Convention as well as the 1979 UN Convention Against the Taking of Hostages.[65] An *ad hoc* preparatory committee was established in accordance with the unanimous decision of the IMO Council that the matter was appropriate for consideration by the IMO and that it required urgent attention.[66]

After a year of deliberation, using the draft text submitted by the three countries as a basis, the committee concluded a draft Convention, titled 'the Convention for the Suppression of Unlawful Acts Against the Safety of Maritime Navigation' (1988 SUA Convention). The Convention was adopted by consensus on 10 March 1988 by a diplomatic conference held in Rome. In addition, a Protocol for the Suppression of Unlawful Acts Against the Safety of Fixed Platforms Located on the Continental Shelf was adopted by the conference (1988 SUA Convention Protocol).

This was a result of a proposal by the United States, supported by other coastal states that have fixed platforms on their continental shelves, proposing that such installations be protected from terrorist acts.[67] In accordance with Article 18, stating " ... *enter into force ninety days following the date on which fifteen States have either signed it without reservation, acceptance or approval, or have deposited an instrument of ratification, acceptance, approval or accession...*"[68]

---

64 IMO, 'Convention for the Suppression of Unlawful Acts Against the Safety of Maritime Navigation, Protocol for the Suppression of Unlawful Acts Against the Safety of Fixed Platforms Located on the Continental Shelf,' available at http://www.imo.org/en/About/conventions/listofconventions/pages/sua-treaties.aspx.

65 Tuerk(n 57), p. 344.

66 *Ibid.* p. 345.

67 Brad, J. Kieserman, 'Preventing and Defeating Terrorism at Sea: Practical Considerations for the Implementation of the Draft Protocol to the Convention for the Suppression of Unlawful Acts Against the Safety of Maritime Navigation (SUA),' in *Recent Developments in the Law of Sea and China* (Myron H. Nordquist, John Norton Moore & Kuen-chen Fu, eds. 2005), cited in Tuerk(n 57).

68 The SUA Convention 1988, Art. 18.

The 1988 SUA Convention entered into effect on 1 March 1992. As of 2018, there are 166 state parties, the combined merchant fleets of which constitute approximately 95.16 percent of the gross tonnage of the world's merchant fleet.[69] The 1988 SUA Convention Protocol also came into effect on the same day, and the number of contracting states is 156 countries, which represent 94.8 percent of the gross tonnage of the world's merchant fleet.[70]

The 1988 SUA Convention

1 Introduction

The SUA Convention was designed to ensure that appropriate action is taken against persons committing unlawful acts against ships by facilitating the establishment of criminal jurisdiction, as well as the establishment of rules regarding extradition and prosecution of the offenders. In order to ensure that the offenders are held accountable, state parties are obliged to either prosecute or extradite the offenders. The SUA Convention is a significant accomplishment of the international community in an effort "to develop international cooperation between states in devising and adopting effective and practical measures for the prevention of all unlawful acts against the safety of maritime navigation and the prosecution and punishment of their perpetrators."[71]

The SUA Convention in substance is based on previously existing terrorism conventions, with their provisions adapted to the maritime field.[72] The Convention has served as an essential legal framework in rallying international cooperation in fighting maritime terrorism. In this section, the legal arrangements of the 1988 SUA Convention are examined in depth.

2 Provisions

- **Definition of Terms**

In the Convention, the term 'ship' is defined. Ship is referred to as "a vessel of any type whatsoever not permanently attached to the sea-bed, including dynamically supported craft, submersible, or any other floating craft."[73] Despite the fact that the Convention is in substance a counter-maritime terrorism convention, the term 'maritime terrorism' is not mentioned in the Convention.

---

69 IMO, 'Status of multilateral Conventions and instruments in respect of which the International Maritime Organization or its Secretary-General performs depositary or other functions,' 13 September 2017, available at http://www.imo.org/en/About/Conventions/StatusOfConventions/Documents/Status%20-%202017.pdf.

70 *Ibid.*

71 The 1988 SUA Convention, Preamble.

72 Tuerk (n 57), p. 347.

73 The 1988 SUA Convention, Art. 1.

Furthermore, there was no attempt to create such a definition at the diplomatic conference.[74] Instead, the term 'offence' which *de facto* describes acts of maritime terrorism, is used. This might be due to consideration of the controversies over the definition of terrorism, as described earlier, and to avoid a delay in concluding the Convention given an urgency to create a legal regime for counter-maritime terrorism.

– **Application**

The SUA Convention applies to ships navigating or scheduled to navigate into, through, or from waters beyond the outer limit of the territorial sea of a single state or beyond the outer limit of the territorial sea with adjacent states, or when the alleged offender is found in the territory of a state.[75] Thus, the SUA Convention is applicable to ships engaged on an international voyage operating or scheduled to operate seaward of any state's territorial sea.[76] Ships engaged in cabotage that takes place exclusively within the territorial sea of a coastal state are thus excluded, and any unlawful act directed against them is governed solely by national laws.[77] In conformity with the general law of sovereign immunities, the Convention is not applied to warships or government ships operated for non-commercial purposes.[78]

– **Offences**

The SUA Convention followed the approach of other sectoral terrorism treaties. It dealt with only a particular type of terrorist activity and was focused on the establishment of those activities as crimes over which the state with pertinent connections to the offences could exercise jurisdiction.[79] The offences set forth as crimes in the Convention were drawn from the existing terrorism treaties, and adapted to the maritime context.[80] The Convention provides for a number of unlawful acts that constitute the offences. If any person commits unlawfully and intentionally any of acts below, that person commits an offence.[81]

74 Tuerk (n 57), p. 347.
75 The 1988SUA Convention, Art. 4(1) & (2).
76 Tuerk (n 57), p. 348.
77 David Freestone, 'The 1988 International Convention for the Suppression of Unlawful Acts Against the Safety of Maritime Navigation,' 3 *Int'l J. Marine & Coastal L.* 305, 308(1988), cited in Tuerk (n 1).
78 The 1988 SUA Convention, Art. 1(1) & (2).
79 Tullio Treves, 'The Rome Convention for the Suppression of Unlawful Acts Against the Safety of Maritime Navigation' in Natalino Ronzitti (ed), *Maritime Terrorism and International Law* (Martinus Nijhoff, Dordrecht, 1990), cited in Natalie Klein, *Maritime Security and the Law of the Sea* (Oxford University Press, New York, 2011), p. 147.
80 See Klein (n 79), p. 152.
81 The 1988 SUA Convention, Art. 3(1).

(i) seizes or exercises control over a ship by force or threat thereof or any other form of intimidation
(ii) performs an act of violence against a person on board a ship if that act is likely to endanger the safe navigation of that ship
(iii) destroys a ship or causes damage to a ship or its cargo which is likely to endanger the safe navigation of that ship
(iv) places or causes to be placed on a ship, by any means whatsoever, a device or substance which is likely to destroy that ship, or cause damage to that ship or its cargo which endangers or is likely to endanger the safe navigation of that ship
(v) destroys or seriously damages maritime navigational facilities or seriously interferes with their operations, if any such act is likely to endanger the safe navigation of a ship
(vi) communicates information which he knows to be false, thereby endangering the safe navigation of a ship
(vii) injures or kills any person, in connection with the commission or the attempted commission of any of the offences (set forth above)

Along with the direct commission of the offences above, attempts, complicity, abetment, or threatening of committing these offences fall within the offences under the SUA Convention.[82] The offences set forth in Article 3 of the Convention are principally *mutatis mutandis* those provided for in the existing aviation treaties.[83] At the initiative of the U.S., a new principal offence was added for injuring or killing a person in connection with the commission or attempted commission of any of other principal offences.[84]

– **Establishment of Jurisdiction**

The jurisdiction established by a state party is distinguished into two types, namely obligatory and discretionary. A state party is required to establish its jurisdiction when the offence is committed:[85]

(i) against or on board a ship flying the flag of the state at the time the offence is committed; or
(ii) in the territory of that state, including its territorial sea; or
(iii) by a national of that state

82 *Ibid.*, Art. 3(2).
83 Glen Plant, 'The Convention for the Suppression of the Unlawful Acts Against the Safety of Maritime Navigation,' 39 *International & Comparative Law* Quarterly, 27(1990), cited in Tuerk (n 57).
84 See Klein (n 79), p. 153.
85 The 1988 SUA Convention, Art. 6(1).

A state party, in its discretion, may establish its jurisdiction over any such offence when:

(i) it is committed by a stateless person when habitual residence is in that state; or
(ii) during its commission a national of that state is seized, threatened, injured, or killed; or
(iii) it is committed in an attempt to compel that state to do or abstain from doing any act

Reflecting a common goal of the international community to punish the offenders, the Convention provides for an obligation for state parties to establish jurisdiction over the offences in cases where the alleged offender is present in its territory and the state does not extradite him to any of the state parties that have established their jurisdiction in accordance with the above provisions.[86]

– **Custody**

In order to ensure that the offender is punishable, the Convention imposes on state parties some obligations, which are necessary for jurisdiction, extradition and prosecution. If any offender or alleged offender is present in the territory of any state party, the state is obliged to take the offender into custody or take other measures to ensure his presence for such time as is necessary to enable any criminal or extradition proceedings to be instituted.[87] The state having him under its custody is obliged to immediately make a preliminary inquiry into the facts.[88] The state has also an obligation to immediately notify the states which have established jurisdiction.[89]

– **Master's Delivery**

The master of a ship of flag state is allowed to deliver any alleged offender to the authorities of other state party.[90] For delivery, the master is required to give prior notification to the receiving state before entering its territorial sea.[91] The receiving state is required to accept the delivery, except the acts are outside the application of the Convention.[92]

– **Prosecution and Extradition**

In order to prevent the offender from avoiding punishment in a safe haven in any territories of those states that are parties to the Convention, the

86 *Ibid.*, Art. 6(4).
87 The 1988 SUA Convention, Art. 7(1).
88 *Ibid.*, Art. 7(2).
89 *Ibid.*, Art. 7(5).
90 *Ibid.* Art. 8(1).
91 *Ibid.*, Art. 8(2).
92 *Ibid.*, Art. 8(3).

Convention provides for an obligation of prosecution and extradition. In terms of prosecution, any state party is obliged to submit the case without delay to the competent authorities for the purpose of the prosecution of the offender or the alleged offender.[93] The authorities are required to deal with the case in the same manner as in the case of any other offence of a grave nature of the law of that state.[94]

Despite the provision of prosecution, there is no absolute obligation for the state party to prosecute the offender under the Convention. The provision, which corresponds to other anti-terrorism conventions, has been called a deficiency of the SUA Convention since it arguably allows terrorists to escape punishments.[95]

Concerning extradition, the offences set forth in the Convention are deemed to be extraditable offences in any extradition treaty existing between any of the state parties.[96] Where there is no specific extradition treaty in force between the requesting and requested states, the requested state may at its option consider the Convention as a legal basis for extradition.[97] This provision is substantially the same as the corresponding provision of the International Convention Against the Taking of Hostages. Likewise in prosecution, there is no absolute obligation to extradite. This might be due to a consideration of the possibility of non-extradition for political offences as well as the right to grant asylum.[98]

– **Cooperation**

States are required to cooperate in the prevention of the offences by:[99] (i) taking all practicable measures to prevent preparation for the commission of offences within or outside their territories; (ii) exchanging information and coordinating administrative and other measures taken as appropriate to prevent the commission of offences. States having information about the possible commission of the offences are also required to furnish the information to the relevant states which are believed to have established jurisdiction.[100]

---

93 *Ibid.*, Art. 10(1).

94 *Ibid.*

95 Tullio Treves, 'The Convention for the Suppression of Unlawful Acts Against the Safety of Maritime Navigation,' 2 SING, *J. INT'L & COMP. L.* 541, 542(1998), cited in Tuerk (n 57).

96 The 1988 SUA Convention, Art. 11(1).

97 *Ibid.*, Art. 11(2).

98 See Tuerk (n 57), p. 349.

99 The 1988 SUA Convention, Art. 13(1).

100 *Ibid.*, Art. 14.

Positions of East Asian Countries

Out of 166 contracting parties (as of 2018) to the 1988 SUA Convention, the participation of South and East Asian countries seems relatively low, compared to other regions. Out of 173 IMO member states, Malaysia, Indonesia, Thailand and North Korea are among the Asian states that have yet to join the Convention. Allegedly the Southeast Asian states in particular are concerned about the possible infringement of their sovereign rights of punishment over the offences which are subject to mandatory jurisdiction of state parties.[101] Their participation is very significant in combating piracy and maritime terrorism in South Asian waters, given their geographical locations in relation to the Malacca Strait, which is one of the hotspots of piracy across the world.

1 China

Among East Asian countries, China was among the first countries to ratify the Convention. China, one of 42 signatories, was quick to ratify the Convention in August 1991, with a reservation: "*The People's Republic of China shall not be bound by paragraph 1 of Article 16 of the said Convention.*"[102] China, like some other countries, made a reservation that it is not bound by the provision of mandatory jurisdiction of the International Court of Justice with respect to the peaceful settlement of disputes.

China has no separate laws to accommodate the SUA Convention, and the punishment of unlawful acts committed by ships operating on the seas is pursuant to the Criminal Law. While China has no specific regulations regarding the SUA Convention, the requirements under the convention are implemented by the Public Security, Border Police, the People's Liberation Army and the customs agency.

2 Korea

Unlike China, Japan and Korea — neither of which were signatories — were slow to accede to the Convention. Korea became a state party by accession in May 2003. For Korea, the 9/11 terrorist attacks in 2001 served as a wake-up call in becoming a party to the Convention. In the wake of the terrorist attacks and the UN Security Council Resolution 1373 thereof,[103] urging "member states to become parties to the relevant international conventions and protocols

---

101 Suk Kyoon Kim, '*Building a Multilateral Framework to Combat Piracy in Asia: From a Global Governance Perspective*' (doctoral dissertation, Hanyang University, Seoul, Korea, 2005), pp. 47–48.

102 IMO, 'Status of IMO Treaties,' 16 November 2018.

103 UN Security Council, S/RES/1373(2001), adopted on 28 September 2001.

relating to terrorism," the Korean government sought approval from the National Assembly of the 1988 SUA Convention and the Protocol for the Suppression of Unlawful Acts Against the Safety of Fixed Platforms Located on the Continental Shelf. In the debate at the Foreign Affairs and Unification Committee, there was a controversy over the possible infringement of sovereignty by the provision of the SUA Convention: "State Parties undertake to include such offences as extraditable offences in every extradition treaty to be concluded between them."[104] Some lawmakers were concerned that the provision might clash with 'a political offence exception' in any extradition treaties.[105] Eventually it was cleared by the government's explanation that under any bilateral extradition treaty to which Korea is a party, the offences are extraditable, if extradition is required in any other multilateral conventions.[106]

In order to nationally accommodate the convention and its protocol, the Korean government enacted the 'Punishment for Damaging Ships and Maritime Structures Act' in the same year of accession to expand jurisdiction to acts committed by foreign nationals against Korean ships and maritime structures outside the Korean territory.

The Act also provides for the process of extradition of criminals and defines specific acts of the offence. More specifically, it provides for: (i) the punishment of foreign nationals for criminal acts committed against ships and maritime structures outside of the territory of Korea (Art. 3); (ii) extradition of a criminal by the master to a SUA Convention state party pursuant to the approval of the minister of justice (Art. 4); and (iii) inclusion of unlawful acts such as murder or infliction of injury upon persons on ship or maritime structures, as well as the hijacking of ships, damage to ships and others, placement of dangerous objects, delivery of false information, threats, and so on (Arts. 5 &13).

3 Japan

Though Japan is a state party to the 1988 SUA Convention, there are no national laws that have accommodated the convention. It has yet to become a party to the 2005 SUA Protocol, as of 2018. Japan is known to have been reluctant to join the protocol on the grounds that when joining the protocol, it would be required to have its vessels inspected while navigating foreign waters (although it, too, would be able to inspect suspicious foreign vessels in the high seas near Japan).

---

104 1988 SUA Convention, Art. 11.

105 Foreign Affairs and Unification Committee, National Assembly of Korea, the minutes of the 238th Assembly (*translated by author*), 16 April 2003.

106 *Ibid.*

Conclusion

The 1988 SUA Convention is an initial legal response at the global level to the growing risk of maritime terrorism. The Convention is designed to provide a legal framework to cope with an emerging trend of unlawful acts at sea which did not fall under the provisions of piracy in the UNCLOS. The Convention represents a significant extension of a cooperative international legal regime to fight terrorism in the maritime domain. In the absence of previous treaties concerning maritime terrorism, the Convention built on existing conventions on aviation and land-based terrorism. The provisions of the Convention were adapted from those conventions to the extent that the Convention is called a reproduction of land-based terrorism conventions.

As illustrated, the triggering event for the adoption of the Convention was the *Achille Lauro* hijacking incident. Despite its purpose to serve as a legal framework in the prevention and suppression of maritime terrorism, the Convention has presented a number of weaknesses and limitations. Primarily, the Convention is focused on measures to punish the offenders, such as jurisdiction, prosecution and extradition, and thus is concentrated on reactive measures, rather than preventive ones.

The Convention, in the same context, failed to provide for enforcement measures in the prevention and suppression of terrorist acts, including the right of visit and search of vessels suspected of being involved in terrorism. As such, the limitation became evident when the international community was challenged by a new kind of terrorist activity posing a grave threat to the safety of international shipping.

In terms of cooperation between the states, the obligation of states is not explicit as to what measures should be taken, as the Convention simply provides that states are obliged to take "all practical measures to prevent preparation for, or commission of terrorist attacks within or outside their territories." The Convention in substance is reactive rather than preventive of maritime terrorism, and as a result, a new legal framework was required to address new maritime threats, such as the proliferation of weapons of mass destruction (WMD).

The 2005 SUA Protocol

1 Introduction

In the aftermath of the 9/11 attacks in 2001, the international community feared that the maritime domain could be a target of catastrophic terrorist attacks. Recognizing the vulnerability of international shipping by potential maritime terrorist attacks, and seeing "an urgent need to take additional effective measures to prevent the proliferation of nuclear, chemical or biological weapons and their delivery,"[107] the international community sought to update and revise the 1988 SUA Convention.

Prior to the revision of the SUA Convention, the international community, at the initiative of the United States and the IMO, as part of counter-terrorist measures, amended the International Convention for the Safety of Life at Sea (SOLAS) and created the International Ship and Port Facility Security (ISPS) Code in 2002, which aims to develop a culture of threat-based security throughout the maritime cargo supply chain on which the global economy depends.[108] The matter of the ISPS Code will be discussed in Chapter 6 in depth.

The amendments to the SUA Convention and its related protocol by incorporating various developments in a wide array of land-based terrorism treaties[109] were adopted by the Diplomatic Conference on the Revision of the SUA Treaties on 14 October 2005. The amendments were adopted in the form of protocols to the SUA treaties, namely the 2005 SUA Protocols, and entered into force on 28 July 2010.

In undertaking the negotiations to amend the 1988 SUA Convention, the critical task was how to strike a balance between the need to respond to new threats to the security of shipping and the protection of pre-eminent authority of the flag state over its vessels.[110] Ultimately, the 2005 SUA Convention creates a tighter balance between response to the new threats and the right of flag states.

---

107 The 2005 SUA Protocol, Preamble.

108 Thomas A. Mensah, 'The Place of the ISPS Code in the Legal International Regime for the Security of International Shipping,' *WMU Journal of Maritime Affairs* (2004), 3(17), pp. 26–27, cited in James Kraska, 'Effective Implementation of the 2005 Convention for the Suppression of Unlawful Acts against the Safety of Maritime Navigation,' *Naval War College Review* (2017), 70(1), p. 12.

109 The land-based conventions include: the Convention on Offences and Certain Other Acts Committed on Board Aircraft 1963; the Convention for the Suppression of Unlawful Seizure of Aircraft 1970; the Convention for the Suppression of Unlawful Acts against the Safety of Civil Aviation 1971; the Convention on the Prevention and Punishment of Crimes against Internationally Protected Persons, including Diplomatic Agents; the International Convention against the Taking of Hostages 1979; the Convention on the Physical Protection of Nuclear Material 1979; the Protocol for the Suppression of Unlawful Acts of Violence at Airports Serving International Civil Aviation 1988; the Protocol for the Suppression of Unlawful Acts against the Safety of Fixed Platforms Located on the Continental Shelf 1988; the Convention on the Making of Plastic Explosives for the Purpose of Detection 1991; the International Convention for the Suppression of Terrorist Bombing 1997; the International Convention for the Suppression of the Financing of Terrorism 1999; and the International Convention for the Suppression of Acts of Nuclear Terrorism 2005.

110 See Klein (n 79), p. 171.

2 Amendments

– Definition of Terms

The 2005 SUA Convention has added a number of terms concerning weapons of mass destruction (WMD) in particular, in accordance with the expansion of its coverage to the proliferation of WMD by sea. The definition of 'ship' remains unchanged. The definition appears to include an unmanned underwater vehicle (UUV) or unmanned surface vehicle (USV) under "a vessel of any type whatsoever."[111] The legal standard of "serious injury or damage" is defined[112] as: (i) serious bodily injury; or (ii) extensive destruction of a place of public use, state or government facility, infrastructure facility, or public transportation system; or (iii) substantial damage to the environment. The 2005 SUA Protocol is unique among counter-terrorism conventions in that it covers the misuse of dual-use materials — the transport on board a ship of legitimate items, products and materials intended to cause or threaten to cause death, serious injury or damage.[113]

BCN weapons are defined as those including biological weapons, chemical weapons, nuclear weapons and other nuclear explosive devices.[114] Biological weapons are microbial or other biological agents, toxins or weapons, equipment or means of delivery designed to use such agents or toxins for hostile purposes.[115] Chemical weapons are toxic chemicals and their precursors, except those intended for:[116](i) industrial, agricultural, research, medical, pharmaceutical or other peaceful purposes; (ii) protective purposes, namely those purposes directly related to protection against toxic chemicals and to protect against chemical weapons; (iii) military purposes not connected with the use of chemical weapons and not dependent on the use of the toxic properties of chemicals as a method of warfare; and (iv) law enforcement.

– Offences

Among the unlawful acts covered by the 1988 SUA Convention in Article 3, several are: (i) the seizure of ships by force; (ii) acts of violence against persons on board ships; and (iii) the placing of devices on board a ship which are likely to destroy or damage it. The offences under the Convention are expanded to

111 James Kraska, 'Effective Implementation of the 2005 Convention for the Suppression of Unlawful Acts against the Safety of Maritime Navigation,' *Naval War College Review* (2017), 70(1), p. 17.
112 The 1988 SUA Convention, Art. 1(1)(c).
113 Kraska (n 111), p. 14.
114 The 2005 SUA Convention, Art. 1(1)(d).
115 *Ibid.*
116 *Ibid.*

incorporate offences involving weapons of mass destruction, including BCN (biological, chemical and nuclear) weapons. The 2005 SUA Protocol adds a new Article *3bis*, which describes the circumstances under which a person commits an offence within the meaning of the Convention:

- when the purpose of the act, by its nature or context, is to intimidate a population, or compel a government or an international organization to do or to abstain from doing any act by committing the following acts: (i) uses against or on a ship or discharges from a ship any explosive, radioactive material or BCN weapon in a manner that causes or is likely to cause death or serious injury or damage; or (ii) discharges, from a ship, oil, liquefied natural gas, or other hazardous or noxious substances, in such quantity or concentration that causes or is likely to cause death or serious injury or damage; or (iii) uses a ship in a manner that causes death or serious injury or damage; or (iv) threatens to commit an offence set forth in (i),(ii), or (iii).
- when transport on board a ship: (i) any explosive or radioactive material, knowing that it is intended to be used to cause or in a threat to cause, death, or serious injury or damage for the purpose of intimidating a population, or compelling a government or an international organization to do or abstain from doing any act; or (ii) any BCN weapon, knowing it to be a BCN weapon; or (iii) any source material, special fissionable material, or equipment or material especially designed or prepared for the processing, use or production of special fissionable material, knowing that it is intended to be used in a nuclear explosive activity or in any other nuclear activity not under safeguards pursuant to an IAEA comprehensive agreement; or (iv) any equipment, materials or software or related technology that significantly contributes to the design, manufacture or delivery of a BCN weapon, with the intention that it will be used for such purpose.

Article 3*bis* comprehensively prohibits the shipping of materials ranging from BCN weapons, explosives and radioactive material, to software or related technology which is intended to contribute to the design, manufacture or delivery of a BCN weapon. A problem arising from this comprehensive prohibition concerns how to determine whether the goods on board a ship are dual-use goods. In most situations, a seafarer would not know what goods are on board a ship or what their purpose is. A typical seafarer would not know what is in a container, as it is ordinarily sealed and loaded at port.[117]

The transport of nuclear material is not considered an offence if such an item or material is transported to or from the territory of, or is otherwise

117 Tuerk (n 57), p. 349.

transported under the control of, a state party to the Treaty on the Non-Proliferation of Nuclear Weapons.[118] Any person commits an offence if that person unlawfully and intentionally transports another person on board a ship knowing that the person has committed an act that constitutes an offence set forth under the SUA Convention or an offence set forth in any treaty listed in the Annex[119] and intending to assist that person to evade criminal prosecution.[120]

The offender is culpable in relation to nine other counter-terrorism treaties that are included in a new annex to the 1988 SUA Convention under Article 7 of the 2005 SUA Convention. The scope of this provision accounts for the linkage of maritime security with security on land.[121] The 2005 SUA Protocol also makes it an offence if any person: (i) unlawfully and intentionally injures or kills any person in connection with the commission of any of the offences in the Convention: (ii) attempts to commit an offence; (iii) participates as an accomplice; (iv) organizes or directs others to commit an offence; (v) or contributes to the commissioning of an offence.[122]

The 2005 SUA Protocol requires state parties to take necessary measures to enable a legal entity located in their territory or organized under their laws to

---

118 The 2005 SUA Protocol, Art. *3bis* (2).

119 The treaties listed in the Annex include:

1. Convention for the Suppression of Unlawful Seizure of Aircraft, done at The Hague on 16 December 1970.
2. Convention for the Suppression of Unlawful Acts against the Safety of Civil Aviation, done at Montreal on 23 September 1971.
3. Convention on the Prevention and Punishment of Crimes against Internationally Protected Persons, including Diplomatic Agents, adopted by the General Assembly of the United Nations on 14 December 1973.
4. International Convention against the Taking of Hostages, adopted by the General Assembly of the United Nations on 17 December 1979.
5. Convention on the Physical Protection of Nuclear Material, done at Vienna on 26 October 1979.
6. Protocol for the Suppression of Unlawful Acts of Violence at Airports Serving International Civil Aviation, supplementary to the Convention for the Suppression of Unlawful Acts against the Safety of Civil Aviation, done at Montreal on 24 February 1988.
7. Protocol for the Suppression of Unlawful Acts against the Safety of Fixed Platforms Located on the Continental Shelf, done at Rome on 10 March 1988.
8. International Convention for the Suppression of Terrorist Bombings, adopted by the General Assembly of the United Nations on 15 December 1997.
9. International Convention for the Suppression of the Financing of Terrorism, adopted by the General Assembly of the United Nations on 9 December 1999.

120 The 2005 SUA Protocol, Art. 3*ter*.

121 See Klein (n 79), p. 173.

122 The 2005 SUA Convention, Art. 3*quater*.

be held liable and to face sanctions when a person responsible for management or control of that legal party has, in that capacity, committed an offence under the convention.[123] State parties are also obliged to ensure that legal entities liable are subject to effective, proportionate and dissuasive criminal, civil or administrative sanction, including monetary sanctions.[124]

– **Ship Boarding Procedure**

As illustrated earlier, the lack of enforcement measures to prevent and suppress the commission of offences has been referred to as a weakness of the 1988 SUA Convention. The lack of effective means to prevent and suppress offences made the Convention, to a certain extent, merely provide a lawful base to establish jurisdiction, ultimately making the Convention a weak legal instrument. The 2005 SUA Protocol, reflecting such weaknesses, adopted a ship boarding procedure that allows states to board ships flying the flag of another state.

The inclusion of the ship boarding procedure was seriously considered during the negotiations at the IMO, in relation to the underlying traditional principles governing the use of oceans, i.e., the freedom of navigation on the high seas and the exclusive jurisdiction of a flag state over their vessels. The ship boarding procedure was ultimately accepted by recognizing that the principle of flag state jurisdiction must be respected to the utmost extent and a boarding by another state on the high seas could only take place in exceptional circumstances.[125]

Article 8*bis* of the 2005 SUA Protocol sets forth a process for cooperation and procedures for boarding a ship flying the flag of another state party. For boarding a ship flying the flag of another state party or displaying marks of registry of another state, the Protocol sets forth the prerequisites that need to be fulfilled. First, the suspected ship that a state party desires to board should be located outside the territorial sea of any state.[126] By limiting the location of boarding outside the territorial sea, this provision purports not to interfere with coastal state's exercise of sovereignty over its territorial sea. Second, a state must have reasonable grounds to suspect that the ship or a person on board the ship is, has been, or is about to be involved in the commission of an offence under the Convention.[127]

---

123 *Ibid.*, Art. 5*bis* (1).

124 *Ibid.*, Art. 5*bis* (2).

125 See IMO Legal Committee, 'Repot of the Legal Committee on the Work of its Eighty-Ninth Session' (4 November 2004), 89th Session of IMO DOC LEG/89/16, paras. 36–60.

126 The 2005 SUA Convention, Art. 8*bis* (5).

127 *Ibid.*, Art. 8*bis* (4).

Over the request to board a ship, the requested states have an obligation to cooperate to "the fullest extent possible" and respond to the request as "expeditiously as possible."[128] Any request to board is required to contain, if possible, the information on the suspected vessel[129]: (i) name of the suspected ship; (ii) IMO ship identification number; (iii) port of registry; (iv) ports of origin and destination; and (v) any other relevant information.

States are required to consider "the dangers and difficulties" involved in boarding a ship at sea and searching its cargo and to give consideration to whether other measures could be taken in the next port of call or elsewhere.[130] This provision is a reminder that it is often impossible to conduct a thorough inspection of either a small craft or a large commercial vessel at sea, and often the best course of action is to bring the ship into port to facilitate inspection.[131]

– **Consent to Ship Boarding**

When it comes to the consent of the flag state, there are two types of authorization, namely prior authorization and *ad hoc* authorization. In terms of prior authorization, a state party may notify the IMO Secretary-General, upon or after depositing the instrument of ratification, acceptance, approval or accession, that it would allow authorization to board and search a ship flying its flag and its cargo and persons on board if there is no response from the flag state within four hours.[132] A state can also notify that it authorizes a requesting state to board and search the ship, its cargo and persons on board, and to question the persons on board to determine if an offence has been, or is about to be committed.[133]

Concerning an *ad hoc* authorization over the request to board the suspected ship, if the nationality of the ship is confirmed, the flag state may have the following options:[134] (i) authorize the requesting state to board and take appropriate measures, including stopping, boarding and searching the ship; (ii) conduct the boarding and search with its own law enforcement or other officials; (iii) conduct the boarding and search together with the requesting state, subject to any conditions it may impose; or (iv) decline to authorize a boarding and search.

---

128 The 2005 SUA Convention, Art. 8*bis*.
129 *Ibid.*, Art, 8*bis* (2).
130 *Ibid.*, Art. 8*bis* (3).
131 Kraska (n 111), p. 17.
132 The 2005 SUA Convention, Art. 8*bis* (5)(d).
133 *Ibid*, Art. 8*bis* (5)(e).
134 *Ibid*, Art. 8*bis* (5)(c).

When the requesting state boards a foreign-flagged ship and finds evidence of offences under the Convention, the flag state may further authorize the requesting state to detain the ship, cargo and persons on board pending receipt of its disposition instructions.[135] In any case, the boarding state is required to promptly inform the flag state of the results of a boarding, search and detention.[136] The requesting state is not allowed to take additional measures without the express authorization of the flag state, except when necessary to relieve imminent danger to the lives of persons or where those measures derive from relevant bilateral or multilateral agreements.[137]

The authorization for another state to board the ship does not mean that that state now exercises jurisdiction over the ship. For all boardings, the flag state has the right over a detained ship, cargo or other items and persons on board, including seizure, forfeiture, arrest and prosecution.[138] The boarding provision does not affect other types of boardings that are generally accepted in international law, seaward of territorial sea of any state, such as boardings as for the right of visit, rendering assistance to persons, ship in distress or an authorization from the flag state to take law enforcement or other actions.[139]

In order to facilitate and expedite the boarding procedures under the 2005 SUA Protocol, state parties may conclude agreements or arrangements.[140] For the U.S., both prior and subsequent to the adoption of the 2005 SUA Protocol, it has sought to enter into ship-boarding agreements with states holding the largest shipping registries, hence having the greatest number of flag vessels under their control and exclusive jurisdiction.[141]

The U.S. has signed ship-boarding agreements with the Bahamas, Belize, Croatia, Cyprus, Liberia, Marshall Islands, Malta, Mongolia and Panama. The combination of states that have signed bilateral ship boarding agreements with the U.S., with the commitments made by other Proliferation Security Initiative (PSI) partners under the Statement of Interdiction Principles, accounts for 60 percent of the global commercial shipping fleet deadweight tonnage.[142]

– **Safeguards**

A number of safeguard are provided in Article 8*bis* to ensure that the boarding is conducted consistent with international law standards. In this regard, the

135 *Ibid.*, Art. 8*bis* (6).
136 *Ibid.*
137 *Ibid.*, Art. 8*bis* (7).
138 *Ibid.*, Art. 8*bis* (8).
139 *Ibid.*, Art. 8*bis* (11).
140 *Ibid.*, Art. 8*bis* (13).
141 Klein (n 79), p. 184.
142 *Ibid.*, p. 185.

use of force, in particular, is provided separately from the provision of other safeguard measures. This may reflect greater weight accorded on the use of force of safeguard measures, given the significance of regulating the use of force in undertaking boarding. When carrying out the authorized actions by the boarding state, the use of force should be avoided.[143]

The use of force is permitted in exceptional circumstances where it is necessary to ensure the safety of its officials and persons on board, or where the officials are obstructed in the execution of the authorized actions.[144] Any use of force should not exceed the minimum degree of force which is necessary and reasonable in the circumstances.[145] The Protocol sets forth the duties of the boarding state, which include:[146] (i) to take due account of the safety of life and the safety and security of the ship and its cargo; (ii) to ensure that basic human rights are respected; (iii) to comply with international law in boarding; (iv) not to prejudice the commercial or legal interest of the flag state; and (v) to avoid a ship being unduly detained or delayed. In addition, the boarding state is liable for any damage, harm or loss attributable to it.[147] The boarding state has also an obligation that it should not interfere with or affect the right and obligation and the exercise of costal states.[148]

– **Extradition**

Article 11*ter* is added to set forth an obligation of states with respect to the extradition of a political offence. An obligation of extradition or affording mutual legal assistance does not apply if the request for extradition is believed to have been made for the purpose of prosecuting or punishing a person on account of a person's race, religion, nationality, ethnic origin, political affiliation or gender, or that compliance with the request would cause prejudice to that person's position for any of these reasons.

Article 12*bis* of the protocol requires state parties to afford one another assistance in connection with criminal proceedings brought in respect of the offences under the SUA Convention. In accordance with Article 12*bis*, a person who is being detained or is serving a sentence in the territory of one state may be transferred to another state for the purposes of identification, testimony, or otherwise providing assistance in obtaining evidence for the investigation or prosecution of offences when the following conditions are met: (i) the person

143 The 2005 SUA Convention, Art. 8*bis* (9).
144 *Ibid.*
145 *Ibid.*
146 *Ibid.* Art. 8*bis* (10).
147 *Ibid.*
148 *Ibid.*

freely gives informed consent; and (ii) the competent authorities of both states agree.

Positions of East Asian Countries

None of East Asian states has become a party to the 2005 SUA Protocols. It appears that Japan and Korea's reluctance, in particular, to join the convention is attributable to the following elements: (i) concern about the possible infringement of their sovereignty by reinforced preventive and enforcement measures under the Protocol; and (ii) the view that participation in the PSI enables them to intercept transport of WMD by ship or enforce other preventive measures. These elements are as equally applicable to the Protocol of 2005 as to the Protocol for the Suppression of Unlawful Acts against the Safety of Fixed Platforms Located on the Continental Shelf. For these considerations, East Asian countries are not likely to accede to the Protocols in the near future.

Conclusion

The 2005 SUA Protocol ensures that the maritime security framework established under the SUA treaties enables parties to respond to new contemporary maritime threats. The Protocol enables ship boarding and law enforcement measures over vessels that are suspected of committing the offences under the convention.

As such, the Protocol is regarded as a significant legal framework to enhance maritime security against maritime terrorism and the concern over the proliferation of WMDs. Addressing the legal lacuna of the 1988 SUA Convention, which lacks the effective means of enforcement to prevent and suppress maritime terrorism and the proliferation of WMD s by ship, the Protocol provides for the lawful means for the exercise of ship boarding on the suspect foreign flagged vessels and ships suspected of carrying WMD s and related materials.

Despite its effectiveness as a legal instrument to fight maritime terrorism and the proliferation of WMD s, it faces a number of challenges that need to be addressed.

First, a significant problem is a slow implementation of the Protocol. As of November 2018, the number of contracting states is only 45, which accounts for 39.06 percent of the gross tonnage of the world's merchant fleet.[149] Since its entry into force in 2010 by depositing an instrument of ratification of 12 states,[150] there has been a slow ratification of the Protocol. It is in stark contrast to the 1988 SUA Convention, to which contracting states are 166, accounting for

149 IMO (n 102).

150 The 2005 SUA Convention, Art. 18.

95.16 percent of the world's merchant fleet. As with much of international law, the success of the 2005 SUA Protocol hinges on its implementation, not merely its adoption at the international level.[151] In order to utilize the Convention as an effective instrument to enhance maritime security, state parties, with a commitment to counter maritime terrorism, need to make necessary domestic arrangements to implement the legal instrument.

Second, another fundamental challenge is how to ensure the utility of the ship boarding on the suspected vessel, which requires the express consent of the flag state. The concern arises from the delay in authorization and the possibility of obstructive conditions in conducting a boarding.[152] In this regard, the interactions between the flag state and the requesting state are facilitated through the designated competent authority of the flag state, and the success of cooperation hinges on responsive and iterative engagement.[153] State parties are required to designate the authority and notify the Secretary-General of IMO within one month of becoming a party,[154] but only four states, including Latvia, San Marino, Sweden and the U.S., made a notification.[155]

VI Conclusion

In this chapter, we have discussed the matters concerning maritime terrorism, terrorist organizations and legal regimes to counter maritime terrorism. Compared with land-based terrorism, the number of maritime terrorism has been relatively quite small over the past decades. Apart from a lesser public attention on maritime terrorism, a number of challenges in the maritime domain lie ahead of international efforts to reinforce counter-maritime terrorism capabilities.

As with terrorism, the definition of maritime terrorism has not been agreed upon. The definitions of maritime terrorism made by scholars and various agencies are mostly concerned with the extension of land-based terrorism. In addition, the scope of maritime terrorism, under the definitions, is very broadly and inclusively defined to the extent that various kinds of unlawful acts at sea may fall into maritime terrorism. This may pose a risk that can blur the line between maritime terrorism and other unlawful acts at sea.

151 Kraska (n 111), p. 20.
152 See Klein (n 79), p. 191.
153 Kraska (n 111), p.18.
154 The 2005 SUA Convention, Art. 15.
155 Kraska (n 111), p.18.

The international community needs to come up with an agreed upon definition of maritime terrorism, given distinctive features of maritime terrorism in relation to piracy and other acts of unlawful acts. Due to quite a few occurrences and the nature of the maritime domain, which is out of public sight, it is likely that a lesser public attention is paid or even the threat of maritime terrorism is ignored. However, maritime terrorism poses the gravest threat to the safety and security of maritime domain, along with piracy. As illustrated in a number of maritime terrorism in the past, the impact and significance of maritime terrorism is enormous and far-reaching.

Likewise terrorism on land, maritime terrorism is inherently transnational, involving various elements beyond the boarder. While remaining vigilant over maritime terrorism at the national level, a closer international cooperation at the regional and global levels is required beyond the national interests. As with international efforts to combat piracy, a closer cooperation among coast guard agencies, in particular, responsible for counter-maritime terrorism, is required at the regional level.

Regarding the SUA Convention regime, the largest challenge in taking counter-measures at the international level, either proactive or responsive, against maritime terrorism might be concerned with how to strike a balance with the exclusive right of flag state control. Under the 2005 SUA Protocol, over the request to board a ship, the requested states have an obligation to cooperate to “the fullest extent possible” and respond to the request as “expeditiously as possible. However, flags of convenience out of the total world shipping fleets account for 70.2 percent. Under this circumstance, it would not be easy to expect a prompt and effective response for counter-terrorism measures, mainly ship boarding, from open registries.

The open registries are mostly small island countries or least developed countries which are largely interested in registration fees. Thus there should be authorization procedures under which ship boarding requests can be more promptly and effectively handled while not undermining the underlying tenet of the exclusive flag state control. Given that shipping is increasingly used for transporting weapons of mass destruction and smuggling illicit goods, more participation in the 2005 SUA Protocol which comprehensively prohibits the shipping of materials concerned with weapons of mass destruction should be encouraged.

Most importantly, the issue of maritime terrorism cannot be properly addressed as a separate issue from land-based terrorism or terrorist organizations since maritime terrorism is committed by terrorist organizations which have capabilities to operate at sea. The vast majority of maritime terrorism acts were committed by terrorist organizations whose principal activities were performed on land. In this context, the legal regimes to deal with maritime terrorism have an inherent limitation that only touches on the 'acts' of terrorism at sea, leaving the illegality of terrorist organizations itself uncovered. Maritime terrorism is inherently linked to terrorism on land and thus legal instruments to deal with maritime terrorism should extend their coverage beyond acts of terrorism at sea, and maritime terrorism should be approached in the context of terrorism as a whole, as well as in view of the uniqueness of the maritime domain.

CHAPTER 5

Contemporary Piracy: Nature and Reality

I Emergence of Contemporary Piracy

Piracy is undoubtedly the oldest threat to safe navigation and seafaring. The origin of piracy goes back to ancient times, and corresponds with the history of shipping. Varying with regions and times, piracy had been prevalent across the oceans throughout the history of the world. Piracy was at its peak in the era of the Age of Discovery between the late 15th and 17th centuries, during which time pirates attacked Spanish and Portuguese merchant fleets carrying treasures and valuable goods looted from the New World. At the time, Asian waters were not an exception to piracy attacks, either. Southeast Asian seas and the Indian Ocean were a hotspot of piracy in Asia.

Piracy was believed to have disappeared in the early 19th century across the oceans, as a result of enormous counter-piracy efforts. In the absence of piracy threats, the oceans remained stable and secure during the past century. Pirates, meanwhile, became a popular subject of novels, dramas, movies and other literary works, in which pirates and their life were described as romantic and adventurous. This has helped people have a misconception of pirates, who were outlaws and committed heinous atrocities at sea. However, piracy has never been eradicated throughout the history of the mankind. It would be right to argue that piracy over that period had merely been latent due to strong anti-piracy measures. Unfortunately, this proved to be merely a short-lived respite. In the 1970s, less than a century after piracy's supposed demise, a steady rise in the number of attacks ushered in the present phenomenon of modern-day piracy.[1]

Contemporary piracy, taking advantage of advanced information technologies and weapons, appears in many different forms. The loss of life and damage to property, as well as costs incurred by piracy to the shipping industry at the global level, are tremendous. Piracy has emerged as the gravest threat to the safety of navigation and seaborne trade, becoming an urgent global security issue that the international community needs to address together. The phenomenon of contemporary piracy has not appeared out of nowhere. This is

1 Maximo Q. Mjia, Pierre Cariou & Francois-Charles Wolff, 'Ship Piracy: Ship Type and Flag,' in Wayne K. Talley, *Maritime Safety, Security and Piracy* (informa, London, 2008), p. 103.

 | DOI:10.1163/9789004389908_006

the result of an interaction between a wide range of international and regional factors and stakeholders. The factors that have contributed to the emergence of contemporary piracy may be identified as follows.

First, a booming shipping trade, in tandem with the expansion of seaborne trade in the era of globalization, has served as a primary factor. Valuable cargoes, particularly of energy resources, are a tempting target for pirates. Second, the collapse of maritime supremacy in the post-Cold War era brought about a power vacuum in the oceans, and this has resulted in the weakening of policing and deterrence of piracy. Third, the unstable political situations in some coastal states have helped contribute to the problem. Many of piracy attacks are committed by rebels in those countries to finance their activities. Furthermore, those coastal states lack resources for law enforcement and the capability to prevent and suppress piracy. Lastly, geographical conditions suited for piracy, and a long-held tradition of piracy for livelihoods, are also important contributing factors.

The problem of contemporary piracy extends beyond a particular region or a single coastal state — it is a common concern of the international community. The purpose of this chapter is to explore various aspects of acts of piracy and unravel the nature and reality of the global piracy issue from a multi-faceted perspective. This chapter examines definitional aspects of piracy in international law and provides an overview of the global trend of piracy attacks. It also presents global counter-piracy efforts at the international and governmental as well as industry level.

II Definitions of Piracy and their Distinction from other Unlawful Acts at Sea

Introduction

The definition of piracy varies with the perspectives and interests of those concerned. The most challenging problem with defining the term 'piracy' might be that there exists a considerable degree of disparity between the legal definition of piracy and its general usage in journalism or elsewhere. The common usage of the word 'piracy' by the public, which is supposedly derived from the historical context, refers to any unlawful acts of violence at sea or in coastal areas against ships, crews and locals, irrespective of the elements that constitute the legal term. Outside piracy, there are different forms of violence at sea, such as armed robbery, terrorism and other unlawful acts. This occasionally brings about confusion in the distinction between the definition of piracy and other acts of violence at sea.

In legal terms, the definition of piracy in international law is very restrictive, covering certain aspects of unlawful acts at sea. Thus, what constitutes an act of piracy in international law has remained controversial. For this reason, it is crucial to identify the legal elements of acts of piracy in international law, and to separate them from other acts of maritime violence in terms of law enforcement and criminal jurisdiction. The below critically examines the definitions of piracy and other acts of violence at sea and their relationships from a legal perspective.

Various Piracy Definitions

1 Hall's Definition

Hall, English lawyer who had published influential works on international law in the 19th century, defines piracy as follows: *"acts of violence done upon the ocean or unappropriated lands or within the territory of a state through descent from the sea, by a body of men acting independently of any politically organized society."*[2] His definition's main elements include[3]: (i) acts of violence in the ocean or within the territorial waters of a state; (ii) committed by persons not linked to any organizations with political goals. Under the Hall's definition, it is hard to distinguish attacks occurring in the territorial waters from those on the high seas. Although Hall intended to restrict piracy to acts of violence, independent of political intent, piracy cannot be free from a political context since pirates are often motivated from political goals or at least piratical attacks have political repercussions.[4]

2 Harvard Research Draft Convention[5]

As an exercise in proposing legal formulations taking into due account of the confusions of the period regarding the concept of "piracy," the Harvard Research Draft has had a major impact on the development of legal thought.[6] The 1932 Draft Convention defines piracy as follows:

> Piracy is ---------, committed in a place not within the territorial jurisdiction of any state; any act of violence or of depredation, committed with

2 William Edward Hall, *A Treatise on International Law*, 8th ed. (Clarendon Press, Oxford, 1924).

3 Suk Kyoon Kim, '*Building a Multilateral Framework to Combat Piracy in Asia: From a Global Governance Perspective*' (doctoral dissertation, Hanyang University, Seoul, Korea, 2005), p 7.

4 *Ibid.*, pp. 7–8.

5 Hall (n 2).

6 Alfred P. Rubin, *The Law of Piracy*, 2nd ed. (Transnational Publishers, New York, 1998), p. 341.

> intent to rob, rape, wound, enslave, imprison, or kill a person or with intent to steal or destroy property, for private ends without a bona fide purpose of asserting a claim of right, provided that the act is connected with an attack on or from the sea or in or from the air. If the act is connected with an attack which starts from on board ship, either that ship or another ship which is involved must be a pirate ship or a ship without national charter.

The weaknesses of the draft are apparent in that there seem to be no cases supporting the inclusions of the substance of the offenses such as "rape", "wound", "enslave" and "imprison."[7] However, the Harvard Research Draft Convention was very significant in developing the legal concept of piracy since it served as a source of discussions of piracy at the International Law Commission which had been responsible for preparing a text of the law of the sea under the auspices of the United Nations.

3 Definition of Piracy Under 1958 Geneva Convention on the High Seas

The International Law Commission (ILC) began its discussion of piracy in May 1955, with the text prepared by the Rapporteur of the International Law Commission, much of which was the translations of the Harvard Research draft. The final text of ILC was drafted after numerous meetings and discussions and was approved by the General Assembly of UN in May 1956. The final text was adopted in the 1958 Geneva Conference, with some non-substantive changes from the original draft text.

Article 15. Piracy consists of any of the following acts:

(1) Any illegal acts of violence, detention or any act of depredation, committed for private ends by the crew or the passengers of a private ship or a private aircraft, and directed:
  - (a) On the high seas, against another ship or aircraft, or against persons or property on board such ship or aircraft;
  - (b) Against a ship, aircraft, persons or property in a place outside the jurisdiction of any State;

(2) Any act of voluntary participation in the operation of a ship or of an aircraft with knowledge of facts making it a pirate ship or aircraft;

(3) Any act of inciting or of intentionally facilitating an act described in subparagraph 1 or subparagraph 2 of this article.

---

7 *Ibid.*, p. 342.

4 Definition of Piracy under the UNCLOS

The articles adopted in Geneva in 1958 were inserted with minor changes in the UNCLOS and appear as articles 100–107. Only a significant change was to amend to narrow the scope for possible abuse, as follows[8]: "A seizure on account of piracy may be carried out only by warships or military aircraft, other ships or craft *clearly marked and identifiable as being* on government service *and* authorized to that effect." The definition of piracy under Article 101 of the UNCLOS is restrictive, but precise and detailed. The definition of piracy under the UNCLOS serves as a framework that is referenced by international organizations represented by the International Maritime Organization (IMO), as well as national legislations when they define piracy. The UNCLOS defines piracy as acts consisting of any of the following elements.

(a) Any illegal acts of violence or detention, or any act of depredation, committed for private ends by the crew or the passenger of a private ship or a private aircraft, and directed;
   (i) On the high seas, against another ship or aircraft, or against persons or property on board such ship or aircraft;
   (ii) Against a ship, aircraft, persons or property in a place outside the jurisdiction of any state.
(b) Any act of voluntary participation in the operation of a ship or of an aircraft with knowledge of facts making it a pirate ship or aircraft;
(c) Any act of inciting or of intentionally facilitating an act of described in subparagraph (a) or (b). The acts of piracy, as defined in article 101, committed by a warship, government ship or government aircraft whose crew has mutinied and taken control of the ship or aircraft are assimilated to acts committed by a private ship or aircraft.

Exploring the legal elements that constitute the definition of piracy at sea under the UNCLOS, the key points include: (i) illegal acts of violence or detention, or any act of depredation; (ii) motivated by private ends; (iii) committed by the crew or passengers on board a private ship; (iv) directed against another vessel, or the persons and property on board ship; and (v) committed on the high seas or outside the jurisdiction of any state.

Despite being a universally accepted legal term, a number of problems with the definition of piracy are identified. A principal argument in this regard is that the definition does not take into account the development of various modern maritime zones and remains trapped in a period where the high seas were only three miles from the shore.[9] The problems become more apparent

8 *Ibid.*, p. 372.
9 Mjia, Cariou & Wolff (n 1), p. 105.

when the definition is applied to the trend of piracy attacks worldwide in recent years.

First, the criterion of 'private ends' appears to be inapplicable to an increasing number of piracy attacks in South Asia and West Africa supposedly committed by terrorist groups fighting for political ends or religious beliefs.

Second, the two ship-rule requires that at least two ships must be involved in a piracy attack. This requires that a piracy attack should be committed by a ship against another ship. However, the *modus operandi* of piratical acts in South Asia, in which in many cases locals and a small group of people are aboard rubber dinghies and canoes, is unable to meet the requirement. Under this criterion, the growing piratical incidents in West Africa, concentrated in the Gulf of Guinea, in which pirates attack oil and gas tankers and offshore oil rigs for oil theft, are not qualified as piracy defined in the UNCLOS.

Third, the criteria of 'on the high seas' and 'outside the jurisdiction of any state' make the suitability of piracy very restrictive. Given that the majority of unlawful acts at sea take place inshore or offshore, either in the territorial sea or in port, the criteria do not correspond with what is happening, particularly in South Asia. This serves the argument that all states could claim that piracy no longer exists.[10] Also, controversy remains as to what exactly 'outside the jurisdiction of any state' means.

Concerning the interpretation of the phrase 'outside the jurisdiction,' it remains unclear whether the 'jurisdiction' of a state applies to the exclusive economic zone (EEZ) or is simply limited to the territorial sea. My view is that the phrase should be interpreted as the areas beyond the territorial waters on the grounds that (i) the EEZ is equivalent to the high seas in terms of navigation; (ii) hot pursuit pursuant to Article 111 of the UNCLOS is allowed up to the territorial sea; and (iii) coastal states' jurisdiction over piracy should be permitted as restrictedly as possible, given the nature of piracy as a universal crime.

The criterion that the place of the crime is restricted to the high seas is ill-suited for Southeast Asia, where states are situated adjacent or opposite in an archipelagic geography. The underlying tenet of the criterion is understood to declare that the unlawful acts of violence committed within states' jurisdictions can be enforced by coastal states. However, in many cases, unlawful acts of violence at sea — even within a state's jurisdiction, such as off the coast of Somalia — are transnational and beyond a state's capability. The reason that

10 Mejia, 'Maritime Gerrymandering: Dilemmas in Defining Piracy, Terrorism and Other Acts of Maritime Violence,' (2003)2(2), *Journal of International Commercial Law*, 153–175, p. 160.

the UNCLOS definition of piracy is so problematic is due to a lack of agreement among scholars involved in various attempts in the 20th century to codify the crime of piracy in international law.[11]

5 Definitions of Piracy and Armed Robbery against Ships by the IMO and the IMB

The IMO has coped with the difficulties of classifying piratical acts that do not seem to meet the criteria under the UNCLOS by using the compound 'piracy and armed robbery against ships.'[12] Following the definition of piracy under the UNCLOS, the IMO defines 'armed robbery' as any of the following acts[13]:

> any illegal act of violence or detention or any act of depredation, or threat thereof, other than an act of piracy, committed for private ends and directed against a ship or against persons or property on board such a ship, within a State's internal waters, archipelagic waters and territorial sea; any act of inciting or of intentionally facilitating an act described above.

The key elements of the IMO's definition of armed robbery include: (i) any offences, other than piracy; (ii) directed against a ship or against persons on board; and (iii) within a state's jurisdiction. Under such a broad definition, any offences, not piracy under the UNCLOS, against ships or persons within the jurisdiction of a state may fall within the act of armed robbery. Adopting the definitions of piracy under the UNCLOS and armed robbery by the IMO, the International Maritime Bureau (IMB) of the International Chamber of Commerce (ICC) defines piracy and armed robbery as:

> An act of boarding or attempting to board any ship with the apparent intent to commit theft or any other crime and with the apparent intent or capability to use force in the furtherance of that act.

Without complicated legal elements being embedded, the IMB's definition of piracy and armed robbery against ships is simple and clear. The IMB's definition has no legal ground and is only for statistical purposes. The IMB applies the simple definition since the vast majority of unlawful acts against ships take place within the jurisdiction of states, and the definition of piracy under the UNCLOS does not address this aspect. On the other hand, it is argued that since

11 *Ibid.*, p. 161.
12 *Ibid.*, p. 163.
13 IMO Resolution A.1025(26), Adopted on 18 January 2010.

the IMB is an industry-funded organization, it intentionally adopts a rather broader definition of piracy that results in high numbers of piracy acts, which could be used to justify their rate structure and special premiums of primary piracy regions.[14]

Maritime Terrorism

Despite the constant threat of terrorism at sea, the issue of terrorism, which was previously discussed in Chapter 4, is not addressed in the definitions of piracy under the UNCLOS and of armed robbery against ships by the IMO. In the absence of a universally agreed-upon definition of maritime terrorism in international law, the conceptual distinction between the acts of piracy under the UNCLOS and the acts of maritime terrorism has been controversial.

Generally, the distinction between piracy and maritime terrorism is predicated on the motive behind the unlawful acts. That is, maritime terrorism is for a political or religious purpose, whereas piracy is motivated by private ends, mostly financial gain. The dichotomy is not always obvious since maritime terrorism is often camouflaged as piracy and piracy has increasingly become a good means of terrorism, as noted earlier. The motive behind unlawful acts is blended in some cases, so that it is not easy to draw a clear line between them. In terms of the location of attacks, apart from the motive, maritime terrorism differs from the act of piracy in that it is not restricted to any maritime zone — unlike in the act of piracy, which is limited to either on the high seas or outside the jurisdiction of any state.

Relationships between Piracy and Other Unlawful Acts at Sea

Despite the fact that piracy and armed robbery are conceptually distinctive, it is not easy to distinguish between the two acts of violence at sea in terms of threats to safe navigation and the shipping community. However, the matter of where unlawful acts are committed has significant implications with regard to law enforcement and criminal jurisdiction. For acts of piracy, all states are authorized to seize a pirate ship or arrest pirates, irrespective of the maritime zones of piracy attacks. The state that has seized the pirate ship or the pirates may impose penalties and take action on ships or property.[15] All states are obliged to cooperate to "the fullest extent possible" in the repression of piracy.[16]

---

14 White, B. L. & Wydajewski, K. J., 'Commercial Ship Self-Defense Against Piracy and Maritime Terrorism,' (2002) 2, *Oceans 2002*, pp. 1164–1171.

15 UNCLOS, Art. 105.

16 *Ibid.*, Art. 100.

Piracy is considered *hostis humani generis*, i.e., enemies of all mankind, and all states are granted the right to exercise law enforcement and criminal jurisdiction. States accepted universal jurisdiction over piracy because pirates: (i) attacked the ships of all states and were thus a threat to all states; and (ii) were not subject to the authority of any state, and therefore no state could be held responsible for their acts. These created the practical need and provided the theoretical justification for the exercise of universal jurisdiction.[17]

In contrast, since the act of armed robbery against ships is a national crime committed within the jurisdiction of a state, primary responsibility for enforcement falls on coastal states. Criminal jurisdiction of armed robbery against ships is subject principally to laws and regulations of a state where the unlawful act is committed.

Armed robbery against ships also constitutes an offence under the 1988 SUA Convention and in some cases the 2000 United Nations Convention against Transnational Organized Crime. Thus, it is hard to draw a clear distinction between armed robbery and the act of terrorism in term of violence, but they are distinctive in the purpose of violence and the establishment of criminal jurisdiction. Whereas the establishment of criminal jurisdiction over armed robbery is limited to the state where the unlawful act is committed, the SUA Convention enables states to facilitate the establishment of criminal jurisdiction over the act of terrorism when the offences, regardless of where they happened, are committed — against a ship flying the flag of the state; against a ship in the territory of that state; or by a national of that state.

III Typology of Contemporary Piracy

Introduction

The traditional types of pirates, particularly in the period of the Age of Discovery, might be classified into privateers, buccaneers, corsairs and Barbary pirates based on their relationships to state power, geographical location and country of origin. For contemporary piracy, a number of international organizations involved in maritime affairs have developed their own criteria to classify various types of piracy attacks to serve their activities. The followings are the examples of some of those classifications.

17 Mejia (n 10), p. 167.

1. Baltic and International Maritime Council (BIMCO), the North Atlantic Treaty Organization (NATO), International Chamber of Shipping (ICS):[18]
   (i) Armed robbery: For the most part, the intention is to take valuables from the safe or to steal IT equipment and personal effects.
   (ii) Cargo theft: Vessels are hijacked for several days and cargo is transferred to a smaller vessel.
   (iii) Kidnapping: Robbery is often the prime objective, but the occasional kidnapping of crew members can occur.
2. Best Management Practices 4 (BMP4), developed by BIMCO, ICS, IMB and INTERCARGO, among others: The BMP 4 distinguishes between the definitions of piratical acts based on differing levels of pirate activity.
   (i) Pirate attacks: A piracy attack is where a vessel has been subjected to an aggressive approach by a pirate craft, and weapons have been discharged.
   (ii) Hijack: A hijacking is where pirates have boarded and taken control of a vessel against the crew's will.
   (iii) Illegal boarding: An illegal boarding is where pirates have boarded a vessel but have not taken control. Command remains with the master.
3. International Maritime Bureau (IMB): The IMB Piracy Reporting Centre following the UNCLOS piracy definition & the IMO armed robbery definition classifies the types of attack:
   (i) Attempted
   (ii) Boarded
   (iii) Fired Upon
   (iv) Hijacked
4. Oceans Beyond Piracy (OBP): the OBP program of One Earth Future Foundation puts forward three models of piracy:
   (i) Robbery: Robbery is defined as any incident in which the intent is to board the vessel and steal ship stores, equipment, and/or the crew's personal effects.
   (ii) Kidnap for ransom: This occurs when pirates carry out an attack with the explicit intent to hijack the vessel and hold the crew hostage while they negotiate a ransom payment.

18 BIMCO, 'Guidelines for Owners, Operators and Masters for Protection against Piracy in the Gulf of Guinea Region,' p. 4, available at http://www.imo.org/en/OurWork/Security/WestAfrica/Documents/Guidelines_for_protection_against_Piracy_in_the_Gulf_of_Guinea_Region.pdf.

(iii) Oil theft: Vessels carrying refined oil products are targeted and attacked specifically for the value of the oil cargo.

Typology of Contemporary Piracy

By taking account of the classifications of piracy by various international organizations, a number of different categories of piracy attacks, based on *modus operandi*, geographic location, violence level, and faciliatory factors, etc. are put forward.

1 Petty Theft

The goal of this type of attack is to quickly steal movable items on ships, which appear to be valuable and profitable, while ships are in their berths or at anchor. For the most part, the intention of theft is to steal cash and valuables from the safe, or to steal IT equipment, personal effects and ship stores. This type of attack is the most typical in South Asia, particularly in Indonesia. Robbers take advantage of relatively relaxed security of many small ports in the region. The typical method is that robbers approach near the bow or stern and attempt to board, usually with grappling hooks. The robbers are usually not armed and robbers flee when they are noticed, and thus this type of crime is generally considered to be less violent. Robbers are mostly locals and generally operate in a small group.

This type of robbery has been a way of earning a livelihood in the coastal areas of South Asia. Cases of theft of cash or personal effects have generally less significant impacts compared to armed robberies. According to the Regional Cooperation Agreement on Combating Piracy and Armed Robbery Against Ships in Asia (ReCAAP), which classifies unlawful acts at sea based on their level of violence, this type of attack is classified 'minimally significant.' The IMB defines this type of piracy as low-level robbery. Out of the 86 incidents reported in the waters of Asia in 2016, 59 incidents occurred on board ships while at anchor or in their berths.[19]

2 Armed Robbery: Maritime Mugging

This type of attack occurs when pirates armed with weapons board the ship and steal ship stores, equipment and the crew's personal effects. Attacks are committed against ships while at anchor/berth or underway. This type of attack is a common form of piracy in Southeast Asia. The purpose of these 'shoot

19 'ReCAAP ISC Annual Report 2016,' p. 6, available at http://www.recaap.org/DesktopModules/Bring2mind/DMX/Download.aspx?Command=Core_Download&EntryId=421&PortalId=0&TabId=78.

and scoot' pirate attacks is to rob cash and valuables from the safe, the crew, and ship stores, rather than commit more serious acts such as hijacking entire ships and their cargoes.[20]

Attacks committed against ships that are underway usually take place within a short distance from the territory of coastal states, especially in the Malacca Strait where ships sail at low speeds due to narrow sea lanes and underwater features. The typical method of these attacks is that first the target ship is approached by one or more small craft that varies from primitive, homemade vessels to modern high-speed motorboats. The ship underway is boarded alongside or near the stern, depending on the freeboard and ease of access.

In general, ships with low freeboard that sail at a relatively low speed are prime targets for piracy attacks.[21] Pirates heavily armed with various weapons, including knives, machetes, pistols and automatic weapons, board during the night when ships slow down while they go through the narrow sea lanes off the coast. This type of pirate attack involves threatening, assault, serious injury, and even kidnapping and killing of the crew. A large number of pirates, who belong to organized syndicates, are engaged in an attack, and the level of violence is higher than with petty theft, in which the perpetrator flees upon being noticed.

This type of pirate incident is considered more significant because it involves large vessels as well as a high probability for use of force. Of the 85 incidents reported in 2016 in Asia, 26 attacks were classified as this type of pirate attack. They are concentrated in the waters of the Philippines — half of all incidents occurred there — and the rest occurred off East Malaysia, Indonesia, the South China Sea and the Malacca Strait.

3 Phantom Ship: Hijacking of Vessels and Conversion

The phantom ship indicates that an entire ship has been hijacked by pirates, and it has been re-born as a 'phantom' ship. The typical *modus operandi* is that cargo on board a ship is seized, and the crews are killed and thrown overboard or, if they are lucky, set adrift in boats. Then, the ship is renamed, repainted, re-crewed, registered over several times, and made available in international maritime trade. The phantom ship is given a temporary certificate through the ship registration office in an Asian port. The ship is then fraudulently re-registered — typically under the nationality of Honduras, Belize, Panama or Liberia — and issued with false documents to enable them to board a fresh

20 T. Arbuckle, 'Scourge of Piracy Returns to Southeast Asia' (1998), 29, *Jane's Intelligence Review*, pp. 26–29.

21 White & Wydajewski (n 14).

payload. The new shipper loads his cargo onto the pirate vessel and receives his bill of lading. The ship, instead of heading for the port named on the bill of lading, sails to a different port, unloads the cargo to a conspirator or an unsuspecting buyer, then sheds its temporary registration for another.[22] Phantom ships are often used for smuggling and other unlawful acts at sea.

The phantom ship may illustrate the transnational nature of piracy, given that these piracy attacks are pre-meditated, well-organized and committed by crime syndicates across borders, involving a large number of operatives at each stage. The crime syndicates are well-resourced and carefully laid-out international criminal networks, and the operatives are highly trained, heavily armed and fully prepared to use firearms.

Phantom ship piracy attacks, which had been prevalent until the early 2000s in Southeast Asia, were a grave concern in the region and among the shipping community. Southeast Asia accounted for the vast majority of phantom ships worldwide, recording 48 incidents out of a total of 53 incidents in the period between 1996 and 2013. Phantom ship piracy culminated in 2003 and began to sharply decline since 2005.[23] This type of attack has not been reported in Southeast Asia in recent years. A case of a phantom ship incident that occurred in Southeast Asian waters is presented here as an example:

Ten Yu Ho incident: On 27 September 1998, a Panama-registered cargo ship owned by a Japanese citizen, the *Ten Yu Ho* disappeared three hours after departing from Kuala Tanjong, Indonesia. The ship, loaded with a cargo of 3,000 tons of aluminum ingots, was bound for Incheon, Korea. Three months after the ship disappeared, it was found in Zhangjiagang in Jiangsu Province, China, repainted, re-crewed, and renamed the *SANE-1*. The renamed ship was identified as the *Ten Yu Ho* by confirmation of the engine number. Fourteen crewmen (12 Chinese and two Koreans) and cargo still remain missing.

4 Hijacking, Hostage-Taking and Ransom-Seeking

The typical method of this type of piracy attack is to hijack a vessel while it is underway and bring it to the pirates' base. There, the pirates will hold the crew hostage for a period of time and negotiate a ransom payment with a shipowner in exchange for the release of the crew and ship. This has been most prevalent off the Somali coast and the Gulf of Aden over the last decade. Piracy attacks in the region, which is perceived as the symbol of contemporary piracy, are at the most significant level in all aspects, such as scale of attack, level of

22 Arbuckle (n 20).

23 Keun Soo Jeong, 'Diverse Piracy Patterns and Different Control Mechanisms,' Presented to the ISA Global South Caucus Conference 2015, p. 8.

sophistication, degree of violence, damage inflicted, and impact on the international community.

Unlike in traditional piracy attacks, the crews are held hostage for a relatively extended period of time and released after a ransom is paid. The use of violence is not common against crews, although pirates carry weapons. This happens because piracy is motivated by the prospect of large monetary gains from ransom payments. This type of attack is usually committed by a relatively large number of pirates under the command of a well-organized criminal network — for instance, one that is connected to rebel groups in Somalia.

These piracy attacks have become a business model involving a complex web of interactions between numerous stakeholders, including financers, instigators and the pirates themselves.[24] The missions of stakeholders are well coordinated and each participant has a role to play, including planning, recruitment, funding, information-gathering, commission of the attack, hostage management and negotiation for ransom, using advanced information technologies and equipment. These piracy attacks are committed against ships that are underway far from offshore or on the high seas by using a mother ship and one or two skiffs, which are small and fast-moving.

5 Hijacking, Hostage-Taking and Cargo Theft

Unlike Somali pirates seeking a ransom payment, West African pirates, concentrated in the Gulf of Guinea, are engaged in hijacking, hostage-taking and cargo theft. Unlike off the coast of Somalia, which has been in a state of anarchy over the last decade, the piracy-prone region in West Africa is under the rule of developed central governments and is subject to in-port policing. Under these stable circumstances, pirates lack the capacity to capture ships and hold them for a ransom for an extended period of time. Thus, they have developed a combined model of armed robbery, kidnapping for ransom and cargo theft, of which the concentration is on cargo theft.

The prominent feature of such piracy is oil theft. Vessels carrying refined oil products are targeted and attacked specifically for the value of the oil cargo that they carry. When the vessel is hijacked, the crew is often forced to navigate the vessel to an unknown location where the cargo can be lightered to another vessel or to a storage facility on land. The refined oil product then finds its way onto the black market. Eventually, the oil product makes its way back into the clean, mainstream supply and is sold domestically or in the global marketplace.[25]

---

24 UNCTAD, 'Maritime Piracy' (2014) 2, *Studies in Transport Law and Policy*, p. 2.

25 Oceans Beyond Piracy, 'The State of Maritime Piracy 2013' (2013), p. 52.

IV Aspects of Contemporary Piracy Attacks: Trends, Features and Violence

Piracy is a complex and global phenomenon, despite regional variations, and these features may change over time and over space. This section explores and compares the various aspects of contemporary piracy attacks worldwide, including the frequency of piracy occurrences, regional concentrations, contributing factors, *modus operandi* and damage inflicted.

Overview of Piracy Attacks in Recent Years

The occurrences of piracy attacks have an irregular trend, varying with geographical location and time. In terms of a global trend of piracy occurrences, piracy attacks had been constantly on the rise since the mid-1990s and peaked in the period of 2000–2004, averaging 350–450 incidents annually.[26] Over the last decade (2008–2017), a total of 3,010 incidents worldwide were reported to the International Maritime Bureau (IMB), of which Asia and Africa account for 1,325 and 1,455 incidents, respectively.[27] The figures show that piracy attacks are concentrated on the two continents, each accounting for 44 percent and 48 percent of global piracy attacks.

After a peak in 2010 with 445 incidents, as Fig. 9 shows, piracy attacks worldwide have dramatically declined. Over the five years since 2013, average annual piracy attacks have numbered 225 incidents, which is a significant drop from the past decade. Of particular note is that in 2016, record low occurrences, with 180 incidents overall, were reported. It remains to be seen whether a global trend of piracy reduction will continue or not.

Nonetheless, it may indicate a positive sign that piracy attacks are curbed in piracy-prone regions such as the Somali coast and the Malacca Strait. The statistics of piracy occurrences are based on the data reported to the IMB, which employs a broad piracy definition encompassing the acts of piracy under the UNCLOS and armed robbery together. However, the actual occurrences of piracy are believed to be higher than the statistics of the IMB, given non-reporting or under-reporting.

Under-reporting is due to concerns over increases in insurance premiums, disruption of shipping schedules during an investigation, and fears that the ship company and shipmaster will gain a reputation for incompetence. A survey by the Nippon Foundation shows that there is a large gap between the

26 The statistics are adapted from IMB Annual Piracy Reports.

27 *Ibid.*

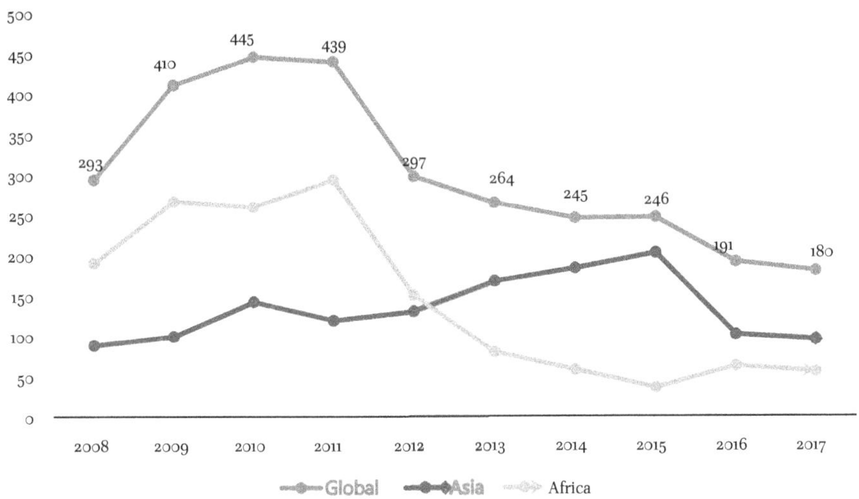

FIGURE 9 Trend of global piracy occurrences (2008–2017)
SOURCE: ADAPTED FROM IMB ANNUAL PIRACY REPORTS

number of reported incidents and actual occurrences; it found that 20 Japanese vessels were attacked when the foundation surveyed 201 Japanese shipping companies in 1997. This was 10 times larger than IMB's figures of Japanese victims, for which only two incidents were reported.[28]

Features of Piracy Attacks by Region

The problem of piracy is a global phenomenon, reported in the seas of 62 countries in four out of five continents. Of those countries, it is highly concentrated in a number of countries, including Indonesia, Yemen, Malaysia, Somalia, Nigeria, Oman, Bangladesh and India.[29] This part explores the features of piracy attacks by region.

1 Southeast Asia

Southeast Asia has been a traditionally piracy-prone region since ancient times. The vast majority of piracy attacks in Asian waters are concentrated in Southeast Asian seas. In the period from the early 1990s to the mid-2000s, two-thirds of piracy attacks worldwide were concentrated in the waters of Asia. The waters of Southeast Asia were one of the riskiest shipping routes. In

28 Yamada, *Maritime Terrorism (in Japanese)*, (Php Shinsho, Tokyo, 2003), pp. 107–108.

29 Dugato, M & Berlusconi, G, 'Maritime Piracy Worldwide' (2015) N.1/2015, *Transcrime Research in Brief*.

particular, the Malacca Strait, which is one of the busiest shipping lanes in the world (with an annual traffic volume of over 50,000 ships), as well as a strategic chokepoint for the global seaborne trade, has been the most vulnerable in the region.

But since the mid-2000s, piracy attacks in Southeast Asia have been dramatically reduced. This change was driven by the littoral states of the Malacca Strait, such as Singapore, Malaysia and Indonesia, along with other regional and user states. The stable piracy situation in Southeast Asia has changed since 2010, with the waters off Indonesia reemerging as a hotspot of piracy. In 2015, 201 piracy attacks in Southeast Asia were reported, accounting for 82 percent of a total 246 incidents worldwide. The gravity of the piracy issue in this region may be illustrated by the 2016 figures of piracy occurrences: four incidents (out of a total of seven) of ship hijackings and 34 (out of a total of 34) crew kidnapping occurred in that region.[30]

The features of piracy attacks in Asian waters in recent years are identified as follows. First, armed robbery and kidnapping of the crew onboard ships that are underway have been constantly on the rise, while traditional petty theft remains dominant. This may indicate that piracy attacks in that region are becoming increasingly violent. Second, the growing *modus operandi* is that a group of pirates, composed of maximum of 17 people, armed with rifles and knives on board a fast-moving boat, hijack fishing boats or tug boats that have a low freeboard, and kidnap the crew for a ransom.

A notable trend is that kidnapping of general cargo ships and crude oil carriers, attributed to the Philippines militant group the *Abu Sayyaf*, have been significantly increasing. Third, the Sulu-Celebes Seas off the Philippines have newly emerged as a piracy-prone spot. As recently as in October 2016, the ten gunmen of the *Abu Sayyaf* boarded a 11,391-ton Korean cargo ship off Tawi-Tawi Island and kidnapped the Korean master and a Filipino crew and abandoned ship.[31]

The rise in piracy attacks in Southeast Asia can be attributed to some contributing factors: (i) permissive environment toward piracy as a source of livelihood for locals; (ii) archipelagic geography dotted with small islands; (iii) channel for funding militant groups; (iv) lack of law-enforcement capability of littoral states; and (iv) bad economic and unstable political situation and relaxed counter-piracy efforts.

---

30 See IMB, 'Piracy and Armed Robbery Against Ships Annual Report 2016.'

31 'Sulu-Celebes Sea Increase in Pirate Attacks & Crew Abductions,' *The Standard Club*, 17 January 2017.

2 East Africa

The region of the Somali coast and the Gulf of Aden have been hotspots of piracy over the last decade. The shipping industry and the international community have greatly suffered from tremendous damages inflicted by piracy attacks in that region. As illustrated earlier, a distinctive feature of piracy in that region has been a hijack-for-ransom business model, which depends for its success on a supporting infrastructure on land and which attaches a high economic value to hostages.[32]

As Fig. 10 indicates, the number of piracy attacks in that region continued to rise until 2010, with 111 incidents in 2008 (of a total of 293), 197 (of a total of 410) in 2009, 192 in 2010 (out of 445), which accounted for one-third of piracy attacks worldwide.[33] Unlike in other regions, where piracy attacks tend to occur in coastal waters or nearby trade lanes, Somali pirates have widened their geographical presence and are moving farther away from the coast and territorial waters into the Indian Ocean, the Red Sea, the Gulf of Oman, the Mozambique Channel, the Maldives and Indian territorial waters.[34] Thus the list of countries directly affected by piracy has become extensive, including the Comoros, Djibouti, India, Iran, Kenya, Madagascar, Mozambique, Oman, Qatar, Seychelles, Tanzania, Arab Emirates and Yemen.

The piracy problem in that region has dominated other regions in the scale, scope, severity and damage of the attacks. Several pirate groups have operated in Somali waters, according to a study of the UN and independent sources.[35] Reports suggest that there may be seven to 10 distinct gangs or 'pirate action groups' financed by so-called 'instigators' who organize the funding and delegate operations to group leaders.

These groups operate from Xabo on Puntland's northern coast, along Puntland's eastern coast out of ports from Garacad south to Hobyo, and from Harardhere in central Somalia to Kismayo.[36] Poverty, lack of employment, environmental hardship, pitifully low incomes, reduction of pastoralist and maritime resources due to drought and illegal fishing and a volatile security and political situation are attributed to Somali piracy.[37] In some cases, it is believed that Somali businessmen and international support networks provide

32 UNCTAD, 'Maritime Piracy,' *Studies in Transport Law and Policy,* (2014) 1, p.8.
33 IMB (n 30).
34 *Ibid.*
35 US Congressional Research Service, 'Piracy Off the Horn of Africa, April,' (2011), p. 5.
36 *Ibid.*
37 *Ibid.*, p. 6.

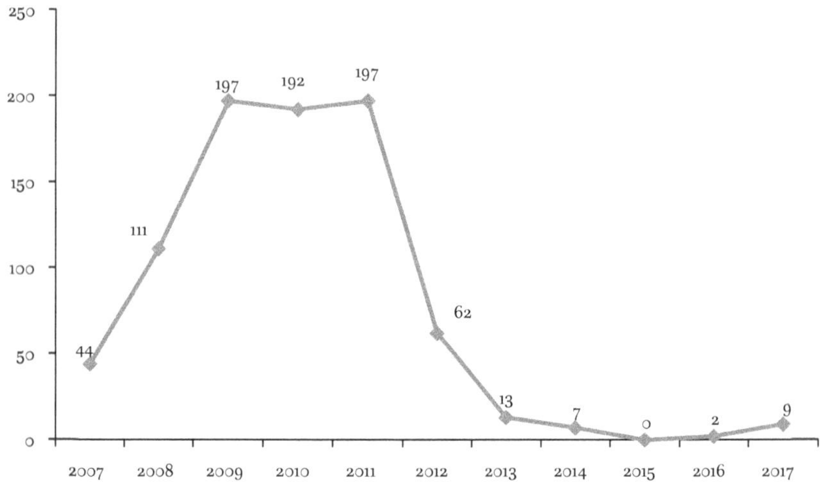

FIGURE 10 Status of piracy attacks off the Somali coast (2007–2017)
SOURCE: ADAPTED FROM IMB ANNUAL PIRACY REPORTS

pirate groups with financing and supplies in return for shares of ransom payments that are also distributed among pirates themselves.[38]

Somali pirate groups have developed highly sophisticated operational capabilities. The typical Somali pirate team is equipped a variety of small arms, including AK-47 rifles and rocket-propelled grenade (PRC) launchers. Many pirate teams use fishing skiffs powered with large outboard motors to give chase to larger but slower-moving tankers, cargo ships, yachts, cruise ships, barges and tug boats. Local Somali fishermen are often forced to support pirate activities in some cases, while in other cases, coastal Somalis lend their fishing boats, equipment and navigational expertise to teams of would-be pirates from inland communities.[39]

The damage and costs incurred by Somali pirates will be discussed in a later section. Piracy attacks in that region have been dramatically curbed since 2011. Over the last few years, piracy attacks have been drastically reduced, with only a small number of attacks being reported. For instance, there were no reported attacks in 2015. Various counter-piracy measures implemented by the international community and the shipping industry, which will be discussed in detail, are credited with the dramatic reduction. Among those, combined naval

38 *Ibid.*, p. 10.
39 *Ibid.*

patrols and escorts and the employment of armed guards onboard ships in the high-risk areas off the Somali coast and the Gulf of Aden are the most salient and successful, deterring piracy attempts and greatly reducing the success rate of piracy attacks as well.

Despite the significant drop in piracy attacks since 2012, piracy is expected to remain a major concern in East Asian waters. This is because Somali pirates may not have totally given up on piracy as a source of revenue — they may be changing their strategy by increasingly targeting ships at anchorage.[40]

3 West Africa

Of particular concern is the recent escalation of piracy attacks in the Gulf of Guinea, which has newly emerged as a hotspot of piracy in West Africa. The littoral states in the Gulf include Benin, Cameroon, Gabon, Ghana, Guinea and Nigeria. A total of 43 incidents were reported in four countries in 2016, an upsurge from 20 incidents in the previous year.[41] Piracy in that region is highly concentrated in Nigeria, which accounted for 92 percent (33) out of total 36 incidents in 2017.

The share of the Gulf out of overall reported incidents in Africa has also been sharply increasing over recent years, accounting for 23 percent (35) in 2012, 44 percent (35) in 2013, 42 percent (24) in 2014, 57 percent (20) in 2015, 69 percent (43) in 2016 and 60 percent (33) in 2017. Of growing concern is that piracy attacks committed by militant groups, such as *Boko Haram* and *the Movement for the Emancipation of the Niger Delta*, are increasing. The militant groups commit piracy to finance their activities. The *modus operandi* in that region tends to be more violent than any other region, as indicated in statistics that show the number of armed incidents and kidnapping in Nigeria were the highest in the world with 27 and 29 incidents in 2016. The second-highest ranking is held by the Philippines, with five and 18 incidents, respectively.[42]

A distinctive feature of piracy attacks in that region is that pirates are increasingly targeting oil production infrastructure and tankers carrying oil, usually in territorial waters. Pirate networks appear to be generally well informed about the operations of the oil industry and to have access to important information, including the names of ships, intended voyage courses, the value of the cargo, whether or not armed guards are aboard, and the extent of the

40 *Ibid.*, p. 10.
41 IMB (n 30).
42 *Ibid.*

insurance coverage.[43] Given the gravity of the piracy situation, the region was designated by the insurance industry as a 'war risk zone' for shipping, with Benin, Nigeria and Togo waters being identified as 'high risk' areas — that is to say, in the same risk category as Somalia.[44]

Types of Violence, Weapons and Victim Vessels

Overall, the degree of violence has tended to decrease over the past five years (2013–2017), in comparison with the previous five years (2008–2012), in terms of types of arm used and violence against crew members. Concerning the types of arm used during piracy attacks over the last five years, the share of incidents involving guns was 24 percent (266) of a total of 1,126 incidents, a significant reduction from 52 percent (983) of 1,884 cases over the previous five years.

The use of guns peaked in 2011, with 245 incidents, and began to diminish significantly onward, with an increasing use of knives in the same period. In terms of the types of violence to crews over the last decade, hostage-taking was more frequent, with 78 percent (1,259) of a total 1,612 incidents in the past five years, and 89 percent (4,500) of a total 5,005 incidents in the previous five years. (see Fig. 11)

The sharp decline in the number of hostage-taking incidents is attributable to an overall reduction of piracy incidents in recent years. The disparity in the lethality of violence between the two periods is apparent given that the victims of killing (including missing persons) in the past five years was greatly reduced, to 11 crews from 72 crews, compared to the previous five years. Kidnapping for a ransom is a primary source of violence and has seen an increase from the previous five years. The reduction in killing is attributed to a higher rate of ransom payment for the release of hostages, along with greater policing and law enforcement.

Concerning the types of victim vessel, Fig. 12 indicates that over the last six years chemical tankers, bulk carriers, containers, crude oil tankers, general cargo and tugs were the primary targets of pirates. Amongst those, chemical tankers and bulk carriers are identified the most vulnerable to piracy attacks. The high-value cargoes that those ships carry are highly likely to be attractive to pirates. In addition, their strategic role in the global merchandise and

43 Tom Thomson, 'Piracy May be Getting Worse, Not Better,' *The Maritime Executive* (May 2013).

44 Mark McNames, 'Piracy on the Rise in the Gulf of Guinea as Niger Delta Militants Move Offshore' (2012),10(15), *Terrorism Monitor*, p. 6, available at https://jamestown.org/program/piracy-on-the-rise-in-the-gulf-of-guinea-as-niger-delta-militants-move-offshore/.

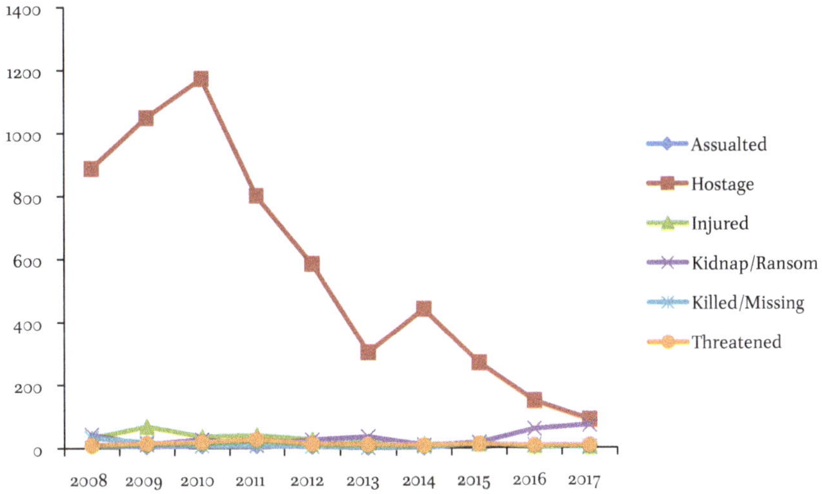

FIGURE 11 Types of violence to crew (2008–2017)
SOURCE: ADAPTED FROM IMB ANNUAL PIRACY REPORTS

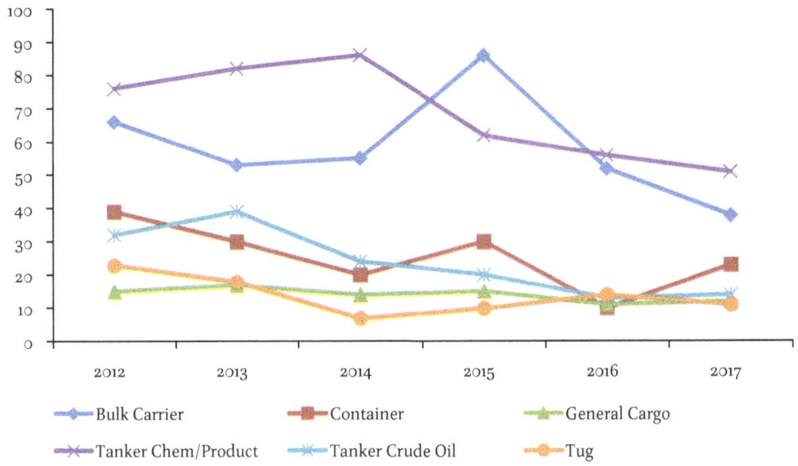

FIGURE 12 Types of vessels attacked (2012–2017)
SOURCE: ADAPTED FROM IMB ANNUAL PIRACY REPORTS

energy trades might be a contributing factor for ransom-seeking. An added factor in the case of tankers and bulkers is the relatively lower speed at which they operate and their relative low height, which facilitates boarding by pirates.[45]

45 UNCTAD (n 32), p. 6.

V Costs of Piracy

The global costs of piracy, including the cost of piracy off eastern Africa, remain uncertain. Studies of global piracy costs tend to primarily focus on calculating first-order costs such as the cost of ransoms, security deterrence equipment and naval forces deployment.[46] The secondary costs of piracy, including the effects on foreign investment in the affected and neighboring regions, or on commodity prices, remain uncovered due to difficulties in estimating the scope of the effects and related costs.

The costs associated with piracy vary with research organizations or institutions, with divergent estimates and conclusions. The RAND Institute and the IMB, for example, have estimated piracy costs to range between $1billion to $16 billion per year. The One Earth Future (OEF) Foundation, as part of its Oceans Beyond Piracy (OBP) Project, estimates that the total cost of Somali piracy was at $7 billion to $12 billion in 2010, $6.6 billion to $6.9billion in 2011, and $5.7 billion to $6.1 billion in 2012.[47] While over 80 percent of these costs were estimated to be borne by the shipping industry, 20 percent were estimated to be borne by governments. Averaging out all related expenses, the cost per incident was valued at $82.7 million in 2012, a total 189 percent increase from $28.6 million estimated for 2011.[48] In 2013, the World Bank has estimated the global economic cost of piracy off the coast of Somalia at $18 billion, with a margin of error of roughly $6 billion.[49] The following is a breakdown of first-order costs arising from piracy off the coast of Somalia, as found by the OEF.[50]

1 Ransoms and Recovery

In 2012, OBP estimates that $31.75 million dollars in ransoms were paid to Somali pirates. This represents an 80.1 percent decline in ransoms from 2011, when $159.62 million was paid. The reduction in ransoms is due to the lower number of vessels captured and released in 2012, as well as a lower average ransom than the previous year. Between 2005 and 2012, the value of ransoms paid for ships and/or seafarers kidnapped by Somali-based pirates is estimated at $339 million and $413 million.

The amount of ransoms paid to pirates has escalated over recent years. The average ransoms soared to $3.4 million, $4 million, $5 million and $3.96 million

46 *Ibid.*, p. 13.

47 *Ibid.*

48 *Ibid.*

49 *Ibid.* p, 14.

50 One Earth Future Foundation, 'The Economic Cost of Somali Piracy 2012,' Working Paper, *Oceans Beyond Piracy Project*, 2013.

in 2009, 2010, 2011 and 2012 respectively.[51] While in 2010 the total amount of ransoms paid was $176 million, this amount fell to $160 million in 2011 and $31.7 million in 2012.

The Korean tanker *Samho Dream,* which was carrying oil from Iraq to the U.S., was hijacked by Somali pirates on 4 April 2010. On 6 November 2010, after being held for 217 days, the ship was released from pirate control in exchange for a ransom of about $9 million, which was the largest ransom payment at the time. As the value of ransoms paid has increased, so have the duration of negotiations and of captivity. Up from 55 days in 2009, seafarers are being held hostage for an average of duration of three to four months.[52]

2 Military Operations

The incremental cost of vessel deployments, vessel protection detachments, the administrative budgets of naval operations, and other expenses amounted to $1.09 billion in 2012. Operationally, the major change that took place between 2011 and 2012 is a decrease in naval assets deployed by the three major naval missions, including EUNAVFOR's Operation Atlanta, NATO's Operation Ocean Shield and the Combined Task Force's CTF-151, alongside a corresponding increase in the assets provided by independent deployers, such as China, India, Japan, Russia and Korea.[53]

3 Security Equipment and Guards

Ships are increasingly equipped with security equipment, personnel and guards. The total cost of security equipment and guards incurred to the shipping industry is estimated to range between $363 million and $2.5 billion in 2010, $1.06 billion and $1.16 billion in 2011, and $1.65 billion and $2.06 billion in 2012.[54] Greater acceptance of armed guards by both flag states and shipowners and operators has contributed to driving up the costs. The number of armed guards used to protect merchant ships transiting the piracy-affected areas has increased together with the proportion of ships employing armed guards.[55]

4 Rerouting

To avoid piracy attacks in the high-risk area in the Gulf of Aden, the shipping industry chooses to divert from the traditionally favored route, the Suez Canal,

51 UNCTAD (n 32), p. 15.
52 *Ibid.*, p. 16.
53 One Earth Future Foundation (n 50).
54 UNCTAD (n 32), pp. 19–21.
55 *Ibid.*

to alternative shipping routes, including the Cape of Good Hope. During the surge of piracy in East Africa, some ships, such as *A.P. Moller-Maersk* tankers, rerouted to avoid the high-risk area in the Gulf of Aden. Rerouting necessarily requires shipping companies to spend higher costs for additional shipping days, charge higher shipping rates, and lower trade competitiveness. Diverting fleet and trade from the Suez Canal to the Cape of Good Hope on a trip from the Middle East to Europe doubles the typical transport time.[56] It is estimated that the shipping industry pays around $2.3 billion to $3 billion per year to reroute ships to avoid piracy each year.[57]

5 Increased Speed

According to the OBP estimate, shipping companies spent an extra $1.53 billion on fuel costs associated with steaming at faster-than-optimal speeds in order to prevent pirate attacks. The cost of this practice dropped 43.3 percent from 2011, which is a result of reduction in the proportion of ships going through the high-risk area at a faster speed as well as a decrease in ships steaming at faster-than-optimal speeds.[58]

6 Additional Labor Costs

Piracy results in direct costs related to labor in the form of hazard pay and payment for seafarers while they are being held hostage on the captured ship. Hazard pay offers seamen the right to obtain double pay while transiting the high-risk areas. In 2012, these costs totaled $471.6 million, an upsurge from $195.1 million in 2011.[59]

7 Prosecutions and Imprisonment

As some countries highly affected by piracy may have limited capacity to undertake prosecutions, the international community has provided some financial aid to allow countries such as Kenya and the Seychelles to build their capacity thereof. OBP estimated that the cost of prosecution and imprisonment of pirates totaled $14.89 million in 2012, a significant drop from $31 million in 2010.[60] The reduction in prosecution costs appears to be largely due to a decrease in the number of suspects prosecuted, while an increase in the cost of imprisonment

56 *Ibid.*

57 Kennedy K. Mbekeani & Mthuli Ncube, 'Economic Impact of Maritime Piracy' (2011), 2(10), *Africa Economic Brief*, African Development Bank.

58 One Earth Future Foundation (n 50).

59 *Ibid.*

60 *Ibid.*

reflects the long-term imprisonment of pirates. In early 2013, over 1,000 suspects were reported to be awaiting prosecution in around 20 countries.[61]

8 Insurance

The increase in piracy attacks in the high-risk areas has affected insurance premiums and coverage. Ships that continue to pass through the Gulf of Aden and the Suez Canal require a war-risk coverage. Since the Gulf of Aden was designated as a war-risk area by the insurance industry in 2008, the cost of war-risk premiums has increased significantly, from $500 per ship, per voyage, up to $150,000 per ship, per voyage in 2010.[62] In contrast, it was estimated that the cost of insurance in 2012 was up to $550.7 million, a 23 percent decline from $634.9 million in the previous year. The drop is attributable to the increased presence of private armed guards aboard merchant vessels and the resulting premium discount.[63]

9 Counter-Piracy Organizations

The cost of various counter-piracy organizations, ranging from UN agencies to independent NGOs, was estimated at $24.5 million in 2010 and at $24.08 million in 2012.[64]

VI Global Counter-Piracy Efforts and Policy Reponses

The Global Level

With growing concern over the piracy problem across the oceans, the international community has struggled to combat piracy, undertaking a wide range of anti-piracy measures and policies. The international efforts to respond to the threat of piracy have taken on a multi-faceted approach. International counter-piracy efforts are driven by the UN and the IMO, in collaboration with principal state stakeholders, including coastal states of regions with high piracy rates, the U.S., and other major trade states.

1 UN Security Resolution

The UN Security Council has issued a series of resolutions since 2008 to facilitate an international response to Somali piracy. Among those, Resolution 1816

---

61 UNCTAD (n 32).

62 *Ibid.*

63 One Earth Future Foundation (n 50).

64 *Ibid.*

(June 2008), which was issued first in this regard, authorized relevant states to exercise the right of pursuit into the territorial waters of Somalia for a period of six months. It states that states acting in cooperation with the Somali government are granted to "enter the territorial waters of Somalia for the purpose of repressing acts of piracy and armed robbery at sea" and to "use, within the territorial waters of Somalia, in a manner consistent with action permitted on the high seas with respect to piracy under relevant international law, all means to repress acts of piracy and armed robbery."[65] This measure, by which the period was extended to one year and has been renewed on a yearly basis, has been a principal international cooperative mechanism in fighting pirates.

Resolution 1838 (October 2008) calls on states with military capabilities to "take part actively in the fight against piracy on the high seas off the coast of Somalia, in particular by deploying naval vessels and military aircraft."[66] The UN Security Council has also adopted Resolutions to facilitate the prosecution of the Somali pirates. Resolution 1897 (December 2009) encouraged states to conclude special agreements or arrangements that would allow governments to embark law enforcement officials ('shipriders') to facilitate the investigation, and allowed for prosecution of persons detained as a result of anti-piracy operations.[67]

Resolution 1918 (April 2010) calls on states to "criminalize piracy under their domestic law and favorably consider the prosecution of suspected, and imprisonment of the convicted, pirates apprehended off Somalia."[68] Resolution 1976 (April 2011) decides to consider the establishment of Somali courts to try suspected pirates both in Somalia and in the region.[69]

2 CGPCS

Based on UN Security Resolution 1851 (December 2008), which encourages states to establish an international cooperation mechanism to act as a common point of contact on all aspects of combating piracy at sea off Somalia,[70] the Contact Group on Piracy off the Coast of Somalia (CGPCS) was created in 2009. The CGPCS, composed of approximately 60 member governments, 20 international organizations, and shipping associations, has four working groups.

65 UN Security Council, S/Res/1816 (2008), para. 7.

66 *Ibid*, S/Res/1838(2008), para. 3.; this was re-urged by Resolution 1851 (December 2008).

67 *Ibid.*, S/Res/1897(2009), para. 6.

68 *Ibid.*, S/Res/1918(2010), para. 2.; this was re-urged by Resolution 2015(December 2011).

69 *Ibid.*, S/Res/1976(2011), para. 26.

70 *Ibid.*, S/Res/1851(2008), para. 4.

The CGPCS is tasked with: (i) improving operational and informational support to counter-piracy operations; (ii) establishing a counter-piracy coordination mechanism; (iii) strengthening judicial frameworks for arrest, prosecution and detention of pirates; (iv) strengthening commercial shipping self-awareness and other capabilities; (v) pursuing improved diplomatic and public information efforts; and (vi) tracking financial flows related to piracy. The CGPCS has established a trust fund, contributed to by member governments, international organizations, non-governmental organizations and shipping associations to support the activities of states combating piracy off Somalia.

3 IMO

The IMO has had a program to combat piracy off Somalia and has successfully engaged on a multilateral basis in other regions to improve anti-piracy cooperation. To assist in the implementation of international instruments to fight piracy, the IMO has promulgated a number of circulars on guidance to ship owners, ship operators and crews on preventing and suppressing piracy, and recommendations to governments for preventing and suppressing piracy. The IMO has adopted the Code of Practice for the Investigation of Crimes of Piracy and Armed Robbery Against Ships (Resolution A. 99(22)).[71]

The IMO has also held seminars and regional training programs to assist states in developing the appropriate national framework for combating piracy. As part of those efforts, an IMO-sponsored international meeting in Djibouti in 2009 adopted a code of conduct concerning the repression of piracy in the western Indian Ocean and the Gulf of Aden.

In accordance with the code, three regional facilities were established to support information-sharing: (i) the Maritime Coordination Center in Mombasa, Kenya; (ii) the Sub-Regional Coordination Center in Dar es Salaam, Tanzania; (iii) and a new regional maritime information center in Sana'a, Yemen. The parties also agreed to the establishment of a regional training center in Djibouti. In addition, based on collected data and experience by the military, the IMO has developed detailed guidance and recommendations, commonly known as best management practices for governments and commercial vessels in seeking to prevent, deter and respond to pirate attacks.[72]

71 UN, 'Oceans and the Law of the Sea 2009.' p. 20 para. 61.

72 'Best Management Practices for Protection against Somalia based Piracy' (version 4-2011),' developed and sponsored by IMO and other international maritime organizations, available at http://eunavfor.eu/wp-content/uploads/2013/01/bmp4-low-res_sept_5_20111.pdf.

Southeast Asia

1 ReCAAP

In order to combat piracy in the Malacca Strait and other Asian waters, the littoral states and other Asian countries formed a multilateral cooperative framework, known as the Regional Cooperation Agreement on Combating Piracy and Armed Robbery against Ships in Asia (ReCAAP).[73] The agreement provides: (i) general obligations of member countries for the prevention and suppression of piracy and armed robbery, and arrest of perpetrators and seizures of pirate ships or aircraft; (ii) rescue of victims of piracy attacks; (iii) establishment of an Information Sharing Center (ISC); (iv) cooperation in the arrest and extradition of pirates; and (v) mutual legal assistance and cooperation in capacity-building.

The ReCAAP, initiated by Japan in 2001, was concluded on 11 November 2004, and came into force on 4 September 2006. As of 2017, the contracting parties include 20 countries, including five extra-regional countries such as Denmark, Netherland, Norway, the U.K and the U.S.[74]

The ISC, based in Singapore and composed of one representative from each member state, plays a pivotal role in piracy reporting and response coordination among the participating countries. As a core body of ReCAAP, the roles include[75]: (i) to serve as a platform for information exchange with the ReCAAP focal points via the Information Network System; (ii) to analyze and provide accurate statistics of piracy and armed robbery incidents; (iii) to facilitate capacity-building efforts that help improve the capability of member countries in combating piracy and armed robbery in the region; (iv) to cooperate with organizations and like-minded parties on joint exercises, information-sharing, capacity-building programs, or other forms of cooperation.

2 Operation MALSINDO

The littoral states of the Malacca Strait, including Indonesia, Malaysia and Singapore, have conducted a trilateral patrol, called Operation MALSINDO, a year-round, coordinated naval patrol launched on 20 July 2004. The three littoral states agreed to patrol their respective waters in the 900-km strait with 17 ships

73 See RECAAP Web site, available at www.recaap.org/index_home.html.

74 The participating countries include: Australia, Bangladesh, Brunei, Cambodia, China, Denmark, India, Japan, Korea, Laos, Malaysia, Myanmar, Netherland, Norway, Philippines, Singapore, Sri Lanka, Thailand, the United Kingdom, the U.S. and Vietnam. Indonesia and Malaysia have declined to become a party to RECAAP, citing sovereignty concerns.

75 RECAAP, 'Regional Guide to Counter Piracy and Armed Robbery Against Ships in Asia,' p. 51.

and to coordinate their moves through a 24-hour communications link.[76] The arrangement addresses the legal challenge in the narrow strait that the right of hot pursuit is restricted to beyond the territorial sea of the vessel's state or of a third state[77] by allowing warships into one another's waters when pursuing pirates.[78]

3 Eyes in the Sky

In September 2005, the three littoral states launched coordinated aerial surveillance, named the Eyes in the Sky (EIS) initiative, pursuant to which each country patrols twice per week along the Malacca and Singapore Straits and each flight carries a maritime patrol team made up of military personnel from each participating state.[79] To improve the effectiveness of the naval and air patrols, terms of reference and standard operating procedures were agreed on in April 2006, and the combined efforts were renamed the Malacca Straits Patrols (MSP).

The MSP has three elements: (i) the Malacca Straits Surface Patrols (MSSP); (ii) EIS; and (iii) the Intelligence Exchange Group (IEG). The IEG developed the Malacca Straits Patrols Information System (MSP-IS) to improve coordination and situational awareness at sea among the three countries.[80] In September 2008, the MSP was given a boost with the participation of Thailand in both the MSSP and the EIS. Thailand's area of operation is the northern approaches to the Malacca Strait in the Andaman Sea.[81]

East Africa

The European Union (EU), the African Union, the League of Arab States and the North Atlantic Treaty Organization (NATO) are actively engaged in combating piracy off the coast of Somalia and the Gulf of Aden. Naval ship patrols are viewed as one of the most effective deterrents to piracy attacks, as demonstrated in the significant drop in the figures of piracy incidents in recent years in this region. Over 40 countries are engaged in counter-piracy operations in East Africa, either in a national capacity or through joint forces.[82] Naval

---

76 Kim (n 3), p. 93.
77 UNCLOS, Art. 111(3).
78 Kim (n 3), p. 93.
79 Ian Storey, 'Maritime Security in Southeast Asia: Two Cheers for Regional Cooperation' (2009), *Southeast Asian Affairs 2009*, p. 41.
80 *Ibid.*
81 *Ibid.*, p. 42.
82 UNCTAD (n 32), p. 10.

operations to combat piracy in the region include: Operation Ocean Shield by NATO; Operation Atlanta by EU; and Combined Task Force 151 led by the U.S.

– Operation Ocean Shield

The NATO first deployed a maritime group in 2008 to conduct an anti-piracy operation off the coast of Somalia, with its principal aim of the protection of World Food Program (WFP) assistance shipments in the region. In August 2009, NATO replaced the operation with a new anti-piracy mission, called 'Operation Ocean Shield.' While participating in capacity-building efforts with regional countries, three to five naval ships on a daily basis patrolled the high-risk areas, and these efforts have made a great contribution to suppressing piracy in the region. As piracy attacks off the coast of Somalia greatly diminished, the NATO decided to terminate the mandate for Operation Ocean Shield in December 2016.

– Operation Atlanta

In December 2008, the EU launched EU NAVFOR 'Operation Atlanta,' its first naval operation under the framework of the European Security and Defense Policy.[83] Operation Atlanta, involving approximately 1,200 personnel, four to six ships and two to three aircraft, has been tasked with providing protection for World Food Programme vessels and merchant vessels in the south of the Red Sea, the Gulf of Aden and the Indian Ocean.

For this purpose, it is authorized to employ the necessary measures, including the use of force, to deter, prevent and intervene in order to bring an end to acts of piracy and armed robbery.[84] In May 2012, the aircraft of EU NAVFOR for the first time attacked a land base of pirates in Harardhere, Somalia. In November 2016, the EU extended the mandate for EU NAVFOR to December 2018.

– CTF 151

Combined Task Force (CTF) 151 is one of three task forces operated by Combined Maritime Forces (CMF), which is a multi-national naval partnership composed of 31 member states. CMF is commanded by the U.S. Naval Forces Central Command, which covers the Arabian Gulf, the Red Sea, the Gulf of Oman and parts of the Indian Ocean. CTF 151, established in January 2009 and replacing CTF 150, is tasked with counter-piracy missions in these regions under the authority of UN Security Council's Resolutions 1816, 1838, 1846, 1851 and 1897. CTF 151 is a multinational force commanded in rotation by participating countries on an approximately three-to-six-month basis.

The force flow in CTF 151 is constantly changing, as ships and aircraft from a variety of countries assign vessels, aircraft and personnel to the task

83 U.S. Congressional Research Service, 'Piracy off the Horn of Africa,' April 2007, p. 27.

84 *Ibid.*

force.[85] CTF 151, in conjunction with other counter-piracy operations from NATO and the EU, carries out counter-piracy missions, including patrols and escorts of merchant vessels transiting the Internationally Recommended Corridor in the Gulf of Aden.[86] CTF 151 has played an essential role in combating piracy off Somalia and the Gulf of Aden.

West Africa

Of various counter-piracy efforts in West Africa, the establishment of a sub-regional Integrated Coast Guard Network (ICGN) has been underway. In the absence of a sub-regional agreement on the right of hot-pursuit across national maritime boundaries, sub-regional countries lack an effective means to pursue and interdict pirates and armed robbers. Against this backdrop, the Maritime Organization for West and Central Africa (MOWCA), with the support of the IMO, developed a Memorandum of Understanding on the Establishment of a Sub-regional ICGN in West and Central Africa, which was adopted in Senegal in July 2008.

The planned ICGN would enable sub-regional countries to collectively respond to unlawful acts at sea, addressing legal challenges in combating pirates. The planned ICGN divides the sub-region into four Coastguard Zones, in which not more than five coastal member states are in a coastguard zone in order to ensure more effective zone coordination. As of 2017, it has been signed by 15 of its 20 coastal member states.

In June 2013, 25 West and Central African countries adopted the Yaounde′ Code of Conduct, developed with technical support from the IMO. The primary objective is to manage and considerably reduce the adverse impacts of piracy, armed robbery against ships and other illicit maritime activities.

The Shipping Industry

The private sector and shipping industry have struggled to cope with the threat of piracy in various ways. With a growing piracy threat off the coast of Somalia, some vessels opted to circumnavigate south of the Cape of Good Hope, rather than risk piracy attacks in the Gulf of Aden while transiting the Suez Canal. Ships are recommended to operate at speeds above 15 knots when transiting high-risk areas. The shipping industry has developed a spate of counter-piracy measures and best practices and employed a variety of security equipment to prevent and abort pirates' attacks.

---

85 Combined Maritime Forces, 'CTF 151: Counter Piracy,' available at https://combinedmaritimeforces.com/ctf-151-counter-piracy/.

86 *Ibid.*

1 Security Equipment

- Radar and GPS: A ship's radar is used to track nearby ships for contact avoidance. Global positioning systems (GPS) allow the shipowner to monitor their ships and to be notified when the ship is in danger.
- Alarms: Sounding the ship's alarms/whistles serves to inform the ship's crew that a piracy attack has commenced and demonstrates to any potential attackers that the ship is aware of the attack and is reacting to it.[87]
- Sonic weapons: A sonic weapon, which blasts earsplitting noise, is used to ward off the attackers. The sonic device was developed by the U.S. Navy in the wake of the terrorist attack on the *USS Cole* in Yemen in 2000 as a way to keep operations of small boats from approaching warships.
- Electric fences: Electric fences are installed onboard ships as an anti-piracy defense mechanism. Attackers are shocked with a non-lethal electric shock of 9,000 volts.
- Razor wires: Known as barbed tapes, razor wires are installed to prevent attackers from boarding a ship by using barbs with piercing effects.
- Water cannons and fire hoses: Water cannons are designed to deliver water in a vertical sweeping arc, thus protecting greater part of the hull. The water from high-pressure fire hoses is used to repel small boats and boarding pirates. The U.S. Navy has used high-pressure fire hoses to deter unauthorized boarders in port and at sea.[88]
- Citadels: A citadel refers to a room where the crew of the ship can hide in case there is a pirate attack on the ship or when the pirates are aboard the ship. The use of citadels has proven to be a successful mechanism for avoiding capture in several cases. However, there are several aspects that need to be noted about using a citadel as anti-piracy method.[89]

The citadel requires having not just food and water supplies but also effective communication channels to be able to communicate with the outside world, along with a proper system of ventilation and a first aid kit. The room can be fitted with CCTV cameras and should have controls for switching off both main and auxiliary engines. The citadel needs to be properly planned and constructed, given that it is a last attempt of crews to escape from the pirates.

87 'Best Management Practices for Protection against Somalia based Piracy' (n 72).

88 Wayne K. Talley & Ethan M. Rule, 'Piracy in Shipping,' in *Maritime Safety, Security and Piracy* (Infoma: London, 2008), p. 96.

89 Sharda, 'What is "Citadel" Anti-Piracy Method?' *Marine Insight*, July 21, 2016.

2 Carriage and Use of Firearms

In response to the growing violence of pirate attacks, some assert that crews need to be armed for self-protection. However, the shipping community and the international community are opposed to the argument, largely due to a concern that it may lead to an escalation of violence and incur tremendous costs as well.

Recognizing such concerns, the IMO advises that the carriage and use of firearms by crews for protection of personnel or ship is strongly discouraged.[90] It is also concerned that the carriage of arms on board may encourage attackers to carry firearms, thereby escalating an already dangerous situation, and that any firearms on board may themselves become an attractive target for an attacker.[91]

Another concern is that the use of firearms requires special training and proficiency, and thus the risk of accidents with the use of firearms by under-trained crews would be great. In this connection, a worrisome scenario is that if crews equipped with firearms are unable to repel pirate attacks, this may lead to serious casualties in retaliation, such as kidnapping and killing.

There is also fear that an exchange of fire between the crews on board a ship carrying chemicals, oil or other flammable substances with pirates who are themselves heavily armed with automatic rifles and rocket propelled grenade (PRC) launchers could inflict disastrous casualties. By all accounts, the carriage and use of firearms by crews as a way of self-protection against piracy attacks is discouraged in the shipping community.

3 Privately Contracted Armed Security Personnel

With the increased threat to shipping, shipowners employ Privately Contracted Armed Security Personnel (PCASP) to protect vessels, cargo and crews against piracy attacks. The employment of PCASP appears to be quite effective in preventing and suppressing pirate attacks, given that Somali pirates tend to avoid attempts to attack a ship when PCASP is verified on board the ship. In the absence of applicable international regulations to govern the employment of PCASP on board ships, the positions and policies of states vary significantly.

Some coastal states that are highly affected by piracy, including Oman, Djibouti, Durban and Sri Lanka, allow ship owners to employ PCASP on board ships.[92] It is believed that the increased presence of PCASP has contributed to

90 IMO, 'Guidance to Shipowners and Ship Operators, Shipmasters and Crews on Preventing and Suppressing Act of Piracy and Armed Robbery Against Ships' (MSC/Circ. 623/Rev. 3).

91 *Ibid.*

92 Suk Kyoon Kim, *The Oceans and Pirates (in Korean)*, (Ocean & Ocean: Seoul, 2014), pp. 496–501.

a significant drop in Somali piracy. There are reportedly over 140 companies providing armed protection to vessels, employing a minimum of 2,700 armed guards.[93] The proportion of ships employing PCASP has sharply increased in recent years, rising from 20 percent in 2011 to 50 percent in 2012.[94]

While not endorsing the use of armed guards, the IMO, which recognizes the growing number of Private Maritime Security Companies (PMSC) and PCASP, as well as the need for international standards to govern them, has issued a number of recommendations in the form of Maritime Safety Committee (MSC) circulations.

The list of circulations includes: (i) Revised Interim Guidance to Shipowners, Ship Operators and Shipmasters on the Use of Privately Contracted Armed Security Personnel on Board Ships in the High Risk Area (MSC. 1/Circ. 1405/Rev.2); (ii) Revised Interim Recommendations for Flag States Regarding the Use of Privately Contracted Armed Security Personnel on Board Ships in the High Risk Area (MSC.1/Circ. 1406/Rev.2); (iii) Revised Interim Recommendations for Port and Coastal States Regarding the Use of Privately Contracted Armed Security Personnel on Board Ships in the High Risk Area (MSC. 1/Circ. 1408/Rev.1); (iv) Interim Guidance to Private Maritime Security Companies Providing Privately Contracted Armed Security Personnel on Board Ships in the High Risk Area (MSC. 1/Circ. 1443); and (v) Interim Guidance for Flag States on Measures to Prevent and Mitigate Somalia-Based Piracy (MSC.1/Circ. 1444).

In terms of the use of force, the IMO advises that force should be used only after PCASP takes all necessary steps to avoid the use of force. If force is used, it is advised that it should not exceed what is strictly necessary and reasonable under the circumstances.[95] Although the employment of PCASP on board ships serves as an effective counter-piracy measure, it gives rise to legal challenges in practice in terms of accountability and human rights violations.

A legal problem may concern who has to be held accountable about possible incidents where PCASP wrongly identifies innocent fishermen as pirates and kills the fishermen. These types of situation may give rise to complicated legal matters of accountability, human right violations, criminal jurisdiction as well as sovereign rights between flag state and victim state. The *Enrica Lexi*

93 Tondini, M., 'Some Legal and Non-Legal Reflection on the Use of Armed Protection Teams on Board Merchant Vessels: An Introduction to the Topic' (2012), 51(1), *Military Law and the Law of War Review*, pp. 7–19.

94 One Earth Foundation (n 50).

95 IMO, 'Revised Interim Guidance to Shipowners, Ship Operators and Shipmasters on the Use of Privately Contracted Armed Security Personnel on Board Ships in the High Risk Area' (MSC. 1/Circ. 1405/Rev.2), para. 5.14.

incident[96] may be a case in point, in which two Indian fishermen were allegedly killed by shots from an Italian oil tanker.

VII Efforts of East Asian Countries to Combat Piracy

Overview of Counter-Piracy Efforts

China, Japan and Korea, which are wholly dependent on sea lanes of communication for import-export commodities and energy transport, have been greatly endeavoring to secure the sea lanes of communication. Japan played a vital role in creating the Regional Cooperation Agreement on Combating Piracy and Armed Robbery against Ships in Asia (ReCAAP), which came into force in 2006. The three East Asian states, in line with UN resolutions calling for an international response, have been committed to the international counter-piracy operations off Somalia and the Gulf of Aden by deploying their naval vessels over the last decade.

The Korean government decided to send a naval unit, named *Cheonghae,*[97] to participate in international counter-piracy efforts and protect its vessels passing through the region. In March 2009, Korea deployed the *Cheonghae Unit* to these operations for the first time. The deployment consisted of one DDH-II destroyer of 4,000 tonnage class, with a crew of several hundreds that included a UDT team, along with a Lynx helicopter. The deployment, on rotation every six months, continues to maintain the initial level of force. The *Cheonghae Unit* conducts weekly convoys, largely for Korean-flagged vessels traveling through the Gulf of Aden, and participates in CTF-151 operations. As illustrated earlier, the Combined Task Force (CTF) 151 is one of three task forces operated by the Combined Maritime Forces (CMF), which is a multi-national naval partnership and composed of 31 member states.

---

96 On 15 February 2012, an Indian fishing boat, the *St. Antony,* engaged in fishing activity in India's Exclusive Economic Zone at a distance of about 20.5 nautical miles off the Indian coast at Kollam, Kerala, faced a volley of bullets fired from sophisticated automatic firearms from two uniformed persons on board an oil tanker ship. The Italian oil tanker the *MV Enrica Lexie* was about 200 meters away from the fishing boat operating in clear weather. Two fishermen on *St. Antony* were fatally hit by the bullets fired from the *Enrica Lexie,* and the lives of nine other fishermen on the boat were endangered due to the firing. India requested the exercise of criminal jurisdiction over two Italian marines from the Italian Navy who were believed to have fired at the fishing boat. The incident is pending at the Permanent Court of Arbitration.

97 The Naval Unit named after a naval base established by General Jang Bogo during the Silla dynasty to protect the kingdom's commercial ships and coastal population from pirates.

Despite these efforts, the Korean warship is able to escort only 13 percent of flagged ships that pass through the region. The most prominent accomplishment of the *Cheonghae Unit* was the successful Operation 'the Gulf of Aden Daybreak' in 2011, which was to suppress a piracy attack on the *Samho Jewelry*, a 10, 000 tonnage, Korean-owned tanker, and to rescue crew onboard the tanker seized in waters between India and Oman.

The rescue operation began on 15 January when 13 Somali pirates seized the *Samho Jewelry*. The following day, Korea's warship *Choi Yong*, the DDH-II on duty at the time, was sent to the area. As a rescue team — composed of 10 members of navy commando units aboard a speed boat — attempted to raid the *Samho Jewelry*, the pirates opened fire, wounding three of commandos and foiling the rescue attempt.

With the warship providing covering fire, the rescue team attacked and retook control of the ship in a five-hour operation that required them to move cabin by cabin to root out the pirates. The rescue operation freed the ship's crew of 21 with none of them killed and only the *Samho Jewelry's* captain wounded. Eight of the 13 Somali pirates onboard were killed in the operation; five were captured and brought to Korea for trial. The successful counter-piracy operation made a good accounting of itself. Of the pirates who were brought to trial in Korea, a pirate who had shot the captain was sentenced to life in prison and the other pirates were sentenced to 13 to 15 years of prison.

Japan has deployed two Japan Maritime Self-Defense Force destroyers with Japan Coast Guard law enforcement officers onboard since 2009. As of June 2015, the deployed unit has escorted 3,577 ships in 621 escort missions.[98] Japan has also been deploying two P-3C maritime patrol aircraft to the Gulf of Aden. Japan observes that although a marked reduction has been seen in the number of piracy attacks and hijackings in the region since 2012, the underlying causes of piracy remain in place and the current decline is inherently reversible.[99] In line with such a prospect, Japan is committed to continuing with its efforts to ensure maritime security and to work together with international partners in order to improve stability in Somalia and build law enforcement capacity in its neighboring countries.[100]

In 2008, China also decided to join the international counter-piracy operation in the Gulf of Aden, spurred by a sharp increase in piracy attacks against its vessels traveling in the region. A fifth of 1,265 Chinese-owned, -cargoed, or

98 Ministry of Foreign Affairs of Japan, 'Japan's Actions against Piracy off the Coast of Somalia.'

99 *Ibid.*

100 *Ibid.*

-crewed ships transiting Somali waters in 2008 underwent piracy threats, of which seven were attacked.[101] The People's Liberation Army Navy (PLNA) unilaterally deployed an escort task force (ETF), composed of three ships (two combat ships and one oiler). This marked China's biggest naval expedition outside the Pacific region since the 15th century when Zheng He made expeditionary voyages to South Asia and East Africa from 1405 to 1433.

Additionally, the PLNA deployed Z-9C helicopters to the ETF, which provided better situational awareness and were better suited to special operations forces in counter-piracy operations. Despite improved cooperation with the other task forces, the Chinese ETF never participated in any coalition. This is attributable to two factors[102]: (i) China's desire to be able to alter operations without needing to involve the other members of a coalition; and (ii) China's intention to avoid exposing its capabilities to an uncomfortable degree. However, the PLNA's increasing participation in the coordinated operation, called Shared Awareness and Deconfliction (SHADE), and improved cooperation with the other navies demonstrated the Chinese wish to be seen as a responsible stakeholder vis-à-vis piracy.[103]

The PLNA remained cautious and never changed its restrictions on armed rescue, prisoners, or searches for captured vessels. Nonetheless, the PLNA was escorting any kind of merchant vessels without considering the nature of her flag.[104] Furthermore, it was cooperating with the other navies in the region through the SHADE or by VHF. Since January 2012, the PLNA has started to coordinate its actions in the region with other navies.[105]

National Anti-Piracy Legislations

1 Korea

Acts of piracy are punishable under the Criminal Act and the Punishment for Damaging Ships and Maritime Structures Act (hereinafter "Punishment for Damage Act"). Acts of piracy are also punishable under the Criminal Act as maritime robbery, which is defined in Article 340 as: "the forcible seizure of a ship or another's property after intruding upon a ship through the threat of collective force on the sea;" and "causing injury, killing or raping." At the same time, more broadly defined acts of piracy, that threaten Korean vessels or the safety

101 S. A. Erickson, *Chinese Sea Power in Action*, cited in Jerome Henry, 'China's Military Deployments in the Gulf of Aden: Anti-Piracy and Beyond,' Center for Asian Studies.

102 S. A. Erickson, *No Substitute for Experience*, cited in Jerome Henry (n 101).

103 B. Barton, "The EU's Engagement of China in the Indian Ocean," The RUSI Journal 158, no. 6, 2013, cited in Jerome Henry (n 101).

104 Henry (n 101).

105 Erickson (n 102).

of maritime infrastructure on the continental shelf outside the jurisdiction of Korea, are punishable under the Punishment for Damage Act.

Because Korea does not have separate regulations punishing acts of piracy like in the U.S. or Japan, some legal challenges arose in instituting proceedings against the *Samho Jewelry* pirates. There was a need to strengthen the legal grounds for the anti-piracy activities of the navy in the Gulf of Aden. To be more specific, under Korea's legal systems, there is a potential for confusion in dealing with piracy. This is largely because the Criminal Act's definition of maritime robbery is muddled, and also because there is a gap between that definition and the definition of piracy under the UNCLOS. The issues that arise from the differing components constituting the act of piracy under the UNCLOS and maritime robbery under the Criminal Act are as follows:

- The UNCLOS limits the purpose of piracy to "private ends," while no such restrictions exist under the Criminal Act;
- Acts of piracy under the UNCLOS must meet the two-ship rule where one pirate ship commits an act against another ship, while no such rule exists under the Criminal Act;
- The UNCLOS does not indicate whether the act of piracy must be committed by more than one person; thus, it appears that even an act by a single person can meet the requirement of being piracy. The Criminal Act, however, requires a "collective force," which may be difficult to establish in the case of an act committed by a single person;
- The UNCLOS includes acts of voluntary participation or of inciting or intentionally facilitating piracy, while no such rule exists under the Criminal Act;
- While the UNCLOS defines the location as "on the high seas, or in any other place outside the jurisdiction of any state," the Criminal Act only states "in the sea," thereby having no such limitation. While the UNCLOS limits act of piracy to the high seas and places beyond the jurisdiction of any state, the International Maritime Organization (IMO) describes crimes committed within the jurisdiction of a state as sea robbery, thereby differentiating the two.

As mentioned earlier, several issues were raised due to the gap between national and international law, as well as the limitations of the national justice system, in the process of bringing the *Samho Jewelry* pirates to justice. Although it was a Maltese-flagged vessel, there were no issues regarding Korea's exercise of jurisdiction pursuant to the universal jurisdiction provision of UNCLOS Article 105.[106]

106 UNCLOS Art. 105 states, "…[E]very State may seize a pirate ship or aircraft, or a ship or aircraft taken by piracy and under the control of pirates, and arrest the persons and seize the property on board. The courts of the State which carried out the seizure may decide upon the penalties to be imposed …"

Rather, in the process of the trial, the legality was questioned regarding: (i) the arrest and transfer of the pirates by the Korean Navy; (ii) request for the warrant after the arrest and transfer; and (iii) the assistance of legal counsel.

More specifically, first, with regard to the arrest of the pirates by the Korean Navy, the Criminal Procedure Act, Article 213 (Delivery of Arrested Flagrant Offender) was an issue that was raised. It provides in Paragraph 1 that "In cases where a person other than a public prosecutor or judicial police officer arrests a flagrant offender, he shall immediately hand over the offender to a public prosecutor or judicial police officer." In the application of this provision, there were many arguments as to whether the nine days it took for the pirates to be handed over by navy officers — who were not judicial police officers — to the Korea Coast Guard officers could be qualified as being "immediate."

Regarding this issue, the Busan District Court, recognizing certain circumstances such as the refusal of neighboring states to receive the pirates and the difficulty in finding flights for their transfer, held that "the nine days it took for the *Cheonghae Unit* to bring the defendants to Korea was inevitable due to spatial and material limitations" and therefore falls within the definition of "immediately."[107]

The second issue raised was whether a warrant was requested within the time period provided in Criminal Procedure Act, Art. 203-2(5), stating that where a flagrant offender arrested is sought to be detained, a warrant of detention must be requested within 48 hours. On this point, the Busan District Court cited Art. 200–2(5) in holding that while the provision applies to situations in which a public prosecutor or judicial police officer arrests a flagrant offender, and in special cases where the transfer to the judicial institution following the arrest exceeds 48 hours as was in this case, it would be proper to view the above 48 hours as starting when the judicial institution receives the flagrant offender.[108] The third issue raised was the point at which the suspects should have received legal assistance. The Busan District Court held that the moment of receipt of the flagrant offender by a judicial institution is when the right to legal counsel should be guaranteed.[109]

While decisions of the court regarding the above points appears to be generally reasonable, some argue that it is not proper to equate the arrests made by the navy operating in Somali waters with those of "private individuals," given that the arrest of pirates is an exercise of public power, premised on criminal punishment. The application of the "immediacy" provision to pirates may

107 2011 Go-Hap 93 Pangyeolmun [Verdict] (Busan Dist. Ct. 2011).

108 *Id.*

109 *Id.*

need to be modified, considering potential factors that might lead to a delay, such as the political situation of adjacent states, bad weather conditions, the arrest of other pirates afterwards and so on.[110] On the other hand, some claim that further breaking down the legal provisions is undesirable because the arrest and treatment of suspects are inevitably unpredictable and inconsistent, as they are premised on military operations against heavily armed pirates.

In the future, the possibility of further arrest and transfer of pirates to the country cannot be ruled out and the same issues raised in the *Samho Jewelry* piracy case could resurface. In order to address the legal problems described above, the following options are suggested: (i) amendments to the relevant provisions of the Criminal Act, Criminal Procedure Act, Punishment for Damaging Ships and Maritime Structures Act, etc.; (ii) enactment of namely 'the Special Act regarding Judicial Actions in the Anti-piracy Operations of the Navy in the Somali Waters' to facilitate judicial proceedings of pirates seized by the navy; and (iii) enactment of a separate regulation regarding counter-piracy

As recently as December 2016, Korea enacted legislation known as the Prevention of Piracy Damages to Vessels engaged on International Voyages Act (hereinafter "Piracy Damage Prevention Act"), to ensure the safety of vessels engaged on international voyages and maritime installations from piracy threats and to prevent damages thereof. The Act, which has not addressed the problems arising from legal proceedings of pirates, as discussed above, is aimed at providing preventive measures that the government and the shipping industry must employ.

The principal provisions are outlined: (i) shipowners are required to submit a Piracy Prevention Plan to the Minister of Oceans and Fisheries[111]; (ii) shipowners are required to install a citadel on ships engaged on international voyages[112]; (iii) ships engaged on international voyages transiting the risk areas are allowed to employ privately contracted armed security guards (PCASP).[113]

The Act provides for standards and rules to be complied with when security guards use firearms against pirates: (i) the master and others have a final authority to allow the use of firearms; (ii) the use of firearms is permitted in the face of an imminent and inevitable situation where harm cannot be prevented otherwise; (iii) security guards are required to seek all reasonable means to avoid the use of firearms and should not use firearms except where crew

110 SOUTH REGIONAL HEADQUARTERS OF THE KOREA COAST GUARD, WHITE PAPER ON THE INVESTIGATION OF *SAMHO JEWELRY* PIRACY CASE 292 (2011).

111 Piracy Damage Prevention Act, Art. 9.

112 *Ibid.*, Art. 12.

113 *Ibid*, Arts. 15 – 28.; the risk areas are designated in the ordinances of the Act.

and security guards are lethally threatened; and (iv) where security guards use firearms, they should follow the procedures and comply with the principle of proportionality.

Separate legislation regarding the handling of pirates and their arrests, like in Japan, would balance out the piracy provisions in the UNCLOS and thus help settle the gap between national and international legal provisions. While it may also settle the limitations exposed in the capture and trial process of the pirates, the burden of enacting a new legislation still remains. Although the gravity of piracy issues raised the need for a separate counter-piracy legislation, the counterargument that the current legal system is sufficient for judicial action is also given much weight.

2 Japan

In the aftermath of the *Alondra Rainbow* incident in 1999,[114] Japan hosted an international anti-piracy conference in April 2004 in Tokyo for joint action against piracy and armed robbery, with representatives from 15 Asian states in attendance. At the conference, the 'Anti-Piracy Action Plan' and the 'Asia Anti-Piracy Challenge 2000' were adopted. Together with the Japanese Ministry of Land, Infrastructure, Transport and Tourism (MLIT), the Japan Coast Guard (JCG) took the lead in strengthening anti-piracy cooperation with the littoral states of Southeast Asia.

To this end, it also hosted an experts meeting with the coastal states surrounding the Malacca Strait in order to run cooperative programs for piracy information-sharing, vulnerable open waters patrol through the deployment of patrol boats and aircrafts, joint exercises and boarding training with port states, training of maritime security institutions and technology assistance for the enhancement of maritime enforcement capacities.

Prior to the enactment of the 'Act of Punishment and Countermeasures against Piracy' (海賊行爲の處罰及び海賊行爲への對處に關する法律) (hereinafter 'Punishment and Countermeasures against Piracy Act') in June 2009,

114 The *Alondra Rainbow*, a 7,762-ton Japanese cargo ship registered in Panama, departed from Kuala Tanjong of Sumatra, Indonesia, bound for Japan, on 22 October 1999 carrying aluminum ingots. It was hijacked by pirates armed with guns and knives. At the time, there were two Japanese — the captain and the chief engineer — and 15 Filipino crew members onboard. Following the initial attack, the 15 pirates moved the crew to the pirate ship and confined them for six days, after which they were set free on a life boat on October 29. After drifting on the seas for 11 days, they were discovered by a fishing boat near the coast of Phuket, Thailand and were safely rescued. On 16 November, the pirate ship was captured by the Indian Coast Guard and Navy while sailing in the high seas of southern India with all 15 of the Indonesian pirates captured.

Japan applied the provisions of the Penal Code to punish acts of piracy. However, after having deployed two Japan Maritime Self-Defense Force ships in March 2009 to the Somalia waters and the Gulf of Aden, Japan quickly enacted the above law to provide a legal basis for intervention in instances of damage to foreign vessels and harm to foreign nationals by pirates and to address the potential legal problems that could arise from law enforcement by its military in the region. Its major points are outlined as follows:

- The Act applies to "ships" regardless of nationality, thereby strengthening the legal basis for protection or other measures against piracy committed against foreign vessels. However, the scope of "ships" excludes warships and other government ships.
- In defining piracy, its purpose has been limited to "private ends," identical to that of the UNCLOS. As for location, while the UNCLOS limits it to the "high seas, or in any other place outside the jurisdiction of any state," the Act extends the scope of location not only to the high seas but to territorial and internal waters as well (Art. 2). The high seas were defined to include exclusive economic zones, thereby leaving no room for controversy regarding its scope.
- There are no provisions regarding acts of voluntary participation or of inciting or intentionally facilitating piracy, while there is a penalty clause for the crime of attempting piracy. Further, while the UNCLOS defines piracy as "any illegal acts of violence or detention, or any act of depredation … against another ship or aircraft, or against persons or property on board such ship or aircraft," the Punishment and Countermeasures against Piracy Act defines acts of piracy, in a specific yet broader manner, as: (i) seizing another ship in navigation or taking control of the operation of another ship by rendering persons irresistible by assault, intimidation or any other means; (ii) kidnapping a person on board another ship in navigation for the purpose of taking the person hostage for depredation; (iii) demanding any property, any other unobligated action or abstaining exercise of person's right while taking hostage; (iv) intruding into or damaging another ship in navigation; (v) obstructing sailing of a ship for the purpose of committing the act of piracy; and (vi) preparing weapons and operating a ship for the purpose (Art. 2, paras. 1 to 7).
- The JCG was designated as a lead agency responsible for counter-measures against piracy, though allowing the Self-Defense Force to take action when necessary, so that the relationship was clear among the agencies involved (Arts. 5 and 7). In other words, the JCG would normally be in charge of taking counter-measures against piracy; but in special circumstances where the JCG alone is not capable of responding to piracy as in cases of Somali piracy,

the Self-Defense Force may take measures necessary with the approval of the prime minister.

Where the Self-Defense Force takes counter-piracy measures, the Japan Coast Guard Law is applied to the execution of the duties of the Maritime Self-Defense officers at the rank of Petty Officer 3rd Class or higher, while relevant provisions of the JCG Law are applied *mutatis mutants* with regard to the use of weapons (Art. 8, paras. 1 to 3) in order to address potential legal issues that may arise in the process of responding to piracy by the Self-Defense Force having no law enforcement authority.

The Japan Coast Guard has eight international investigators, in six-month rotations, aboard two conveyors dispatched to Somali waters; and the JCG is also carrying out long-distance flight training on a yearly basis for the Middle East and European regions in preparation for the possible transfer of pirates.

In 2013, Japan enacted a national law permitting privately contracted armed security personnel (PCASP) aboard Japanese flagged vessels. The legislation is titled the 'Special Measures Act for the Security of Japanese Vessels in Pirate Infested Waters' (海賊多發海域における日本船舶の警備に關する特別措置法) (hereinafter 'Japanese Guarding Act'). Previously, Japanese-flagged vessels had been prevented from employing PCASP aboard in accordance with the Japanese Swords and Firearms Control Law of 1958. The orders of the Act prescribe: (i) embarking PCASP is allowed only for a Japanese-flagged tanker carrying crude oil and meeting certain requirements as set down in the ordinances. The requirements to qualify for armed security guard permission include: (i) an oil tanker must have a maximum speed no faster than 18 knots fully loaded, and have a freeboard of less than 16 meters; (ii) a ship must have a secure citadel where crew members can seek refuge and continue external communication in the event of an attack, along with primary preventative measures including a water discharging system and razor wire along exposed areas of the deck; (iii) shipowners must submit to the MLIT the Designated Guarding Plan for permission to employ PCASP aboard their vessel; (iv) the use of PCASP is allowed only within the designated high sea area in the Gulf of Aden and the Indian Ocean along with a passing area at Bab-el-Mandeb, the entrance to the Red Sea.

While priority areas are shifting to West Africa and the Malacca Strait from the Somali coast and the Gulf of Aden, the Japanese government accepted the correlation of increased use of PCASP with decreased pirate boarding in this region.[115]

115 Marex, 'Deciphering the Japanese Ship Guarding Act,' *Posidonia 2018*, July 2014.

3 China

As China and its vessels have been incurred much damage in Somali waters, it has engaged in the international efforts to fight piracy by deploying a fleet of two destroyers and a supplier; but China's national justice system regarding piracy is still very much lacking.

Under the Chinese judicial system, there are no provisions of law regarding "pirates (海盜)"; rather the punishment for acts of piracy are in accordance with Arts. 8, 9 and 263 of the Criminal Law of the People's Republic of China. Art. 8 states: "This Law may be applicable to any foreigner who commits a crime of not less than three years in prison outside the territory and territorial waters against People's Republic of China or any of its citizens"; while Art. 9 provides that "This Law shall be applicable to crimes which are stipulated in international treaties concluded or acceded to by the People's Republic of China and over which the People's Republic of China exercises criminal jurisdiction within the scope of obligations, prescribed in these treaties it agrees to comply." These two provisions form the basis for the exercise of criminal jurisdiction over acts of piracy committed against China or foreign ships in the waters outside Chinese jurisdiction.

While piracy is punishable as robbery (强劫罪) under Art. 263 of the Criminal Act, there are no specific provisions regulating robbery at sea. Among those listed under robbery, acts that may be applicable to pirates include: (i) those causing serious injuries or death while robbing (para. 5); (ii) those committing robbery using guns (para. 7); and (iii) those robbing materials for military use, or materials for fighting disasters or relieving disaster victims (para. 8).

4 Conclusion

As seen above, Japan has enacted separate counter-piracy legislation entitled 'Act of Punishment and Measures against Piracy' in order to provide the legal basis necessary for the activities of the Self-Defense Force to fight and handle pirates in foreign waters; but Korea and China punish acts of piracy pursuant to their Criminal Codes and other relevant laws.

Korea, Japan and China are parties to the UNCLOS and therefore do not have legal problems in exercising jurisdiction over pirate attacks against their own or foreign vessels in the Somali waters. However, as demonstrated in the *Samho Jewelry* case, procedural issues in the process of exercising jurisdiction remain yet to be settled in Korea. It has also been pointed out that under the current justice system relating to piracy in Korea and China, the legal basis for providing escorts to and intervening in foreign vessels is weak.

The possible solutions to these issues might include enacting special laws granting law enforcement authority to naval officers on duty in foreign waters, or enacting separate anti-piracy or other related laws to facilitate criminal procedures for bringing pirates to justice. This must be decided after having considered legislative concerns, such as the effectiveness of the existing piracy-related laws and the actual effect of new legislation, in a greater context within the judicial systems of the states concerned.

As for Korea, it is of the position that the legislative issues were already addressed by the Punishment for Damaging Ships and Marine Structures Act and thus does not require separate legislation. However, the legal problems raised while bringing the Somali pirates to justice have remained unsettled. In contrast, Japan addressed the problem of no judicial authority of navy officers on counter-piracy missions in Somali waters by applying *mutatis mutants* relevant provisions of the Japan Coast Guard Law. In addition, coast guard officers are aboard the warships in operation in the region to provide assistance in law enforcement against pirates.

Of particular note is that both Japan and Korea have enacted legislations permitting the employment of PCASP aboard their vessels transiting piracy-prone areas. Their moves appear to be in line with their recognition that the use of PCASP has contributed to the decrease in piracy attacks in Somali waters and the Gulf of Aden in recent years, as well as with a growing need for a greater role of the shipping industry for combating piracy. It appears that the Japanese government's intention is to minimize the scope of ships eligible for the employment of PCASP by limiting it only to Japanese-flagged oil tankers.

However, the provision does not appear to correspond with of the realities of piracy attacks, given that other types of cargo ship are also vulnerable. Japan allows the employment of PCASP in the risk areas designated by the MLIT, which covers the traditional risk areas of piracy, but it is not applicable to newly piracy-prone areas such the Malacca Strait and parts of the Southeast Asian seas. It is expected that the Japanese government will modify the specific geographic areas as needed to adapt to fluid operational and threat conditions.

Following the Japanese legislation, Korea also enacted a law permitting the employment of PCASP aboard its vessels transiting risk areas. A number of potential problems are envisaged with respect to the enforcement of the provisions of the Piracy Damage Prevention Act. A potential problem is that it is not explicit who is responsible for mis-use of firearms and who is the final decision-maker between the master and a person in charge of PCASP to use firearms. Furthermore, the requirements of the use of firearms are complicated and thus disputes with regard to the legality of their usage are likely.

VIII Conclusion

Contemporary piracy, called the 'scourge of the 21st century,' has had far-reaching and extensively negative effects on the shipping industry and sea-borne trade, and furthermore the safety and security of the sea. Recognizing the gravity of problems posed by piracy, the international community has engaged in combating it across the oceans.

By virtue of international anti-piracy efforts, overall the incidents of piracy have been in decline since the mid-2010s. Of particular note is that the situations off the coast of Somalia and the Gulf of Aden appear to be under control, as demonstrated by a sharp decline in piracy occurrences in recent years in that region. The reduction is attributable to persistent and concerted counter-piracy efforts at the global, regional and shipping-industry level.

However, it is too early to state that the piracy problem in that region is under control based solely on the figures of recent piracy incidents. Rather, it remains to be seen whether such trends can be sustained or not, given that the underlying causes of piracy in that region, such as the attractive rewards of piracy, a poverty-stricken economy, a chaotic political situation and a lack of counter-piracy capacity of coastal states, have remained unsettled. As such, it is likely that piracy in that region would resurge if stakeholders retreat from the commitment of counter-piracy efforts or allow any chance for pirates to revive their efforts.

Contrary to the significant reduction in piracy attacks at the global level, Southeast Asia and West Africa have undergone an upsurge in recent years. In particular, piracy in Southeast Asia has seen an increase in incidents and a marked rise in the violence and sophistication of pirate activity. The typical Asian piracy, that is, cargo theft while ships are in ports, has tended to shift to hijacking and ransom demands. West Africa, especially in the Gulf of Guinea, has emerged as a piracy-prone region, with growing pirate efforts to hijack oil tankers and seize cargo aboard, or attack oil rigs to steal oil and equipment.

Lastly, some suggestions have been put forward to address the piracy issue. First, the activities of the stakeholders involved in various counter-piracy measures need to be further coordinated and organized in a concerted manner. Piracy is a complicated and multi-faceted problem that involves a wide range of factors. The problem cannot be addressed by only the efforts of governments. As such, governments, the shipping community, and other related civilian sectors need to share burdens in combating piracy together. Second, the international community needs to be more concerned with piracy problems in Southeast Asia and West Africa. At the global level, the UN and international organizations need to be more concerned with and enhance support for regional counter-piracy efforts. Third, the international community needs to formulate regulations to govern the increasing employment of armed security guards aboard ships. Fourth, the establishment of a regional integrated coast guard in South Asia needs to be considered for joint patrols, escorts and law enforcement in high-risk areas of piracy if the regional situation gets worse.

CHAPTER 6

ISPS Code and Port & Cargo Container Security

I Introduction

The 9/11 terrorist attacks dramatically affected the world of trade and shipping, serving as a wake-up call to maritime security. Shocked by the catastrophic attacks, the international maritime community, at the initiative of the International Maritime Organization (IMO), sought to address the mounting concern of maritime terrorism and as such engaged in devising a new target-focused maritime security framework. Ports and ships were charged to focus on improving maritime security. Given that ports are the place where international shipping interfaces with the production and delivery of goods, the disruption due to a terrorist attack would seriously hinder international trade. The unavailability or reduced capacity of a port could negatively affect other ports in the transport chain.[1]

Prior to the 9/11 attacks, there was an attempt in 1986 by the IMO to adopt a circular to improve security of ships both at port and at sea, but the recommendations contained therein were voluntary and were not at all widely adopted by the governments of operators. However, this situation was to be significantly redressed subsequent to the 9/11 terrorist attacks.[2] Against this backdrop, an initial and key outcome of international efforts to enhance port and ship security is the International Ship and Port Facility Code (ISPS Code), which requires the implementation of security policies, plans and procedures for ports and ships.

The global cargo supply chain offers terrorists many significant targets of opportunity. Of particular concern is the possible use of a supply chain or a maritime transportation conveyance to deliver weapons of mass destruction (WMD). Cargo containers are especially vulnerable to terrorist and criminal manipulation.[3] One of the most frequently envisioned scenarios is that of a container vessel laden with WMD exploding in a heavily populated port area or near a critical offshore infrastructure involving liquefied natural gas (LNG)

1 Natalie Klein, *Maritime Security and the Law of the Sea* (Oxford University Press, New York, 2011), p. 157.
2 *Ibid.*
3 Michael McNicholas, *Maritime Security: An Introduction* (Elsevier, Burlington, 2008), p. 90.

 DOI:10.1163/9789004389908_007

tankers or ships carrying flammable or hazardous and noxious substances (HNS).[4]

Apart from international efforts to enhance port and ship security, the United States has formulated a number of its own port and cargo container security policies. The newly adopted maritime security initiatives by the U.S since the 9/11 terrorist attacks include: (i) the Container Security Initiative (CSI); (ii) the Customs-Trade Partnership Against Terrorism (C-TPAT); (iii) the Secure Freight Initiative (SFI); and (iv) the 24-Hour Advance Manifest (24-Hour Rule). These initiatives, focused on preventive measures, have definitely had a significant impact on global trade and shipping because globally more than 80 percent of cargo transportation is shipped by sea, and the U.S. is the largest trading state in the world.

This chapter will examine global security measures concerning ports, ships and cargo containers, focusing on the ISPS Code and the U.S. cargo container security initiatives. Specifically, this chapter will explore the provisions of the ISPS Code from a legal perspective and the implementation of the U.S. cargo container security initiatives from a practical perspective.

II Adoption of the ISPS Code

Amendment to the 1974 SOLAS Convention

The ISPS Code was created as an amendment to the 1974 Safety of Life at Sea (SOLAS) Convention. The SOLAS Convention was first adopted in 1914 in response to the *Titanic* disaster,[5] the second version was adopted in 1929, with a third and fourth adopted in 1948 and 1960, respectively. The SOLAS Convention provides specific minimum standards for the construction, equipment and operation of ships, compatible with their safety. Flag states are responsible for ensuring that ships under their flag comply with its requirements, and a number

4 Suk Kyoon Kim, 'Maritime Security Initiatives in East Asia: Assessment and the Way Forward' (2011) 42(3), *Ocean Development and International Law*, p, 227, cited in U.S. Department of Homeland Security (DHS) and U.S. Department of Defense (DOD), *the National Strategy for Maritime Security*, September 2005, 2.

5 The sinking of *Titanic* occurred on the night of 14 April through to the morning of 15 April 1912 in the North Atlantic Ocean. *Titanic* was on a four-days' trip from Southampton, England to New York in the U.S. The largest passenger liner in service at the time, *Titanic* had an estimated 2,224 people on board when she collided with an iceberg. Her sinking resulted in the deaths of more than 1,500 people, which made it one of the deadliest peacetime maritime disasters in history.

of certificates are prescribed in the Convention to certify the implementation of the requirements.

The Convention was revised on numerous occasions onward, and the Diplomatic Conference on Maritime Security adopted a full revised version on 1 November 1974, which entered into force on 25 May 1980. The most prominent feature of the 1974 version is the adoption of the tacit acceptance procedure, which provides that an amendment shall enter into force on a specific date, unless before that date objections to the amendment are received from an agreed-upon number of state parties.[6] As a result, the 1974 Convention has been updated and amended on numerous occasions, and the Convention in force today is referred to as SOLAS 1974, as amended.[7]

Following the tragic events of the 9/11 terrorist attacks, the 22nd session of the Assembly of the IMO in November 2001 unanimously agreed to the development of new measures relating to the security of ships and port facilities for adoption by the Conference of the Contracting Governments to the 1974 SOLAS Convention (known as the Diplomatic Conference on Maritime Security). Preparations for the diplomatic conference were entrusted to the IMO's Maritime Security Committee (MSC) on the basis of submissions made by member states, intergovernmental organizations and non-governmental organizations in consultative status with the IMO.[8] Through these processes, the diplomatic conference finally adopted amendments to the existing provisions of the 1974 SOLAS Convention, accelerating the implementation of the requirement to fit Automatic Identification Systems (AIS).

Most importantly, the amendment adopted new regulations in Chapter XI-1 under the title of "Special Measures to Enhance Maritime Safety." The chapter covers the marking of the ship's identification number, port state control on operational requirements, and the carriage of a continuous synopsis record.[9] The existing Chapter XI was amended and re-identified as Chapter XI-1, and a new Chapter XI-2 was adopted on special measures to enhance maritime security under the title of "Special Measures to Enhance Maritime Security." Regulation 3 of Chapter XI-2 enshrines the ISPS Code.

The ISPS Code

The ISPS Code, which stands for the International Code for the Security of Ships and of Port Facilities, is a comprehensive set of measures to enhance

6 IMO, 'International Convention for the Safety of Life at Sea (SOLAS), 1974.'
7 *Ibid.*
8 ISPS Code, Preamble, para. 2.
9 *Ibid.*,para. 3.

the security of ships and port facilities, developed in response to the perceived threats to ships and port facilities in the aftermath of the 9/11 terrorist attacks in the U.S. The Code consists of Part A, the provisions of which shall be treated as mandatory, and of Part B, the provisions of which shall be treated as recommendatory, as adopted on 12 December 2002, by Resolution 2 of the Conference of Contracting Governments to the 1974 SOLAS Convention.[10] The Code went into effect on 1 July 2004. Part A outlines detailed maritime and port security-related requirements to which contracting governments, port authorities, and shipping companies must adhere in order to be in compliance with the code. Part B provides a series of recommendatory guidelines on how to meet the requirements and obligations set out within the provisions of Part A.[11]

As illustrated earlier, the SOLAS Convention is designed to provide specific minimum standards for the construction, equipment and operation of ships to ensure the safety of navigation. The primary purpose of the ISPS Code is to identify and deter security threats to ships and ports and take preventive measures through an interface between ships and port personnel. The two Conventions do not align in terms of objectives, scope and application. Nevertheless, the rationale that the 1974 SOLAS Convention be extended to cover port facilities was fueled by:[12] (i) an urgent need to enhance port security after the 9/11 terrorist attacks and to create a new comprehensive mandatory security regime; (ii) a consideration that the 1974 SOLAS Convention offers the speediest means of ensuring the necessary security measures to enter into force quickly, by virtue of the tacit acceptance procedure.

It was agreed among the contracting states that the provisions of the ISPS Code should not extend to the actual response to attacks or to any necessary clean-up activities after such an attack.[13] In drafting, care has been taken to ensure compatibility with the provisions of the International Convention on Standards of Training, Certification and Watchkeeping and Certification for Seafarers (STCW), 1978, as amended, and the International Safety Management (ISM) Code and the harmonized system of survey and certification.[14]

The provisions of the ISPS Code represent a significant change in the approach of the international maritime industries to the issue of security in the maritime sector.[15] The implementation of the provisions requires continuing

10 1974 SOLAS Convention, XI-2/1.

11 IMO (n 6).

12 Suk Kyoon Kim, *Maritime Safety & Maritime Security (in Korean, translated by author)* (The Sea Garden, Seoul, 2016), p. 356.

13 ISPS Code, Preamble, para. 5.

14 *Ibid.*, para. 6.

15 *Ibid.*, para. 7.

effective cooperation and understanding between all those involved with, or using, ships and port management, as well as national and local authorities with security responsibilities.[16]

III Regulations of the ISPS Code

This section outlines the principal regulations of Part A of the ISPS Code.

Objectives

The objectives of the ISPS Code include[17]:
- to establish an international network involving cooperation between contracting governments, government agencies, local administrations and shipping and port industries to detect security threats and take preventive measures against security incidents affecting ships or port facilities used in international trade;
- to determine the respective roles and responsibilities of all parties concerned with safeguarding maritime security in ports and on board ships at the national, regional and international levels;
- to ensure the early and efficient collection and exchange of security-related information;
- to provide a methodology for security assessments so as to have in place plans and procedures to react to changing security levels; and
- to ensure confidence that adequate and proportionate maritime security measures are in place.

Definitions

The definitions of key terminologies are identified as follows[18]:
- *Ship Security Plan*: A plan developed to ensure the application of measures on board the ship designed to protect persons on board, cargo, cargo transport units, ship's stores or the ship from the risks of a security incident.
- *Port Facility Security Plan*: A plan developed to ensure the application of measures designed to protect the port facility and ships, persons, cargo, cargo transport unit and ship's stores within the port facility from the risks of a security incident.

---

16 *Ibid.*, para. 8.

17 ISPS Code, Part A, Art. 1.2.

18 *Ibid.*, Art. 2.1.

- *Ship Security Officer*: The person on board the ship, accountable to the master, designated by the company as responsible for the security of the ship, including implementation and maintenance of the ship security plan and for liaison with the company security officer and port facility security officers.
- *Company Security Officer*: The person designated by the company for ensuring that a ship security assessment is carried out; that a ship security plan is developed, submitted for approval, and thereafter implemented and maintained; and for liaison with port facility security officers and the ship security officer.
- *Port Facility Security Officer*: The person designated as responsible for the development, implementation, revision and maintenance of the port facility security plan and for liaison with the ship security officers and company security officers.
- *Security Level 1*: The level for which minimum appropriate protective security measures will be maintained at all times.
- *Security Level 2*: The level for which appropriate additional protective security measures will be maintained for a period of time as a result of heightened risk of a security incident.
- *Security Level 3*: The level for which further specific protective security measures will be maintained for a limited period of time when a security incident is probable or imminent, although it may not be possible to identify the specific target.

Application

The Code applies to the following types of ships engaged on international voyages[19]: (i) passenger ships, including high-speed passenger craft; (ii) cargo ships of 500 gross tonnage and upwards; (iii) mobile offshore drilling units. The Code also applies to port facilities serving ships engaged on international voyages.

The contracting governments are required to determine the extent of application of this part to the port facilities within their territory, which are primarily not used to serve the ships engaged on international voyages, but occasionally to serve ships engaged on international voyages.[20] This section makes it clear that the Code does not apply to warships, naval auxiliaries or other ships owned or operated by a contracting government and used only on government non-commercial service.[21]

19 *Ibid.*, Art. 3.1.
20 *Ibid.*, Art. 3.2.
21 *Ibid.*, Art. 3.3.

Responsibilities of Contracting Governments

Contracting governments are required to set security levels and provide guidance for protection from security incidents. Higher security levels indicate a greater likelihood of occurrence of a security incident. Factors to be considered in setting the appropriate security level include[22]:

- the degree that the threat information is credible;
- the degree that the threat information is corroborated;
- the degree that the threat information is specific or imminent; and
- the potential consequences of such a security incident.

Contracting governments may delegate to a recognized security organization certain of their security duties, with the exception of[23]:

- setting the security level;
- approving a port facility security assessment and its amendment;
- determining the port facilities that required the designation of a port facility security officer;
- approving a port facility security plan and its amendments;
- exercising control and compliance measures;
- establishing the requirements for a Declaration of Security.

Declaration of Security

Contracting governments are obliged to determine when a Declaration of Security is required by assessing the risk the ship/port interface or ship-to-ship activity poses to persons, property or the environment.[24] A ship can request completion of a Declaration of Security when[25]:

- the ship is operating at a higher security level that the port facility or another ship it is interfacing with;
- there is an agreement on a Declaration of Security between contracting governments covering certain international voyages or specific ships on those voyages;
- there has been a security threat or a security incident involving the ship or port facility, as applicable;
- the ship is at a port which is not required to have and implement an approved port security plan; or
- the ship is conducting ship-to-ship activities with another ship not required to have and implement an approved port facility or ship.

---

22 *Ibid*, Art. 4.1.

23 *Ibid.*, Art. 4.3.

24 *Ibid.*, Art. 5.1.

25 *Ibid.*, Art. 5.2.

Requests for the completion of a Declaration of Security will be acknowledged by the applicable facility or ship.[26] The Declaration of Security will be completed by the master or the ship security officer on the behalf of the ship(s), and if appropriate, the port facility security officer — or, if the contracting government determines otherwise, by any other body responsible for shore-side security on behalf of the port facility.[27] The Declaration of Security is required to address the security requirements that could be shared between a port facility and a ship (or between ships) and to state the responsibility for each,[28] and the minimum period for which the declarations shall be kept by the port facilities and by ships entitled to fly their flag.[29]

Obligations of the Company

The company is mandated to ensure that the ship security plan contains a clear statement emphasizing the master's authority. The company is required to establish in the ship security plan that the master has the overriding authority and responsibility to make decisions with respect to the safety and security of the ship and to request the assistance of company or of any contracting government as may be necessary.[30] The company is required to ensure that the company security officer, the master and the ship security officer are given the necessary support to fulfill their duties and responsibilities.[31]

Ship Security

A ship is required to act on the security levels set by contracting governments. At Security Level 1, the following activities will be carried out, through appropriated measures, on all ships in order to identify and take preventive measures against security incidents[32]:

- ensuring the performance of all ship security duties;
- controlling access to the ship;
- controlling the embarkation of persons and their effects;
- monitoring restricted areas to ensure that only authorized persons have access;
- monitoring of deck areas and areas surrounding the ship;

26 *Ibid.*, Art. 5.3.
27 *Ibid.*, Art. 5.4.
28 *Ibid.*, Art. 5.5.
29 *Ibid.*, Art. 5.7.
30 *Ibid.*, Art. 6.1.
31 *Ibid.*, Art. 6.2.
32 *Ibid.*, Art. 7.2.

- supervising the handling of cargo ship's stores; and
- ensuring that security communication is readily available.

At Security Level 2, the additional protective measures specified in the ship security plan will be implemented for each activity detailed at Security Level 1.[33] At Security Level 3, further specific protective measures specified in the ship security plan will be implemented for each activity detailed at Level 1.[34] Whenever Security Level 2 or 3 is set by the administration, the ship shall acknowledge the receipt of the instructions on the change of the security level.[35]

Prior to entering a port within the territory of a contracting government that has set Security Level 2 or 3, the ship shall acknowledge receipt of this instruction and confirm to the port facility security officer the initiation of the implementation of the appropriate measures. In the case of Security Level 3, the ship shall report any difficulties in implementation of compliance, and the port facility and ship security officer shall liaise and coordinate the appropriate actions.[36]

Ship Security Assessment

The ship security assessment is an essential and integral part of the process of developing and updating the ship security plan.[37] The company security officer is required to ensure that the ship security assessment is carried out by persons with appropriate skills to evaluate the security of a ship.[38] Subject to the provisions of Section 9.2.1, a recognized security organization may carry out the ship security assessment of a specific ship.[39] The ship security assessment shall include an on-scene security survey and, at minimum, include the following elements[40]:

- identification of existing security measures, procedures and operations;
- identification and evaluation of key ship-board operations and the likelihood of their occurrence, in order to establish and prioritize security measures; and
- identification of weaknesses, including human factors, in the infrastructure, policies and procedures.

---

33 *Ibid.*, Art. 7.3.
34 *Ibid.*, Art. 7.4.
35 *Ibid.*, Art. 7.5.
36 *Ibid.*, Art. 7.6.
37 *Ibid.*, Art. 8.1.
38 *Ibid.*, Art. 8.2.
39 *Ibid.*, Art. 8.3.
40 *Ibid.*, Art. 8.4.

Ship Security Plan

Each ship is required to carry on board a ship security plan approved by the administration. The plan shall make provisions for the three security levels. The administration may entrust the review and approval of ship security plans, or of amendments to a previously approved plan, to a recognized security organization.[41] But the recognized organization shall not have been involved in either the preparation of the ship security assessment or of the ship security plan, or the amendments, under review.[42] The plan will be written in the working languages of the ship. If the language is not English, French or Spanish, a translation into one of these languages will be included and the plan is required to address, at minimum, the following[43]:

- measures designed to prevent weapons, dangerous substances and devices intended for use against persons, ships or ports, the carriage of which is not authorized for being taken on board the ship;
- identification of restricted areas and measures for the prevention of unauthorized access to them;
- measures for the prevention of unauthorized accesses to the ship;
- procedures for responding to security threats or breaches of security, including provisions for maintaining critical operations of the ship or ship/port interface;
- procedures for responding to any security instructions contracting governments may give at Security Level 3;
- procedures for evacuation in case of security threats or breaches of security;
- duties of shipboard personnel assigned security responsibilities, as well as security aspects as they relate to other shipboard personnel;
- procedures for training, drills and exercise associated with the plan;
- procedures for interfacing with port facility security;
- procedures for the periodic review and updating of the plan;
- procedures for reporting security incidents;
- identification of the ship security officers;
- identification of the company security officer, including 24-hour contact details;
- procedures to ensure the inspection, testing, calibration and maintenance of any security equipment provided on board;
- frequency for testing or calibration of any security equipment provided on board;

41 *Ibid.*, Art. 9.2.
42 *Ibid.*, Art. 9.2.1.
43 *Ibid.*, Art. 9.4.

- identification of the locations where the ship security alert system aviation points are provided; and
- procedures, instructions and guidance on the use of the ship security alert system, including testing, activation, deactivation and resetting.

Records

The records of the following activities addressed in the ship security plan will be kept on board for at least the minimum period specified by the administration[44]:

- training, drills and exercises;
- security threats and security incidents;
- breaches of security;
- changes in security level;
- communications relating to the direct security of the ship or to port facilities where the ship has been;
- internal audits and reviews of security activities;
- periodic review of the ship security assessment;
- implementation of any amendments to the plan; and
- maintenance, calibration and testing of any security equipment provided on board including testing of the ship security alert system.

The records should be kept in the working language(s) of the ship, but if the language(s) used are not English, French or Spanish, translation into one of these languages must be included.[45] If the records are kept in an electronic format, they must be protected from unauthorized use or change of any kind.[46] All records must be protected from unauthorized access or disclosure.[47]

Company Security Officer

The company is required to designate a company security officer. A person designated as the company security officer may act as the company security officer for one or more ships, depending on the number of or types of ships the company operates. The duties and responsibilities of the company security officer include, but are not limited to[48]:

- advising on the level of threats likely to be encountered by the ship, using appropriate security assessments and other relevant information;

---

44 *Ibid.*, Art. 10.1.
45 *Ibid.*, Art. 10.2.
46 *Ibid.*, Art. 10.3.
47 *Ibid.*, Art. 10.4.
48 *Ibid.*, Art. 11.2.

- ensuring that ship security assessments are carried out;
- ensuring the development, submission for approval, implementation and maintenance of the ship security plan;
- ensuring that the ship security plan is modified to correct deficiencies and satisfy the security requirements of the individual ship;
- arranging for internal audits and reviews of security activities;
- arranging for the initial and subsequent verifications of the ship by the administration or the recognized security organization;
- ensuring that deficiencies and non-conformities identified during internal audits, periodic reviews, security inspections and verification of compliance are promptly addressed and dealt with;
- enhancing security awareness and vigilance;
- ensuring adequate training for personnel responsible for the security of the ship;
- ensuring effective communication and cooperation between the ship security officer and the relevant port facility security officers;
- ensuring consistency between security requirements and safety requirements;
- ensuring that, if sister-ship or fleet security plans are used, the plan for each ship reflects the ship-specific information accurately; and
- ensuring that any alternative or equivalent arrangements approved for a particular ship or group of ships are implemented and maintained

Ship Security Officer

A ship security officer should be designated on each ship. The duties and responsibilities of the ship security officer include, but are not limited to[49]:

- undertaking regular security inspections of the ship to ensure that appropriate security measures are maintained;
- maintaining and supervising the implementation of the ship security plan, including any amendments to the plan;
- coordinating the security aspects of handling of cargo and ship's stores with other shipboard personnel and with the relevant port facility security officers;
- proposing modification to the ship security plan;
- reporting to the company security officer any deficiencies and non-conformities identified during internal audits, periodic reviews, security inspections and verifications of compliance, and implementing any corrective actions;

49 *Ibid.*, Art. 12.2.

- ensuring that adequate training has been provided to shipboard personnel;
- reporting all security incidents;
- coordinating implementation of the ship security plan with the company security officer and the relevant port facility officer; and
- ensuring that security equipment is properly operated, tested, calibrated and maintained.

Port Facility Security

A port facility is required to act upon the security levels by the contracting government within whose territory it is located. Security measures and procedures will be applied at the port facility in such a manner as to cause a minimum of interference with, or delay to, passengers, ship, ship's personnel and visitors, goods and services.[50] At Security Level 1, the following measures will be carried out through appropriate measures in all port facilities in order to identify and take preventive measures against security incidents[51]:

- ensuring the performance of all port facility security duties;
- controlling access to the port facility;
- monitoring the port facility, including anchoring and berthing area(s);
- monitoring restricted areas to ensure that only authorized persons have access;
- supervising the handling of cargo;
- supervising the handling of ship's stores; and
- ensuring that security communication is readily available.

At Security Level 2, the additional protective measures specified in the port facility plan will be implemented for each activity detailed at Security Level 1.[52] At Security Level 3, further specific protective measures specified in the port facility security plan will be implemented for each activity detailed at Security Level 2.[53]

Port Facility Security Assessment

The port facility security assessment will be carried out by the contracting government within whose territory the port facility is located.[54] A contracting government may authorize a recognized security organization to carry out the port facility security assessment of a specific port facility. When the port

50 *Ibid.*, Art. 14.1.
51 *Ibid.*, Art. 14.2.
52 *Ibid.*, Art. 14.3.
53 *Ibid.*, Art. 14.4.
54 *Ibid.*, Art. 15.2.

facility security assessment has been carried out by a recognized security organization, the security assessment will be reviewed and approved for compliance with requirements by the contracting government.[55] The port facility security assessment shall include, at minimum, the following elements[56]:
- identification and elevation of important assets and infrastructure;
- identification of possible threats to the assets and infrastructure and the likelihood of their occurrence, in order to establish and prioritize security measures;
- identification, selection and prioritization of countermeasures and procedural changes and their level of effectiveness in reducing vulnerability; and
- identification of weaknesses, including human factors, in the infrastructure, policies and procedures.

Port Facility Security Plan

A port facility security plan will be developed and maintained for each port facility on the basis of a port facility security assessment. The plan shall make provisions for the three security levels.[57] The port facility security plan will be approved by the contracting government in whose territory the port facility is located. The plan will address, at minimum, the following[58]:
- measures designed to prevent weapons or any other dangerous substances and devices intended for use against persons, ships or ports, the carriage of which is not authorized in the port facility or on board a ship;
- measures designed to prevent unauthorized access to the port facility, to ships moored at the facility, and to restricted areas of the facility;
- procedures for responding to security threats or breaches of security, including provisions for maintaining crucial operations of the port facility or ship/port interface;
- procedures for responding to any security instructions the contracting government may give at Security Level 3;
- procedures for evacuation in case of security threats or breaches of security;
- duties of port facility personnel assigned security responsibilities and of other facility personnel on security aspects;
- procedures for interfacing with ship security activities;
- procedures for the periodic review and updating of the plan;
- procedures for reporting security incidents;

55 *Ibid.*, Art. 15.2.1.
56 *Ibid.*, Art. 15.5.
57 *Ibid.*, Art. 16.1.
58 *Ibid.*, Art. 16.3.

- identification of the port facility security officer, including 24-hour contact details;
- measures to ensure the security of the information detained in the plan;
- measures designed to ensure effective security of cargo and the cargo-handling equipment at the port facility;
- procedures for auditing the port facility security plan;
- procedures for facilitating shore leave for ship's personnel or personnel changes, as well as access of visitors to the ship, including representatives of seafarers' welfare and labor organizations.

Port Facility Security Officer

A port facility security officer shall be designated for each port facility. A person may be designated as the port facility security officer for one or more port facilities. The duties and responsibilities of the port facility officer include, but are not limited to[59]:

- conducting an initial comprehensive security survey of the port facility, taking into account the relevant port facility security assessment;
- ensuring the development and maintenance of the port facility security plan;
- implementing and exercising the port facility security plan;
- undertaking regular security inspections of the port facility to ensure the continuation of appropriate security measures;
- recommending and incorporating modifications to the port facility security plan in order to correct deficiencies and to update the plan to take into account relevant changes to the port facility;
- enhancing security awareness and vigilance of the port facility personnel;
- reporting to the relevant authorities and maintaining records of occurrences that threaten the security of the port facility;
- coordinating implementation of the port facility security plan with the appropriate company and ship security officer(s);
- coordinating with security services;
- ensuring that standards for personnel responsible for security of the port facility are met;
- ensuring that security equipment is properly operated, tested, calibrated and maintained, and;
- assisting ship security officers in confirming the identity of those seeking to board the ship when requested.

---

59 *Ibid.*, Art. 17.2.

Training, Drills and Exercises in the Port Facility Plan

The port facility security officer and appropriate port facility security personnel are required to have appropriate knowledge and training.[60] Port facility personnel with specific security duties are required to understand their duties and responsibilities for port facility security as described in the port facility security plan, and they are required to have the sufficient knowledge and ability to perform their assigned duties.[61]

To ensure the effective implementation of the port facility security plan, drills will be carried out at appropriate intervals, taking into account the types of operations of the port facility, port facility personnel changes, the types of ships the port facility is serving, and other relevant circumstances.[62] The port facility security officer is required to ensure the effective coordination and implementation of the port facility security plan by participating in exercises at appropriate intervals.[63]

Verification and Certification for Ships

Each ship is subject to verifications specified below[64]:

- an initial verification before the ship is put into service or before the certificate required is issued for the first time, which is to include a complete corroboration that its security system and any associated equipment as mentioned in the approved ship security plan is in place. This verification will ensure that the security system and any associated equipment fully comply with the requirements of the code and the ship security plan, and that they are in satisfactory condition.
- a renewal verification at intervals specified by the administration, but not exceeding five years. This verification will ensure that the security system and any associated security equipment fully comply with the applicable requirements of the code and the ship security plan, and that they are in satisfactory condition.
- at least one intermediate verification. If only one intermediate verification is carried out, it shall take place between the second and third anniversary date of the certificate. The intermediate verification shall include inspection of the security system and any associated security equipment of the ship to ensure that it remains satisfactory.

---

60 *Ibid.*, Art. 18.1.

61 *Ibid.*, Art. 18.2.

62 *Ibid.*, Art. 18.3.

63 *Ibid.*, Art. 18.4.

64 *Ibid.*, Art. 19.1.

The verifications of ships will be carried out by the officers of the administration, which may entrust the verifications to a recognized security organization.[65] The security system and any associated security equipment will be maintained to conform with the provisions of regulations XI-2/4.2 and XI-2/2/6 of the code and the ship security plan.[66] After verification, no changes will be made to the security system or in any associated security equipment, or in the approved ship security plan without the sanction of the administration.[67]

An Internal Ship Security Certificate is issued after the initial or renewal verification. Such a certificate is issued or endorsed either by the administration or by a recognized security organization acting on behalf of the administration.[68] Another contracting government may, at the request of the administration, cause the ship to be verified, and if satisfied that the provisions comply with this section, it shall issue a certificate to the ship. A certificate issued shall contain a statement to the effect that it has been issued at the request of the administration.[69] If the language used in the text of certificate is not in English, French or Spanish, the text will include a translation into one of these languages.[70]

Duration and Validity of Certificate

An International Ship Security Certificate shall be issued for a period specified by the administration which will not exceed five years. When the renewal verification is completed within three months before the expiry date of the existing certificate, the new certificate shall be valid from the date of completion of the renewal verification to a date not exceeding five years from the date of the expiry of the existing certificate.[71] A certificate becomes invalid in any of the following cases[72]:

- if the relevant verifications are not completed within the specified periods;
- if the certificate is not endorsed in accordance with specified procedures;
- when a company assumes the responsibility for the operation of a ship not previously operated by the company; and
- upon transfer of the ship to the flag of another state.

65 *Ibid.* Art. 19.1.2.
66 *Ibid.*, Art. 19.1.4.
67 *Ibid.*
68 *Ibid.*, Art. 19.2.3.
69 *Ibid.*, Art. 19.2.3.2.
70 *Ibid.*, Art. 19.2.4.
71 *Ibid.*, Art. 19.3.2.
72 *Ibid.*, Art. 19.3.8.

An Interim International Certificate is granted when all requirements are met for the purpose of:

- a ship without a certificate, on delivery or prior to its entry or reentry into service;
- transfer of a ship from the flag of a contracting government to the flag of another contracting government;
- transfer of a ship to the flag of a contracting government from a state which is not a contracting government; or
- when a company assumes the responsibility for the operation of a ship not previously operated by the company.

An Interim International Certificate will be valid for six months, or until the certificate required is issued, whichever comes first, and may not be extended.[73]

Conclusion

As examined above, the ISPS Code is a risk-assessment-based security framework to protect the security of ships and port facilities against threats such as terrorism, stowaways, piracy, smuggling and vandalism. The primary objective of the ISPS Code is to establish standard requirements for the maritime industry's efforts in taking preventive measures against potential security incidents that could affect ships or port facilities used in international trade.[74]

For this purpose, the Code requires vessels and port facilities to conduct security assessments, develop security plans and employ security officers responsible for the implementation of security plans. By adopting the ISPS Code, which standardizes the security requirements of ships and port facilities in a unified security framework, the international community has increased its ability to prevent maritime terrorism. For non-compliant ships, penalties such as serious delay or possible denial of entry to certain ports are likely to be imposed.

Nonetheless, as with other international treaties, compliance with the requirements of the ISPS Code fully rests upon state parties. Overall, it is believed that state parties have made efforts to adopt the requirements within their legislative systems by enacting laws and regulations, and to implement them by improving port security infrastructure, increasing security personnel and acquiring security equipment. For further consolidation of the ISPS Code as a national security framework, the requirements under the Code are needed to be incorporated into the national security strategies of state parties.

73 *Ibid.*, Art. 19.4.4.

74 McNicholas (n 3), p. 90.

Another challenge concerns how to fill the gap between developed and under-developed countries in terms of compliance with the code, which requires a large investment of expense and infrastructure.

IV Implementation of the ISPS Code of East Asian Countries

Korea

Following the full implementation of the ISPS Code, as of January 2011, 1,004 ships of Korean nationality obtained the security certificates, and 28 trade ports utilized by ships engaged on international voyages became the target of the ISPS Code. The Korean government in 2003 legislated and implemented the regulation regarding Security of Ships and Port Facilities in the form of a public notice of the Ministry of Oceans and Fisheries, due to time constraints until the amendment of the SOLAS Convention's entry into force.

Since the accommodation of the ISPS Code into a national legislation was a legislative matter which was directly related to the rights and duties of citizens, the legal basis of the public notice to implement such duties was considered inadequate. Thus, in August 2007, the legal grounds were strengthened by the enactment of the Security of Ships and Port Facilities Engaged on International Voyages Act.

The Act provides for: (i) setting of the security level of ships and port facilities engaged on international voyages (Arts. 5 & 6); (ii) designation of a general security officer and ship security officer by the owner of the ship engaged on international voyages (Arts. 7 & 8) and the acquisition of international ship security certificates (Arts. 11 & 12); (iii) port state control of foreign ships by the verification of international ship security certificates (Art. 19, para. 1); (iv) requirement to submit ship security information 24 hours prior to the entry of foreign ships into a port of the Republic of Korea and the related authority to limit movement, request modification, investigate ships or refuse their entry (Art. 19, paras. 4 & 6); (v) designation of a port security officer by the owner of the port facility and the implementation of a security evaluation (Arts. 23 & 24) and so on.

Japan

For the implementation of the ISPS Code, Japan enacted the Law regarding Security of International Voyage Ships and International Port Facilities (国際航海船舶及び国際港湾施設の保安の確保等に関する法律) in April 2004. Under the Law, security measures are required for ships on international voyages and in international port facilities, and the advance notification of ship security information must be transmitted when entering Japanese ports from abroad for control of ships that have a higher possibility of harming security.

The ordinances of the Law require ships on international voyages entering Japanese ports for the first time to notify the port security office of ship security information regarding 28 items, 24 hours prior to its entry (Arts. 74 & 75). Pursuant to the Japan Coast Guard Law (海上保安庁法) (Art. 2), the Japan Coast Guard is also responsible for tasks related to ship security information, maritime order, and crime prevention and suppression.

Japan also enacted the Act of Special Measures relating to the Prohibition of Entry of Designated Ships in June 2004 that would allow it to prohibit port entry of designated ships and ships from designated states in consideration of the international political situation surrounding Japan (特定船舶の入港の禁止に関する特別措置法). Designated ships include: (i) ships of designated foreign nationality as determined by the cabinet; (ii) ships having called at designated foreign ports during the period prohibited by the cabinet; and (iii) ships that have similar relationships with designated foreign states in terms of the above provisions (Art. 2). Such decisions of the cabinet regarding the above provisions must obtain approval from the parliament (Art. 5).

China

China also actively participated in the amendment of the SOLAS Convention. China, as a contracting party to the SOLAS Convention, enacted two laws in 2003 to implement the requirements under the amendments to the convention for ships and port security — the Port Facility Security Regulation and the International Ships Security Regulation, which came into force in November 2003 and April 2004, respectively.[75]

In China, there are 130 trade ports and about 10,000 port facilities. Maritime transport security is managed by the Maritime Transport Bureau under the Ministry of Communication. With regard to port security, pursuant to the reformed Port Management System as instituted by the Port Law amended in 2003 and implemented on 1 January 2004, port management authority was transferred to regional governments so that port authorities were no longer in charge of administrative functions.

75 Zhang Shoguo, Department of Water Transport, Ministry of Communication, China, 'Playing an Active Role in Fulfilling Maritime Security Obligations,' presented at OECD Workshop on Maritime Transport (Apr. 2004).

In other words, it transformed from a complex, dual port management system by the central and regional governments to a 'One Port-One Government (一港一政) system where a regional government took charge of the safety management of a port, thereby establishing a unified regional-government port management system (Art. 6).[76] Chapter 4 of the Port Law provides that the port operator and the port administration are in charge of the safety and security of the port. The Port Facility Security Regulation sets forth security level, security evaluation, education and training of security officers and so on. In order to effectively implement the law, China promulgated the International Ship Security Regulation and has taken other necessary measures such as notification of the port facility security fee and so on.[77]

Conclusion

After having passed a new resolution regarding ships and port facility security at the 22nd IMO general meeting in November 2001, the amendment to the existing SOLAS Convention was unanimously adopted at the 1974 SOLAS Convention Conference of Contracting States (Diplomatic Conference) in December 2002. The very fact that an amendment to an international convention was adopted within one year, and that the ISPS Code was fully implemented within a year and half, was very exceptional, given the need for various preparations necessary for national implementation such as the examination of relevant legislations, security evaluation, education and training and so on. It may be credited to a concerted effort of the international community taken upon recognition of the urgent need to strengthen the security of ships and port facilities in the wake of the 9/11 terrorist attacks.

China and Japan enacted national laws to provide legislative support for the national implementation of the ISPS Code prior to the code's entry into force. Korea, however, as observed earlier, did not have legislative support within the limited time period prior to the implementation of the ISPS Code and thus had to enact a public notice at the ministerial level. Continued controversies that a ministerial notice provided insufficient legal grounds for the national implementation of the ISPS Code led to the enactment of the Security of Ships and Port Facilities Engaged on International Voyages Act in 2007.

76 See Jae Ho Yoon, ZhengHui Chen, Myong Sop Pak, 'A Study on the Development of Chinese Port System and the Improvement of China's Port Law,' 35 J. *KOREA TRADE* 290–96 (June 2010).

77 Jae sun choi, 'STUDY ON THE ESTABLISHMENT OF STATE LOGISTICS SECURITY SYSTEM,' 141–42 (Korea Maritime Institute 2006).

The ship and company security system provided by the ISPS Code, in some aspects, overlaps with the International Safety Management Code (ISM Code)[78] that has been in effect since 1 July 1998 for maritime safety, accident prevention and environmental protection, and can thus add to the burden of shipping companies. Furthermore, given that there is no legal framework that supports the container security measures in place, a legal basis through enactment or amendment of relevant regulations needs to be provided.

V U.S. Maritime Security Legislations

Introduction

As stated earlier, the 9/11 terrorist attacks have changed the paradigm of security in the world. In response to an imminent threat that the cargo supply chain is highly likely to be a target of massive terrorism or used as an instrument of terrorism, the international community, driven by the United States, rushed to the development of maritime security measures. Along with the international requirements of the ISPS Code, the United States has implemented its own domestic maritime security measures in accordance with the Maritime Transportation Security Act (MTSA), which provides for a baseline of security for U.S. ports.

Furthermore, the U.S., concerned about the vulnerability of containerized cargo exported and imported through ports, has developed security measures for overseas trade. The new security framework, outlined as a 'layered security approach,' focuses on the security of cargo containers transported from foreign seaports. The layered security approach employs different security measures that ensure there are protective measures in place from one end of a sea-based journey to the other.[79]

The layered security measures are designed to protect the three phases of the journey of cargo containers: (i) overseas; (ii) in transit; and (iii) in U.S. waters and on U.S. shores. The security measures overseas, enacted in the Security and Accountability for Every Port Act of 2006[80] (SAFE Port Act), include: (i)

78 The IMO primarily focused on improving the structure and installations of the ships themselves as well as the crew qualifications for the safe navigation of ships and the protection of the marine environment. However, after having realized that the majority of accidents on the seas were caused not by vessel defects but rather human error, it established the International Safety Management Code (ISM Code). Korea amended its Maritime Traffic Safety Act in February 1999 to provide for the relevant matters in Articles 10 and 21.

79 U.S. Department of Homeland Security, 'Secure Seas, Open Ports: Keeping Our Waters safe, Secure and Open for Business,' 21 June 2004.

80 Security and Accountability for Every Port Act of 2006, U.S. Public Law 109–347.

the 24-Hour Advance Manifest; (ii) Container Security Initiative (CSI); (iii) Customs-Trade Partnership Against Terrorism; (iv) the ISPS Code; (v) International Port Security Program; and (vi) Operation Safe Commerce.

The set of U.S. maritime security measures in the cargo supply chain has inevitably had a significant impact on the security policies of its foreign trading partners and by extension the world commerce generally, given that the U.S. is the largest trading state and a leading country in fighting terrorism. This section outlines a number of major U.S. security measures prescribed in the MTSA and within the layered security approach.

The Maritime Transport Security Act of 2002

As an integral part of measures to enhance security for ports and the cargo supply chain in the aftermath of 9/11, the U.S. enacted the Maritime Transport Security Act (MTSA) 2002, amending the Merchant Marine Act 1936 to newly establish security programs and implement the ISPS Code.[81] Recognizing that 361 public ports in the U.S. are an integral part of its economy (they handle over 95 percent of U.S. overseas trade; the top 50 ports account for about 90 percent of all the cargo carriage; ports are a major locus of grave crimes and are vulnerable to terrorism),[82] the MTSA sets forth maritime security measures for U.S seaports. The primary security programs set forth in the MTSA include:

- *Port and Vessel Vulnerability Assessment*: A detailed vulnerability assessment conducted by the secretary of the Department of Homeland Security (DHS) must include: identification and evaluation of critical assets and infrastructures; identification and evaluation of those assets and infrastructures; and identification of weaknesses in physical security, passenger and cargo security, structural integrity, protections systems, etc.[83]
- *Maritime Transportation Security Plan*: The secretary of DHS is required to prepare a National Maritime Transportation Security Plan for deterring and responding to a transportation security incident. The plan is intended to provide efficient, coordinated and effective action to deter and minimize damage from a transportation security incident.[84]
- *Transportation Security Card*: An individual entering an area of a vessel or facility that is designated as a secure area is required to hold a biometric transportation security card issued by the secretary.[85]

81 Maritime Transport Security Act, U.S. Public Law 107–295.
82 *Ibid.*
83 *Ibid.*, §70102.
84 *Ibid.*, §70103.
85 *Ibid.*, §70105.

- *Foreign Port Assessment*: The secretary is required to assess the effectiveness of the antiterrorism measures maintained at a foreign port from which foreign vessels depart on voyages to the U.S., and any other foreign port that poses a security risk to international commerce.[86]
- *Actions When Foreign Ports Do Not Maintain Effective Antiterrorism Measures*: If a foreign port is found to be not maintaining effective antiterrorism measures, the secretary may prescribe conditions of entry into the U.S. for any vessel arriving from that port, or any vessel carrying cargo or passengers originating from or transported through that port.[87]
- *Enhanced Crewmember Identification*: Foreign crewmembers on vessels calling at U.S. ports are required to carry and present any identification on demand.[88]
- *Automatic Identification System (AIS)*: Commercial vessels over 65 feet in length are required to install the AIS.[89]
- *Long-Range Vessel-Tracking System*: The secretary may implement a long-range automated vessel tracking system for all vessels in U.S. waters that are equipped with the Global Maritime Distress and Safety System.[90]
- *U.S. Coast Guard Sea Marshall Program*: The Ports and Waterways Safety Act (33 U.S.C. 1226(b)) is amended to dispatch armed coast guard personnel on vessels and public or commercial structures or adjacent to waters under U.S. jurisdiction to deter or respond to acts of terrorism or transportation security incidents.[91]
- *Maritime Security Professional Training*: The secretary is required to develop standards and curricula to allow for the training and certification of maritime security professionals.[92]

The Security and Accountability for Every Port Act of 2006

The Security and Accountability for Every Port Act[93] of 2006 (SAFE Port Act) was enacted to improve maritime and cargo security through enhanced layered defenses. The Act was enacted in the wake of the Dubai Ports World controversy, which arose as a national security debate as the U.S. government

86 *Ibid.*, §70108.
87 *Ibid.*, §70110.
88 *Ibid.*, §70110.
89 *Ibid.*, §70114.
90 *Ibid.*, §70115.
91 *Ibid.*, SEC. 107.
92 *Ibid.*, SEC. 109.
93 The Security and Accountability for Every Port Act, U.S. Public Law 109–347.

tried to sign the management contracts of six major U.S. ports with a company based in the United Arab Emirates (UAE).

While the Act was designed to improve port security, it was also aimed at stopping key U.S. ports from falling into the hand of foreign owners. The Act was signed into law on 13 October 2006. The Act, which builds on the MTSA, codified a number of programs to improve the security of U.S. ports. The port security programs include:

- additional requirements for maritime facilities, including inspections of maritime facilities and enhanced security requirements for facilities[94];
- establishment of interagency operational centers for port security. The secretary of DHS is mandated to establish interagency operational centers for port security at all high-priority ports[95];
- scanning of containers by radiation detection equipment[96];
- establishment of the Container Security Initiative (CSI)[97];
- launch of Customs-Trade Partnership Against Terrorism[98]

VI U.S. Port and Cargo Container Security Programs

This section highlights a number of major port and cargo container security programs established by the U.S. in response to the 9/11 terrorist attacks. The U.S.-launched security programs have had a significant impact on the security policy of its trading partners and global trade generally.

Container Security Initiative

1 Background

In accordance with the Security and Accountability for Every Port Act (SAFE Port Act), the Container Security Initiative (CSI) was launched by the U.S. Customs and Border Protection (CBP) in January 2002. As part of anti-terrorism programs, the CBP created the CSI within three months of the terrorist attacks. The primary goal of the CSI is to enhance security for container cargo shipped to the U.S. by ensuring all containers that pose a potential risk for terrorism are identified and inspected at foreign ports before they are placed on vessels destined for the U.S.

---

94 *Ibid.*, SEC. 102–104.

95 *Ibid.*, §70107A.

96 *Ibid.*, SEC. 121.

97 *Ibid.*, SEC. 205.

98 *Ibid.*, SEC. 211–223.

Annually over 80 percent of global shipments are transported by ship, and over 180 million cargo containers are transported among seaports around the world, constituting the most critical component of global trade. All trading nations depend on containerized shipping for the transportation of manufactured goods. For the U.S., over 11 million maritime containers arrive on ships and are offloaded at U.S. seaports each year. Under this circumstance, the vulnerability of cargo containers has come under scrutiny.

2 Elements of CSI

According to the Container Security Initiative Strategic Plan of CBP, the four elements of CSI include[99] the following directives:

- *Identify High-Risk Containers*: The CBP uses automated targeting tools to identify containers that pose a potential risk for terrorism, based on advance information and strategic intelligence.
- *Pre-Screen and Evaluate Containers before they are Shipped*: Containers are screened as early in the supply chain as possible, generally at the port of departure.
- *Use Technology to Pre-Screen High-Risk Containers to ensure that Screening can be done Rapidly without Slowing Down the Movement of Trade*: This technology includes large-scale X-ray and gamma ray machines and radiation detection devices.
- *Use Smarter, More Secure Containers*. This will allow CBP officers at U.S. ports of arrival to identify containers that have been tampered with during transit.

3 Deployment of CSI Officials Overseas

In order to implement the CSI program, U.S. customs officials are stationed at foreign seaports of countries that have bilaterally agreed to implement the CSI program. They, in collaboration with participant countries, identify cargo containers that pose a potential risk for terrorism and inspect those containers at the foreign ports before they are shipped to the U.S. U.S. customs officials work with host customs administrations to establish security criteria for identifying high-risk containers.

Those administrations use non-intrusive inspection (NII) and radiation detection technology to screen high-risk containers before being shipped to U.S. ports. The implementation of the CSI program is built on a reciprocal basis with participating countries. This means that the host countries are allowed to

99 U.S. Customs and Border Protection, 'Container Security Initiative: 2006–2011 Strategic Plan,' available at file:///C:/Users/%EA%B9%80%EC%84%9D%EA%B7%A0/Downloads/nps03-121306-12.pdf.

send their customs officials to major U.S. ports to target ocean-going, containerized cargo being exported to their countries. Japan and Canada station their customs officials in some U.S. ports as part of the CSI program.

4 Participating Ports in the CSI Program

In fiscal year 2010, more than 10.1 million shipments were reviewed in CSI ports before arriving at U.S. seaports, an average of 27,000 shipments a day. Since its launch in 2002, the CSI, which was first implemented in ports shipping the highest volume of containers to the U.S., has expanded to include strategic ports around the world. The World Customs Organization (WCO), the European Union (EU), and the G8 support CSI expansion and have adopted resolutions implementing CSI security measures introduced at ports throughout the world.[100] As of 2018, the CSI program is operational in 58 ports in North America, Europe, Asia, Africa, the Middle East and Latin and Central America (Table 7). Over 80 percent of all maritime cargo imported into the U.S. is subject to prescreening.[101]

24-Hour Advance Manifest Rule

Effective on 2 December 2002, the U.S. CBP enacted a new rule, the '24-Hour Advance Manifest Rule,' which requires all ocean carriers or non-vessel operating common carriers (NVOCCs) to transmit a complete cargo manifest to U.S. Customs at least 24 hours prior to cargo loading if that vessel is calling at a U.S. port directly. In practice, most shipping lines close their cargo booking 48 hours prior to container loading, which allows a time cushion of 24 hours before the required reporting to the CBP.[102] The 24-hour rule allows CBP officers to prescreen and target high-risk shipments and containers before they arrive in a U.S. port.

This initiative is in support of the CSI program and permits CBP teams in CSI ports an adequate opportunity to evaluate and screen all cargo container documentation for indicators of heightened risk while still at the foreign port.[103] The rule extends not only to U.S. imports but also cargo transiting U.S. ports and remaining on board the vessel for subsequent discharge at a non-U.S. port.

The 24-hour period is measured against the scheduled commencement of loading for each non-U.S. port to a vessel destined or transiting a U.S. port. Failure to comply with this rule could result in cargo being held at an origin port,

100 U.S. Customs and Border Protection, 'Container Security Initiative in Summary,' 2011.
101 U.S. Customs and Border Protection, 'CSI: Container Security Initiative: CSI Ports Map.'
102 McNicholas (n 3), p. 126.
103 *Ibid.*

TABLE 7 CSI operational ports

Region	Ports
America and Caribbean	– Canada: Montreal, Vancouver & Halifax
	– Brazil: Santos
	– Argentina: Buenos Aires
	– Honduras: Puerto Cortes
	– Dominican Republic: Caucedo
	– Jamaica: Kingston
	– The Bahamas: Freeport
	– Panama: Balboa, *Colón* & Manzanillo
	– Colombia: Cartagena
Europe	– The Netherlands: Rotterdam
	– Germany: Bremerhaven & Hamburg
	– Belgium: Antwerp & Zeebrugge
	– France: Le Havre & Marseille
	– Sweden: Gothenburg
	– Italy: La Spezia, Genoa, Naples, Giota Tauro & Livorno
	– U.K: Felixstowe, Liverpool, Thamesport, Tilbury & Southampton
	– Greece: Piraeus
	– Spain: Algeciras, Barcelona & Valencia
	– Portugal: Lisbon
Asia	– Singapore: Singapore
	– Japan: Yokohama, Tokyo, Nagoya & Kobe
	– Hong Kong: Hong Kong
	– Korea: Busan
	– Malaysia: Port Klang & Tanjung Pelepas
	– Thailand: Laem Chabang
	– United Arab Emirates: Dubai
	– China: Shenzhen & Shanghai
	– Taiwan: Kaohsiung & Chi-Lung
	– Sri Lanka: Colombo
	– Oman: Port Salalah
	– Pakistan: Port Qasim
	– Israel: Port of Ashdod & Port in Haifa
Africa	– South Africa: Durban
	– Egypt: Alexandria

SOURCE: ADAPTED FROM U.S. CBP, *CSI FACT SHEET*

significant penalties against the carrier or NVOCC, along with the removal of containers for inspection by U.S. Customs and/or the denial of permission to unload vessel cargo and the possibility of returning the cargo to the load port.

Secure Freight Initiative

The Secure Freight Initiative (SFI) is a joint container security program of the Department of Homeland Security and the National Nuclear Security Administration under the Department of Energy. The SFI program was mandated by the provisions of the Security and Accountability for Every Port Act of 2006[104] and the Implementing Recommendations of the 9/11 Commission Act of 2007[105] that require, by 2012, all maritime cargo containers originating outside of the U.S. and unloaded at a U.S. port to be screened and scanned prior to reaching a U.S. domestic port.

In accordance with the provisions, the CBP has established the Secure Freight Initiative, which is testing the feasibility of moving from a risk-based approach to 100 percent scanning of all cargo containers bound for U.S. ports. The SIF builds on the two ongoing programs, the CSI and the Megaports Initiative, to strengthen cargo screening. The Megaports Initiative (MI), implemented by the Department of Energy, is designed to work with foreign customs, port authorities, port operators and/or other relevant entities in partner countries to systematically enhance detection capabilities for special nuclear and other radioactive materials in containerized cargo.[106]

The goal of the MI is to scan as much container traffic as possible (including imports, exports and transshipped containers) regardless of destination and with minimal impact to port operations. The MI seeks to equip 100 seaports with radiation detection systems by 2015, scanning approximately 50 percent of global maritime containerized cargo.[107]

Through the SFI program, data from radiation detection equipment provided by the MI program, and non-intrusive inspection (NII) equipment provided

104 SEC. 121 (Domestic Radiation Detection and Imaging): "(a) Scanning Containers-Subject to section 1318 of title 19, United States Code, not later than December 31, 2007, all containers entering the United States through 22 ports through which the greatest volume of container enter the United States by vessel shall be scanned for radiation. To the extent practicable, the Secretary shall deploy next generation radiation detection technology."

105 Implementing Recommendation of the 9/11 Commission Act of 2007, U.S. Public Law 110–153.

106 National Nuclear Security Administration, U.S. Department of Energy, 'Megaport Initiative', available at https://nnsa.energy.gov/aboutus/ourprograms/nonproliferation/programoffices/internationalmaterialprotectionandcooperation/-5.

107 *Ibid.*

by the Department of Homeland Security or the host government, is integrated with manifest data.[108] Under the SFI program, integrated nuclear detection devices, X-ray or gamma ray imagining machines, and container-identifying optical character recognition devices are deployed to foreign seaports. This equipment scans for nuclear and radiological material.[109]

The concept of SFI is that data collected during the scanning will be transmitted in near real-time to CBP personnel in foreign ports and the DHS National Targeting Center. As with the CSI goal, SFI's objective is to provide information for investigation and resolution in foreign ports prior to the cargo being loaded on U.S.-bound ships.[110]

Customs-Trade Partnership against Terrorism (*C-TPAT*)

In the wake of the 9/11 attacks, the United States has established a government-private sector cooperation program for container security, named the Customs-Trade Partnership Against Terrorism (C-TPAT). The C-TPAT is a voluntary public-private partnership program which recognizes that the CBP can provide the highest level of cargo security only through close cooperation with the principle stakeholders of the international supply chain, such as importers, carriers, consolidators, licensed customs brokers and manufacturers.[111]

The C-TPAT aims at strengthening the overall security of the international supply chain and facilitating the movement of cargo by encouraging private companies to actively guard against arms and weapons smuggling, trade in illicit goods that fund terrorist activities, and the smuggling of terrorists with shipments of goods.[112]

The C-TPAT launched in 2007 with the participation of seven major U.S. companies. The Security and Accountability for Every Port Act (SAFE Port Act) of 2006 provided a statuary framework for the C-TPAT program and imposed strict program oversight requirements. Under the SAFE Port Act, the program classifies the participants into three tiers: Tier 1, Tier 2, and Tier 3. An applicant seeking to participate in the program needs to meet minimum requirements, and participants are accorded different benefits in accordance with their tier. Private companies meeting or exceeding the program requirements are

108 CBP, 'Secure Freight Initiative: Vision and Operations Overview,' released on 7 December 2006, available at http://www.dhs.gov/xnews/releases/pr 1165943729650.shtm.

109 McNicholas (n 3), p. 127.

110 *Ibid.*

111 U.S. Customs-Trade Partnership against Terrorism Web site, available at www.cbp.gov/border-security/ports-entry/cargo-security/c-tpat-customs-trade-partnership-against-terrorism.

112 *Ibid.*

provided with benefits, including reduced scrutiny over their shipments, front-of-the-line inspections, and possible exemption from stratified exams.

The C-TPAT is not intended to duplicate the security measures created under the ISPS Code and other security measures, such as the Container Security Initiative. Rather it seeks to build on the ISPS Code and other security measures in place and require additional security measures and practices that enhance overall security throughout the international supply chain.[113] Participation in the C-TPAT continues to grow and as of 2017, more than 11,400 certified partners are participating in the program.[114]

VII Conclusion

This chapter has examined the international statuary framework for the security of the cargo supply chain as well as the U.S. maritime security measures. Since the adoption of the ISPS Code, it has served as a legal framework of port and vessel security around the world. It is believed that the ISPS Code has greatly contributed to the enhancement of cargo and port security around the world by providing minimum standards and obligations that state parties are required to meet or fulfill. The prominent feature of the ISPS Code is to enhance security against threats through the interface of vessels and port personnel.

Beyond the implementation of the ISPS Code, the U.S., which has led the creation of the Code, has employed a number of domestic maritime security measures subject to U.S. laws. It is worth noting that most maritime security measures at the global level have been driven by the U.S., in response to potential threats of terrorism in the maritime domain after the 9/11 terrorist attacks. The ISPS Code, in particular, is a key outcome of such U.S.-led efforts to enhance maritime security on the globe. In the global cargo supply chain, a set of U.S maritime security measures has had a far-reaching effect on U.S. trading partners. Given that they are heavily dependent on trade with the U.S., they had no choice but to comply with the requirements imposed by the U.S.

I think that it is not desirable that global maritime security measures are led by a single country and are further subject to its domestic security measures. In other words, the U.S. security measures *per se,* not by the international rule making process, have become global standards or norms for maritime security. Although the rule-making process in multilateral negotiations is lengthy and

113 McNicholas (n 3), p. 120.
114 U.S. Customs-Trade Partnership against Terrorism website (n 111).

laborious, global maritime security measures need to build on the consensus of the international community. This is because they are universally applicable security norms, once established. As such, the international community should continue to endeavor to enact those globally implemented standards and security measures into an existing or new international agreement to strengthen their legal basis.

CHAPTER 7

Enforcement of Proliferation Security Initiative (PSI) and Challenges

I Evolution of the Proliferation Security Initiative

Emergence of New Security Threats and Counter-Proliferation

During the post-Cold War period of the 20th century, the threat of massive destruction from conflict between nuclear-armed superpowers has significantly diminished. But in its place, the contemporary world has witnessed the rise of non-conventional threats posed by terrorist groups or rouge states which seek to have weapons of mass destruction (WMD) for use as a tool of terrorism. Rogue states and transnational terrorist groups now threaten the security of the world. Challenged by these evolving threats, the international community has come up with new security strategies to strengthen the traditional regime of non-proliferation of WMD.

Over the past three decades, the international community has established a number of legally binding agreements against nuclear proliferation as well as biological, chemical and radiological. Those non-proliferation treaties, which focus on preventing the spread of WMD, weapons technology, and related materials, include: (i) the 1968 Non-Proliferation Treaty (NPT)[1]; (ii) the 1972 Biological Weapons Convention[2]; and (iii) the 1993 Chemical Weapons Convention.[3] Despite its contribution to the prevention of proliferation of

1 The Treaty on the Non-Proliferation of Nuclear Weapons, referred to as the 'Non-Proliferation Treaty' (NPT) is an international treaty established to prevent the spread of nuclear weapons and weapons technology, to promote cooperation in the peaceful uses of nuclear energy, and to further the goal of achieving disarmament. The NPT entered into effect in March 1970. The parties in May 1995 agreed to extend the treaty indefinitely. North Korea, which acceded in 1985, announced its withdrawal from the NPT and never came into compliance. As of 2017, the members of NPT are up to 191.

2 The Convention on the Prohibition of the Development, Production and Stockpiling of Bacteriological (Biological) and Toxin Weapons and on their Destruction is commonly referred to as the 'Biological Weapons Convention' (BWC). Effective in March 1975, the BTC is the first multilateral disarmament treaty which aims to ban the development, production and stockpiling of an entire category of weapons. As of 2017, the number of BTC parties is 179.

3 The Convention on the Prohibition of the Development, Production, Stockpiling and the Use of Chemical Weapons and on their Destruction, referred as the 'Chemical Weapons Convention' (CWC), comprehensively prohibits the use, development stockpiling and transfer of

 | DOI:10.1163/9789004389908_008

WMD over the past decades, the traditional non-proliferation regime has exposed its limitations and shortcomings in addressing the new contemporary security environment.

Of those, importantly, the non-proliferation regime is applicable only to the state parties to the conventions and sovereign states, but limited to non-state parties and non-state actors. More specifically, the three categories of actors that lie outside the international community constitute a proliferation threat more dangerous and difficult to control than at any time in the past.[4]

First, North Korea and Iran both defied international norms of nuclear non-proliferation and respect for treaties and the United Nations Security Council Resolutions by conducting a series of missile launches and pursuing nuclear development. Second, terrorist groups are actively pursuing WMD, and are not likely to be deterred or dissuaded from using them. Third, despite successes in dismantling the *Al Qaeda* network, facilitators of proliferation still exist, motivated by financial gains. The problem is compounded by states such as North Korea, which views proliferation as an important revenue source — including as a way to finance their own WMD programs.[5] Fourth, adding to the complexity and the danger is the widespread availability of the materials, technology, equipment and basic knowledge required to develop and produce WMD and delivery systems.[6]

Against this backdrop, the international community has engaged in developing new strategies to address the shortcomings of the existing non-proliferation regime. As such, the strategy of counter-proliferation, which builds on non-proliferation, has been developed. The Proliferation Security Initiative (PSI) has constituted a key policy instrument to implement the strategy of counter-proliferation.

The counter-proliferation strategy focuses on intelligence, law enforcement and sometimes military action to prevent and deter the spread of WMD — as opposed to non-proliferation, which relies primarily on traditional measures such as diplomacy, arms control, and multilateral agreements that seek to dissuade or impede proliferation states and terrorist networks. The counter-proliferation strategy involves more aggressive actions

chemical weapons. Any chemical used for warfare is considered a chemical weapon by the convention. The CWC was effective in April 1997. The number of parties to the convention is 192 as of 2017.

4 U.S. Department of Defense, National Institute, 'The Proliferation Security Initiative: A Model for Future International Collaboration,' released in August 2009.

5 *Ibid.*

6 *Ibid.*

to prevent and deter the proliferation of WMD than non-proliferation, which is considered somewhat passive by relying primarily on controlling exports of WMD.[7]

Creation of the PSI

The Proliferation Security Initiative (PSI) is a global effort that aims to stop trafficking of WMD, as well as their delivery systems and related materials to and from states and non-state actors of proliferation concern.[8] It was devised as a response to the growing challenges posed by the proliferation of WMD, their delivery systems, and related materials worldwide.[9]

The PSI was initiated by the U.S. in the aftermath of the 9/11 terrorist attacks. The U.S. involvement in the PSI stems from the U.S. National Strategy to Combat Weapons of Mass Destruction, issued in December 2002,[10] which outlined the principal pillars of the U.S. strategy to combat weapons of mass destruction, including: (i) counter-proliferation to combat WMD use; (ii) strengthened non-proliferation to combat WMD proliferation, and; (iii) consequence management to respond to WMD use. Indeed, the strategy was a declaration that the U.S. has identified proliferation as a grave threat and set counter-proliferation as a higher priority on its security agenda. The strategy provides 'interdiction,' along with 'deterrence,' and 'defense and mitigation,' as an operational capability needed to counter the threat and use of WMD by states and terrorists.

On this basis, the PSI launched on 31 May 2003. Previously, an interdiction of a North Korean freighter, the *So San*, provided the critical impetus for the U.S. to initiate the creation of the PSI. The interdiction of the *So San* occurred on 9 December 2002 on the high seas, some 600 miles off the coast of Yemen. The Spanish frigate *Navarra*, part of the international coalition patrolling the Arabian Sea in search of fleeing members of *Al Qaeda* and the *Taliban*, spotted the *So San*, which was unflagged, and stopped and boarded for the purpose of checking the registration. The ship was registered in Cambodia and had a North Korean crew onboard.

---

7 See Suk Kyoon Kim, *Maritime Safety & Maritime Security* (*in Korean*) (The Sea Garden, Seoul, 2016), pp. 371–372.

8 U.S. Department of State, Bureau of International Security and Nonproliferation, 'Proliferation Security Initiative,' available at https://www.state.gov/t/isn/c10390.htm.

9 U.S. Department of State, Bureau of International Security and Nonproliferation, 'Proliferation Security Initiative (PSI), Fact Sheet,' 2008, available at https://2001–2009.state.gov/t/isn/rls/fs/105217.htm.

10 U.S. Department of State (n 8).

The *So San,* which had departed from the North Korean port of Nampo, was heading for Yemen. Spanish troops boarded by helicopter, with the assistance of the U.S. Navy, and discovered 15 Scud missiles, 24 tanks of rocket fuel additive, and 85 drums of chemical materials hidden under the sacks of cement that were the *So San*'s declared cargo manifest. When a U.S. warship started to escort the *So San* to Diego Garcia (where a U.S. naval base is located in the central Indian Ocean), the government of Yemen strongly protested to the U.S. and Spanish governments, claiming that the Scud missiles were legally purchased from North Korea.

However, the Yemen government could not explain why the missiles were hidden and why the ship did not have the proper paperwork. After a few days, the *So San* was ultimately released to continue to Yemen, affirming that there was no legal authority to seize the shipment of Scud missiles, nor was Yemen prohibited from taking delivery of such weapons from North Korea.

As in the incident of the *So San,* the increasingly aggressive efforts by proliferators to stand outside or to circumvent existing non-proliferation norms and to profit from such trade justified a need for new and stronger action by the international community. In particular, U.S. security officials were convinced of the limitation on interception and the need for the development of a new strategy within the existing international law and framework.

On 31 May 2003, speaking in Krakow, Poland, U.S. President George W. Bush announced a new counter-proliferation initiative[11]: "When weapons of mass destruction or their components are in transit, we must have the means and authority to seize them. So today I announce a new effort to fight proliferation called the Proliferation Security Initiative. The United States and a number of our close allies.... have begun working on new agreements to search planes and ships carrying suspect cargo and to seize illegal weapons or missile technologies. Over time, we will extend this partnership as broadly as possible to keep the world's most destructive weapons away from our shores and out of the hands of our common enemies."

Over the following weeks, meetings including representatives of 11 states, including Australia, France, the U.S., the U.K, Germany, Italy, the Netherlands, Portugal, Poland, Spain and Japan, were held in Madrid, Spain on 12 June 2003, and subsequently in Brisbane, Australia, on 9 July 2003, leading to a meeting in Paris, France. On 4 September 2003, a core group of the 11 states met in Paris and detailed the principles governing the PSI and

11 George W. Bush's speech, delivered on 31 May 2003 in Krakow, Poland. Full text is available at http://www.presidency.ucsb.edu/ws/index.php?pid=64354.

adopted the 'Statement of Interdiction Principle,' which will be discussed in detail below.

However, the core group was disbanded in August 2005 after India[12] complained of discrimination among PSI participants. The Operational Experts Group (OEG) was established in its place. The OEG, composed of 21 states, is a group of military, law enforcement, intelligence, legal and diplomatic experts from participating states that meet regularly to develop operational concepts, organize the interdiction exercise program, share information about legal authorities, and pursue cooperation with key industry sectors.[13] The states of the OEG include: Argentina, Australia, Canada, Denmark, France, Germany, Greece, Italy, Japan, the Netherlands, New Zealand, Norway, Poland, Portugal, Republic of Korea, Russia, Singapore, Spain, the U.K and the U.S.

PSI in the Trump Administration in Relation to North Korea

Launched in the Bush Administration in 2003, the PSI program is faced with a new security environment in relation to North Korea. In the wake of the historic summit held in Singapore on 12 June 2018 between the leaders of the United States of America and Democratic People's Republic of Korea (North Korea), a new security circumstance has emerged. The two leaders, U.S. President Donald Trump and North Korean leader Kim Jong-Un, signed a joint statement,[14] agreeing to: (i) establishing new relations for peace and prosperity; (ii) building a lasting and stable peace regime on the Korean Peninsula; (iii) reaffirmation of the complete denuclearization of the Korean Peninsula; and (iv) recovery of U.S soldier remains.

The talks between the U.S. and North Korea, following the South and the North summit on 27 April 2018, de-escalated tensions wreaked by North Korea's nuclear tests and launches of intercontinental ballistic missiles which are capable of hitting the whole mainland of the U.S. North Korea was referred to as one of 'rogue states' which severely restrict human rights, sponsor terrorism and seek to proliferate WMD. The practices of rouge states concerned with sponsoring terrorism and proliferation of WMD prompted the creation of the PSI program and thus they have been the primary target thereof.

North Korea was believed that it has involved in proliferating WMD and related materials. President George W. Bush of U.S. referred to North Korea as part of "axis of evil" during his 2002 State of the Union address. While the

12 As of 2017, India has not endorsed the PSI interdiction principles.

13 U.S. Department of State (n 8).

14 'Trump and Kim's Joint Statement,' *Reuters*, June 12, 2018.

Six-Party Talks[15] for the denuclearization of North Korea were underway, North Korea was taken off from the list of the State Sponsors of Terrorism. In the wake of the launch of North Korea's first intercontinental ballistic missile in July 2017, however, the U.S. added North Korea back to its State Sponsors of Terrorism list, with its own economic sanctions as well as intensified UN Security Council sanctions.

Regarding the U.S. posture over the PSI, the Obama administration, which pursued a policy of 'strategic patience' toward North Korea, "inexplicably jettisoned the effective multilateral program upon entering office."[16] Vice President Mike Pence of the Trump administration during his visit to Seoul in April 2017 said that "the era of strategic patience was over."[17] However, it is not apparent whether the Trump administration has brought back the PSI. Given U.S.'s tougher stance regarding security concerns in the Trump administration, the PSI is likely to serve as a vital multilateral framework for the U.S. to deter the proliferation of WMD.

Meanwhile, the UN Security Council has imposed a series of sanctions on North Korea which have been intensified as North Korea has continued to conduct nuclear and missile tests in violation of its resolutions over the past years. In relation to the PSI concerned with North Korea, the implementation of the UN sanctions would reinforce the PSI on North Korea since they target the ships suspected of carrying illicit items from and to North Korea.

It remains to be seen how de-escalation of tensions and further development of relations between the U.S. and North Korea would affect the enforcement of the PSI and UN sanctions on North Korea. However, it is apparent that it depends on North Korea's implementation of its commitment to denuclearization. My view in this regard is that a combination of dialogue and sanctions toward North Korea should be undertaken until the completion of

15 The six-party talks participated by North Korea, South Korea, the U.S., Japan, China and Russia aimed to find a peaceful resolution to the security concerns as a result of the North Korean nuclear weapons program. Five rounds of talks were held in the period between 2003 and 2007, producing little progress toward North Korea's denuclearization. North Korea agreed to shut down its nuclear facilities in exchange for fuel aid and steps towards the normalization of relations with the United States and Japan. The six-party talked ended when North Korea unilaterally declared on April 14, 2009 that it would pull out of the talks on the pretext of UN Security Council's statement condemning North Korea's failed satellite launch.

16 Albert B. Wolf, 'How Trump Can Pressure North Korea with the Stroke of a Pen' *The Diplomat*, February 01, 2017.

17 Juliana Rose Pignataro, 'What Is Strategic Patience? US Policy Toward North Korea Is Over, Says Pence,' *International Business Times*, April 17, 2017.

denuclearization of North Korea. In the context, the PSI would play a vital role of being an international instrument of sanctions and pressure on North Korea to comply with international law and order at sea.

II Nature of the PSI

A look at its history reveals that the PSI is quite different from typical treaties or international organizations in its formulation. The very nature of the PSI is likely to become more explicit by outlining a number of key elements.

First, the PSI is a political commitment of participating states to international counter-proliferation efforts against WMD at sea, in the air, or on land. The PSI is not a formal agreement or treaty, but merely a coalition of willing of participating states to stop the proliferation of WMD around the world. The states that agree to the need for a cooperative approach to combating the proliferation of WMD are committed to the enforcement of the interdiction principles.

Second, the PSI is not a formal treaty-based organization, but an activity. Thus, the PSI has no organizational structure to support the enforcement of the PSI. The PSI is an action that takes specific steps to effectively interdict WMD-related shipments and prevent proliferation.

Third, the PSI works within the existing national and international law and frameworks. The enforcement of the PSI is subject to the national legal authorities of participating countries and relevant international law and frameworks.

Forth, participation in the PSI relies on voluntary actions of member states that are consistent with national legal authorities and relevant international law and frameworks. PSI participants use existing national and international authorities to put an end to WMD-related trafficking and take steps to strengthen those authorities as necessary.[18] A country's decision to participate in an interdiction is completely voluntary, and the endorsement of the PSI interdiction principles is the only requirement for participation. The endorsement does not obligate participating countries to take any specific actions.

Fifth, the PSI is a proactive approach to prevent the proliferation of WMD. The PSI, which is enforced as a preventive tool at any time, is distinguished from 'preventive strike' or 'preemptive strike,' which is a military action to deter or stop the imminent threat of WMD.

18 *Ibid.*

Giving an account of how the PSI works, as described by the U.S. Department of State,[19] will be helpful to better understanding of the nature of the PSI. The PSI works in three primary ways. First, it channels international commitment to stopping WMD-related proliferation by focusing on interdiction as a key component of a global proliferation strategy. Endorsing the PSI Statement of Interdiction Principles provides for a common view of the proliferation problem and a shared vision for addressing it.

Second, the PSI provides participating countries with opportunities to improve national capabilities and authorities to conduct interdictions. A robust PSI exercise program allows participants to increase their interoperability, improve interdiction decision-making processes, and enhance the interdiction capabilities and readiness of all participant states.

Third, and of the most immediate importance, the PSI provides a basis of cooperation among partners on specific actions when the need arises. Interdictions are information-driven and may involve one or several participating countries, as geography and circumstances require. By working together, PSI partners combine their capabilities to deter and stop proliferation whenever and wherever it takes place.

III Interdiction Principles and Participation in the PSI

PSI Interdiction Principles[20]

PSI participants are committed to the following interception principles to establish a more coordinated and effective basis through which to impede and stop shipments of WMD, their delivery systems and related materials flowing to and from states and non-state actors of proliferation concern, consistent with national legal authorities and relevant international law and frameworks, including the UN Security Council. They call on all states concerned with this threat to join in similarly committing to:

- Undertake effective measures, either alone or in concert with other states, for interdicting the transfer or transport of WMD, their delivery systems, and related materials to and from states and non-state actors of proliferation concern. "States or non-state actors of proliferation concern," which generally refer to those countries or entities that the PSI participants establish should

19 U.S. Department of State (n 9).

20 The PSI interdiction principles and the annotations described here are from the 'Statement of Interdiction Principles' provided by U.S. Department of State, 2003, available at https://www.state.gov/t/isn/c27726.htm.

be subject to interdiction activities because they are engaged in proliferation through: (i) efforts to develop or acquire chemical, biological or nuclear weapons and associated delivery systems; or (ii) transfers (either selling, receiving or facilitating) of WMD, their delivery systems or related materials.

- Adopt streamlined procedures for the rapid exchange of relevant information concerning suspected proliferation activity, protecting the confidential character of classified information provided by other states as part of this initiative, dedicate appropriate resources and efforts to interdiction operations and capabilities, and maximize coordination among participants in interdiction efforts.
- Review and work to strengthen their relevant national legal authorities where necessary to accomplish these objectives, and work to strengthen when necessary international law and frameworks in appropriate ways to support these commitments.
- Take specific actions in support of interdiction efforts regarding cargoes of WMD, their delivery systems or related materials, to the extent their national legal authorities permit and consistent with their obligations under international law and frameworks, to include:
  (i) Not to transport or assist in the transport of any such cargoes to or from states or non-state actors of proliferation concern, and not to allow any persons subject to their jurisdiction to do so.
  (ii) At their own initiative or at the request and good cause shown by another state, to take action to board and search any vessel flying their flag in their internal waters or territorial seas, or areas beyond the territorial seas of any other state, that is reasonably suspected of transporting such cargoes to or from states or non-state actors of proliferation concern, and to seize such cargoes that are identified.
  (iii) To seriously consider providing consent under the appropriate circumstances to the boarding and searching of its own flag vessels by other states, and to the seizure of such WMD-related cargoes in such vessels that may be identified by such states.
  (iv) To take appropriate actions to (a) stop and/or search in their internal waters, territorial seas, or contiguous zones (when declared) vessels that are reasonably suspected of carrying such cargoes to or from states or non-state actors of proliferation concern and to seize such cargoes that are identified; and (b) to enforce conditions on vessels entering or leaving their ports, internal waters or territorial seas that are reasonably suspected of carrying such cargoes, such as requiring that such vessels be subject to boarding, search and seizure of such cargoes prior to entry.

(v) At their own initiative or upon the request and good cause shown by another state, to (a) require aircraft that are reasonably suspected of carrying such cargoes to or from states or non-state actors of proliferation concern and that are transiting their airspace to land for inspection and seize any such cargoes that are identified; and/or (b) deny aircraft reasonably suspected of carrying such cargoes transit rights through their airspace in advance of such flights.

(vi) If their ports, airfields or other facilities are used as transshipment points for shipment of such cargoes to or from states or non-state actors of proliferation concern, to inspect vessels, aircraft or other modes of transport reasonably suspected of carrying cargoes, and to seize such cargoes that are identified.

Participation in the PSI

Starting with 11 states, over the years the parties to the PSI have expanded to 105 states. The growing number of participants is not merely the expansion of participating states, but is a demonstration of broader support for values and goals of coherent and concerted international efforts to prevent the proliferation of WMD, their delivery systems and related materials. This may indicate that the PSI has been positioned as a critical global maritime security initiative to address the growing concern of proliferation of WMD and related materials.

More importantly, the growing participation is likely to strengthen the legal basis of the PSI, which was formed outside the international rule-making process. States can participate in the PSI in a variety of ways[21]:

- Formally committing to and publicly endorsing the PSI and the Statement of Interdiction Principles and indicating willingness to take all steps available to support PSI efforts.
- Undertaking a review and providing information on current national legal authorities to undertake interdictions at sea, in the air or on land, and indicating willingness to strengthen authorities where appropriate.
- Identifying specific national 'assets' that might contribute to PSI efforts (e.g., information sharing, military and/or law enforcement assets).
- Providing points of contact for PSI assistance requests and other operational activities, and establishing appropriate internal government processes to coordinate PSI responses efforts.
- Being willing to actively participate in PSI interdiction training exercises and actual operations as opportunities arise.

21 U.S. Department of State (n 9).

- Being willing to conclude relevant agreements (e.g., boarding agreements) or otherwise to establish a concrete basis for cooperation with PSI efforts.

Participants in the PSI are to comply with the Statement of Interdiction Principles and encouraged to enact legal statutes to facilitate effective interdiction of WMD and related materials. Participation in PSI activities include Operational Experts Group meetings, live exercises, command post exercises, tabletop exercises, workshops and other WMD interdiction trainings.

As illustrated in Table 8, the members of the PSI include 106 states (as of 2018). The latest participant is the Republic of Palau that joined in December 2018. The overall number of participants accounts for 55 percent out of all 193 UN member states, which is a relatively low participation level compared with other globally adopted treaties in maritime security, such as the Convention for the Suppression of Unlawful Acts Against the Safety of Maritime Navigation (SUA Convention), whose contracting states are 166. Geographically, the distribution of the participating states is uneven. Participating states are mostly concentrated in Europe and Asia/Pacific, of which the largest participating region is Europe with 48 participants, followed by Asia/Pacific with 38 states.

In contrast, other regions are underrepresented. In the Asia/Pacific region, in particular, a lingering challenge is that some of major regional countries, including China, India, Indonesia and Pakistan, have been reluctant to join the PSI for various reasons. China has, for example, questioned the legality of the PSI, claiming that it is not consistent with the right of innocent passage by allowing interdiction in territorial waters.[22]

However, it appears that China's intention is somewhat concerned with its reluctance to be part of the U.S.-led global security framework. China also appears to be conscious of North Korea, a traditional ally of China and one of the primary proliferation concern states that the PSI targets. Furthermore, China's bitter experience with the U.S. with respect to the enforcement of the PSI might have discouraged its participation in the U.S.-led PSI. A Chinese cargo vessel *Yinhe* (銀河) was interdicted by the U.S. Navy on the high seas in 1993 on suspicion of carrying the chemicals thiodiglycol and thionyl chloride, which can be used to manufacture mustard gas, a chemical warfare agent. It was believed that these chemicals would be delivered to the Iranian port of Bandar Abbas.

The U.S. Navy forced the *Yinhe* to stop on the high seas of the Indian Ocean for three weeks. The Chinese government subsequently agreed to have the ship

22 Charles Wolf, Jr., Brian G. Chow & Gregory S. Jones, 'U.S. Combat Commands' Participation in the Proliferation Security Initiative,' Technical Report, RAND National Defense Research Institute, 2009.

searched in Dammam, Saudi Arabia by a joint Saudi-U.S. team in the presence of Chinese representatives. The inspection took place from 26 August to 4 September 1993. The inspection report stated: "The complete inspection of all the containers aboard the *Yinhe* showed conclusively that the two chemicals thiodiglycol and thionyl chloride were not among the ship's cargo."[23]

China accused the U.S. of obstructing the vessel's normal shipping operations and of seriously infringing China's sovereignty and right to the freedom of navigation on the high seas. However, the U.S. refused to apologize, claiming that "the U.S. had acted in good faith on intelligence from a number of sources, all of which proved to be wrong."[24]

Indonesia, a coastal state of the Malacca Strait as well as a major stakeholder in maritime security in Southeast Asia, is not joining the PSI. This is presumably due to concerns over the infringement of sovereignty, as with the SUA Convention. India and Pakistan, which both possess nuclear weapons, are concerned that the PSI might be directed against them, which is one reason behind their reluctance to join the PSI.[25]

Of particular note is that only four African states are joining the PSI. Given that demands for North Korean weapons or others are likely to be higher due to civil wars underway, as demonstrated in the interdiction of the *So San*, the very low participation of African countries in the PSI is a significant challenge to the evolution of the PSI toward a global security norm.

Participation of South Korea in the PSI[26]

The participation of South Korea had a great significance in the evolution of the PSI because South Korea is in a strategic position in relation to North Korea, which is a primary state of proliferation concern as well as a target state under the PSI program. On the Korean Peninsula, the two Koreas have remained hostile to each other while having been technically in a state of war since they were divided at the end of World War II.

Despite various international efforts to deter North Korea's nuclear development, it has aggressively pursued nuclear capabilities over past years

23 Ministry of Foreign Affairs of China, 'Statement by the Ministry of Foreign Affairs on the *Yinhe* Incident,' released on 4 September 1993.

24 Patrick E. Tyler, 'No Chemical Arms Aboard China Ship,' *The New York Times*, 6 September 1993, available at http://www.nytimes.com/1993/09/06/world/no-chemical-arms-aboard-china-ship.html.

25 Wolf, Chow & Jones (n 22).

26 For further information, See Suk Kyoon Kim, 'Korean Peninsula Maritime Issues,' *Ocean Development and International Law*, (2010)41(2), pp. 179–180.

TABLE 8 Status of PSI participants (as of 2018)

America and Caribbean (17)	– Antigua and Barbuda – Argentina – Bahamas – Belize – Canada – Chile – Colombia – Dominica – Dominican Republic – El Salvador – Honduras – Panama – Paraguay – St. Lucia – St. Vincent and the Grenadines – Trinidad and Tobago – United States
Europe (47)	– Albania – Andorra – Armenia – Austria – Azerbaijan – Belarus – Belgium – Bosnia – Bulgaria – Croatia – Cyprus – Czech Republic – Denmark – Estonia – Finland – France – Georgia – Germany – Greece – Holy See

	– Liechtenstein – Lithuania – Luxembourg – Macedonia – Malta – Moldova – Montenegro – Morocco – Netherlands – Norway – Poland – Portugal – Romania – Russia – San Marino – Serbia – Slovakia – Slovenia – Spain – Sweden – Switzerland – Hungary – Iceland – Ireland – Italy – Ukraine – United Kingdom
Asia/Pacific (38)	– Afghanistan – Australia – Azerbaijan – Bahrain – Brunei – Cambodia – Fiji – Libya – Malaysia – Marshall Islands – Mongolia – New Zealand

TABLE 8 (*cont.*)

	– Oman
	– Palau
	– Papua New Guinea
	– Philippines
	– Qatar
	– Samoa
	– Saudi Arabia
	– Singapore
	– Sri Lanka
	– Iraq
	– Israel
	– Japan
	– Jordan
	– Kazakhstan
	– Korea, Republic of
	– Kyrgyzstan
	– Kuwait
	– Tajikistan
	– Thailand
	– Turkey
	– Turkmenistan
	– United Arab Emirates
	– Uzbekistan
	– Vanuatu
	– Vietnam
	– Yemen
Africa (4)	– Angola
	– Djibouti
	– Liberia
	– Tunisia

SOURCE: ADAPTED FROM U.S. DEPARTMENT OF STATE, *'PROLIFERATION SECURITY INITIATIVE PARTICIPANTS'*

by conducting a series of nuclear tests and launching missiles. Furthermore, North Korea has shipped weapons and arms to conflict regions across the world, particularly in the Middle East and Africa, while importing materials needed for nuclear development from states of proliferation concern such as

Pakistan and Iran. Since North Korea's first nuclear test in October 2006, the UN has imposed on North Korea a wide range of sanctions banning the trade of illicit items which can be used for nuclear development and military purposes.

Despite requests from the United States and other participating countries, which considered South Korea's participation vital to the success of the PSI, South Korea had been reluctant to fully join the PSI. Instead, it had remained a like-minded country by sending observers to the PSI training exercises. Even when the UN Security Council 1718 — which prevented North Korea from illicit trafficking of WMD, their means of delivery and related materials — was adopted in October 2006, South Korea adhered to its position of not being a full participant in the PSI.

South Korea's position was due to concern that its full participation might provoke a military conflict with North Korea, given a volatile situation on the Korean Peninsula. In addition, South Korea was of the view that participation in the PSI did not align with its engagement policy with North Korea. On this basis, South Korea referred to the Agreement on Maritime Transportation between the South and the North, claiming that the Agreement would bring the same effect as joining the PSI.[27]

Nevertheless, South Korea dramatically changed its position in the wake of North Korea's nuclear test on 25 May 2009, deciding to fully participate in the PSI. Currently, South Korea is one of the Operational Experts Group and plays a vital role in the implementation of UN sanctions on North Korea and the enforcement of the PSI on the Korean Peninsula.

IV The PSI and International Law

The Statement of Interdiction Principles provides that actions should be taken to the extent their national legal authorities permit and be consistent with their obligations under international law and frameworks.[28] Despite its

27 Under the Agreement on Maritime Transportation between the South and the North, which entered into force in August 2005, the South and the North allowed shipping through the designated shipping lanes in their respective territorial waters. Under the Agreement, the South and the North can stop and search in the designated shipping lanes only merchant ships suspected of violating obligations and carrying weapons and parts of weapons. Any ship suspected of undertaking prohibited activities is subject to boarding and inspection. When any violations are confirmed, the ship is forced to leave the designated shipping lanes.

28 The Statement of Interdiction Principles, Art. 4.

enforcement within national and international laws, the legality of the PSI was challenged by some states on the ground that the PSI was created outside the international law-making process, and interdiction in territorial waters is not consistent with the UN Convention on the Law of the Sea (UNCLOS). This part deals with issues concerning PSI's consistency with international law, specifically the regimes in the UNCLOS, and furthermore examine the international efforts to bolster the legality of the PSI.

UN Security Council Resolutions

UN member states "confer on the Security Council primary responsibility for the maintenance of international peace and security"[29] and "agree to accept and carry out the decisions of the Security Council."[30] In accordance with these provisions of the UN Charter, the resolutions of the UN Security Council (UNSC) are legally binding, and the member states have responsibilities and duties to carry out and comply with obligations. The below are relevant UN Security Council resolutions, which are often referred to as the legal basis of the enforcement of the PSI program, although they make no mention of the PSI therein.

– **UNSCR 1540**

United Nations Security Council Resolution (UNSCR) 1540, adopted on 28 April 2004, calls on all states: (i) to refrain from providing any form of support to non-state actors that attempt to develop, acquire, manufacture, posses, transport, transfer or use nuclear, chemical or biological weapons and their means of delivery;[31] (ii) to adopt and enforce appropriate effective laws which prohibit any non-state actor to manufacture, possess, develop, transport, transfer or use nuclear, chemical or biological weapons and their means of delivery for terrorist purposes; and (iii) to take and enforce effective measures to establish domestic controls to prevent the proliferation of nuclear, chemical or biological weapons and their means of delivery.

The purpose of UNSCR 1540 is very similar to that of the PSI, but is distinguished from the PSI in that it only refers to non-state actors, whereas the PSI interdiction principles are applicable to both state and non-state actors. The original purpose of UNSCR 1540 was to endorse the PSI and to provide authority for interdiction of the high seas, but the final text makes no mention of the

29 UN Charter, Art. 24(1).
30 *Ibid.*, Art. 25.
31 UNSCR 1540, Art. 1.

PSI and provides no authority for the interdiction of ships on the high seas because of a threatened Chinese veto.[32]

– **UNSCRs on Iran**

The UNSC adopted a number of resolutions aimed at preventing Iran from developing a nuclear weapon capability and further helping the PSI to stem the nuclear flow into Iran. UNSCR 1737, adopted on 23 December 2006, aims to make Iran suspend all enrichment-related and reprocessing activities, including research and development. For interdiction, especially with carriers not flying PSI-participant flags or in areas where PSI participants do not have indisputable jurisdiction, UNSCR 1737 helps the PSI in two ways[33]: (i) it calls for all states to take necessary measures, possibly including interdiction, to prevent Iran from obtaining the proscribed nuclear items; (ii) its annex lists the names of entities and individuals designated by the Security Council as being engaged in, directly associated with, or providing support for Iran's proliferation sensitive nuclear activities and for the development of nuclear weapon delivery systems.

The UNSC adopted another resolutions on Iran, including UNSCR 1803, on 2 March 2008, to reinforce its commitment to prevent Iran from developing a nuclear weapon capability, further helping PSI to stem the nuclear flow from Iran.[34]

– **UNSCR s on North Korea**

Over the last decade, the UN Security Council has adopted a number of resolutions imposing sanctions on North Korea, which has continued to conduct nuclear tests and missile launches in violation of relevant treaties and resolutions of the Security Council. The resolutions on North Korea include: Resolution 825(1993), Resolution 1695(2006), Resolution 1718(2006), Resolution1874 (2009), Resolution 1887(2009), Resolution 2087(2013), Resolution 2094(2013), Resolution 2270(2016), Resolution 2321(2016), Resolution 2356(2017), Resolution 2371(2017) and Resolution 2397(2017).

Interdiction on North Korean vessels that are believed to carry illicit items has a significant implication in relation to the PSI. Given that North Korea is a primary state of proliferation concern, the interdiction of vessels carrying prohibited items to and from North Korea, pursuant to the UNSC resolutions,

---

32 William Hawkins, 'Chinese Realpolitik and the Proliferation of Security Initiative,' cited in Charles Wolf, Jr., Brian G. Chow, Gregory S. Jones, 'U.S. Combat Commands' Participation in the Proliferation Security Initiative,' Technical Report, RAND National Defense Research Institute, 2009.

33 Wolf, Chow & Jones (n 22).

34 *Ibid.*

TABLE 9 UNSCRs on North Korea

Resolution (adoption)	Violation (date)	Sanctions
1718 (14 Oct., 2006)	First nuclear test (14 Oct., 2006)	– Prohibit North Korea from conducting future nuclear tests or launching a ballistic missile – Call for North Korea to completely abandon all nuclear weapons and existing nuclear program – Ban on trade of a wide range of illicit goods, including large-scale arms, missiles, nuclear technology materials and equipment, by using member states' flagged vessels and aircraft
1874 (12 June, 2009)	Second nuclear test (25 May, 2009)	– Reinforce the sanctions under Resolution 1718 by banning all imports and exports of weapons to and from North Korea – Call upon member states to inspect all cargo to and from North Korea in their territories if there are reasonable grounds to believe it contains illicit items – Call upon member states to inspect vessels, with the consent of the flag state, on the high seas, if they have reasonable cause to believe that the cargo of ship contains prohibited items – Authorize member states to seize and dispose of illicit items that are identified in inspections – Prohibit bunkering services to North Korean vessels which are believed to carry illicit items
2087 (22 Jan., 2013)	Satellite launch (12 Dec., 2012)	– Call upon member states to implement fully their obligations pursuant to the previous resolutions 1718(2006) and 1874(2009)

2094 (20 Mar., 2013)	Third nuclear test (12 Feb., 2013)	– Strengthen the existing sanctions, expand the scope of material covered and increase measures for states to enforce and monitor the implementation of sanctions and the transport of materials to or from North Korea through their territories – Call upon member states to inspect all cargo within or transiting through their territories that originated from North Korea or that is destined for North Korea, if the state has reasonable grounds to believe that the cargo contains illicit items – Deny entry to member states' ports over any vessels refusing to allow an inspection after inspection has been authorized by the vessel's flag state
2270 (2 Mar., 2016)	Forth nuclear test (6 Jan., 2016)	– Expand the scope of weapons prevented from the direct or indirect supply, sale or transfer to North Korea to all arms and related materials, including small arms and light weapons and their related materials – Call upon member states to inspect all cargo within or transiting through their territories if the cargo originated from or is directed to North Korea (a reasonable suspicion is not necessary to conduct a cargo inspection) – Call upon member states to prohibit their nationals from leasing or chartering their flagged vessels to North Korea and from registering, owning, leasing, operating or providing any vessel classification in North Korea – Prohibit the entry into member states' ports of any vessel owned by a designated individual and entity or that contains prohibited cargo – Blacklist 31 ships owned by the North Korean shipping firm Ocean Maritime Company, and the ships on the blacklist are banned from entry into ports of member states

TABLE 9 *(cont.)*

Resolution (adoption)	Violation (date)	Sanctions
2321 (30 Nov., 2016)	Fifth nuclear test (9 Sept., 2016)	– Call upon member states to reinforce their commitment to the implementation of measures imposed by the previous resolutions – Prohibit member states' nationals from procuring vessel and aircraft crewing services from North Korea – Prohibit North Korea from supply, sell, transfer, directly or indirectly, from its territory or by its nationals or using its flag vessels or aircraft, cooper, nickel, silver and zinc – Prohibit member states from the procurement of such materials from North Korea by their nationals, or using their flag vessels or aircraft whether or not originating in the territory of North Korea
2371 (5 Aug., 2017)	Launch of ballistic missiles (3 July and 28 July, 2017)	– Prohibit North Korea from the export of coal, iron, iron ore, lead, lead ore and seafood from its territory or by its nationals or using its flag vessels or aircraft – Prohibit member states from the procurement of such items from North Korea by their nationals, or using their flag vessels or aircraft – Request the Security Council's North Korea Sanctions Committee to identify additional conventional arms-related and proliferation-related items to be banned for transfer to and from North Korea – Enable the committee to designate vessels tied to violations of Security Council resolutions and prohibit their international port access

2375 (11 Sept., 2017)	Sixth nuclear test (2 Sept.,2017)	– Reduce about 30% of oil provided to North Korea by cutting off over 55% of refined petroleum products going to North Korea – Ban all North Korea textile exports – Call upon member states to inspect vessels with the consent of flag state, on the high seas, if they have reason to believe that the cargo of such vessels contains prohibited items – Call upon member states to cooperate with inspection: (1) if the flag state does not consent to inspection on the high seas, the flag state shall direct the vessel to proceed to an appropriate and convenient port for inspection by the local authorities; (2) if a flag state neither consents to inspection on the high seas nor directs the vessel to proceed to the port or if the vessel refuses to comply with flag state direction to permit inspection on the high sea or proceed to such a port, the committee is required to designate the vessel for the measures imposed by previous resolutions and the flag state is required to immediately deregister that vessel
2397 (22 Dec., 2017)	Ballistic missile launch (28 Nov., 2017)	– Call upon member states to reduce to 500,000 barrels from an annual cap of 2 million barrels that North Korea can import refined petroleum each year – 100,000 North Korean workers working overseas will be expelled within two years – Call upon member states to inspect and freeze any vessel in their ports and territorial waters that are involved in the shipping of coal and other prohibited items, and ship-to-ship transfers of petroleum

SOURCE: ADAPTED FROM *UNSCR RESOLUTIONS*

supplements and reinforces the implementation of the PSI. The matters of the PSI on the Korean Peninsula will be discussed in greater detail below.

Consistency with the UNCLOS

Despite PSI's contribution to the prevention and deterrence of proliferation of WMD, its legality has been challenged. The legality of actions for interdiction is questioned in relation especially to the UNCLOS. In such context, the Statement of Interdiction Principles intends participants to take actions to "the extent their national legal authorities permit and consistent with their obligations under international law and frameworks," and "strengthen their relevant national legal authorities and international law and framework in appropriate ways to support these commitments."

Interdictions under the PSI, which are undertaken in different maritime zones under the UNCLOS, including internal waters, territorial waters, contiguous zone, exclusive economic zone and the high seas, are subject to legal restrictions in accordance with the legal nature of respective maritime zones. Most importantly, the PSI is immediately constrained by the traditional requirement of exclusive flag state control and the freedom of the high seas.

The consistency with the UNCLOS in enforcing interdiction is a key value of the PSI because it is subject to the maritime order established by the UNCLOS, and consistency with the UNCLOS may have a great significance for the evolution of the PSI into customary law. On this basis, this part will deal with legal challenges arising from the enforcement of interdictions in the maritime zones.

1 Ports and Internal Waters

Internal waters of a state, which are defined as the waters on the landward side of the baseline of a state, are subject to a full sovereignty of the state. Ports are assimilated to the land territory of a state, and as such, states may control what vessel enters their ports and under what conditions. A similar situation exists in respect of internal waters.[35] Thus, if states have the appropriate national legislation in place, authority will exist to board, search, and even seize cargo that is prohibited under national law.[36]

The Statement of Interdiction Principles intends the participant states to be committed to taking appropriate actions[37] in internal waters: (i) stopping,

35 Natalie Klein, *Maritime Security and the Law of the Sea* (Oxford University Press, New York, 2011), p. 199.

36 Joyner, 'The Proliferation Security Initiative,' cited in Natalie Klein, *ibid.*

37 Statement of Interdiction Principles 4(d).

boarding and search of vessels that are reasonably suspected of carrying illicit cargoes to or from states or non-state actors of proliferation concern, and seizure of such cargoes; (ii) enforcing conditions on vessels entering or leaving their ports, internal waters or territorial waters.

The use of a flexible standard, such as 'reasonable suspicion,' is intended to enhance the deterrent value of the PSI.[38] It is not completely novel, but is comparable to the standard imposed in relation to permissible interdictions where there are 'reasonable grounds' for suspecting a ship is engaged in the slave trade, piracy or unauthorized broadcasting.[39]

Although participant states are able to enforce the Statement of Interdiction Principles in their ports or internal waters in accordance with their national legislation, limitations also exist. The largest restriction is found in sovereign immunity, according to which port states have no authority to inspect any warships and government vessels used only for non-commercial purposes.[40] One of the key difficulties in this regard is that the participant states in the PSI would not want to create an exception to the complete immunity of warships and non-commercial government vessels for the purposes of inspections, as a target state may then similarly rely on this exception to interfere with the warships of a PSI participant state.[41]

2 Territorial Waters and Contiguous Zone

The Statement of Interdiction Principles commits participants to taking appropriate actions, including stopping and searching vessels in the participant states' territorial seas and contiguous zones.[42] The issue of what conditions allow for interdictions in the territorial seas is very significant because the UNCLOS grants foreign vessels the right of innocent passage.

Thus, unlike in internal waters where interdictions are permissible without restrictions, the legal authority of coastal states to interdict foreign vessels in their territorial waters or contiguous zones is constrained by the right of innocent passage: "Every state has the right to establish the breadth of its territorial sea up to a limit not exceeding 12 nautical miles,"[43] and enjoys almost complete

38 Lehrman, 'Enhancing the Proliferation Security Initiative' cited in Klein (n 35), p. 198.
39 *Ibid.*
40 Joyner (n 36).
41 Kaye, 'The Proliferation Security Initiative,' cited in Natalie Klein (n 35), p. 199.
42 Statement of Interdiction Principles 4(d).
43 UNCLOS, Art. 3.

sovereignty in its territorial waters. "Ships of all states enjoy the right of innocent passage through the territorial sea."[44]

However, the right of innocent passage is constrained by the conditions that the exercise of innocent passage should not be prejudicial to the peace, good order or security of the coastal state; the exercise of rights and the fulfillment of duties under the UNCLOS should be conducted in a peaceful way.[45] If coastal states have a reasonable suspicion that a foreign vessel transiting or in their territorial waters is carrying WMD and related materials, the coastal states may interdict the foreign vessel for inspection in accordance with their national legislation.[46] This is supported by the provisions of the UNCLOS that "a coastal state may take the necessary steps in its territorial sea to prevent passage which is not innocent" and "suspend temporarily in specified areas of its territorial sea the innocent passage of foreign ships if such suspension is essential for the protection of its security, including weapons exercises."[47]

Coastal states may declare a contiguous zone to their territorial seas up to 24 nautical miles from the baselines, and "exercise the control necessary to: (i) prevent infringement of its customs, fiscal, immigration or sanitary laws and regulations within its territory or territorial sea; (ii) punish infringement of the above laws and regulations committed within its territory or territorial sea."[48] Participant states are allowed to operate within existing law if the passage of WMD and associated materials through this zone could be characterized as a violation of customs laws.[49] However, if the vessel is merely transiting the contiguous zone of a participant state without stopping in its ports or entering its territorial sea, there would be no justification for the interdiction of the vessel for customs law violations.[50]

With regard to the authority of a coastal state to "take the necessary steps in its territorial sea to prevent non-innocent passage," legal challenges arise in relation to interdictions in territorial waters. They are primarily concerned with the extent and scope of innocent passage. The enforcement of the PSI on a vessel which is suspected of carrying WMD or related materials and merely

44 UNCLOS, Art 17.
45 *Ibid.*, Arts. 19, 25, & 301.
46 See Yann-Huei Song, 'The U.S-Led Proliferation Security Initiative and UNCLOS: Legality, Implementation, and Assessment,' *Ocean Development and International Law* (2007), vol. 38, p. 117.
47 UNCLOS, Art. 25(3).
48 *Ibid.*, Art. 33.
49 Kaye, cited in Klein (n 35), p. 202.
50 Klein (35), p. 202.

transiting territorial waters, with no actions that pose a threat to the coastal state, is likely to be a violation of the right of innocent passage.

The UNCLOS lists activities that are considered not innocent, including any threat or use of force and any exercise or practice with weapons of any kind.[51] Under the UNCLOS, the criterion of being 'innocent' on the territorial sea is based primarily on the 'activity' of a ship, as set forth in Article 19(2) " ... *engaged in any of the following activities,*"[52] not based on the cargo on board. Accordingly, the enforcement of the PSI based on the cargo on board appears to be inconsistent with the innocent passage regime.

However, some commentators take the position that the violation of the right of innocent passage does not require a specific action or violation of any law, including the laws of the coastal state.[53] The different views of the scope of innocent passage in relation to the PSI seem to be closely concerned with how to strike a balance between the innocent passage regime and the need to protect the security of coastal states, and furthermore prevent the proliferation of WMD.[54]

My view is that given that innocent passage is a principal pillar of the UNCLOS, which allows free navigation, the extent and scope that innocent passage is allowed should not be compromised by an emerging norm. Once the innocent passage regime retreats from its substantial purpose and scope because of an emerging security initiative or norm, the values of the UNCLOS are highly likely to be undermined. As a consequence, the underlying tenet of UNCLOS could be shaky. Another challenge is concerned with how to deal with dual use materials found in interdictions. Since most of the materials used for manufacturing WMD and related materials are dual use, it is difficult to identify the intentions of transport of those materials.

3 Exclusive Economic Zones and the Straits Used for International Navigation

Under the UNCLOS, coastal states are entitled to declare their exclusive economic zones 200 nautical miles from the baselines.[55] Coastal states have sovereign

51 UNCLOS, Art. 19(2).

52 *Ibid.*

53 Churchill and Lowe, cited in Natalie Klein (n 35), p. 201.

54 A similar challenge is posed by the enforcement of UN Security Council resolutions on North Korea. Resolution 2270 requires all member states to inspect the cargo that has originated in North Korea or that is destined for North Korea, with no mention of the activity of the vessel carrying the cargo. For further information, see Suk Kyoon Kim, *Maritime Disputes in Northeast Asia: Regional Challenges and Cooperation* (Brill, Boston, 2017), pp. 177–178.

55 UNCLOS, Art. 57.

rights for the purpose of exploring and exploiting, conserving and managing the natural resources in their EEZ, and have jurisdiction on: (i) the establishment and use of artificial islands, installations and structures; (ii) marine scientific research; and (iii) the protection and preservation of the marine environment.

Other than those rights, all states are allowed to enjoy the freedoms of navigation and overflight in the EEZ s.[56] The EEZ is equivalent to the high seas in terms of navigation. Accordingly, unless a vessel navigating the EEZ of a coastal state violates the sovereign right or laws and regulations of the coastal state, especially marine pollution, any form of interdiction is not justified. In the same context, coastal states are not allowed to interdict vessels transiting their EEZ s for the purpose of the PSI without the consent of the flag state.[57]

Transit passage is applied in the straits used for international navigation between one part of the high seas or an exclusive economic zone and another part of the high seas or an exclusive economic zone.[58] The regime of innocent passage is applied where transit passage is not applied or in between a part of the high seas or an exclusive economic zone and the territorial sea of a foreign state.[59] The regime of passage through the straits used for international navigation does not affect exercise of sovereignty or jurisdiction by the states bordering the straits.[60] Accordingly, participant states, pursuant to the Statement of Interdiction Principles, may interdict foreign vessels through the straits used for international navigation if the vessels are believed to carry WMD or related materials.[61]

4 The High Seas

On the high seas, states have the right of freedom of navigation and the exclusive jurisdiction over the vessel of their flags under the UNCLOS[62] and customary international law. However, the exercise of freedom of the high seas is subject to obligations under the UNCLOS, including: (i) due regard for the interests of other states[63]; (ii) the high seas should be reserved for peaceful purposes[64]; (iii) rights, jurisdiction and freedoms should not be abused;[65] (iv) the exercise

56 *Ibid.*, Art. 56.
57 See Song (n 46), p. 118.
58 UNCLOS, Art. 37.
59 *Ibid.*, Art. 45.
60 *Ibid.*, Art. 34.
61 Song (n 46), p. 118.
62 UNCLOS, Arts. 87 & 92.
63 UNCLOS, Art. 87.
64 *Ibid.*, Art. 88.
65 *Ibid.*, Art. 300.

of rights and fulfillment of duties should refrain from any threat or use of force against the territorial integrity or political independence of any state, or in any other manner inconsistent with the principles of international law.[66]

A warship is allowed to exercise the right of visit on a foreign vessel when it is engaged in[67]: (i) piracy; (ii) the slave trade; (iii) unauthorized broadcasting, or; (iv) being without nationality. Except for those circumstances described above, states are entitled to exercise the freedom of the high seas. Thus, states are not allowed to interdict foreign flagged vessels for the purpose of the PSI, without the consent of the flag states, on the high seas.

Bilateral Ship-Boarding Agreements

For the purpose of facilitating the interdiction of suspected foreign flagged vessels on the high seas, the U.S. has entered into a number of bilateral ship-boarding agreements with states holding the largest shipping registries. As a result, the U.S. has the greatest number of flag vessels under its control and exclusive jurisdiction.[68] The agreements are intended to facilitate bilateral cooperation to prevent illicit shipments by establishing points of contact in each state as well as setting out procedures to board and search vessels in international waters.[69]

This approach enables the U.S. to establish authority that it would not otherwise have to board vessels suspected of carrying illicit shipments of WMD and related materials.[70] According to the Bureau of International Security and Nonproliferation under the U.S. State Department, the U.S. has signed bilateral ship-boarding agreements with the Bahamas, Belize, Croatia, Cyprus, Liberia, Malta, Marshall Islands, Mongolia and Panama between 2004 and 2007. The flags of these nine states are often used by shippers as 'flags of convenience,' and a majority of the world's shipping operate under these flags: about 70 percent of total tonnage, comprising about 300 million gross registered tons.[71]

Under these agreements, if a vessel registered in the U.S. or the partner country is suspected of carrying proliferation-related cargo, either one of the parities to this agreement can request the other to confirm the nationality of the ship in question, and if needed, authorize the boarding, search and possible detention of the vessel and its cargo.[72] However, the

66 *Ibid.*, Art. 301.
67 *Ibid.*, Art. 110.
68 Natalie Klein (n 35), p.184.
69 U.S. State Department, Bureau of International Security and Nonproliferation, 'Ship Boarding Agreements,' available at https://2001-2009.state.gov/t/isn/c12386.htm.
70 Klein (n 35), p. 184.
71 Wolf, Chow & Jones (n 22).
72 U.S. State Department (n 8).

agreements do not necessarily allow cargo seizure.[73] Under these agreements, a vessel may be searched as little as two hours after a request has been made.[74]

In 2008, for example, the U.S. signed a ship-boarding agreement with the Bahamas,[75] which is the world's third-largest flag registry of merchant ships in terms of gross tonnage. The below is part of the agreement concerning ship-boarding procedures in international waters:

Article 4
Operations in International Waters

1 **Authority to Board Suspect Vessel**

Whenever the Security Officials of one Party ("the requesting Party") encounter a suspect vessel claiming nationality in the other Party ("the requested Party") located in international waters, the requesting Party may request through the Competent Authority of the requested Party that it:

a. confirm the claim of nationality of the suspect vessel; and
b. if such claim is confirmed:
   (i) authorize the boarding and search of the suspect vessel, cargo and the persons found on board by Security Force Officials of the requesting Party; and
   (ii) if evidence of proliferation by sea is found, authorize the Security Force Officials of the requesting Party to detain the vessel, cargo and persons on board, pending instructions conveyed through the Competent Authority of the requested Party as to the exercise of jurisdiction in accordance with Article 5 of this Agreement.

2 Contents of Requests
Each request shall contain the basis for the suspicion, the geographic position of the vessel, and, if available, the name of the suspect vessel, the registration

73 Sharon Squassoni, 'Proliferation Security Initiative (PSI),' *CRS Report for Congress*, updated on 14 September 2008.

74 Wolf, Chow & Jones (n 22).

75 Agreement Between the Government of the Commonwealth of the Bahamas and the Government of the United States of America Concerning Cooperation to Suppress the Proliferation of Weapons of Mass Destruction, Their Delivery Systems, and Related Materials by Sea, signed 11 August 2008.

number, the IMO number, home port, the port of origin and destination, and any other identifying information. If a request is conveyed orally, the requesting Party shall confirm the request in writing by facsimile or e-mail as soon as possible.

3 Responding to Requests

a. If the nationality is verified, the requested Party may:
   i. decide to conduct the boarding and search with its own Security Force Officials;
   ii. authorize the boarding and search by the Security Force Officials of the requesting Party;
   iii. decide to conduct the boarding and search together with the requesting Party; or
   iv. deny permission to board and search.

b. A requested Party shall make best efforts to respond to requests pursuant to this Article as expeditiously as possible, and in any case shall confirm or refute the claim of nationality within 2 hours of the initial request.

4 Right of Visit

Notwithstanding the foregoing paragraphs of this Article, the Security Force Officials of one Party ("the first Party") are authorized to board suspect vessels claiming nationality in the other Party that are not flying the flag of the other Party, not displaying any marks of its registration or nationality, and claiming to have no documentation on board the vessel, for the purpose of locating and examining the vessel's documentation. If documentation or other physical evidence of nationality is located, the foregoing paragraphs of this Article apply. If no documentation or other physical evidence of nationality is available, the boarding Party may assimilate the vessel to a ship without nationality in accordance with international law.

5 Use of Force

The authorization to board, search and detain includes the authority to use force in accordance with Article 9 of this Agreement.

6 Shipboarding Otherwise in Accordance with International Law

Except as expressly provided herein, this Agreement does not apply to or limit the right of either Party to conduct boardings of vessels or other activities consistent with international law whether based, *inter alia*, on the right of visit, the rendering of assistance to persons, vessels, and property in distress or peril, or an authorization from the flag or coastal State to take law enforcement action.

High Seas Interdiction under the UNCLOS

In practical terms, the freedom of the high seas means that a ship on the high seas is subject to the jurisdiction of the state to which the ship is registered (that is, the flag state) but may not be interfered with by the ships of other states.[76] However, freedom of the high sea is subject to a few exceptions. The types of the limited circumstances in which these exceptions are permitted are outlined below.[77]

1 Interdiction by Permission

An effective way to ensure that PSI operations conform with international law is to obtain from other states express permission to interdict their ships upon reasonable suspicion that they carry illicit WMD or related materials. Such permission can take the form of a treaty as described in U.S. bilateral ship-boarding agreements, or by the exchange of diplomatic notes specifying the circumstances in which interdiction would be permitted and the consequences in the event that WMD materials or missiles are discovered.

2 Interdiction of Stateless Vessels

As stated earlier, the UNCLOS makes it clear that ships without nationality may be visited by other ships to inquire into their status.[78] Some dispute the claim that stateless ships are subject to the interdiction of all states, including interdiction for the purpose of the PSI. But the U.S. has consistently asserted the jurisdiction of all states in other contexts, e.g., narcotics trafficking and drift net fishing.

3 Interdiction by the Flag State

The flag state is free to interdict ships of its own registry. Where there is reasonable suspicion to believe that the flag flown by an apparently foreign ship is false and that the ship in truth is registered to the interdicting state, a warship is permitted to stop it and confirm its nationality.

4 Interdiction to Suppress Prohibited Activities

The UNCLOS specifies three types of undesirable activities justifying interference with freedom of navigation: (i) piracy; (ii) slave trading; and (iii) unauthorized broadcasting.[79] Although the PSI itself might mark an important development

---

76 Robert Chesney, 'The Proliferation Security Initiative and WMD Interdiction on the High Seas,' *National Strategy Forum* (2003), 13(1).

77 *Ibid.*

78 UNCLOS, Art. 110.

79 *Ibid.*

in the evolution of such an exception, proliferation concern is not recognized in customary international law as an undesirable activity for which there is an exception to free navigation. None of the WMD treaties expressly authorize *ad hoc* enforcement through interdiction. In addition, there is little or no support for a proliferation exception to freedom of navigation in past state practice.

5 Interdiction as a form of Preemptive Self-Defense

The legal principle of self-defense, called the *Caroline*[80] test, states that the necessity for preemptive self-defense must be "instant, overwhelming" need for self-defense, "leaving no choice of means" and "no moment for deliberation." Applying the principle to the PSI, it seems that the PSI lacks the imminence element to justify the interdiction program, except in extreme circumstances such as a shipment bound for a state on the verge of engaging in hostilities with the interdicting state.

6 Interdiction under the SUA Convention

As discussed in Chapter 4, Article 8*bis* of the 2005 SUA Protocol sets forth a process for cooperation and procedures for boarding a ship flying the flag of another state party. For boarding a foreign flagged ship, the suspected ship should be located outside the territorial sea of any state,[81] and a state must have reasonable grounds that the ship or a person on board the ship is, has been, or is about to be involved in the commission of an offence under the convention.[82]

V Enforcement of Interdictions

Cases of Maritime Interdiction

As in the event of the *So San* incident, the legality of interdictions often becomes controversial as to whether they are consistent with international law.

80 The *Caroline* was an American ship destroyed in 1837 by the British on the theory that it was going to be used to aid a Canadian insurrection. This action outraged the United States. In retaliation, a group of American and Canadian raiders attacked a British ship and destroyed it. The diplomatic crisis was defused by the negotiations that led to the Webster-Ashburton Treaty in 1842 where both the Americans and British admitted to wrongdoing. In the aftermath, the incident led to the legal principle of the *Caroline* test. The principle states that the necessity for preemptive self-defense must be "instant, overwhelming, and leaving no choice of means, and no moment for deliberation," as formulated by Daniel Webster in his response to British claims that they attacked the *Caroline* in self-defense.

81 The 2005 SUA Convention, Art. 8*bis* (5).

82 *Ibid.*, Art. 8*bis* (4).

Interdictions are concerned with the security interests of states involved. This may explain why only a few cases of interdictions are revealed, and access to information on interdictions is very limited. The cases below were part of the interdictions undertaken before or after the creation of the PSI.

The cases, to some extent, contributed to the justification of the PSI. They may also demonstrate the importance of intelligence-sharing and cooperation among states concerned in the undertaking of interdictions. Of particular note is that North Korean vessels in violation of UN sanctions appear to be a primary target of interdictions. However, it is worth noting that the interdictions of North Korean vessels are mostly undertaken in accordance with the UN Security Council Resolutions, not within the framework of the PSI.

1 Kuwolsan

On 30 June 1999, the North Korean freighter *Kuwolsan* docked at the Indian port of Kandala to unload a consignment of sugar. Indian customs agents attempted to board and search the ship. The North Korean crew physically impeded them, but eventually, at gunpoint, relented. Because the customs officials lacked the expertise needed, experts from Indian's missile establishment were called in to examine the items found. Hidden inside crates labeled "water refinement equipment" was an entire assembly line for ballistic missiles. This included tips of nose cones, sheet metal for rock frames, machine tools, guidance systems, and engineering drawings labeled "Scud B" and "Scud C." The Indians seized all of these items despite North Korean protests. The intended recipient of the shipment was Libya, according to U.S. intelligence officials.[83]

2 BBC China

In October 2003, Germany obtained information that the 5,548-ton general cargo ship *BBC China,* flagged under Antigua and Barbuda but owned by Germany, was transporting nuclear-related materials to Libya on behalf of the *Abdul Qadeer Khan* proliferation network. The U.S., the U.K, Germany and Italy worked together to halt and inspect the shipment of the *BBC China.* The inspection revealed that the ship's container number was fabricated and the ship was carrying nuclear-related equipment (centrifuge components) destined for Libya. The interdiction was a few weeks after the issuance of the Statement of Interdiction Principles. While that interdiction was a notable achievement

83 Jo Warrick, 'On North Korean Freighter, a Hidden Missile Factory,' *The Washington Post*, 14 August 2003.

in itself, it also played a major part in two broader counter-proliferation efforts: the unravelling of the *A.Q. Khan* network and Libya's decision to abandon its WMD and longer-range missile programs.[84]

3 Kang Nam

The North Korea ship *Kang Nam*, a 2000-tonnnage freighter suspected of carrying illicit cargo banned by the UN Security Council, was tracked by the U.S. Navy. Immediately after the ship left the North Korean port of Nampo, the U.S Navy began pursuit. The ship, sailing along the Chinese coastline, was believed to be destined for Myanmar. North Korea warned that forced inspection of the ship would be considered "an act of war" and that it would react accordingly.[85] However, when it neared the Malacca Strait, it turned around during 28–29 June 2009 and began to travel back toward North Korea, without explanation. The *Kang Nam* was the first North Korean vessel monitored under UN Security Resolution 1874, adopted in June to punish North Korea for its May 25 nuclear test.

4 South Korea's Seizure of North Korean Containers

On 22 September 2009 at the port of Busan, South Korea seized four North Korean containers shipped by North Korea on a Panama-registered freighter. At the request of intelligence authorities, the Korea Coast Guard ordered the freighter, which left the port of Busan for Dalian, China, to return, and it seized the containers. Reportedly, the search could be part of Seoul's participation in a U.S.-led counter-proliferation campaign, or part of an attempt to enforce UN sanctions (Resolution 1874).[86] The containers contained protective clothing used to protect against chemical weapons.

5 Thailand's Seizure of a North Korean Shipment

In December 2009, acting on a tip from U.S. intelligence, Thailand authorities seized a shipment of arms and sophisticated missiles from North Korea. U.S. intelligence had been tracking the shipment since it was loaded in Pyongyang. The ultimate destination was not determined. However, it was speculated to be heading for either Iran and passed on later to *Hezbollah or Hamas*, or to Pakistan, which has a long history of purchases from North Korea.[87]

---

84 U.S. Department of Defense, National Institute (n 4).

85 Choe Sang-Hun, 'Test Looms as U.S. Tracks North Korean Ship,' *The New York Times*, 21 June 2009.

86 'Seized N. K Containers Had Chemical Weapons Items,' *The Dong-A Ilbo*, 6 October 2009.

87 Thomas Fuller & David E. Sanger, 'Officials Seek Destination of North Korean Arms, *The New York Times*, 13 December 2009.

6 Failed Interdiction of a North Korean Vessel

In June 2011, the U.S destroyer USS *McCampbell* intercepted the Belize-flagged North Korean vessel *MV Light* suspected of transporting missile technology to Myanmar in the international waters south of Shanghai. The U.S. Navy requested boarding, but the North Korean operator refused, despite the granting of authority from Belize, consistent with the U.S.-Belize Ship Boarding Agreement. The North Korean crew claimed that the ship was carrying industrial chemical to Bangladesh. The failure of the North Korean crew to comply with the consent of its flag arguably made it a 'stateless' vessel under international maritime law.

During a pursuit lasting several days, international diplomatic efforts were coordinated, aided by the presence in Washington of the Association of Southeast Asian Nations (ASEAN) delegation. Singapore and Malaysia gave assurances that they would detain the vessel if it made port. Before reaching Southeast Asian waters, however, the *MV Light* stopped and retraced its course back to North Korea, tracked by U.S. surveillance aircraft.[88] The ship was ultimately allowed to return to North Korea. Although the materials were not 'interdicted' or even inspected to verify a violation, the fact that the commodity never reached its planned target made it a 'success' for the PSI.

7 Interdiction of North Korean Ship in the Panama Canal

In July 2013, the Panama government interdicted a 14,000-ton North Korean cargo vessel, the *Chung Chon Gang*, while it was passing through the Panama Canal. The ship was on the way back to North Korea after leaving from Cuba. The container ship was stopped on July 15 under suspicion that it was carrying drugs. It had disappeared from satellite tracking for a few days as it approached the Cuban capital Havana, having departed from Russia's eastern coast three months earlier. Upon a search of the vessel, officials found military hardware including two Soviet-era MIG-21 fighter aircraft, air defense systems, missiles and command and control vehicles hidden under the sacks of sugar.[89]

8 Seizure of a Ship Involved in Ship-to-Ship Transfer of Oil to North Korea

In December 2017, South Korea seized the Hong Kong-flagged oil tanker *Lighthouse Winmore* on the suspicion of transferring of 600 tons of refined oil to a North Korean ship in international waters in violation of UN Security Council

88 Euan Graham, 'Maritime Counter-Proliferation: The Case of MV Light,' *RSIS*, 29 June 2011.

89 'N Korean ship seized with Cuban Weapons Returns to Cuba,' *BBC News*, 15 February 2014.

Resolution 2397. The Resolution requires member states to prohibit direct or indirect transactions of oil with North Korea, noting that North Korea is illicitly exporting coal and other prohibited items through deceptive maritime practices and obtaining petroleum illegally through ship-to-ship transfers.[90]

Allegedly on October 15, the *Lighthouse Winmore,* which called in the port of Yeosu, South Korea, to load 14,039 tons of refined petroleum, departed for Taiwan. Instead, the *Lighthouse Winmore* transferred the refined oil to four other ships in international waters, including the transfer of 600 tons to the North Korean ship *Sam Jong 2* on October 2. Previously, the U.S Department of Treasury released satellite photos showing a ship-to-ship transfer involving another North Korean ship, *Rye Song Gang 1*.

VI Challenges to the PSI

Lack of Legality

The largest challenge of the PSI might be concerned with its legality to serve as a global maritime security norm. Critics argue that the enforcement of interdictions on the high seas is not consistent with the doctrine of the freedom of the high seas under the UNCLOS and international customary law. Although the Statement of Interdiction Principles requires that interdictions should be conducted to the extent that national legal authorities and international law and frameworks permit, the international legal basis for interdictions on the high seas are not robust enough.

Criticism of its probable lack of legality comes from the fact that it was created outside the UN and the international law-making process. Furthermore, the PSI does not fall under any UN committee or body. Thus, controversy is likely to arise if participant states, without national legal authorities of interdiction, are able to detain and seize vessels carrying WMD and related materials, relying on only the interdiction principles.

Limited Application

A key challenge in the PSI framework is that it is applicable only to commercial, not government, transportation, pursuant to the doctrine of state immunity. Warships and non-commercial government vessels on the high seas are granted complete immunity from inspections of any states other than the flag state.[91] The possible use of vessels entitled to state immunity to ship WMD and

90 UNSC Resolution 2397, para. 9.

91 UNCLOS, Arts. 96 & 96.

related materials to states or non-state actors remains unchallenged in any of the legal frameworks developed in response to concerns regarding maritime terrorism and proliferation at sea.[92] The PSI, bilateral ship-boarding agreements, and the 2005 SUA Protocol make no attempt to change this principle.[93]

Under the doctrine of state immunity, government vessels used for non-commercial service cannot be legally interdicted on the high seas. Thus, the doctrine could be abused by states of proliferation concern to avoid interdictions. Of particular concern is North Korea, whose merchant vessels are subject to comprehensive and tough sanctions imposed by the UN Security Council. For example, an event that the missile shipments picked up by a Pakistani C-130 in 2002 in North Korea could not have been intercepted under the PSI[94] may demonstrate the concern.

Low and Uneven Participation

Launched with 11 states in 2003, participation in the PSI has greatly expanded to 106 states over the years. However, as examined earlier, participation remains relatively low out of 193 UN member states, and furthermore participant states are unevenly represented by region. A majority of the participants are European states. Only four out of 55 African states are joining the PSI, and a large number of Asian states are not parties to the PSI. Some key states in the continents, such as Brazil, China, Egypt, India, Indonesia, Pakistan and South Africa, remain out of the PSI framework. In order to strengthen the international basis of the PSI, the quality and quantity of the membership of the PSI should be enhanced. More active involvement of participants should also be encouraged, with increased political will and commitment, to achieve the goals of the PSI.

Strengthening of the Structural Basis

As described earlier, the PSI is not an organization, but an activity, and it has no formal mechanism to deal with secretariat affairs. The PSI is led by the Operational Experts Group (OEG), composed of 21 states. The OEG plays an essential role in ensuring the effectiveness of the PSI by[95]: (i) leveraging related counter-proliferation efforts; (ii) contributing customs, law enforcement, military and other security experts and assets to interdiction exercises; (iii) hosting

---

92 Klein (n 35), p. 209.

93 *Ibid.*

94 Squassoni (n 73).

95 U.S. Department of State, 'Proliferation Security Initiative,' available at https://www.state.gov/t/isn/c10390.htm.

PSI meetings, workshops and exercises with other PSI participants, and; (iv) working with specific states to improve their capacity to combat the proliferation of WMD.

OEG delegations initially were dominated by personnel from defense ministries. Over time, however, experts expanded to include breakout groups on intelligence, customs, law enforcement and legal authorities. Without a formal mechanism, the OEG, in its place, *de facto* serves as the secretariat of the PSI while undertaking the aforementioned duties. However, the OEG has limitations on playing the role of a secretariat due to not a standing structure and legal authority as well as budget constraints.

The creation of a secretariat for the PSI needs to be considered to address this problem. Furthermore, the leadership of major regional states should be strengthened and they should play a greater role in formulating the PSI as a multilateral security cooperation framework in the region.

Difficulties in Enforcement of Interdiction at Sea

To interdict a vessel underway is, in practice, a very risky job because a great deal of danger is involved in the conduct of interdiction at sea. This will be particularly the case when a vessel refuses to comply with interdiction. Without compliance from a suspect vessel, it would be extremely challenging to force a suspect vessel underway to stop and be boarded and searched, given that a ship engaged in an international voyage is a physically enormous structure. Furthermore, it would be an extremely hard job to search the ship and discover illicit materials hidden in general cargo at sea. Thus, a ship needs to be brought to a port and the cargo onboard needs to be discharged and inspected by experts of various fields. As demonstrated in the interdictions of vessels from states of proliferation concern, especially North Korea, a suspect vessel is not likely to comply with instructions in a good manner.

For North Korea, its merchant ships are believed to be owned by the North Korean government, and crews are military or government personnel and are armed, as demonstrated in the *Dai Hong Dan* incident, which occurred on 29 October 2007. When the North Korean cargo ship was attacked by Somali pirates who were disguised as guards and boarded the ship, the armed North Korean sailors fought to beat back the pirates' attack.[96] Given this circumstance, there could be armed conflicts when interdiction is enforced on suspect vessels from North Korea.

96 See 'N. Korea Thanks U.S. for Piracy Aid,' *Associated Press*, 9 November 2007.

VII Conclusion

Over the years, the international community in the new security environment has been increasingly convinced of the need for action to implement and advance shared security goals. Devised as a security instrument to address new security threats, the PSI is an important contribution to global non-proliferation efforts and is a strong deterrent to proliferation-related trafficking. The efforts to be consistent with national legislation and international law and frameworks appears to defuse, to a large extent, concerns that the PSI would undermine the formal treaty and agreement framework.

Despite an initial success, however, many challenges lie ahead of the PSI, *inter alia,* with regard to formulating the rules for interdiction of WMD. The foremost challenge might be concerned with how to promote the participation of strategic regional states and strengthen the legal basis of the PSI. Another important challenge is to address the perception of the PSI as a U.S.-led security regime. The U.S.'s roles and contributions to the establishment and evolution of the PSI should be highly recognized. However, such perception deters, to a certain extent, the PSI from evolving into a global security norm with much broader participation. As demonstrated in a number of previous interdictions, participating states greatly rely on intelligence provided by the U.S. Without addressing an intelligence gap between the U.S. and other participating states, the PSI is likely to continue to remain a U.S. led-security initiative.

If the PSI continues to be dominated by the U.S., this would make it harder for the PSI to evolve into a customary global security norm, which is an ultimate goal of the PSI. A solution to this challenge would be to strengthen the leadership of strategic regional states, and to encourage more active participation of regional states. On this basis, the PSI needs to become a global security mechanism that rallies cooperation of participating states in preventing and deterring the proliferation of WMD and related materials.

CHAPTER 8

Growing Roles of Coast Guards in East Asia

I Introduction

Apart from the race for a naval buildup in East Asia in the post-Cold War era, a notable trend in the maritime security domain is the expansion of the functions and roles of coast guards. With a growing need to protect their rights in extended maritime jurisdictions and respond to increasing maritime disputes, East Asian countries have built up the capacities of their own coast guards. Notably, regional coast guards, which are at the forefront of maritime disputes, serve as a principal instrument of regional states to support their claims and protect maritime interests and resources.

Beyond the typical missions of offshore law enforcement and search and rescue, regional coast guards are tasked with the protection of rights and the safeguarding of maritime sovereignty in a wide range of maritime disputes. As a result, the roles of regional coast guards have expanded beyond policing tasks offshore — now, they frequently take on a conflict-management role in the international maritime domain. Furthermore, non-traditional security threats such as piracy, maritime terrorism, marine pollution and illegal fishing have emerged as grave challenges to the safe and secure use of the sea.

Given the greater importance and suitability of coast guards in dealing with these challenges, and given that intensifying maritime disputes involve law enforcement with wide powers to arrest both foreigners and national citizens,[1] East Asian countries have sought to build up the capability of coast guards by empowering them with more authority, expanding their functions, allocating them more resources or even creating a new coast guard. The expansion of coast guards in the region is spearheaded by China, which is in dispute with other countries in the East and South China Seas. China's assertiveness in maritime disputes, with an aggressive buildup of coast guard forces, has triggered a coast guard buildup race throughout East Asia. Japan, Korea and Southeast Asian countries engaged in maritime disputes with China are joining the race.

---

1 Sam Bateman, 'Coast Guards: New Forces for Regional Order and Security,' (2003) 65, *Asia Pacific Issues, Analysis from the East-West Center*.

 | DOI:10.1163/9789004389908_009

Despite the greater roles of coast guards, the status of coast guards in national politics is generally weaker than competing agencies such as the navy and the police, and as a result, they are often swayed by national political circumstances. This is well demonstrated in the case of the Korea Coast Guard, which has undergone organizational disbandment and reinstatement over the last two years.

Against this backdrop, this chapter aims to explore the greater roles and functions of coast guards in East Asia in relation to maritime disputes. It will examine the various different types of coast guards in the region and their responsibilities and duties, and their legal status from a comparative approach. This chapter also aims to explore how maritime disputes lead to the expansion of regional coast guards and what factors affect this expansion.

II Overview of Coast Guards in East Asia

Definitions of 'Coast Guard'

In a common usage, a coast guard is generally referred to as a maritime law enforcement agency of a particular country. Among various maritime enforcement agencies, a coast guard is a pivotal institution used to ensure maritime safety, security and law and order at sea. For this purpose, a coast guard carries out a wide range of duties at sea, and thus is described as an amalgam of diverse maritime services. The term 'coast guard' is believed to derive from the United Kingdom's Waterguard, established in 1809, and the United States Coast Guard, which was renamed the Coast Guard in 1915 when the Revenue Cutter Service merged with the U.S. Life-Saving Service.[2]

There is no definition of coast guard in international law. The general usage of the word 'coast guard' or 'coast guard agency' is used to indicate various different types of maritime enforcement agencies. As such, various maritime enforcement agencies, which are tasked primarily with policing offshore and conducting search and rescue operations, with the authority to enforce maritime laws and regulate maritime activities over civilians and foreigners, are described as a coast guard.

Maritime enforcement agencies in East Asia, which are mostly named 'coast guard' in English, have their own service names in their respective languages. The names indicate more apparently organizational characteristics and the

2 United States Coast Guard, 'The Coast Guard through History,' available at website of USCG, https://www.gocoastguard.com/about-the-coast-guard/learn-the-history.

priority of multi-missions. The description of a coast guard may become more distinctive when compared with the description of a navy.

Relationship with the Navy

The coast guard appears similar to the navy, and people sometimes get confused about the differences. The confusion might be derived from their similarities in many respects. Both are uniformed, armed, and operate ships (coast guard ships are described as the 'white hull,' as opposed to the 'grey hull' for naval ships).

However, their duties and missions are distinctive, in addition to differences in their size, assets, organizational structure, and the status of personnel. While the navy is tasked primarily with fighting wars and deterring aggression in the name of national defense, the coast guard is responsible for law enforcement and safety and security in the seas under the national jurisdiction. Traditionally, naval ships have played an essential role in the projection of maritime power of the state and have been regarded as the extension of national sovereignty. Thus, their engagements in maritime disputes have significant implications. While a standoff of coast guard ships is generally viewed as an operational and law enforcement conflict, a naval ships' confrontation could be seen as a showdown between the parties.

In terms of the level of armament, the differences are remarkable. Whereas naval ships are heavily armed with heavy and high-technology weapons, coast guard ships are lightly armed for law enforcement and, to a lesser extent, for self-defense. The coast guard and the navy are subject to a different ethos and set of rules, under which the navy is governed by military doctrines while the coast guard falls under civilian discipline and law.

In terms of law enforcement authority, coast guard officers are authorized to enforce national maritime laws on national citizens and foreigners, while military forces in many countries are prohibited from being involved in policing duties against national citizens for constitutional and political reasons.[3] In the United States, for example, the military is constrained by the *Posse Comitatus* Act, which embodies the traditional American principle of separating civilian and military authority and prohibits the use of the military in civilian law enforcement.[4]

Before the emergence of the coast guard, the navy performed both warfighting and constabulary missions. In East Asia, in particular, coast guards

3 Bateman (n 1).

4 *Ibid.*

were spawned off from the navy or were newly created, with a growing need for a separate maritime enforcement agency responsible for constabulary tasks. While coast guards come to the forefront in maritime disputes, the navies in peacetime expand their roles to coast guard-type missions, including the protection of sea lanes of communication, anti-piracy, protection of the marine environment and disaster relief. Thus, the roles and functions of the coast guard and the navy tend to be, to a certain extent, convergent to each other.

Despite their differences in roles and missions, the coast guard and the navy are complementary to each other, constituting the core maritime bodies of a state. The growing need for cooperation in coping with a wide range of maritime challenges requires the two maritime bodies to build a close working relationship — sharing platforms, assets and doctrines.

In East Asian countries, in which there exists a tradition that coast guards are considered as a subordinate body of the navy, the challenge is how to build a cooperative relationship between the two bodies on the basis of mutual respect. Principally, the way to balance the two maritime bodies may depend on national factors such as national security priorities, political demands, resources strategic culture, etc.

Typology of Coast Guards

Coast guards in East Asia are diverse, varying with the unique circumstances of their nations' historical background, judicial system, military structure, law enforcement system, security situation, priority of maritime affairs, etc. Given these elements, countries have either developed their own coast guard systems, which are regarded as suitable for their national circumstances, or they have opted not to have a separate coast guard.

In this context, coast guards across the world are country-specific, to the extent that the duties and functions are asymmetrical, depending on the priority of mandates. There are a number of different types of coast guards in East Asia, which differ with respect to organizational characteristics, authority, mission, armament and relationships with military and law enforcement agencies. Given these factors, regional coast guards can be classified as several different categories.

1 Military Force

This type of coast guard is typically a branch of a nation's military services and is subject to a military ethos and principles. The personnel are soldiers who are commissioned and mandated by military rules and are assisted by career civilians who provide services in technical fields. The organization of the coast guard parallels that of the navy, and the coast guard ranks and ratings are generally identical to those of the navy. The military-force type coast guard is mandated to fulfill the combined duties of law enforcement and other typical coast guard missions in peacetime as well as military operations under the command of the navy in wartime.

In terms of the level of armament, however, the military-force type coast guard carries lighter arms than the navy, and is only armed to the extent that it is capable of protecting itself and carrying out the mission of assistance to the navy. This is because the coast guard is principally not a war-fighting force, but a complementary force to the navy to assist in wartime. While military-force type coast guards undertake typical coast guard missions, they primarily serve as a defense force.

The United States Coast Guard (USCG) is regarded as the prototype of a military-force type coast guard. The USCG is one of the nation's five military services, along with the Navy, Army, Air Force and Marine Corps. In times of peace, the USCG operates as part of the Department of Homeland Security, carrying out the enforcement of all federal laws at sea, protection of the marine environment, the safeguarding of coastline and ports, and lifesaving missions. In times of war, or at the direction of the president of the U.S., the USCG is subject to control of the Navy.[5]

Despite being a military force, the scope of duties of the USCG is very comprehensive and far reaching, even extending into civilian affairs — in other words, being responsible for almost all the tasks of maritime safety and security. For example, the captain of the port, who is designated by the commandant of the USCG, is a uscg officer who is usually the commander of a sector. This person is responsible for port safety and security and marine environmental protection regulations, including regulations for the protection and security of vessels, harbors and waterfront facilities; anchorages; security zones; safety zones; regulated navigation areas; deepwater ports; water pollution; and ports and waterways safety.[6]

5 See 14 U.S. Code §3 (Department in which the Coast Guard Operates): (a)IN GENERAL: The Coast Guard shall be a service in the Department of Homeland Security, except when operating as a service in the Navy.

(b)TRANSFERS: Upon the declaration of war if Congress so directs in the declaration or when the President directs, the Coast Guard shall operate as a service in the Navy, and shall so continue until the President, by Executive order, transfers the Coast Guard back to the Department of Homeland Security. While operating as a service in the Navy, the Coast Guard shall be subject to the orders of the Secretary of the Navy, who may order changes in Coast Guard operations to render them uniform, to the extent such Secretary deems advisable, with Navy operations.

6 33 CFR. Code § 6.01-3.

This type of coast guard was common in East Asia before coast guards became civilian agencies that were no longer part of the navy. The Indian Coast Guard (ICG) falls within the realm of military force. The ICG was created in 1978 as an independent armed service of the Indian Union, becoming the fourth armed force under the Ministry of Defense. The need for a separate maritime service apart from the navy to undertake anti-smuggling and law enforcement tasks led to the establishment of the ICG. The duties and functions are defined in the Coast Guard Act enacted in 1978.

2 Paramilitary Force

Unlike military-force type coast guards, the coast guards under this category are not a military branch but a civilian service. Although they are not part of the military, they can be said to be a military force in nature, because they are an armed force and subject to the military ethos in many respects. They are armed to the extent that they are capable of acting in self-defense and enforcing laws against illegal acts at sea. For this purpose, coast guard officers are allowed to carry light firearms, and vessels are equipped with weapons such as deck-mounted auto-cannons that range in caliber from 20 to 76mm and machine guns, depending on the size of the vessels.

The coast guard officers under this type are principally civilians whose responsibilities and authorities are subject to relevant laws. They perform multiple roles: as a police officer when engaged in enforcing criminal laws, and as an agent of a particular administrative office when enforcing the laws and rules under its jurisdiction at sea. The authority of coast guard officers in this regard are strictly constrained to the fulfillment of the responsibilities defined by those laws and rules. Most coast guards in East Asia fall within the category of paramilitary force.

The primary example of this type of coast guard may be the Japan Coast Guard (JCG). The JCG was founded in 1948 as a civilian law enforcement entity, called the Maritime Safety Agency, which was the outer bureau of the Ministry of Transportation. The JCG is currently under the Ministry of Land, Infrastructure and Transportation. In accordance with the provision of the JCG Law, the JCG is not permitted to be trained or organized or function as an armed force.[7]

The provision exists because the Soviet Union representative of the Allied Council strongly opposed the establishment of the JCG and proposed the provision. Allegedly the Soviet Union's opposition was due to bitter experiences

7 JCG Law, Art. 25: "Nothing contained in this Law shall be construed to permit the Japan Coast Guard or its personnel to be trained or organized as a military establishment or to function as such."

with the Japanese Navy's response to the Soviet Union's enforcement on Japanese fishing activities in the Sea of Okhotsk.[8] In relationship to the navy, all or part of the JCG falls under the command of the Minister of Defense through the commandant of the JCG when a Defense Action Order is issued. When a Maritime Security Order is issued, the navy is authorized to conduct the mission of the JCG, in accordance with the Japan Coast Guard Law.[9]

In terms of criminal investigation, JCG officers, in accordance with the direction of the commandant of the JCG, undertake the duties of judicial officials in dealing with sea crimes.[10] While JCG officers are engaged in enforcing law and order, they are deemed officials of the agency responsible for undertaking those duties.[11]

The Philippine Coast Guard (PCG) may fall within this category. The PCG is an armed and uniformed service tasked primarily with enforcing laws, ensuring maritime safety and security and protecting the marine environment — missions which are similar to typical coast guards. The PCG was first created in 1967 as a part of the Philippine Navy, and was commanded by a flag officer. The functions of the PCG were later transferred from the navy. Eventually the civilian nature of the PCG led to the creation of a separate coast guard agency from the navy in 1998, and the PCG was transferred to the Department of Transportation.

The Indonesian Coast Guard (ICG) may also be categorized as a paramilitary force. The origin of the ICG is traced back to the Maritime Security Coordinating Board (MSCB), formed in 1972 by a joint decree of several government agencies, including the Ministry of Defense and Security, the Armed Forces, the Ministry of Communications, the Ministry of Finance and the Ministry of Justice. The increasing need for a designated maritime law enforcement agency led to the transformation of the MSCB into the Maritime Security Agency (*Bakamla* or Coast Guard) in 2004. Not limited to the coordination of the multiple agencies, the newly reborn ICG expanded its roles, ranging from early detection of unlawful acts to enforcing the law using its own cutters.[12]

---

8 Fumio Ota, 'The Relationship between the Japan Coast Guard and the Maritime Self Defense Force' in 'Navies, Coast Guards, the Maritime Community and International Stability' (eds by Ian Bowers & Collin Koh), *RSIS Policy Brief*, S. Rajaratnam School of International Studies, Nanyang Technological University, March, 2017, p. 31.

9 *Ibid.*, p. 33.

10 JCG Law, Art. 31.

11 *Ibid.*, Art. 15.

12 Muhamad Arif, 'Inward-Looking Navy and Expanding Bakamla: The Indonesian Case of Navy-Coast Guard Nexus,' in 'Navies, Coast Guards, the Maritime Community and International Stability' (eds by Ian Bowers & Collin Koh), *RSIS Policy Brief*, S. Rajaratnam School of International Studies, Nanyang Technological University, March, 2017, p. 48.

A particular feature in relation to maritime law enforcement is that the Indonesian Navy shares the roles of law enforcement at sea. This results in a dualism in the national maritime law enforcement system and hinders the achievement of national maritime interests. Drawing a proper demarcation of roles and functions between the two agencies remains a challenge to the maritime management of Indonesia.[13]

3 Police Force

In terms of organizational characteristics, the coast guards under this category are either a branch of national police or a separate maritime police. The police type coast guards operate primarily as a maritime policing and law enforcement agency while undertaking typical coast guard missions. They are distinctive in that they are granted more comprehensive judicial authorities than other types of coast guards.

The status of a coast guard officer is as a marine police officer who is authorized to exercise judicial power identical to land police officers, except that their authorities are principally constrained to the sea and sea crimes. The ranking of coast guard officers is identical to the land police, and generally the officers are subject to the same laws as the land police in term of their status and authority. Under certain circumstances, they are transferrable to each other. The primary examples of police coast guards in East Asia are the Korea Coast Guard (KCG) and the Singapore Police Coast Guard (SPCG).

The KCG was founded in 1953 as a unit of the national police, with a principal aim of protecting fishery resources against Japanese exploitation off the Korean Peninsula. The KCG became an independent central agency in 1996, separating from the National Police Agency (NPA) and was placed under the Ministry of Oceans and Fisheries. The National Maritime Police Agency was renamed in English in 2006 as the Korea Coast Guard, while the Korean name remains unchanged.

The renaming was intended to better convey the organization's roles and functions beyond policing and law enforcement offshore, as well as to align with the global trend of greater roles for coast guards. In terms of organizational characteristics, the KCG is a national police agency, responsible for maritime safety and security and law enforcement. Reflecting the nature of the KCG as a police agency, the head is called 'Commissioner,' whose rank is equivalent to the commissioner of the National Police Agency.

---

13 *Ibid.*

The KCG is not necessarily staffed by police officers, but rather the department of marine pollution response is operated by career civilians. Although the KCG differs in organizational hierarchy from the NPA, which falls under the Ministry of the Interior, the KCG and the NPA share much of the same laws and rules related to the status of officers and the authorization of policing and law enforcement. As a police agency, the investigation of sea crimes is an integral part of its wide range of tasks and missions. Notably, its judicial jurisdiction is not necessarily restricted to the sea and can be expanded to the land if deemed necessary.

The Singapore Police Coast Guard (SPCG) is an operational division of the Singapore Police Force (SPC). Previously it was a marine police division of the SPC and underwent a major organizational restructuring, which upgraded the Marine Police to the Police Coast Guard in 1993,[14] and as such its functions were transferred from the navy. The SPCG is a police unit within the SPC, tasked with typical coast guard missions. As such, the officers of the SPCG have the same law enforcement power as the land police force. A higher priority of the SPCG is on preventing illegal immigration, handling foreign government vessel intrusion and guarding the Horsburgh Lighthouse[15] in the Singapore Straits.[16]

4 Civil Service

For coast guards that fall within the realm of civil service, generally only personnel serving on the operational side are uniformed service members. Other than those, these organizations are primarily staffed and administered by career civilians. Coast guard personnel on the operational side, charged with maritime enforcement, are entrusted to enforce maritime laws, but their judicial authorities, in comparison with other types of coast guards, tend to be very limited or nonexistent.

The Canadian Coast Guard (CCG) might be representative of this type of coast guard. The CCG is a civilian service under the Department of Fisheries and Oceans, tasked with non-law-enforcement marine affairs such as search and rescue, navigation aids, icebreaking, marine pollution response and

14 See website of the Singapore Police Force, 'Police Coast Guard,' available at https://www.police.gov.sg/about-us/organisational-structure/specialist-and-line-units/police-coast-guard#content.

15 The Horsburgh Lighthouse is situated on the Pedra Branca Island, located in the eastern entrance to the Straits of Singapore. The sovereignty of Pedra Branca was disputed between Malaysia and Singapore. In May 2008, the International Court of Justice ruled that Singapore has the sovereignty over the island.

16 *Ibid.*

maritime security.[17] The CCG is not entrusted with the responsibilities of law enforcement. Rather, the CCG serves in an operational role in the delivery of maritime law enforcement and security services provided by the federal agencies concerned.[18] Federal maritime laws are enforced by peace officers serving with various federal, provincial or even municipal law enforcement agencies. The enforcement of laws in Canada's territorial sea is the responsibility of the federal police force, the Royal Canadian Mounted Police.[19]

The Malaysian Maritime Enforcement Agency (MMEA), also known as the Malaysian Coast Guard, is part of the Malaysian Civil Service and is under the Prime Minister's Department. In a sense, it may be categorized as a paramilitary force, given that it is an armed service. In a broad sense, however, it can be regarded as a civil service agency in terms of organizational hierarchy. The MMEA was formed in 2004 as a result of a study conducted by the Malaysian government which recognized the need for the restructuring of the maritime enforcement structure. The study concluded that maritime enforcement and search and rescue conducted by eight different government agencies were not efficient because of overlapping functions, overlapping jurisdiction, and an inefficient use of resources.[20]

Based on the study, the Malaysian government decided to establish a new maritime enforcement body, the MMEA. The MMEA was merely an additional civilian agency of the Prime Minister's Department until 2011, when the Malaysian government granted it the status of a sole maritime enforcement agency. This was because some of the government agencies involved were reluctant to transfer maritime enforcement tasks, and continued to deal with maritime enforcement in their own ways.[21]

It is notable that the MMEA shares the tasks of maritime enforcement with the Royal Malaysian Police. The MMEA shares maritime enforcement with the Marine Operation Force of the Royal Malaysian Police (formerly known as the Marine Police) that is tasked with policing ports and rivers.[22] This organization

---

17 See website of the Canadian Coast Guard, 'Canadian Coast Guard,' available at http://www.ccg-gcc.gc.ca/eng/CCG/Home.

18 *Ibid.*

19 *Ibid.*

20 See website of the Malaysian Maritime Enforcement Agency, 'MMEA's Background,' available at https://www.mmea.gov.my/eng/index.php/en/mengenai-kami/latar-belakang.

21 See Dzirhan Mahadzir, 'The Malaysian Case Study,' in 'Navies, Coast Guards, the Maritime Community and International Stability' (eds by Ian Bowers & Collin Koh), *RSIS Policy Brief*, S. Rajaratnam School of International Studies, Nanyang Technological University, March, 2017, p. 40.

22 *Ibid.*

is believed to be a result of negotiations between the newly born maritime enforcement agency and the Marine Police — the Marine Police force was strongly opposed to the establishment of MMEA and refused to be incorporated into it.

5 Volunteer Organization

The prominent feature of coast guard organizations under this category is that maritime rescue services are provided by volunteers. The volunteer coast guard organization, which is not a law enforcement agency, provides search and rescue services to persons or vessels in distress at sea, in collaboration with other agencies such as the police, the navy and air force. The coast guard organization is usually part of a maritime enforcement agency responsible for mobilizing adequate resources and coordinating rescue operations.

Her Majesty's Coastguard (HMCG) of the United Kingdom is a prototype of a volunteer coast guard. The HMCG is a section of the Maritime and Coastguard Agency (MCA), which is a government agency responsible for implementing maritime safety and security policies.[23] The MCA is responsible for the initiation and coordination of resources and maritime search and rescue operations. The search and rescue service is delivered by Coastguard Rescue Officers of the HMCG who are volunteers trained to carry out rescue operations.[24] Volunteer coast guard organizations have been a long tradition in the British Commonwealth of Nations, including in Australia and New Zealand. This type of coast guard organizations is not found in East Asia.

6 Non-Separate Coast Guard

Some small countries have not established a separate coast guard service. The countries have a navy but no coast guard. These countries include Cambodia in East Asia. Table 10 summarizes the typology discussed.

III Roles and Duties of Coast Guards

As discussed above, there exist a variety of different types of coast guards across the world. Coast guards are principally maritime enforcement agencies responsible for ensuring maritime safety and security. However, their roles and responsibilities differ in detail, given the circumstances particular to each nation. The followings are the roles and responsibilities of typical coast guards.

23 See website of the Maritime and Coastguard Agency, available at https://www.gov.uk/government/organisations/maritime-and-coastguard-agency.

24 *Ibid.*

TABLE 10 Typology of coast guards

Typology	Military force	Paramilitary force	Police force	Civil service	Volunteer force	Non-separate coast guard
Country	– U.S. – India	– Japan – China – Philippine – Indonesia	– Korea – Singapore – Vietnam	– Canada – Malaysia	– U.K – Australia – New Zealand	– Cambodia
Feature	– Defense force	– Civilian service	– Comprehensive judicial authority	– Staffed with and administered by civilians	– Rescue services are provided by civilian volunteers	– Small countries do not establish a separate coast guard
	– Subject to military rules and ethos	– Armed for self-defense and law enforcement	– Composed of police officers	– Operational side personnel are armed and uniformed	– Other missions are carried out by maritime enforcement agencies	
	– Undertake typical coast guard missions in peacetime and assist the navy in wartime	– Undertake constabulary duties and typical coast guard missions	– Focus on law enforcement	– Judicial powers are very limited	– Do not exist in East Asia	

	– Composed of soldiers assisted by civilian careers	– Most common type in East Asia	– Maritime enforcement authority is limited		
Name of Service	– Coast Guard (U.S., India)	– Maritime Safety Agency (Japan) – Zhongquo Haijing (中國海警)(China) – Coast Guard (Philippine) – Maritime Security Agency (Indonesia)	– National Maritime Police Agency (Korea) – Police Coast Guard (Singapore) – Maritime Police (Vietnam)	– Coast Guard (Canada) – Maritime Enforcement Agency (Malaysia)	– Her Majesty's Coast Guard (U.K)

SOURCE: THE AUTHOR'S FINDINGS

1 Protection of Maritime Sovereignty

In a broad sense, the protection of maritime sovereignty may best embody the evolving tasks of contemporary coast guards, which are required to play greater roles as the rights and jurisdiction of a coastal state are expanded to the exclusive economic zone (EEZ). With maritime disputes erupting, the primary mandate of coast guards is to protect the maritime rights, marine resources and territorial integrity of states. The protection of fishery and energy resources against illegal foreign exploitation is also a vital task of coast guards in this regard.

2 Law Enforcement

As noted in the preceding, having a law enforcement authority is often pointed to as the most significant distinction between the coast guard and the navy. The law enforcement authority of coast guards varies, to a large extent, with their types of organization. As discussed in the preceding, the police-type coast guards tend to have more comprehensive law enforcement authorities than other types of coast guards. They are usually authorized to arrest and investigate individuals involved in crimes occurring on the sea or crimes related to maritime affairs. Regardless of differences in authority, coast guards tend to be a lead agency among various maritime law enforcement agencies such as customs, immigration and fisheries. This might be due to the capacity of the coast guard, which operates a large number of ships and personnel who specialize in maritime enforcement.

3 Search and Rescue

The duty of life-saving is one of the most fundamental and highly regarded values of coast guards, irrespective of type. The origin of coast guards is derived from the need for a specialized maritime agency to provide professional search and rescue services to mariners in distress. Search and rescue services of coast guards, which build on an old tradition of rendering assistance to mariners in distress, are provided in collaboration with other public agencies and civilian organizations. Internationally, coast guards cooperate with neighboring coast guards in the framework of the Search and Rescue Convention or regional agreements.

4 Ensuring Maritime Safety and Security

Typically, coast guards are responsible for enforcing a wide range of maritime safety and security regimes and institutions. Varying with the range of authority, coast guards are responsible for enforcing a variety of international maritime safety and security regimes adopted by their governments. Coast guards are authorized to enforce their own rules, standards and measures to ensure the safety and security of seafarers, vessels, ports, the marine environment and offshore installations. To ensure the safety of maritime traffic is an integral part of coast guard tasks because it is inherently linked to the safety of life, vessels and the marine environment. For that reason, coast guards in many countries are tasked with the management of aids to navigation such as lighthouse, buoys and Vessel Traffic Services (VTS).

5 Protection of Sea Lanes

The protection of sea lanes of communication from various maritime threats is an essential part of a coast guard's duties. To keep the sea lanes of communication at strategic chokepoints, in particular, open and safe is vital to free navigation and seaborne trade. Notably in Southeast Asia, which has been a hotspot for piracy and armed criminal attacks, the anti-piracy mission is a top priority of regional coast guards.

6 Protection of the Marine Environment

To preserve a clean and safe marine environment is also a vital task of coast guards. Typically, coast guards are tasked with preventive measures to preserve the marine environment. The measures include raising marine environment awareness, controlling pollutants, monitoring pollution, port state control, etc. However, the roles of coast guards in marine pollution incidents differ from state to state. In some cases, marine pollution response is carried out jointly or with other agencies.

7 Role of National Defense

Typically in wartime, most of coast guards, irrespective of their organizational structure, are assigned to the navy and are subject to its command. They could participate in engagements, but normally coast guards are mandated to assist in naval operations by transporting war supplies and troops, as well as protecting naval bases. In peacetime, coast guards are a supplementary force to the navy. Coast guards assist navies in their operations such as border control, anti-spy ship operations, protection of naval bases and offshore military installations, patrolling of military waters, etc.

IV Status of Coast Guard Ships in International Law: Rights and Responsibilities

As the roles of coast guards become significantly more important in dealing with maritime disputes and expanding beyond offshore operations, controversies with regard to the status of coast guard ships in international law have been arisen. This is because the legal status of coast guard ships in the UN Convention on the Law of the Sea (UNCLOS) is less explicit than that of warships. In this section, the legal status of coast guard ships and their rights and responsibilities in the UNCLOS will be discussed. Along with warships, coast guard ships, as government ships, are granted a special status and rights, but are also required to fulfill corresponding responsibilities.

1 Innocent Passage

The UNCLOS stipulates that "ships of all states, whether coastal or land-locked, enjoy the right of innocent passage through the territorial sea."[25] When exercising the right of innocent passage, passage should be 'continuous' and 'expeditious' and should not be 'prejudicial to the peace, good order or security of the coastal state.'[26] Pursuant to the innocent passage provision, which is applicable to all ships, regardless of commercial or government ships, coast guard ships are entitled to exercise the right of innocent passage and subject to the duties thereof.

With the creation of the innocent passage regime, a heated controversy arose as to whether a prior authorization for the passage of warships through the territorial sea should be allowed. The UNCLOS failed to give a definite answer to that question.[27] Under this circumstance, East Asian states take slightly different positions. China requires foreign military ships to obtain permission to enter its territorial sea, but it allows non-military ships to enjoy the right of innocent passage without permission.[28]

Whether the scope of 'non-military ships' encompasses foreign coast guard ships could be controversial. For Korea, 'foreign warships' or 'non-commercial government ships' that intend to pass through its territorial sea are required to give a 3-day advance notice.[29] Unlike China and Korea, Japan remains silent on innocent passage through its territorial sea, providing only the scope of territorial sea, baseline and others.[30] In conclusion, given the nature of coast guard ships, which are a lightly armed maritime enforcement force, the requirement

25 UNCLOS Art. 17.
26 *Ibid.* Arts. 18 & 19.
27 See Suk Kyoon Kim, *Maritime Disputes in Northeast Asia: Regional Challenges and Cooperation* (Brill, Boston, 2017), p. 49.
28 The Law on the Territorial Sea and the Contiguous Zone, Arts. 6 & 8.
29 The Law on the Territorial and Contiguous Zone Art. 5(1) & (2) and the Presidential Decree, Art. 4.
30 Kim (n 27).

of permission for innocent passage appears to be contrary to the underlying tenet of innocent passage.

Another controversy concerns the legal status of the ships of coast guards, which are part of a military force. Applying the definition of warships of Article 29 of the UNCLOS,[31] for example, it could be controversial as to whether U.S. Coast Guard ships are warships or not. A problem may arise with regard to the application of Article 30, which provides a coastal state's right to request any warship to leave the territorial sea immediately when it does not comply with national laws and regulations on innocent passage. Where a coast guard vessel is not a warship it would be subject not to this request but to possible arrest. However, as a coast guard vessel is subject to sovereign immunity the vessel would not be subject to direct law enforcement by the coastal state.

2 Responsibility of the Flag State for Damage Caused by a Coast Guard Ship

The flag state is obliged to bear international responsibility for any loss or damage to the coastal state resulting from the non-compliance by a coast guard ship operated for non-commercial purposes with laws and regulations of the coastal state concerning innocent passage while exercising the right of innocent passage.[32] Other than this immunity, coast guard ships shall be subject to law enforcement of the coastal state.[33]

3 Right and Duties of Transit Passage

Transit passage is the exercise of freedom of navigation and over-flight solely for the 'continuous' and 'expeditious' transit of the strait between one area of high sea or economic zone and another, or in order to enter or leave a state bordering the strait.[34] In accordance with the provision of the UNCLOS stating that "all ships enjoy the right of transit passage, which will not be impeded,"[35] coast guard ships are entitled to enjoy an unimpeded passage through the straits used for international navigation.

---

31 UNCLOS, Art. 29 (Definition of Warships): "For the purposes of this Convention, "warship" mean a ship belonging to the armed forces of a State bearing the external marks distinguishing such ships of its nationality, under the command of an officer duly commissioned by the government of the State ..."

32 *Ibid.*, Art. 31.

33 *Ibid.*, Art. 32.

34 R.R. Churchill & A.V. Lowe, *The Law of the Sea, 3rd ed.*' (Manchester University Press, Manchester, 1999), p. 107.

35 UNCLOS, Art. 38(1).

Coast guard ships are subject to the duties of ships during transit passage, which include: to proceed without delay; to refrain from threat or use of force; to comply with international safety regulations, procedures and practices; to comply with international regulations for the prevention, reduction, and control of pollution from ships.[36] During transit passage, coast guard ships are obliged to respect sea lanes and traffic separation schemes and not allowed to carry out any research or survey activities during transit passage without the prior authorization of the states bordering straits.[37]

4 Right and Duties of Innocent Passage in Archipelagic Waters

"An archipelagic state may draw straight archipelagic baselines joining the outermost points of islands and drying reefs of archipelago"[38] and "all ships enjoy the right of archipelagic sea lanes passage in such sea lanes."[39] Pursuant to these provisions, coast guard ships are entitled to enjoy the right of innocent passage through archipelagic waters. The duties during innocent passage through the territorial sea are applied *mutatis mutandis* to coast guard ships.[40]

5 Respect for the Safety Zone

In the exclusive zone, the coastal state has the exclusive right to construct artificial islands, installation and structures.[41] The coastal state may establish safety zones around those, which do not exceed a distance of 500 meters.[42] "All ships must respect these safety zones and comply with generally accepted international standards regarding navigation in the vicinity of artificial islands, installations, structures and safety zones."[43] Subject to these provisions, coast guard ships are obliged to respect safety zones and comply with international regulations concerning navigation.

6 Immunity on the High Seas

Pursuant to the provision that "ships owned or operated by a state and used only on government non-commercial service shall, on the high seas, have complete immunity from the jurisdiction of any state other than the flag state,"[44]

---

36 *Ibid.*, Art. 39(1) & (2).
37 *Ibid.*, Arts. 40. & 41(7).
38 *Ibid.*, Art. 53(1).
39 *Ibid.*, Art. 53(2).
40 *Ibid.*, Art. 54.
41 *Ibid.*, Art. 60(1).
42 *Ibid.*, Art. 60(5).
43 *Ibid.*, Art. 60(6).
44 *Ibid.*, Art. 96.

thus coast guard ships enjoy immunity on the high seas and as a consequence of Article 58(2) also in the EEZ.

7 Seizure on Account of Piracy

On the high seas, a coast guard ship is entitled to seize a ship, irrespective of nationality, that is reasonably suspected of being engaged in piracy.[45] However, where the coast guard ship has wrongfully carried out the seizure of the ship without adequate grounds, the state of the coast guard ship must compensate for any loss or damage.[46]

8 Right of Visit and Hot Pursuit

The UNCLOS allows a warship to visit and board a foreign ship on the high seas when there are reasonable grounds to suspect the foreign ship's engagement in prohibited acts such as piracy, slave trading or unauthorized broadcasting.[47] The warship is also entitled to visit a ship that is suspected of being the same nationality as the warship — even though it may be flying a foreign flag, or refusing to show a flag — when it encounters one on the high seas.[48] These provisions apply *mutatis mutandis* to a coast guard ship.[49]

Under customary law, the right of hot pursuit, which allows a warship of a state to pursue a foreign ship that has violated laws within its internal waters or territorial sea and to arrest it on the high seas, has been long recognized.[50] The UNCLOS has extended the right to include hot pursuit from archipelagic waters and also hot pursuit from the EEZ or waters above the continental shelf.

The UNCLOS states that "the right of hot pursuit may be exercised only by warships or other ships clearly marked and identifiable as being on government service." Pursuant to this provision, a coast guard ship may exercise the right of hot pursuit and arrest the ship which has violated the laws and regulations of the state of the coast guard ship.[51] The pursuing coast guard ship may use any necessary and reasonable force to effect the arrest, even if this results in the unavoidable sinking of the ship.[52] The right of pursuit ceases as soon as the ship enters the territorial sea of its own or a third state.[53]

---

45 *Ibid.*, Art. 107.
46 *Ibid.*, Art. 106.
47 *Ibid.*, Art. 110(1).
48 *Ibid.*
49 *Ibid.*, Art. 110(4).
50 Churchill & Lowe (n 34), p. 214.
51 UNCLOS, Art. 111.
52 Churchill & Lowe (n 34), p. 215.
53 UNCLOS, Art. 111(3).

V Build-Ups of Coast Guards in East Asia

Rationale for Regional Coast Guard Expansion

This section examines the factors — either global or regional — that have led to the expansion of coast guards in East Asia.

1 Extended Coastal State Jurisdiction

The claims of the UNCLOS, which grants coastal states the 200-nautical mile EEZ, led to extended coastal state jurisdiction.[54] The need to build institutions to exercise sovereign rights, to establish national arrangements for managing offshore areas, and to acquire capabilities for maritime surveillance and enforcement in the extended jurisdiction, became a justification for the capacity-building of coast guards.[55] East Asian countries, which have competed in narrow fishing grounds, had an urgent need to build up the capacity of coast guards to protect against foreign fishing in their claimed EEZs. This led to the buildup of coast guard personnel and assets such as ships and aircraft, which are suitable for undertaking duties in distant waters.

2 Erupting Maritime Disputes

In East Asia, coast guards play an essential role in defending and spearheading the state's claims at the forefront of maritime disputes. A wide array of maritime disputes, ranging from territorial disputes to maritime boundary delimitation, fishing, maritime pollution and marine resources exploitation, are underway in the region. In the South and East China Seas, where disputes over territorial sovereignty and maritime jurisdiction are intensifying, coast guard ships from the disputed countries have become the frontline defenders of their claims. In the East China Sea, Japan and China are vehemently competing for sovereignty over the Senkaku (Diaoyudao) Islands. China and Southeast Asian countries, including the Philippines and Vietnam, are engaged in intense disputes over the jurisdiction of the seas and control of the islands in the South China Sea.

The need for the protection of maritime interests and rights against China's assertiveness serves as a principal justification for the buildup of regional coast guards. The parties to the disputes are deploying their coast guard ships primarily in sensitive areas where there are conflicting claims to maritime jurisdiction or political tensions. This might be due to the strategic consideration

54 UNCLOS Arts. 56 & 58.

55 Bateman (n 1), p. 2.

that coast guard units are more suitable than warships, given that the arrest of a foreign vessel by a warship may be highly provocative — whereas arrest by a coast guard vessel may be accepted as legitimate law enforcement and signal that the arresting party views the incident as relatively minor.[56]

3 Greater Need for Ensuring Maritime Safety

With maritime traffic volumes and offshore activities sharply growing in an increasingly globalized world, there is a greater risk of maritime accidents and oil spills. Maritime accidents, by nature, could have a large number of victims and involve substantial pollution to the marine environment. In East Asia, there has been a sharp increase in the transport of oil and hazardous and noxious substances, in tandem with a rapid economic growth and thus the region is highly vulnerable to oil pollution from ships.

With the need for advanced maritime safety services growing, states are required to provide safety services in a proactive and timely manner. These maritime safety services include the enforcement of ship's safety rules and standards, maritime safety law enforcement, search and rescue, maritime traffic management, navigational information, maintenance of navigational aids, communication systems, prevention and control of marine pollution. Coast guards are a principal agency charged with providing these services.

4 Greater Role for Policing and Security

Coast guards are responsible for establishing law and order against national and transnational sea crimes and unlawful acts at sea. This is concerned with the arrest and seizure of national citizens or foreigners and ships, which violate laws and regulations at sea. Beyond policing offshore, coast guards are tasked to undertake greater policing to protect marine resources in the extended maritime jurisdiction, which is up to 200 nautical miles. As a result, coast guards need to be equipped with more ships, bigger ships, and aircraft suitable for the duties in a wider area of jurisdiction. In addition, the emergence of non-conventional security threats such as piracy, maritime terrorism, and weapons trafficking require a greater role from coast guards.

On top of traditional duties, coast guards are tasked with the implementation of preventive security measures against the new maritime security threats. In response to these threats, a number of maritime security schemes, such as the Proliferation Security Initiative (PSI) and the International Ship and Port Security Code (ISPS Code), are employed. Notably, the UN Security

56 *Ibid.*, p.3.

Council's sanctions on North Korea in the wake of its nuclear development, which involve maritime sanctions such as the inspection and seizure of ships suspected of carrying illicit items from and to North Korea,[57]are being implemented by primarily by coast guards. The new maritime security demands require the acquisition of additional equipment, devices and personnel specialized in those tasks.

VI Reinforcement of Major Coast Guards in East Asia

China

1 A Unified Coast Guard

In 2013 China established a separate coast guard by merging four of its five maritime enforcement agencies, often referred to as the Five Dragons,[58] into a unified agency. The unity, named 'China Coast Guard' (中國海警), is commanded by the State Oceanic Administration (SOA), an agency under the Ministry of Transport, responsible for maritime affairs in the seas under China's jurisdiction. The merged four agencies include: (i) the China Marine Surveillance under the Oceanic Administration; (ii) the China Fisheries Management Bureau under the Ministry of Agriculture; (iii) the Maritime Anti-Smuggling Force under China's Central Administration of Customs; and (iv) the Border Defense Coast Guard under the Ministry of Public Security.

Before the merge, the duties of law enforcement offshore and sovereignty protection in the EEZ were performed separately by the Border Defense Coast Guard and the China Marine Surveillance. The Border Defense Coast Guard (the old China Coast Guard) was comprised of the maritime units of the Border Defense Forces, a branch of the People's Armed Police, and was responsible for law enforcement, fighting crimes, and search and rescue in the territorial waters and contiguous zones. The Border Defense Coast Guard is a paramilitary police force, which is armed and operates like military and has police powers.[59]

57 For further information, see Suk Kyoon Kim, 'Maritime Issues Concerning the Implementation of U.N. Security Council Resolutions on North Korea,' in *Maritime Disputes in Northeast Asia: Regional Challenges and Cooperation* (Brill, Boston, 2017), pp. 171–182.

58 The Five Dragons include the Maritime Safety Administration under the Ministry of Transport, in addition to the four merged agencies.

59 Ryan D. Martinson, 'The Militarization of China's Coast Guard,' *The Diplomat*, 21 November 2014.

The China Marine Surveillance, composed of 8,400 personnel, was in charge of safeguarding maritime rights, surveilling maritime zone uses, and protecting the marine environment. The China Fisheries Management Bureau was responsible for the enforcement of laws concerning fishing and marine resources in Chinese territorial waters and the EEZ, charged with protecting Chinese fishing vessels and fishermen, resolving disputes in fishing activities, preventing illegal fishing, and protecting fishery resources. (Table 11)

In the organizational hierarchy, the China Coast Guard (CCG) belongs to the Department of Coast Guard, a bureaucratic organization of 11 departments within the State Oceanic Administration. The Department of Coast Guard serves as the headquarters of the CCG. However, the CCG is subject to operational guidance from the Ministry of Public Security. The dual commands, to a certain extent, may signify the CCG's organizational characteristics, which is an incorporation of civilian entities and an armed police force.

The need for the creation of a unified China Coast Guard can be examined from a political and operational perspective.

First, the China Coast Guard was created to serve as an instrument of China's maritime strategy, which is to become a maritime power. China has aggressively pursued this goal as part of its national development strategy. President Xi Jinping has elaborated the maritime power strategy by outlining its four components for China to pursue in the maritime domain: (i) the safeguarding of China's maritime rights and interests; (ii) the developing of the marine economy; (iii) the protecting of the marine environment; and (iv) the enhancing of China's capacity for exploiting marine resources. China's Coast Guard was envisioned as carrying out the tasks within the first component.[60]

Second, there was a need for a unified and powerful coast guard in dealing with intensifying maritime disputes in the South and East China Seas. China, in dispute with regional countries over territorial sovereignty and maritime jurisdiction, has perceived that its maritime enforcement agencies were not capable of safeguarding the country's maritime rights.[61] On the other hand, Chinese policymakers employed the coast guard in an attempt to demilitarize territorial disputes, as well as to show rival claimants that China views these disputed areas as sovereign Chinese territory subject to its domestic laws and regulations.[62]

60 Lyle J. Morris, 'Blunt Defenders of Sovereignty: The Rise of Coast Guards in East and Southeast Asia' (2017) 70(2), *Naval War College Review*, p, 85.

61 Gong Jianhua, 'Need for Unified Coast Guard,' *China Daily*, 10 October 2012.

62 Morris (n 60), p. 83.

TABLE 11 Status of the merged maritime enforcement agencies

	China marine surveillance	China fisheries management bureau	Border defense coast guard	Maritime anti-smuggling force
Year of creation	1998	1984	1951	1999
affiliation	Prior to July 2018: State Oceanic Administration/ Ministry of Transport Afterward July 2018: People's Armed Police /Central Military Commission	Ministry of Agriculture	People's Armed Police/ Ministry of Public Security	Customs/ Ministry of Public Security
Jurisdiction	Offshore, EEZ, continental shelf	Fishing ports, fishing grounds, fishing zones	Territorial waters and contiguous zones	Identical with customs jurisdiction
Retention of police power	No	No	Yes	Yes
function	Safeguard of maritime rights, surveillance of use of maritime zones, protection of the marine environment	Protection of fishing ports, fishing vessels, fishermen; prevention of illegal fishing; protection of fishery resources	Law enforcement, combating sea crimes, search and rescue	Anti-smuggling

SOURCE: PARK MOON JIN, 'RESTRUCTURING OF CHINESE MARITIME ORGANIZATIONS AND IMPLICATIONS' (TRANSLATED BY AUTHOR), *DOKDO JOURNAL*, VOL. 21

Third, the overlapping of responsibilities and bureaucratism among maritime enforcement agencies brought about low efficiency and high costs for law enforcement, and difficulty in communicating and cooperating with each other as well as with foreign counterparts. Against this backdrop, the scheme for the unified China Coast Guard became apparent when in March 2013 the 12th National People's Congress passed a Plan for the Institution Reform and Functional Changes of the State Council.

For the past several years after the launch of the China Coast Guard, which is the largest in East Asia, some remarkable changes are identified. The CCG has actively pursued capacity-building by building new large vessels with multiple functions and a higher level of armament. Notably, Chinese Coast Guard ships began to employ more aggressive actions, such as ramming and the use of water cannon inside the cabins of opposing vessels.[63] In August 2017, a Chinese Coast Guard ship rammed a Vietnamese fishing vessel and sank it off the Spratly Islands. Another Chinese Coast Guard ships on the same day destroyed the fishing gear of two Vietnamese fishing vessels and put chemicals into the storage areas, making food and fish inedible.[64]

There are some challenges to the unified China Coast Guard. The internal process of merging the various bureaucracies and cultures appears to be moving slower than expected. It appears that vested interests are preventing full integration of the different agencies.[65] Individual agencies do not seem to be operating as one cohesive whole, with each still executing its own patrols and operating under old command-and-control (C2) structures.[66]

Despite the Chinese government's attempt to make the CCG into a civilian agency, in line with its position in dealing with territorial disputes, the organizational characteristics of the CCG is subject to debate. The CCG's large vessels are equipped with several deck-mounted auto-cannons, including a 76mm, and two auxiliary and two anti-aircraft machine guns.[67] In recent years, alongside China's growing assertiveness on maritime issues, the rapid expansion of the China Coast Guard and its assertive behavior have created alarm in regional countries, triggering a race for coast guard expansion in East Asia.

63 *Ibid.*, p. 87.

64 'Vietnam Fishing Vessel Sank by Ramming of Chinese Coast Guard Ship in the South China Sea (*translated by author*), *Yonhap News*, 17 August 2017.

65 Morris (n 60), p. 86.

66 *Ibid.* p. 87.

67 *Ibid.*, p. 84.

2 Changes to Organizational Structure

In five years since its creation, the China Coast Guard (CCG) has undergone the significant changes to organizational structure. The CCG has been placed under the People's Armed Police, under the supervision of the Central Military Commission (CMC), while being transferred from the State Oceanic Administration and the Ministry of Public Security (MPS).

The decision was adopted by the Standing Committee of the National People's Congress, China's top legislature, on 22 June 2018.[68] The transfer took into effect in July 1, 2018. The transfer of the CCG to the military control aims at "a bigger role in emergencies and crises including war,"[69] "enabling the CCG to be more involved in military drills and daily exercises with People's Liberation Army (PLA) Navy."[70]

Previously, on January 1, 2018, the Chinese government announced major changes to the structure of the People's Armed Police which had been under a dual command of the CMC and the MPS under the State Council, transferring command to the CMC and Chinese Communist Party and removing the State Council's and MPS's oversight powers.[71] Then on March 21, the Chinese government published a follow-on document announcing that the People's Armed Police was to take full control over the China Coast Guard and divest of most non-military functions such as mining, forestry, hydropower, firefighting and security protection.[72] Additionally, a marine police corps under the People's Armed Police will be established to guard China's marine rights and function as a law enforcement body.[73]

The transfer of the CCG to the Central Military Commission, a central state organ under the National People's Congress, being the military branch of the national government, has profound implications in some respects.

First, the transfer to the CMC indicates that the administrative control over the CCG has shifted from civilian to military authority. In terms of organizational affiliation, the CCG was created as an organ of the State Council, while being placed under the State Oceanic Administration along with operational guidance from the Ministry of Public Security which is also under the State Council. While being placed under the People's Armed Police, which removed

68 Xu Hailin, 'China's Military to Lead Coast Guard to Better Defend Sovereignty,' *Global Times*, June 23, 2018.

69 *Ibid.*

70 *Ibid.*

71 Lyle Morris, 'China Welcomes its Newest Armed Forces: The Coast Guard,' *War on the Rock*, RAND Corporation, 4 April, 2018.

72 *Ibid.*

73 *Ibid.*

civilian control, the CCG has become militarized in terms of its organizational identity.

Second, the organizational structure changes of the CCG are likely to be regarded as a buildup of the China's Navy since the reform will likely to enable the CCG to train and equip itself to conduct combat operations alongside the navy during conflict.[74] The CCG is under direct command of People's Armed Police, which is a parallel organ with the People's Liberation Army under the CMC. There is concern that the mandates of the CCG will be focused on military activities as a supplementary force to the navy.

Third, the reform of CCG toward military organization is likely to cause concern of regional states that the CCG would behave more aggressively and coercively in dealing with maritime disputes. In addition, the acts of the CCG under the military control are likely to be regarded as having more political and military implications and could get the navies of disputants involved in maritime disputes.

Fourth, the organizational identity of the CCG as to whether it is a law enforcement body or a military force is unequivocal. Given that the Chinese government plans to establish a marine police corps under the People's Armed Police to guard China's maritime rights and function as a law enforcement body, it is doubted that the activities of the CCG will be limited to the EEZ or defending sovereignty concerned with maritime disputes.

3 Reinforcement

The CCG is composed of approximately 16,200 personnel. In terms of assets, the total vessels of the CCG are estimated to be more than 950, based on the numbers of vessels that the merged agencies had possessed: the Border Defense Coast Guard (250), the Marine Surveillance (400), and the China Fisheries Management Bureau (300). The number of Maritime Anti-Smuggling Force vessels is not available.

In addition to restructuring the coast guard, China has built a dozen of new large ships, many of which have been used to buttress new footholds at the Scarborough Shoal, the Second Tomas, the Luconia Breakers and the Senkaku Islands, and to underwrite economic activities in disputed waters, most notably the two-month drilling operations of HYSY 981 in 2014.[75] In recent years, China has commissioned the largest coast guard vessels in the

74 *Ibid.*

75 Ryan D. Martinson, 'East Asian Security in the Age of the Chinese Mega Cutter,' Center for International Maritime Security, 3 July 2015.

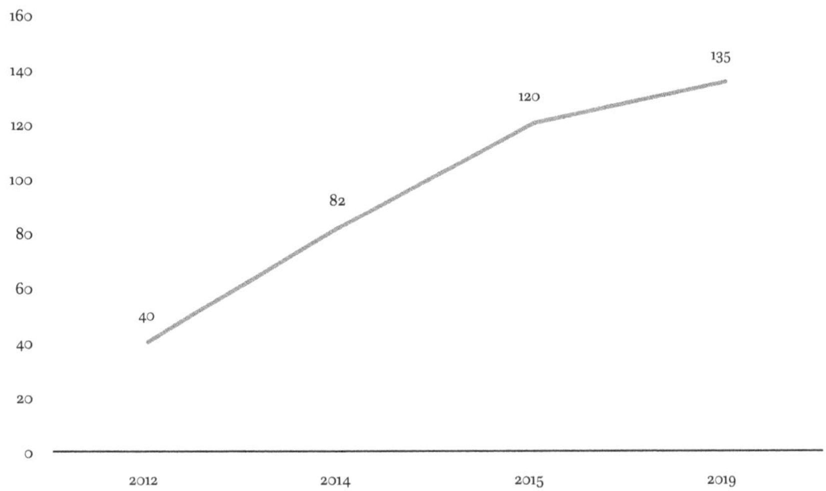

FIGURE 13 Trend of China's increase of large coast guard vessels (1000 tons or greater)
SOURCE: MINISTRY OF FOREIGN AFFAIRS OF JAPAN

world, *Haijing* 2901 and *Haijing* 3901.[76] Both displace 12,000 tons, with a maximum speed of 26 knots, and are armed with a 76mm caliber cannon and two machine guns. *Haijing 2901* and *Haijing* 3901 were deployed in the East and South China Seas, respectively. They are much larger than the previously largest coast guard vessel, which was the Japanese coast guard cutter, the 6,500-tonne *Shikishima*.[77]

In addition, several de-commissioned warships of the Chinese Navy, which displace 4,000 tons, have been transferred to the CCG and rebuilt for the use of coast guard missions. According to the Japanese Foreign Ministry, the CCG has sharply increased its number of large vessels in recent years (See Fig. 13). In 2012, the CCG had a fleet of 40 large coast guard vessels of 1,000 tons or greater. This number tripled in three years and is expected to increase to 135 vessels by the end of 2019.[78]

The reasons for China's vigorously seeking larger coast guard vessels can be outlined as follows. Fundamentally, the commissioning of large coast guard vessels is aimed at performing the duty of 'rights protection' in the Chinese claimed waters. Second, a large coast guard ship has a better capability and

76 The first digit denotes which sea it is to patrol.
77 Ryan D. Martinson (n 75).
78 The Ministry of Foreign Affairs of Japan, 'Status of activities by Chinese government vessels and Chinese fishing vessels in waters surrounding the Senkaku Islands,' available at http://www.mofa.go.jp/files/000180283.pdf.

suitability for operations in the oceans, which require higher endurance and seaworthiness.

On the part of China, the deployment of large coast guard vessels may be required, given the harsh conditions of operations in the disputed waters in the South and East China Seas, which are hundreds of miles away from the shore. Third, the sheer ship size itself is used as a primary instrument of coercion. Smaller opposing vessels are threatened by the sheer large size of CCG vessels, especially given its tactics, such as ramming and firing water cannons. In the 2014 standoff between Vietnam and China over China's attempt to plant an oil-drilling rig in the waters that Vietnam claims to be within its EEZ, the CCG vessels rammed and fired water cannons at Vietnamese vessels. Lastly, the CCG's move to build large vessels and reinforce the armament of its vessels appears to demonstrate its power in the disputed waters.

Japan

The Japan Coast Guard (JCG) has engaged in capacity-building in response to growing tensions over the Senkaku Islands and security threats of maritime terrorism and illegal fishing. Japan argues that since two Chinese Coast Guard ships had intruded into the territorial waters of the Senkaku Islands in 2008, the campaign has continued.

Notably, in the wake of Japan's nationalization of three of the Senkaku Islands in 2010,[79] the CCG vessels more frequently intruded into the territorial waters surrounding the disputed islands, with 188 vessels penetrating the territorial sea in 2013, 88 in 2014, 86 in 2015, and 188 in 2016.[80] Japan perceives China's actions as an intention to violate the sovereignty of Japan and attempt to change the *status quo* through force or coercion.[81] Under this circumstance, the JCG's goal in building additional capacity is to enhance response capability against Chinese Coast Guard vessels' attempts to penetrate the territorial waters of the Senkaku Islands.

As of April 2017, the JCG is composed of 13,744 personnel and a total of 455 vessels, 62 vessels of which are greater than 1,000 tons, including 14 PLH-class[82]

79 The Japanese government purchased three of the Senkaku Islands, including Uotsuri, Kitakojima, and Minamikojima Islands, from private citizens in an effort to bolster its sovereignty over the Senkaku Islands.

80 The Ministry of Foreign Affairs of Japan, 'Trends in Chinese Government and Other Vessels in the Waters Surrounding the Senkaku Islands, and Japan's Response,' available at http://www.mofa.go.jp/region/page23e_000021.html.

81 *Ibid.*

82 It denotes Patrol Vessel Large with Helicopter.

vessels, and 74 aircraft.[83] The JCG is the second largest fleet in tonnage and the second largest in numbers of personnel, and has the most coast guard aircraft in the East Asian region. The largest vessels in the JCG fleet include two PLH-class vessels, with a displacement of 6,500 tons (9,000 tons fully loaded) and two *Mizuho*-class vessels of 5,200 tons.[84] The JCG has by far the largest air fleet in Asia — globally, it is second only to the U.S. Coast Guard — with 26 fixed-wing aircraft and 48 helicopters.[85]

Faced with China's move to deploy large coast guard vessels off the Senkaku Islands and continue its assertive actions, the Japanese government perceives the protection of its territorial waters to be a grave matter of maritime security.[86] As part of its responses, the Japanese government held a cabinet meeting, hosted by the prime minister in December 2016, to discuss measures to strengthen its maritime security capabilities. The Japanese government came up with five measures to strengthen its maritime security, many of which are concentrated on building the capacity of the JCG. These measures include[87]: (i) the strengthening of measures to safeguard the territorial waters of the Senkaku Islands; (ii) the expansion of marine surveillance; (iii) the enhancing of the capabilities to respond to maritime terrorism and other grave security situations; (iv) the strengthening of marine survey; and (vi) infrastructure renovation.

As part of these measures, the Japanese government plans to reinforce the assets of the JCG including deploying six large size patrol vessels, which include three PLH vessels, and a jet engine aircraft and a helicopter, which will cost approximately $200 million. In addition, the JCG plans to add 438 personnel between 2016 and 2017, 207 of whom are assigned to the task of protecting the Senkaku Islands.[88]

Korea

In the particular security situation on the Korean Peninsula, the Korea Coast Guard (KCG) has also sought to enhance its capability to ensure maritime security and safeguard maritime sovereignty. As discussed in the preceding, the KCG is a police-type coast guard, composed of 11,060 personnel, with the assets

83 Japan Coast Guard, 'Japan Coast Guard,' available at http://www.kaiho.mlit.go.jp/e/english.pdf.

84 Morris (n 60), p. 89.

85 *Ibid.*

86 Yoon Sung Soon, 'Need for Strategic Response to Coast Guard Buildups of China and Japan,' *KMI Weekly Report*, January 2017.

87 *Ibid.*

88 *Ibid.*

of 307 vessels and 23 aircraft. While the KCG is responsible for typical coast guard missions such as search and rescue and maritime safety and security, the KCG is also tasked with police missions such as criminal investigation and intelligence gathering related to maritime affairs.

A large number of the tasks concerned with maritime safety and security are undertaken by the Ministry of Oceans and Fisheries (MOF) to which the KCG belongs. This indicates that while the KCG has more constabulary power compared with typical coast guards such as the U.S. Coast Guard and the Japan Coast Guard, the KCG's authority with regard to maritime safety and security is not as far-reaching.

This uniqueness arises from its organizational history. The KCG had been part of the National Police since its creation in 1953. When the MOF was created in 1996, the KCG separated from the National Police Agency and was placed under the MOF as a central government agency.[89] In 2014, the KCG underwent an organizational disbandment in the wake of the *Sewol* ferry disaster.[90] The KCG was restructured, splitting its duties into the National Police Agency and the Ministry of Public Safety and Security, a newly created ministry in the aftermath of the disaster. The restructuring was intended to make the KCG more focused on search and rescue by transferring the duties of criminal investigation and intelligence to the National Police Agency.

However, the disbandment of the KCG, contrary to the global trend of 'big' coast guards, weakened its law enforcement capability at sea and the role of a defense of maritime rights. With the launch of a new administration, the KCG was reinstated as an independent central agency under the MOF in July 2017.

In a volatile security situation on the Korean Peninsula, in which the South and the North have confronted each other across the Demilitarized Zone and tensions over North Korea's nuclear development are high, the focus of the KCG's duties are on ensuring maritime security. Security duties include: (i) the protecting the safety of fishermen and fishing vessels operating off the Northern Limit Lines (NLLs) on the west and east coasts; (ii) enforcing the Proliferation Security Initiative (PSI) and the sanctions measures on North Korea imposed by the UN Security Council;[91] and (iii) the protecting fishery resources against illegal Chinese fishing in the West Sea (Yellow Sea). Above all,

89 Suk Kyoon Kim, 'The *Sewol* Ferry Disaster in Korea and Maritime Safety Management,' (2015)46(4), *Ocean Development and International Law*, p. 10.

90 See footnote 7 in Chapter I.

91 For further information, see Suk Kyoon Kim, 'Maritime Issues Concerning the Implementation of U.N, Security Council Resolutions on North Korea,' in *Maritime Disputes in Northeast Asia: Regional Challenges and Cooperation* (Brill, Boston, 2017).

safeguarding the sovereignty of Dokdo (Takeshima), which has been in dispute with Japan, is a top priority.

The demands for greater responsibility to undertake these tasks required the KCG to expand its roles and functions. Over the past decade, the KCG has increased the number of large vessels greater than 1,000 tons and the number of aircraft. The KCG has 36 large vessels, of which the two largest vessels displace 6,500 tons. Both are deployed to undertake the duties of safeguard of sovereignty: *Sambong 5001* is stationed in the East Sea (Sea of Japan) to protect the sovereignty of Dokdo, and *Lee Chung Ho 5002* is tasked with the protection of Ieodo (referred to as 'Suyan Jiao' in Chinese, or Socotra Rock) in the East China Sea.

Ieodo is a submerged rock situated 4.6 meters underwater, with a surface area of 3.7 square kilometers, in which Korea and China maintain that Ieodo is within their EEZ, in accordance with their claims to the equidistant line and the natural prolongation of the land territory, respectively.[92]

The KCG plans to commission another 6,500-ton class vessel to be deployed in the West Sea. The KCG established a special force, named the Five West Islands Safeguard Unit, in April 2017, tasked with the protection of security of the five West Islands[93] adjacent to the NLL and the suppression of illegal Chinese fishing in the Yellow Sea. The unit is composed of 9 vessels (3 large and 6 medium-size vessels) and 553 personnel.

The Philippines

It is notable that some military force-type coast guards in East Asia, which were a branch of the navy, have converted to a demilitarized civilian service and separated from the navy. The Philippine Coast Guard (PCG) and the Vietnam Coast Guard (VCG) may be the primary examples of the demilitarization of coast guards in the region.

The PCG, which was part of the Philippine Navy (PN), became a separate agency in 1998. Perceiving the need to make the PCG a constabulary force under a civilian authority, the Philippine government, in accordance with the Philippine Coast Guard Law, enacted in 2009, placed the PCG under the Department of Transportation.[94]

---

92 For further information, see Suk Kyoon Kim, 'Disputes over the Delimitation of the EEZ and the Continental Shelf,' in *Maritime Disputes in Northeast Asia: Regional Challenges and Cooperation* (Brill, Boston, 2017).

93 The five West Islands refer to Paekryeong-do, Daechung-do, Socheng-do, Yeonpyeongdo, and Woo-do, situated off the NLL and are under control of South Korea.

94 Morris (n 60)., p. 99.

The separation from the navy means that the PCG is subject to the direct command of the Department of Transportation and the President of the Philippines. In the wake of the Scarborough Shoal incident in April 2012,[95] the PCG has become the primary enforcer of Philippine maritime rights and interests in the country's EEZ, a role that the PN had traditionally filled. The standoff between the China Coast Guard and the PN and the PCG served as an occasion for the Philippine government to reassess both the use of naval assets to conduct maritime law enforcement duties, such as boarding foreign civilian fishing vessels, and the appropriateness of confronting CCG vessels with naval vessels.[96]

As part of its reinforcement efforts, along with the acquisition of patrol vessels from Japan, the Philippine Coast Guard plans to expand its current 9,000 total personnel to 13,500 by 2020.[97] Through the enacting of the Coast Guard Law of 2009 (or Republic Act 9993) and its Implementing Rules and Regulations, the Philippine government also strengthened the PCG's authority and responsibilities by allowing the PCG to take preventive measures in ensuring

95 The Scarborough Shoal, also known as Huangyan Dao in Chinese, is a shoal located between the Macclesfield Bank and the Luzon Island in the South China Sea. The shoal is claimed by China, the Philippines and Taiwan. On 10 April 2012, a Philippine navy ship spotted eight Chinese fishing vessels in the waters of the Scarborough Shoal. The inspection team boarded the Chinese fishing vessels and discovered illegally collected corals, giant clams and live sharks inside the first vessel. The inspection team attempted to arrest the Chinese fishermen but were blocked by China's Marine Surveillance ships. China challenged Philippine territorial waters over a shoal that was 124 nautical miles from the Philippine island of Luzon and well within the Philippine EEZ. Amid growing tensions, the Philippine government decided to replace the naval ship with a coast guard ship in an effort to de-escalate the conflict. The Philippine forces were greatly outnumbered by China in the number of ships present in the scene of the standoff. At one point, China had increased the number of its vessels to 97: five China Coast Guard ships and 92 fishing and auxiliary vessels. Meanwhile, the two countries were engaged in diplomatic rows against each other. China has imposed stricter regulations on its import of Philippine bananas, and Chinese tour agencies suspended tours to the Philippines. In addition, China unilaterally imposed a fishing ban in the South China Sea, lasting from 16 May 2012 to 1 August 2012. The standoff continued for three months until the United States stepped in to mediate a resolution under which both parties agreed to pull back from the shoal. However, the Philippine government accused China of not abiding by the agreement and of maintaining its presence at the shoal, effectively militarizing it. Allegedly, China erected a barrier to the entrance of the shoal to block entry. Currently, China Coast Guard ships continue to maintain a presence in the waters near the shoal, claiming the ownership of it.

96 Morris (n 60), pp. 101–102.

97 Department of Transportation, Republic of the Philippines, 'Philippine Coast Guard Organizational Structure,' September 2014, available at www.dotr.gov.ph/.

the safety of merchant vessels. The law also strengthened PCG's authority to meet challenges and increasing demands for marine resources, technological advancement and climate change.[98]

The shift to a civilian service makes receiving the PCG eligible for foreign aid, which is necessary to improve the capability of the coast guard. A civilian service is more likely to receive foreign aid such as vessels, equipment, technology, training, services and other assistance, which would not be readily offered to a military agency. Japan, for example, has agreed to provide the Philippine Coast Guard 12 multi-role patrol vessels, including two large patrol ships, in the form of an official development assistance (ODA) project.

This is part of the Maritime Safety Capability Improvement for the Philippine Coast Guard Project, under which Japan has agreed to provide a loan of 16,455 million yen (approximately $184 million), to be used to procure vessels and finance the capacity-building of search and rescue operations, marine environment protection, law enforcement, and transport. The project is scheduled to be complete by 2021 when the new vessels under the project are be placed in service.[99]

Vietnam

The Vietnam Coast Guard (CCG) is another prime example of the demilitarization of a regional coast guard. The Vietnamese Maritime Police (VMP) was established in 1998 under the Ministry of Defense (MOD). Before its creation, the Vietnam People's Navy (VPN), in coordination with the Border Defense Force, was responsible for offshore constabulary missions as well as other military missions along the country's long coastline.[100]

In 2008, the Maritime Police was renamed the Vietnam Coast Guard, becoming a separate armed service under the joint command of MOD and the VPN. In 2013, the VCG became a fully independent civilian armed service under the Defense Ministry, separating from the VPN. This happened because there was an increasing need to alleviate the burden on the Navy and to facilitate

98 Homepage of the Philippine Coast Guard, available at http://www.coastguard.gov.ph/index.php/transparency/about-us/legacies.

99 Japan International Cooperation Agency, press release, 'Signing of Japan ODA Loan Agreement with the Republic of Philippines: Further Strengthening the Maritime Capability of the Philippine Coast Guard,' October 26. 2016, available athttps://www.jica.go.jp/english/news/press/2013/131216_01.html.

100 Vu Truong Minh Huy, 'The Vietnam Coast Guard,' in 'Navies, Coast Guards, the Maritime Community and International Stability' (eds by Ian Bowers & Collin Koh), *RSIS Policy Brief*, S. Rajaratnam School of International Studies, Nanyang Technological University, March 2017, p. 37.

enforcing maritime sovereignty and jurisdiction rights under the UNCLOS.[101] Like the equivalent services in the Philippines and the United States, the VCG retains both civilian police powers for law enforcement and military duties during wartime.[102]

In recent years, the Vietnamese government has sought to modernize and strengthen its coast guard in the new maritime security environment. Since 2010, the Vietnam government has vigorously engaged in the capacity-building of its coast guard, composed of approximately 5,500 total personnel, with a small fleet.

Along with renaming the Vietnam Maritime Police as the Vietnam Coast Guard (VCG) and the separation from the navy, more resources were invested in the VCG in order to enhance its capability to respond to territorial disputes with China in the South China Sea. The need for greater roles and functions of the coast guard increased, as China employs aggressive tactics and uses so-called 'maritime militia,' mainly composed of Chinese fishing vessels, as its proxies in maritime disputes. The VCG, which has more than 50 vessels of different classes and three patrol aircraft, is building up its capacity by commissioning more 2000-ton vessels and a 4000-ton vessel, which will be the largest coast guard vessel in Southeast Asia.[103]

The VCG has received foreign aid from other regional coast guards. Japan and Korea have provided the Vietnam Coast Guard with six and one used patrol ships, respectively, as part of their efforts to support VCG capacity-building. Their assistance is preconditioned on the use of the vessels being only constabulary missions and not for military purposes. Japan and Korea, the major users of sea lanes of communication through the seas of Southeast Asia, provide assistance to Southeast Asian coast guards for the enhancement of their capabilities.

Meanwhile, the *Haiyang Shiyou 981* standoff[104]demonstrated the gravity of conflicting claims to maritime jurisdiction between Vietnam and China over

101 *Ibid.*

102 Morris (n 60), p. 95.

103 Vu Truong Minh Huy (n 100), p. 38.

104 The *Haiyang Shiyou* 981 standoff in May 2014 refers to the incident that Vietnam and China coast guard ships were engaged in a standoff over China's attempt to establish an oil platform, called *Haiyang Shiyou*, in waters off the disputed Paracel Islands in the South China Sea. As China moved the oil rig to a location 17 nautical miles from Triton Island, the southwestern-most island of the Paracel Island, Vietnam vociferously protested the move as an infringement of its sovereignty. Soon after the oil rig was deployed, China established a security cordon, with approximately 102–108 Chinese coast guard and fishing vessels 10–11 nautical miles from the rig. In response, Vietnam sent 29 ships to attempt to disrupt the oil rig's placement and operations. Over the next few weeks, China

the Spratly Islands as well as China's assertive actions and the use of fishing vessels as a front-line defender against other countries' government and military vessels. China deployed a greater number of fishing vessels on the front line of the standoff, including maintenance and supply trawlers and tugboats. China also increased the aggressiveness of its tactics, ramming opposing vessels and using water cannons.

Through the incident, the VCG and the VPN found themselves severely outnumbered and the use of Chinese civilian vessels as proxies for China posed a great challenge to the Vietnam government. In the fundamentally new security environment, the Vietnam government appears to seek an answer to the challenge by reinforcing its coast guard capability.

VII Conclusion

East Asian countries have vigorously engaged in a buildup of capabilities of their coast guards. Principally, this was driven by the need for the protection of extended maritime jurisdictions. The concerns over maritime safety and security also serve as a contributing factor. However, above all, intensifying maritime disputes in East Asia are the primary rationale for the expansion of the regional coast guards. The coast guards in East Asia serve as the frontline defender of sovereignty and claims in maritime disputes. The phenomenon of regional coast guard expansion can be described as 'big white hulls,' with the growing deployment of larger coast guard vessels and aircraft.

The mandates and organizational affiliations of the 'big white hulls' in East Asia differs according to the sub-regions. While Southeast Asian countries are engaged in the reinforcement of their coast guards by establishing separate coast guards or the granting of greater authorities and functions to existing coast guards, Northeast Asian countries (China, Japan and Kora) have deployed large coast guard vessels and equipped them with higher levels of armament.

began to employ greater numbers of fishing vessels on the front line of the cordon. China increased the aggressiveness of its tactics, ramming opposing vessels and using water cannons. The standoff brought about massive protests across Vietnam and attacks on Chinese-owned businesses and citizens in the country. The standoff was the most serious dispute in the territorial disputes between the two countries since the Johnson South Reef Skirmish in 1988 in which more than 70 Vietnamese soldiers were killed. Despite Vietnam's attempts to disrupt the China's oil rig establishment in the Vietnam-claimed jurisdiction, the oil rig has been sitting on the Vietnam-claimed continental shelf and on the Vietnamese side of the median line between China and Vietnam.

Such moves have been spearheaded by China, which has aggressively pursued its goal of becoming a maritime power and has been increasingly assertive in maritime disputes. China increasingly deploys vessels larger than warships and uses them as an instrument to project power or coercion against opposing parties to maritime disputes. In particular, the transfer of the China Coast Guard to the military control causes concern that its mandates will be focused on military roles and duties while functioning as the second naval force.

Although coast guard vessels are less political and militarily sensitive than naval vessels, the contentious encounters of large, armed coast guard vessels in the disputed waters could spark a conflict. Given this circumstance, regional states engaged in maritime disputes in particular need to consider preventive measures to avoid conflicts. As part of the measures, the application of a Code for Unplanned Encounters at Sea (CUES) to coast guard ships should be considered. The CUES, recently approved by Chinese and U.S. navies, is an agreement to ensure professional behavior when foreign warships unexpectedly meet while on deployment.[105]

Furthermore, regional coast guards need to foster international cooperation to fight common maritime concerns such as piracy, transnational sea crimes, illegal fishing and maritime security threats. The North Pacific Coast Guard Forum, launched in 2000, which involves China, Japan, Korea, Russia, Canada and the U.S as participants, is a good example of multilateral cooperation framework to facilitate cooperation in information-sharing and combating transnational sea crimes, and developing maritime security regimes.

A coast guard is fundamentally a civilian service, responsible for law enforcement and safety and security at sea. The use of coast guard ships as replacements or stand –ins of warships is contrary to international law. The acts of armed aggression that blur the line between the navy and the coast guard should be discouraged. The coast guard should be used to serve its inherent purpose, which is as a de-escalator of maritime disputes, not an escalator of such disputes.

105 Martinson (n 59).

CHAPTER 9

Conclusion

A wide range of maritime safety and security issues in relation to East Asia were discussed in the previous chapters. We have explored various international maritime safety and security regimes and related issues, starting from the discussion of the definitions of maritime safety and security. As we conclude the discussions, this chapter sheds light on the key points that have been discussed in each chapter.

Chapter 1 attempted to define and distinguish the meanings of the terms 'maritime safety' and 'maritime security' and discussed their applications in practice. Ensuring the safety of ships and the security of navigation might be most challenging in the shipping industry, as shipping involves a great deal of risk from both internal and external factors. Maritime casualties inflicted by natural, accidental or intentional causes often result in a disastrous damage — loss of life or property, as well as pollution to the marine environment. However, although 'maritime safety and security,' are commonly used in the maritime domain, they are not explicitly defined or differentiated from one another. Maritime safety is often applied to encompass the concept of maritime security. Otherwise some argue that the concept of maritime security is wider than that of maritime safety.

The two terms are often used imprecisely, inconsistently, or by cross-referring each other. Further problems occur in translating these terms to and from other languages, where they can have the same, mixed, or overlapping meanings. This occasionally brings about confusion when dealing with maritime issues concerning navigational safety and security. Thus, it is important to attempt to draw a distinction between the two realms of the maritime domain, which are similar but distinctive to some extent.

As discussed in the preceding, both maritime safety and security are principally a set of measures and activities to ensure safe navigation and to protect the marine environment and the rights of a state at sea. While both are activities and tasks, maritime safety is concerned primarily with preventive activities to protect life and property at sea and is primarily the purview of the shipping industry at the operational level. On the other hand, maritime security typically refers to responsive activities to protect life and property at sea and is primarily the task of relevant state agencies. The realm of maritime security is primarily concerned with protecting maritime interests and the rights of a state primarily against external threats.

 | DOI:10.1163/9789004389908_010

On this basis, maritime safety can be defined as "an array of preventive and responsive efforts and activities to protect life and property at sea and preserve the marine environment, by regulating, managing ships and seafarers, and using technological advances, against natural and accidental dangers and harms." On the other hand, maritime security can be defined as "comprehensive preventive and responsive efforts and activities to safeguard the territorial integrity of a state and protect the security of ships, individuals and states, by implementing a variety of security regimes, against intentional and unlawful acts and threats at sea."

A prominent distinction between the two domains might be whether the source of the threat is 'natural,' 'accidental' or 'intentional.' Maritime safety is concerned with efforts or activities at sea to protect life, property and the marine environment from dangers and harms inflicted by 'natural' or 'accidental' causes. Meanwhile, maritime security is principally concerned with measures and activities at sea to address threats and unlawful acts which derive from 'intentional' causes.

In accordance with such a definition, the domain of maritime safety is concerned with safety of ships and crew, safety of navigation, search and rescue, and protection of the marine environment. The domain of maritime security may cover territorial integrity, security of navigation, cargo, ports and on-offshore installation, and the security of marine resources.

Regarding the relationship between maritime safety and security, it is worth to note that whereas maritime security was shed light on due to following factors over the recent past decades — higher vulnerability to maritime terrorism in the aftermath of 9.11 terrorist attacks, the prevalence of piracy, and growing disputes over maritime rights — maritime safety has become a main focus in the maritime domain since the *Titanic* disaster in 1912.

Chapter 2 discussed the legal framework for maritime safety and security and the IMO rule-making process. International maritime safety and security regimes have gradually been formulated since humans were actively engaged in sea-faring and navigation across the oceans. At the early stage, maritime safety and security regimes were established by informal traditions, practices or customs on a regional basis. Most of maritime safety and security regimes codified in international treaties related to shipping were created in the 20th century, during which time international commerce and seaborne trade surged.

Challenged by numerous maritime casualties and marine pollution, the international community engaged in efforts to enhance the safety of navigation and to prevent and control marine pollution. To this end, as a core effort, a large number of international treaties on shipping were adopted from the middle of 19th century onwards. The treaties aimed at setting global safety standards applicable to all shipping around the world and preventing and controlling marine pollution across the oceans.

The International Maritime Organization (IMO), which came into existence in 1958, has served as a core international body in formulating a regulatory maritime framework. In tandem with explosive growth in shipping, the role of the IMO has increasingly become important as a regulatory framework-setter. The IMO has developed a number of new conventions, which have set maritime safety standards to improve safety of ships, crew and instruments to prevent and control maritime pollution.

The IMO has also ensured that existing instruments keep pace with changes in shipping technology and demands in the maritime world. As a result, the IMO has adopted more than 50 international conventions and agreements and also adopted numerous protocols and amendments. The safety regulations adopted by the IMO are mostly multilateral conventions that state parties are required to ratify and enact domestic legislation to implement them. The IMO conventions have been formulated by the consensus of member states. Thus, the rules and standards imposed by the conventions become global norms that have a binding force on member states.

The IMO needs to enhance its authority and capability for the rule-making of safety standards based on a proactive approach. Rather than a responsive rule-making in the aftermath of major maritime accidents, the IMO needs to focus on proactive safety rule -making by leading safety assessment and agenda setting. The IMO also need to be more concerned with the safety of ships under control of flag states. The safety rules and standards applied to ships engaged on international voyages need to be extended to a certain size of ships used for domestic navigation.

The safety rules and standards in legal instruments are subject to the implementation of flag states, coastal states and port states, varying with their jurisdiction. The vast portion of implementation of the rules and standards rests with flag states. More than 70 percent of ships engaged in international shipping are flagged out to foreign states, otherwise known as 'flags of convenience.' The flags of convenience, which operate on an open registry mostly for financial gain, are not capable of ensuring their ships comply with safety regulations. As such, the largest challenge to maritime safety might be how to effectively implement safety standards and rules to prevent substandard ships from being used, and to protect the marine environment.

Chapter 3 discussed the requirements and measures for the safety of navigation and the protection of the marine environment. It intended to give an overall picture of principal safety standards and rules, which are very complex and laid down in various international regulations, as well as safety measures of navigation. It also explored the matters concerned with Port State Control (PSC) that is an essential international legal instrument to ensure compliance with the safety rules and standards set out in conventions and measures for navigational safety and the protection of the marine environment. PSC has played a vital role in ensuring navigational safety and the protection of the marine environment, serving as a supplementary safety net to flag state control.

The significance of PSC has significantly increased over recent years. In fact, PSC, under the umbrella of regional MOU regimes, takes the place of the flag state control. PSC MOUs are not legally binding and are instead merely a cooperative coalition within the MOU region. As a consequence, there are limitations on enforcing harmonized activities within the MOU regions. In order to address such problems, the regional PSC MOUs need to be transformed to multilateral treaties among member states to enhance the enforcement of port state control.

Chapter 4 discussed the matters concerned with maritime terrorism and also examined the SUA regime as a key legal instrument to cope with unlawful acts at sea, in particular, maritime terrorism. In the post-Cold War era, non-conventional security threats derived from racial, ethnic, regional, religious and cultural conflicts have surpassed conventional security threats that had been built on ideological conflicts in the Cold War era. Non-conventional security threats, such as terrorism, piracy, cyber-attacks and weapons of mass destruction (WMD), pose a grave threat to the peace and security of the contemporary world. Of those, the most striking and volatile threat in peacetime must be terrorism.

There exists no universally agreed-upon definition of maritime terrorism in international law. Principally, the concept of maritime terrorism is understood in the context of two global phenomena: terrorism and piracy. The nature of maritime terrorism is understood within the context of terrorism and thus seen as an extension of land-based terrorism.

However, the uniqueness of the maritime domain is highlighted in terms of limited access to the sea. The concept of maritime terrorism was initially understood within the context of piracy, whereby any unauthorized act of violence on the high seas would be characterized as piracy. Whereas piracy is characterized as acts of violence on the high sea or outside the jurisdiction of a coastal state, committed for economic purposes, maritime terrorism is characterized as acts of violence that are perpetrated, irrespective of maritime zones, for political motivations. Nonetheless, the line between piracy and maritime piracy has been blurred. This may happen because terrorist groups are engaged in piracy to finance their activities, as demonstrated in some cases in which terrorists attack ships primarily for financial purposes. It appears that maritime threats have become increasingly intertwined and less discernable.

Judging by its components, maritime terrorism may be described as "acts of violence or the threat of use of violence against vessels, passengers or infrastructures on and offshore to intimidate a population or compel a government or an international organization to do or to abstain from doing any act in order to achieve political or religious objectives."

The maritime domain is perceived to be highly vulnerable to terrorist attacks, as evinced in the number of maritime terrorism incidents in recent years. Damage to vessels, ports, offshore facilities and plants can inflict crippling damage to the economy and shipping of a state, as well as draw wide public attention. Given that the aim of terrorist attacks is to inflict the greatest possible loss of life, economic damage, and fear among the public, this makes maritime targets particularly attractive.

However, the risks and consequences of maritime terrorism appeared not to be underscored in the past, and as a consequence, counter-terrorism efforts were given less attention. This might happen because the risk of terrorism in the maritime domain is not so tangible to the public, and furthermore maritime terrorism is not regarded an imminent threat due to the fact that attacks have been infrequent over the years. However, currently the maritime domain is not only a direct target of terrorism, but it also is used as a channel for terrorist organizations to attempt terrorist attacks on land.

Recognizing the vulnerability and enormous negative impact of maritime terrorism, the international community has exerted a variety of efforts to prevent and combat maritime terrorism. As an integral part of counter-terrorism measures, the international community has adopted a number of multilateral treaties. Amongst these, the Convention for the Suppression of Unlawful Acts Against the Safety of Maritime Navigation (1988 SUA Convention) is a key instrument, serving as a legal base of international cooperation in counter-maritime terrorism efforts.

The 1988 SUA Convention was designed to ensure that appropriate actions are taken against persons committing unlawful acts against ships by facilitating the establishment of criminal jurisdiction, and the extradition and prosecution of the offenders. In order to ensure that the offenders are held accountable, state parties are obliged to either prosecute or extradite the offenders. The SUA Convention in substance is based on previously existing terrorism conventions, with their provisions adapted to the maritime domain.

The 2005 SUA Protocol in the aftermath of the 9/11 attacks was adopted to ensure that the maritime security framework established under the SUA treaties enables states to respond to new contemporary maritime threats. The protocol enables ship-boarding and law enforcement measures over the vessels suspected of the offences under the convention. As such, the protocol is regarded as a significant legal framework to enhance maritime security against maritime terrorism and the proliferation of WMD. Addressing the legal deficiencies of the 1988 SUA Convention, which lacks the effective means of enforcement to prevent and suppress maritime terrorism and the proliferation of WMD by ship, the Protocol provides the lawful means for the exercise of ship-boarding against the suspect foreign-flagged vessels and ships suspected of carrying WMD and related materials.

Despite its effectiveness as a legal instrument to fight maritime terrorism and the proliferation of WMD, it faces a number of challenges that need to be addressed. First, for the SUA Convention regime, the largest challenge in taking counter-measures at the international level, either proactive or responsive, against maritime terrorism might be concerned with how to strike a balance with the exclusive right of flag state control. Second, a significant problem is the slow implementation of the protocol. As of November 2018, the number of contracting states is only 45, which accounts for 39.06 percent of the gross tonnage of the world's merchant fleet. As with much of international law, the success of the 2005 SUA Protocol hinges on its implementation, not merely its adoption at the international level. Third, the issue of maritime terrorism cannot be properly approached while being separated from land-based terrorism or terrorist organizations since maritime terrorism is committed by terrorist organizations which have capabilities to operate at sea. A vast majority of maritime terrorism were committed by terrorist organizations whose principal activities build on land. Fourth, the SUA Convention regime has an inherent limitation that only touches on the 'acts' of terrorism at sea, leaving the illegality of terrorist organizations itself uncovered. Maritime terrorism is inherently linked to terrorism on land. Therefore, the coverage of the SUA Convention should be extended to deal with the issues associated with maritime terrorism beyond the maritime domain.

Chapter 5 explored various aspects of contemporary piracy issues from a global governance perspective. Piracy is undoubtedly the oldest threat to safe navigation and sea-faring. Contemporary piracy, called the 'scourge of the 21st century,' has had far-reaching and extensively negative effects on the shipping industry and seaborne trade and furthermore the safety and security of the sea. Recognizing the gravity of problems posed by piracy, the international community has engaged in combating piracy across the oceans. By virtue of international anti-piracy efforts, overall the incidents of piracy have been in decline since the mid-2010s. Of particular note is that the situation off the coast of Somalia and the Gulf of Aden appear to be under control, as demonstrated in a sharp decline in piracy occurrences over recent years in that region. The reduction is attributable to persistent and concerted counter-piracy efforts at the global, regional as well as shipping-industry level.

However, it is too early to claim that the piracy problem in that region is under control merely by pointing to a recent decrease in incidents. Rather, it remains to be seen whether this trend is sustainable or not, given that the underlying causes of piracy in that region, such as the attractive rewards of piracy, a poverty-stricken economy, a chaotic political situation and lack of counter-piracy capacity, have remained unsettled. As such, it is likely that piracy in that region would resurge if stakeholders retreat from the commitment of counter-piracy efforts or allow any chance for pirates to revive.

Contrary to a significant reduction in piracy attacks at the global level, Southeast Asia and West Africa have undergone an upsurge in recent years. In particular, piracy in Southeast Asia, along with an increase in piracy incidents, has tended to become increasingly violent and sophisticated. The typical Asian-type piracy, that is, cargo theft while ships are in ports, has increasingly shifted to hijacking and ransom demands. West Africa, highly concentrated in the Gulf of Guinea, has also emerged as a piracy-prone region, with growing incidents in which pirates hijack oil tankers and depredate cargo aboard or attack oil rigs to steal oil and equipment.

Some suggestions are put forward to address the piracy issue. First, the activities of the stakeholders involved in various counter-piracy measures need to be further coordinated and organized. Piracy is a complicated and multi-faceted problem that involves a wide range of factors. The problem cannot be addressed only by the efforts of governments and thus, governments, the shipping community, and other related civilian sectors need to share burdens in combating piracy together. Second, the international community needs to be more concerned with the piracy problems in Southeast Asia and West Africa. At the global level, the UN and international organizations should be more concerned with and enhance support for regional counter-piracy efforts. Third, the international community needs to formulate regulations to govern the increasing employment of armed security guards aboard ships. Fourth, the establishment of regional integrated coast guards in South Asia needs to be considered for joint patrols, escorts and law enforcement in the high-risk areas of piracy, if the regional situation gets worse.

Chapter 6 explored the matters concerned with the ISPS Code and Port & Cargo Container Security. The adoption of the ISPS Code or the International Code for the Security of Ships and of Port Facilities and the employment of comprehensive cargo container security measures of the U.S. are a response to the higher vulnerability of port and cargo containers in the aftermath of the

9/11 terrorist attacks. The attacks dramatically changed the world of trade and shipping, serving as a wake-up call to maritime security.

Shocked by the catastrophic attacks, the international maritime community, at the initiative of the IMO, sought to address the mounting concern of maritime terrorism and thus engaged in devising a new target-focused maritime security framework and measures. The focus of improving maritime security was accorded to ports and ships. Given that ports are the place where international shipping interfaces with the production and delivery of goods, the disruption of a port because of a terrorist attack would obviously hinder that interface and international trade.

The ISPS Code is a comprehensive set of measures to enhance the security of ships and port facilities, developed in response to the perceived threats to ships and port facilities in the aftermath of the 9/11 terrorist attacks in the U.S. The code consists of Part A, the provisions of which shall be treated as mandatory, and of Part B, the provisions of which shall be treated as recommendatory, as adopted on 12 December 2002, by resolution of the Conference of Contracting Governments to the 1974 SOLAS Convention. The ISPS Code went into effect on 1 July 2004. Part A outlines detailed maritime and port security-related requirements to which contracting governments, port authorities, and shipping companies must adhere in order to be in compliance with the Code. Part B provides a series of recommendatory guidelines on how to meet the requirements and obligations set out within the provisions of Part A.

Beyond the implementation of the ISPS Code, the U.S., which led the creation of the code, has employed a number of domestic maritime security measures subject to U.S. laws. The U.S. has formulated a number of its own port and cargo container security policies. The newly adopted maritime security initiatives by the U.S since the 9/11 terrorist attacks include: (i) the Container Security Initiative (CSI); (ii) the Customs-Trade Partnership Against Terrorism (C-TPAT); (iii) the Secure Freight Initiative (SFI); and (iv) the 24-Hour Advance Manifest (24-Hour Rule). These U.S. maritime security initiatives, focused on preventive measures, have definitely had a significant impact on the global trade and shipping because globally more than 80 percent of cargo transportation is shipped by sea, and the U.S. is the largest trading state in the world.

It is worth noting that most of the maritime security measures at the global level have been driven by the U.S., in response to potential threats of terrorism in the maritime domain after the 9/11 terrorist attacks. The ISPS Code, in particular, is a key outcome of such U.S.-led efforts to enhance maritime security on the globe. However, it is not desirable that global maritime security measures are led by a single country and are further subject to its domestic security measures. In other words, the U.S. security measures *per se,* not by the international rule-making process, have become global standards or norms for maritime security. The international community should continue to endeavor to enact those globally implemented standards and security measures into an existing or new international agreement to strengthen their legal basis.

Chapter 7 discussed the legal and practical issues concerned with the enforcement of the Proliferation Security Initiative (PSI). While the threat of massive destruction from conflict between nuclear-armed superpowers has been significantly reduced in the post-Cold War period of the 20th century, the contemporary world, has witnessed the rise of non-conventional threats posed by terrorist groups or rogue states which seek to have WMD in their hands and threaten to use them as a tool of terrorism.

The international community has engaged in developing new strategies to address the shortcomings of the existing non-proliferation regimes. As such, the strategy of counter-proliferation, which builds on non-proliferation, has developed. The outcome is the PSI, which is a global effort that aims to stop the trafficking of WMD, their delivery systems, and related materials to and from states and non-state actors of proliferation concern.

The PSI was initiated by the U.S. in the aftermath of the 9/11 terrorist attacks. On 4 September 2003, a core group of 11 states adopted the principles governing the PSI, which is the 'Statement of Interdiction Principle.' The very nature of the PSI is that: First, the PSI is a political commitment of participating states to international counter-proliferation efforts against WMD at sea, in the air or on land; Second, the PSI is not a formal treaty-based organization, but an activity. The PSI is an action that takes specific steps to effectively interdict WMD-related shipments and prevent proliferation; Third, the PSI works within the existing national and international law and frameworks.

The enforcement of the PSI is subject to the national legal authorities of participating countries and relevant international law and frameworks; fourth, participation in the PSI relies on voluntary actions of member states that are consistent with national legal authorities and relevant international law and frameworks; fifth, the PSI is a proactive approach to prevent the proliferation of WMD.

The PSI is an important contribution to global non-proliferation efforts and is a strong deterrent to proliferation-related trafficking. Despite its initial success, however, many challenges lie ahead of the PSI, *inter alia,* with regard to formulating the rules for interdiction of WMD. The foremost challenge is concerned with how to promote the participation of strategic regional states and strengthen the legal basis of the PSI. Another important challenge is to address the perception of the PSI as a U.S.-led security regime.

The U.S.'s roles and contributions to the establishment and evolution of the PSI should be highly recognized. However, such perception deters, to a certain extent, the PSI from evolving to a global security norm and attracting much broader participation.

A solution to this challenge would be to strengthen the leadership of strategic regional states, and to encourage more active participation of regional states. On this basis, the PSI needs to become a global security mechanism that rallies the cooperation of participating states in preventing and deterring the proliferation of WMD and related materials.

Chapter 8 discussed the increasing roles and functions of coast guards in East Asia and their build-ups in relation to growing maritime disputes in the region. A coast guard is generally referred to as a maritime law enforcement agency of a particular country. Among various maritime enforcement agencies, a coast guard is a pivotal institution used to ensure maritime safety, security and law and order at sea. For this purpose, a coast guard carries out a wide range of duties at sea, and thus is described as an amalgam of diverse maritime services. The regional coast guards can be classified into several different categories: (i) military force; (ii) paramilitary force; (iii) police force; (iv) civil service; (v) volunteer organization; and (vi) non-separate coast guard

Typical coast guard roles and responsibilities may include: (i) protection of maritime sovereignty; (ii) law enforcement; (iii) search and rescue; (iv) ensuring maritime safety and security; (v) protection of sea lanes; (vi) protection of the marine environment; and (vii) role of national defense

East Asian countries have vigorously engaged in a buildup of their coast guards' capabilities in recent years. Principally, the expansion of regional coast guards was driven by the need for the protection of extended maritime jurisdictions. Intensifying maritime disputes in East Asia are a primary rationale for the expansion of regional coast guards. The coast guards in East Asia have served as a frontline defender of sovereignty and claims of coastal states in maritime disputes. The phenomenon of regional coast guard expansion can be described as 'big white hulls,' with the growing deployment of large coast guard vessels and aircraft.

The form of the 'big white hulls' in East Asia differs according to the subregions. While Southeast Asian countries are engaged in the reinforcement of coast guards by establishing separate coast guards or granting greater authorities and functions, Northeast Asian countries have deployed large coast guard vessels and equipped them with higher levels of armament. Such moves has been spearheaded by China, which has aggressively pursued the goal of becoming a maritime power and has been increasingly assertive in maritime disputes. China increasingly deploys vessels larger than warships and uses them as an instrument to project power or coerce opposing parties in maritime disputes.

Although coast guard vessels are less political and militarily sensitive, the contentious encounters of large, armed coast guard vessels in disputed waters could spark a conflict. Given this circumstance, regional states engaged in maritime disputes in particular need to consider preventive measures to avoid conflicts. As part of the measures, the application of a Code for Unplanned Encounters at Sea (CUES) to coast guard ships needs to be considered.

Furthermore, regional coast guards need to foster international cooperation to fight common maritime concerns such as piracy, transnational sea crimes, illegal fishing and maritime security threats. The North Pacific Coast Guard Forum, launched in 2000, which involves China, Japan, Korea, Russia, Canada and the U.S as participants, is a good example of multilateral cooperation framework to facilitate cooperation in information-sharing and combating transnational sea crimes, and conducting maritime security regimes.

A coast guard is fundamentally a civilian service, responsible for law enforcement and safety and security at sea. The use of coast guard ships as replacements or stand-ins for warships is contrary to international law. The acts of armed aggression that blur the line between the navy and the coast guard should be discouraged. The coast guard should be used to serve its inherent purpose, which is as a de-escalator of maritime disputes, not an escalator of such disputes.

Index

Abu Sayyaf 112–113, 117, 121–122, 124
Achille Lauro 75, 125–126, 135
Ad hoc authorization 141
Al Qaeda 111, 114, 117, 121–122, 124–125, 229–230
AIS (Automatic Identification Systems) 72, 219
Amoco Cadiz 29, 76, 87
Archipelagic water 38, 109, 154, 284–285
Armed robbery 2, 7, 11–12, 109, 149, 154–158, 161–162, 164, 174–176, 178–179, 183, 189

Ballast water 29, 76–77
BBC China 260
BC Code (Code for Safe Practice for Solid Bulk Cargoes) 34, 41, 70
BLU Code (Code Safe Practice for the Safe Loading and Unloading of Bulk Carriers) 70
Boko Haram 112, 121, 123, 167

Canadian Coast Guard 275
CBP (U.S. Customs and Border Protection) 220–225
China 25, 36, 62–63, 95, 119, 133, 160, 171, 183–185, 192, 215–216, 223, 238–239, 261, 264, 267, 278–279, 282, 288–296, 301–303, 313–314
China Coast Guard 288–289, 291–292, 299, 303
CLL (International Convention on Load Lines) 59, 63
CLC (International Convention on Civil Liability for Oil Pollution Damage) 39, 49, 87
CMF (Combined Maritime Forces) 178, 183
Coast guard 4, 9, 89, 96–98, 119, 146, 179, 195, 267–275, 277–290, 293–298, 300–303, 310, 313–314
Coastal state 15–19, 38, 56, 68, 71, 73, 102, 108–109, 127, 129, 140, 149, 153, 156, 159, 173, 181–182, 189, 194, 239, 251, 253–254, 257, 280, 282–284, 286, 306–307, 313
Company security 201, 203–208, 217
Container security 196–197, 217–218, 220–221, 224–226, 310–311
Contiguous zone 108, 236, 250–252, 288, 290
Contemporary piracy 148–149, 156, 158, 160, 162, 194, 309
Counter-piracy effort 148–149, 164, 173, 179, 183, 194–195, 310
Counter-proliferation 228–231, 234, 261, 264, 312
Convention relating liability in the field of maritime carriage of nuclear material 32, 49
Criminal jurisdiction 126, 128, 150, 155–156, 182, 192, 308
CSCAP (Council for Security Cooperation in the Asia Pacific Working Group) 109
CSC Convention (International Convention for Safe Containers) 45, 69
CSI (Container Security Initiative) 12, 197, 218, 220–225, 311
CSS Code (Code of Safe Practice for Cargo Stowage and Securing) 70
CTF-151 (Combined Task Force-151) 171, 178–179, 183
C-TPAT (Customs-Trade Partnership Against Terrorism) 12, 197, 225–226, 311
CUES (Code for Unplanned Encounters at Sea) 303, 313

DHS (Department of Homeland Security) 218, 229, 225
Diaoyudao 286
Dokdo 298
Double bottom 78
Double hull 61, 78

East Africa 165, 172, 177, 185
EEZ (Exclusive Economic Zone) 18–19, 38, 153, 249, 254, 280, 285–286, 288–290, 293, 2 Establishment of jurisdiction 130, 95, 298–299
EU 90, 177–179, 222
Europe 88–90, 102, 172, 178, 191, 222–223, 238, 240, 264
Exxon Valdes 76

Extradition 116, 126, 128, 131–132, 134, 143, 176, 308
Eyes in the Sky 177

FAO (Food and Agriculture Organization) 14, 21
Ferry boat 2, 54
Flag state 18, 20, 35–38, 55–57, 65, 73, 83, 86, 91, 96, 98, 101–103, 131, 136, 140–143, 145–146, 171, 182, 197, 246–247, 249–250, 254, 258, 263, 283–284, 306–307, 309
Flag of convenience 36, 55, 57, 83
FSI (Freight Security Initiative) 12, 197, 218, 220–221, 226, 311
Free Ache Movement 116, 121, 123
Freedom of the high seas 11, 16, 250, 254–255, 258, 263
FSS Code (Fire Safety System Code) 42, 64

GC Code (Code for the Construction and Equipment of Ships Carrying Liquefied Gases in Bulk) 70
Geneva Convention on the High Seas 37
Gulf of Aden 110–111, 114, 121, 160, 165, 167, 171–173, 175, 177–179, 183–184, 186, 190–191, 193–194, 309

Hebei Spirit 76
Herald of Free Enterprise 29, 60
Hijacking 104, 111, 115–116, 120, 123–126, 134–135, 157, 159–161, 164, 184, 194, 310
HMCG (Her Majesty's Coastguard) 277
Hostage-taking 111, 116, 119, 160–161, 168
Hot pursuit 153, 177, 179, 285
HSC Code (International Code of Safety for High- Speed Craft) 41, 64
Hydrographic service 8, 74

IAEA (International Atomic Energy Agency) 14, 22
IBC Code (International Bulk Chemical Code) 34, 41, 79. 80
ICGN (Integrated Coast Guard Network) 179
IGC Code (International Code for the Construction and Equipment of Ships Carrying Liquefied Gases in Bulk) 41, 69
IHO (International Hydrographic Organization) 14, 22
ILO (International Labor Organization) 21, 57, 70, 86–87
IMB (International Maritime Bureau) 154–155, 157–158, 162–163, 166, 169–170
IMDG Code (International Maritime Dangerous Goods Code) 34, 69, 80
IMSBC Code (International Maritime Solid Bulk Cargoes Code) 43, 69
IMO (International Maritime Organization) 3, 6–7, 13–14, 16, 21–30, 32–35, 37–40, 54–61, 64, 67–72, 77–79, 83, 89, 92, 96, 102, 109, 126–127, 133, 136, 140–141, 145, 152, 154–155, 157, 173, 175, 179, 181–182, 186, 196, 198, 216, 257, 305–306, 311
Indian Coast Guard 273
INF Code (International Code for the Safe Carriage of Packaged Irradiated Nuclear Fuel, Plutonium and High-Level Radioactive Wastes on Board Ships) 42, 70
Innocent passage 11, 15–17, 19, 38, 68, 238, 251–254, 282–284
Interdiction 4, 11, 117, 142, 230, 232, 234–239, 243–245, 250–255, 258–260, 262–266, 312
Interdiction principle 142, 232, 234–238, 243–244, 250–251, 254, 260, 263, 312
International law 7, 11, 14, 18, 22, 34–35, 82–83, 85–86, 89, 105, 107, 142–145, 149–150, 154–155, 174, 186, 231, 234–236, 243–244, 250, 254–255, 257–259, 263, 268, 282, 303, 307, 309, 312, 314
International Law Commission 151
International shipping 1–2, 24, 148–149, 164, 194, 281, 305, 309
International water 19, 82–83, 86, 108–109, 154, 190, 236, 250–251, 285
ISM Code (International Safety Management Code) 29, 42, 59–60, 199, 217
ISPS Code (International Ship and Port Facility Security Code) 40, 42, 85, 136, 196, 199–200, 213–214, 216–218, 226, 287, 310–311
ITLOS (International Tribunal for the Law of the Sea) 37

Japan 25, 62–63, 88, 95, 111, 133–134, 144, 160, 163, 171, 176, 183–184, 189–193,

214–216, 222–223, 231–232, 242, 267, 273–274, 278–279, 282, 286, 294–298, 300–303, 314
Japan Coast Guard 184, 189, 191, 193, 215, 272–273, 295, 297
Jemaah Islamiyah 113, 121, 123

Korea (Republic of) 2, 25, 62–63, 76, 95, 112, 133–134, 144, 160, 171, 183–188, 192–193, 214, 216, 223, 232, 239, 242, 267, 278–279, 282, 296, 298, 301, 314
Korea Coast Guard 187, 261, 268, 274, 296

Law enforcement 9, 111–112, 141–142, 144, 149–150, 155–156, 164, 168, 174, 184, 190–191, 193, 195, 229, 232, 237, 264–265, 267–278, 280, 283, 287–288, 290–293, 297, 299–301, 303, 309–310, 313–314
Liberation Tigers of Tamil Eelam (LTTE) 121, 123–124
London Convention 63, 81
LRIT (Long-Range Identification and Tracking) 72–73, 75
LSA Code (International Life- Saving Appliances Code) 42, 64–65

Malaysian Coast Guard 276
Martine environment 2–11, 13, 19–23, 28–29, 34, 38–40, 56–57, 61, 66, 74–77, 86, 89, 101–103, 114, 254, 270–271, 273, 281, 287, 289, 304–307, 313
Marine pollution 13 14, 19, 22–26, 28, 35, 40, 47–48, 54, 62, 69, 74–76, 81, 83, 96, 254, 267, 275, 281, 287, 305–306
Maritime accident 2, 13, 54, 287, 306
Maritime casualty 1–2, 71, 83, 304–305
Maritime defense 4
Maritime dispute 15, 267–270, 280–281, 286, 289, 293, 301–303, 313–314
Maritime domain 3–4, 8, 10, 14, 16, 22, 104–105, 108–110, 113, 135, 145–147, 226, 267, 289, 304–309, 311
Maritime safety 3–11, 31, 14, 20–29, 33, 38, 40–41, 54, 62, 83, 95, 102, 268, 273–274, 280, 287, 297, 302, 304–306, 313
Maritime security 3–11, 15, 28, 35, 40, 52, 58, 102, 119–120, 130, 144–145, 184, 189, 196, 198, 200, 217–218, 238–239, 276, 288, 296–297, 304–305, 309, 311–312
Maritime Safety Committee (MSC) 6, 23, 25, 29, 33–34, 127, 182
Maritime terrorism 104–105, 107–114, 120–121, 125–129, 133, 135, 144–147, 155, 196, 213, 264, 267, 287, 295–296, 305, 307–309, 311
Maritime terrorist attack 119–120, 135
Maritime terrorist organization 120
Maritime threat 3, 109, 111, 135, 144, 281, 308
Maritime transport 1, 3, 6, 69, 196, 218
Maritime Transport Security Act 218
Maritime zone 37, 39, 108–109, 152, 155, 250, 289–290, 307
MARPOL (International Convention for the Prevention of Pollution from Ships) 29, 35, 39–40, 47, 59, 61–64, 69, 76, 78–81, 83, 100
Merchant Marine Act 218
Merchant Shipping (Minimum Standards) Convention 86–87
MFAG (Medical First Aid Guide for Use in Accidents Involving Dangerous Goods) 70
Military operation 8, 171, 188, 271
Movement for the Emancipation of the Niger Delta 112, 121, 167
M/V Limburg 114, 117, 124

NATO (North Atlantic Treaty Organization) 116, 157, 171, 177–179
National defense 269, 281, 313
Navigation 1, 4, 7, 9–13, 15, 17–19 21, 23–25, 28, 35, 38, 54–58, 62, 64, 66–68, 71, 74, 83, 92, 96, 98, 102, 108, 128, 130, 140, 148, 153, 155, 190, 199, 239, 253 254, 258–259, 281, 283–284, 304–307, 309
Navy 5–6, 111, 115–119, 124, 180, 184–188, 193, 231, 238, 261–262, 268–275, 277–278, 280–281, 292–294, 298, 300–303, 314
NLL (Northern Limit Line) 297–298
9/11 terrorist attacks 12, 104, 106, 124, 133, 196–199, 216–217, 226, 230, 311–312
North Korea 62–63, 133, 229–234, 238–239, 242–249, 260–265, 288, 297
North Pacific Coast Guard Forum 303, 313
NPT (Non- Proliferation Treaty) 228

Open registry 37, 306
Operation MALSINDO 176

OPRC (International Convention on Oil Pollution Preparedness, Response and Co- operation) 47, 62–63
OPRC/HNS (Protocol on Preparedness, Response and Co- operation to pollution Incidents by Hazardous and Noxious Substances) 47, 63

Paris MOU 88–91, 93–96, 100–101
PCASP (Privately Contracted Armed Security Personnel) 181–182, 188, 191, 193
Petroleum 1, 120, 249, 263
Petty theft 158–159, 164
Phantom ship 159–160
Philippine Coast Guard 273, 298–300
Piracy 2, 4, 6–7, 11–12, 21, 104, 108–113, 123–126, 133, 135, 146, 148–195, 213, 251, 255, 2
Pirate 110–112, 116, 125, 148–150, 155–161, 164–175, 177–182, 184, 186–194, 265, 310
Pirate ship 151–152, 155, 176, 186
Pirate attack 157, 159, 172–173, 180–181, 192, 58, 267, 270, 281, 285, 287, 305, 307, 309–310, 314
PMSC (Private Maritime Security Company) 182
Port security 199, 202, 213–215, 218, 220, 226, 287, 311
Posse Comitatus Act 269
Prestige 76, 78
Prior authorization 141
Prosecution 126, 128, 131–132, 135, 139, 142–143, 172–175, 308
PSC (Port State Control) 39, 82–87, 89–90, 92, 96–103, 307
PSI (Proliferation Security Initiative) 11, 117, 142, 144, 228–241, 243–245, 250–255, 258–266, 287, 297, 312–313
PSJ (Port State Jurisdiction) 82

Ransom payment 112, 115, 157, 160–161, 166, 168, 171
ReCAAP (Regional Cooperation Agreement on Combating Piracy and Armed Robbery Against Ships in Asia) 158, 176, 183
Right of visit 135, 142, 255, 257, 295
Russia 25, 95, 116, 171, 232, 241, 262, 303, 314

SAFE Port Act 217, 219–220, 225
Safety zone 18, 271, 284
SAR (Search and Rescue) 4, 11, 47, 62
Sea 1–2, 4–22, 37, 39, 54, 58–59, 62, 67, 69, 71, 74, 76–77, 81–82, 84–85, 105, 108–118, 122–123, 126, 133, 135, 137, 141, 145–152, 155, 160, 174, 177, 179–180, 192, 194, 196–197, 234, 237, 256, 264–268, 271–272, 274, 277, 280, 287, 297, 304–305, 307, 309, 311–313
Sea borne trade 1, 13, 24, 148–149, 164, 194, 281, 305, 309
Sea Empress 76
Sea lanes 1, 17, 68, 159, 183, 270, 281, 284, 301, 313
Security equipment 171, 179–180, 205, 208, 210–213
Senkaku islands 286, 293, 295–296
Ship boarding 140–146, 255–256, 258, 262, 264, 309
Shipping industry 7–9, 21, 33, 56, 77, 148, 165–166, 170–172, 179, 188, 193–194, 304, 309–310
Ships' routeing 66
Ship security 195, 197, 200–216
SOLAS(International Convention for the Safety of Life at Sea) 29, 31, 33–35, 40–41, 44–45, 57–60, 62–66, 69, 71–74, 79–80, 84–85, 100, 136, 197–199, 214–216, 311
Somalia 125, 153, 161, 163, 165, 168, 170, 174–175, 177–179, 182–183, 190, 194, 309
So San 230–231, 239, 259
Southeast Asia 112, 123, 133, 148, 153, 158–160, 163–164, 176, 189, 193–194, 239, 262, 267, 281, 286, 301–302, 310, 313
STCW (International Convention on Standards of Training, Certification and Watchkeeping for Seafarers) 33, 46, 54, 60–61, 63, 79, 87, 199
STCW-F (International Convention on Standards of Training, Certification and Watchkeeping for Fishing Vessels Personnel) 46, 61, 63
Straits used for international navigation 15, 38, 68, 253–254, 283
SUA 1988 (Convention for the Suppression of Unlawful Acts Against the Safety of Maritime Navigation 1988) 40, 52

SUA Protocol 1988 40, 45, 59, 63–64, 127–128, 134, 136
SUA 2005 (Suppression of Unlawful Acts Against the Safety of Maritime Navigation 2005) 52
SUA Protocol 2005 134–140, 142, 144–146, 259, 264, 308–309
Superferry 14 113, 117, 132

Takeshima 298
Transit passage 11, 15, 18, 38, 254, 283–284
Territorial integrity 7–9, 11, 15, 18, 255, 280, 305
Terrorism 4, 6, 11–12, 104–112, 115, 128–129, 132, 134–136, 139, 145–147, 155–156, 213, 217–221, 225–226, 228, 232–233, 307–309, 311–312
Titanic 29, 57, 64, 197, 305
Torrey Canyon 26, 29, 76
Tokyo MOU 88–89, 95–100, 102
Traffic separation scheme 17, 58, 67–68, 284
Transit passage 11, 18, 38, 254, 283–284
Trump administration 232–233
24-hour advance rule 12

UN (United Nations) 5, 7–8, 10–11, 13–15, 18, 22–23, 28, 30, 106, 151, 165, 173, 194, 243, 260, 263–264
UNCLOS (UN Convention on the Law of the Sea) 14–16, 20–22, 32, 37–39, 56, 68, 75, 85–86, 108, 126, 135, 152–155, 157, 162, 186, 189–190, 192, 244, 250–254, 258, 263, 282–283, 285–286, 301
Unlawful acts 2, 4, 8–10, 40, 110–111, 126, 128–129, 133–135, 137, 145–146, 149–150, 153–155, 158, 160, 179, 273, 287, 305, 307–308
UN Security Council 106, 133, 173–174, 178, 233, 235, 243–245, 260–262, 264, 297
U.S. 12, 25, 76, 89, 96–97, 99, 106, 111, 114, 116, 118–120, 126, 130, 142, 145, 171, 173, 176, 178, 186, 197, 199, 217–222, 224–226, 230–233, 235, 238–239, 255–256, 260–262, 266, 268, 271, 278–279, 283, 297, 303, 310–312
U.S. Navy 5–6
USS *Cole* 116, 124, 180
U.S. Coast Guard 89, 96, 119, 219, 283, 296–297

Vienna Convention 30
Vietnam Coast Guard 298, 300–301
VTS (Vessel Traffic Service) 4, 8, 11, 70–71, 281

WMD (Weapons of Mass Destruction) 104–105, 117, 135, 137, 144, 196, 228–230, 232–238, 243, 250, 252–255, 258–259, 261, 263, 265–266, 307, 309, 313, 313
West Africa 112, 153, 161, 167, 179, 191, 194, 310

www.ingramcontent.com/pod-product-compliance
Lightning Source LLC
LaVergne TN
LVHW020633300926
849161LV00004B/687